D0722359

Listening and Longing

DANIEL CAVICCHI

Listening and Longing

MUSIC LOVERS IN THE
AGE OF BARNUM

WESLEYAN UNIVERSITY PRESS

Middletown, Connecticut

WESLEYAN UNIVERSITY PRESS
Middletown CT 06459
www.wesleyan.edu/wespress

© 2011 Daniel Cavicchi
All rights reserved
Manufactured in the United States of America

We gratefully acknowledge the assistance of the Donna Cardamone Jackson Endowment of the American Musicological Society and the Publications Endowment
of the American Musicological Society, supported through the National Endowment for the Humanities. Publication of this book was also supported by a subven-
tion from the Professional Development Fund of Rhode Island School of Design.

Wesleyan University Press is a member of the Green Press Initiative. The paper used
in this book meets their minimum requirement for recycled paper.

5 4 3 2 1

Library of Congress Cataloging-in-Publication Data

Cavicchi, Daniel.
Listening and longing: music lovers in the age of Barnum / Daniel Cavicchi.
p. cm. — (Music/culture)
Includes bibliographical references and index.
ISBN 978-0-8195-7161-8 (cloth : alk. paper) — ISBN 978-0-8195-7162-5 (pbk. : alk. paper) —
ISBN 978-0-8195-7163-2 (e-book)
1. Music—Social aspects—United States—History—19th century.   I. Title.
ML3917.U6C38   2011
780.973'09034—dc23
2011029924

For Bella and Lulu

Instead of huskings now and spelling bees,
The people have such merry times as these,
With concerts gay, and lectures, learned and wise,
That place the wide, wide world before your eyes.
— CHARLES N. HALL, 1854

Contents

◆{⊙}◆

Acknowledgments

✦

This book began with research on uncatalogued sheet music binders at the John Hay Library at Brown University during the summer of 1999. While I never published the paper I wrote based on that research, I soon became interested in the nineteenth-century music culture of the United States. Having an "interest" in a subject and actually writing a book about it, however, are very different things, and I am grateful to all who, during the past decade, have offered their time and insight to help me do the latter.

A request in 2002 from Wayne C. Bowman, editor of *Action, Criticism, and Theory for Music Education*, to write an extended review of Tia De-Nora's *Music in Everyday Life*, gave me my first opportunity to think through some of the topics I wanted to explore. I further refined them in a paper titled "The Musicality of Listening" that I delivered at Experience Music Project's Pop Conference in the spring of 2003. During a walk in Seattle, Paul Théberge kindly suggested that I think more about consumerism; a little later, back home, Marc Perlman expedited things by suggesting that I read Jonathan Rose's *The Intellectual Life of the British Working Classes*.

After receiving a joint grant in 2003 from Rhode Island School of Design's Professional Development Fund and Liberal Arts Humanities Fund, I spent the summer of that year reading diaries, concert programs, and other ephemera at both the Boston Public Library and the American Antiquarian Society. I also made a side research trip to consult archival materials at Cornell University's Kroch Library, Sibley Music Library at the University of Rochester, and the Buffalo and Erie County Historical Society. In early 2004, I made two trips to the New-York Historical Society in New York City and visited the Boston Athenaeum. Much thanks to the librarians at each of these institutions, all of whom were immensely helpful—especially with an ethnographer who had little knowledge about the world of call slips and folios.

An Andrew W. Mellon Short-Term Fellowship at the Massachusetts Historical Society in summer of 2004 enabled me to discover many diaries by music lovers and to make expeditions into Boston to explore still-existing concert venues from the past I was studying. Special thanks must go to fellow Fellow Robb Haberman, who offered his expertise on early American magazines. Thanks also to Director of Research Conrad Wright, who wisely suggested a less linear and more ecological approach to history, a suggestion that still resonates.

I had several opportunities to test and refine my arguments. In 2006, Katherine Bergeron in the Music Department at Brown University invited me to deliver a public talk about the history and theory of music listening and then to teach a semester graduate seminar at Brown on the topic. I am grateful for the generous support offered to me by Bergeron, the faculty in Brown's Music Department, and the students in its ethnomusicology program. Around the same time, Cornel Sandvoss, Jonathan Gray, and C. Lee Harrington all provided insightful comments on an essay about music loving I wrote for their anthology, *Fandom: Identities and Communities in a Mediated World*. During 2007, colleagues offered additional comments and feedback during public presentations of my work at Rhode Island School of Design and at that year's conference of the United States Branch of the International Association for the Study of Popular Music.

After I began writing the manuscript of the book, Nicole Merola, of RISD's English Department, took time to carefully read, edit, and critique several early chapters and thereby prevent despair. Barbara Ryan, of the University of Singapore, invited me to discuss the ideas and methods of the project in a wide-ranging conversation (published on the blog of media studies scholar Henry Jenkins); her provocative questions and responses enabled me to think more clearly about the book's direction. Steven Baur at Dalhousie University offered detailed and constructive comments about the manuscript; his engagement made this a much stronger book than it would have been otherwise. Harry Berger was enthusiastic about the manuscript from the beginning; he and Annie Randall, as the editors of the Music/Culture Series at Wesleyan, read an early version and offered detailed and helpful comments. Parker Smathers, my editor at Wesleyan, has been an enthusiastic, constructive, and good-spirited shepherd throughout.

Overall, my students at Rhode Island School of Design, especially those enrolled in my courses on audience studies, the history of listening, and American history, deserve special thanks; they have for years suffered through my speculations about nineteenth-century musical culture and in return have given me patient and gentle criticism. I would also like to recognize my colleagues in the Department of History, Philosophy, and Social

Sciences at RISD, who daily work to foster a supportive intellectual environment. Teaching liberal arts at an art and design college is a unique academic situation that has only enhanced my writing and thinking.

Finally, thanks to my family. I wrote the initial chapters of this book during a sabbatical at the home of my brother- and sister-in-law, Mark and Laurie Staveski. It was not the first time I had used their residence for a scholarly escape from my own busy household, and I sincerely appreciate it. That a book requires one to be absent so much—seeking quiet, doing research, or simply concentrating on another time—is not necessarily healthy for the daily life of a family. The gratitude I have toward my wife and my children for enabling me to indulge in such an activity is beyond words.

Listening and Longing

Introduction

In Edward Bellamy's 1887 utopian novel, *Looking Backward*, an elite nineteenth-century Bostonian, Julian West, accidentally sleeps until the year 2000 and wakes up to find a wondrous new society. Boston in 2000 is peaceful and efficient, with an industrial economy tempered by rational organization, choice, and self-fulfillment, all of which West interprets as a stark contrast to the poverty and class violence of urban life in the 1880s. By accumulating one awestruck moment after another, West is transformed from a wealthy elite to a radical social activist; the conceit of the novel allows Edward Bellamy to make all sorts of observations about how American society might be reorganized. Some of Bellamy's predictions about the future are rather fanciful; it would not actually come to pass in 2000, for instance, that people would work only between the ages of twenty and forty-five, or that purchased goods would be shipped instantly through an elaborate system of pneumatic tubes. But in one of the more memorable chapters, Bellamy offers an eerily accurate vision of America's future musical life, in which the nineteenth-century world of amateur playing and singing has given way to a new twenty-first-century culture where music is primarily heard and made to order.

Just after realizing that he has awakened in the future, West meets a young woman named Edith, who begins to introduce him to modern life. Edith first surprises West by asking whether he is "fond of music." West, not really understanding the question, eagerly replies that he would be delighted to hear Edith sing. Amused by his assumption, she just laughs and explains: "Professional music is so much grander and more perfect than any performance of ours, and so easily commanded when we wish to hear it, that we don't think of calling our singing or playing music at all. All the really fine singers and players are in the musical service, and the rest of us hold our peace for the main part." Leading West to the "music room," where he is befuddled by the lack of decor or musical instruments, she asks him to choose a selection from a daily schedule of "vocal and instrumental solos, duets, quartets, and various orchestral combinations of music." They sit, Edith touches a button, and West can scarcely breathe as he hears the sound of an organ mysteriously filling the room. After listening to a subsequent violin waltz, Edith wonders aloud "how those among you who depended at all on music managed to endure the old-fashioned system for providing for it," which included ill-performed concerts or, even worse, having to play and sing for oneself in the home. "Yes," West replies, somewhat sadly. "It was that sort of music or none for most of us."[1]

In our time, it is difficult for us to conceive of a world in which being able to simply sit and listen to an accomplished performance is a rare, exciting, and strange event. For the past century, listening to professional musicians perform, whether "live" or through recordings, has been an essential form of musical engagement for Americans, from turn-of-the-century symphony concerts to modern stadium tours, from phonograph societies to college students downloading songs. The music industry has long been based on the consumption of musical performance through listening: concert tours, radio shows, and recordings are all products meant to provide a listening experience, for a price. More recently, listening seems to have taken on even greater cultural significance in the so-called iPod era. Statistics suggest that while contemporary music instrument sales and instrument playing remain relatively steady, they do not match the sales and use of mp3 players, especially among younger generations.[2]

The contemporary ubiquity and ease of music listening—as well as its segregation as a distinct activity—would likely have been foreign to those living in the first several decades of the nineteenth century. There was no recording technology then, obviously; music had to be made painstakingly for it to exist at all. One might have been able to hear music at a parade or public dance, but the concert business was strictly entrepreneurial and notoriously erratic; opera and theater producers regularly went bankrupt, and buildings, productions, and troupes quickly appeared and disappeared. For most Americans—both urban and non-urban, middle and working class— music was primarily something people made together. Everyone knew how to manage a little on an instrument and people would often gather in homes or communal meeting places to play and sing, listen and dance. The most consistent profits to be made on music lay in amateur music making: sheet music sales, instrument sales, and both private and group lessons.

This culture was altered by the advent of national touring by opera stars and instrument virtuosos in the 1840s. Thanks to improved transportation and expanded urbanization, a new, relatively steady, stream of public concerts in America's East Coast cities led small groups of urbanites to become more and more accustomed to having the option of listening to professionals perform. In the decades after the Civil War, the concert business expanded rapidly in places like New York, Philadelphia, Baltimore, St. Louis, Charleston, New Orleans, and Bellamy's Boston. Each city developed a robust and busy musical culture of secular and sacred concerts, operas, recitals, band competitions, minstrel shows, and dances that catered to increasingly large and enthusiastic audiences. Such audiences were encouraged by a burgeoning ideology of middle-class professionalism, which suggested there was limited value in amateur players creating inferior versions of musical pieces.

It is important to note that such public musical performance was a predominantly urban and middle-class affair. The listeners who actively cultivated new audience habits and practices around commercialized public performance comprised a literate audience, interested in and with access to new urban institutions. In particular, clerks and other low-level white collar workers began to make new choices about how to spend their leisure time; rather than engage in the labor of having to practice instruments or take lessons, many used their wages for the more instant gratification of a play or a show. Participation in commercial music performance as an audience member was often difficult for those living in non-urban communities without an entertainment market. It was equally difficult for urban residents routinely denied access to the cultural institutions of the city, especially African Americans and the poor. And, as I will explain further, amateur music making remained strong in diverse American contexts for much of the nineteenth century.

But whether one participated in urban concert-life or not, the possibility of—and desire for—the leisure to shape a musical life exclusively around listening had emerged as a middle-class cultural ideal by the 1850s and continued to serve as a general marker of urban genteel taste until the early 1900s. In 1887, when Edward Bellamy was writing *Looking Backward*, urban concert going had begun to influence institutionalized definitions of musicality, and even of "music" itself, in American society. If more traditional understandings about music consisted mainly of mutual or reciprocal performance at home or with acquaintances, punctuated by occasional attendance at a public performance, concert culture cultivated a different emphasis among those activities, with amateur playing and singing subservient to the reception of professionally made music provided by an arts and entertainment market.

In fact, Thomas Edison explicitly recognized Americans' expanded interest in music listening as an activity when he converted the phonograph from a business machine to an "amusement device" in the 1890s. By abandoning plans to market the phonograph as a recorder for secretaries and instead emphasizing its playback capabilities, Edison was capitalizing on the more immediate late nineteenth-century vogue for mechanized musical playback through music boxes and player pianos, as well as the will of customers who, earlier in the century, had already acquired a taste for habitual listening to music through concerts.[3]

Traditional American music histories have tended to focus on the *making* of music, either in aesthetic terms that account for notable composers, performers, and styles, or in production terms that focus on the development of technologies of distribution such as music publishing, piano manufacturing, recording, and radio.[4] The reception of performances and works, the history of music consumption, the development of audience practices, and the uses of music in daily life—what might collectively be called "audiencing"[5]—figure only secondarily in such a framework. For whom were symphonies, songs, sheet music, instruments, records, and programs produced? In what contexts did various Americans encounter music, and how did those contexts shape their ideas, feelings, and responses? How exactly did people variously integrate these products and experiences into their daily lives? How did composers, performers, and business entrepreneurs cater to—or alter—people's musical behaviors and values?[6]

The absence of examples of audiencing practice in histories of American music is, in part, due to the paucity of primary sources. While the scores, journals, account books, and correspondence of professional composers (and, to a lesser extent, businessmen) have been preserved and deposited in public archives, the everyday experiences and activities of audience members have not enjoyed the same recognition, and thus potential evidence for their musical engagement—descriptive letters, scrapbooks, tickets, or personal collections of sheet music, for example—have been undervalued, overlooked, or lost. This is not all that surprising. In the star system of the Western musical world, composers are expected to attend to the legacy of their work, while audience members remain more anonymous. A concertgoer or sheet music consumer might never have felt the need to record the motivations behind his or her music expenditures or to explain his or her enjoyment of a show.

Nevertheless, musicologists have not attempted to consider historical audiences in depth, as subjects in their own right, until only fairly recently.[7] Stemming from nineteenth-century aesthetic theory that espoused the autonomy of the "work," musicology for much of the twentieth century narrowed its focus to the power of musical texts and the practices of composition and performance that enact such texts. Even while the study of historical reception has notably increased in musicology since the 1990s, thanks to the "cultural turn" in the discipline,[8] the place of reception in our understanding of music remains somewhat limited. Reception has been fitted into enduring intellectual frameworks that continue to privilege composers and works as the drivers of musical culture; research and writing on the aesthetic lives of listeners, for example in the same manner as studies devoted to composers and performers, remain rare.[9]

In this book, I want to offer a fuller understanding of the place of music audiences and listening practices in the history of music in the United States. I will argue that our contemporary culture of listening is not simply the result of twentieth-century technology and mass culture, as is commonly assumed, but rather has origins in a much earlier historical moment, before the iPod, before the stereo system, before even the phonograph. In fact, one might call this a "pre-history" of modern music listening, recovering the moments in which the act of listening to someone else perform first became distinct, marketed, and desired (though not necessarily in that order). In the process, I want to begin building an understanding of American music history from an audience perspective. Such an alternative history hinges not simply on aesthetics or the development of musical institutions but also on a set of equally significant themes, all of which tell the story of how music audiencing became culturally meaningful: the growing separation (both figurative and physical) of performers and audiences; changing frameworks of self, perception, and emotional engagement; shifting notions of talent, literacy, and participation in a culture increasingly shaped by capitalism, and the role of musical experience in shaping daily life and building identity.

Tracing instances of one particular behavior from the vast, disorganized, and incomplete record of everyday human experience is always somewhat maddening, but locating the history of music listening is particularly complicated by issues of definition. First, while processes of commodification since the nineteenth century have rendered music listening a distinct behavior, music listening has nevertheless continued to exist, simultaneously, as a less distinctive act, one that is almost invisibly interwoven with other musical behaviors. So, while a person can choose to occupy the singular role of a listener at a club performance, for example, the players and singers the listener hears may also be listening while they perform. Any dancers present are also evidently listening too, but in a different, physically expressive way. In a broader sense, while some Americans might feel quite comfortable occupying the limited position of a paying audience member, there are those—especially living in communities with musical traditions not primarily shaped by the commercial recording industry—who may not hold a clear distinction between performer and audience; hearing, playing, singing, and dancing are participatory actions that are thoroughly mixed up and interchangeable in the course of any music event.

Charles Keil has coined the terms *consumer listening* and *playing listening* to begin to distinguish these approaches to experiencing music.[10] While the existence of *playing listening* is important in many musical cultures that feature live performance (where it also might be accompanied by the category of *dancing listening*), I am primarily concerned, here, in this history, with Keil's notion of *consumer listening*. I am arguing—following Leon Botstein, in particular—that the extraction of listening from its integral connection to other musical behaviors helped to create modern musical life in the West and, as such, is a process that needs to be interrogated in depth.[11]

Just as it is difficult to isolate music listening in performance, it is difficult to isolate music listening in time. I agree with historian Carole Shammas that cultural revolutions and transformations in history ought to be understood with some skepticism, since their existence stems more from disciplinary conventions—as a narrative shorthand for change—than from a careful weighing of historical evidence.[12] Writing a history of music listening is not as simple as citing a date in the 1850s on which amateur playing ends and listening begins, the product of a cultural revolution after which musical life in the United States was changed forever. Such a narrative would disregard, of course, that Americans listened to music before the nineteenth century, and that piano playing became more prevalent in middle-class homes throughout the United States after the Civil War rather than before. Indeed, in response to the assertion that listening is the dominant form of musical behavior in the United States today, one might reasonably protest that a lot of Americans are still forming bands, applying to music schools, and lining up for singing competitions.

But the rise of commodified listening is better understood as a shift in interrelation rather than a unilateral change from one behavior to another. As ethnomusicologists have shown, a music culture forms a complex ecology, made up of a number of interconnected behaviors and possible avenues for musical expression, including composing, playing, singing, dancing, and listening, not to mention a host of related behaviors in facilitating music making, including instrument making, recording, engineering, promoting, deejaying, selling, teaching, and writing. Changes that affect one part of a music culture—like changes in any complex system—do not necessarily obliterate the entire culture but more subtly invite responses that attempt to recalibrate internal connections and processes. In this case, commodification in the mid-nineteenth century gave the act of listening a new significance that it did not possess before and, through that signification, altered the ecological balance of the country's musical life.

James Johnson has argued, specifically, that types of musical engagement in history develop cumulatively, each overlapping the other, with the social pressures of conformity, exerted over generations, creating gradual shifts of emphasis and value.[13] The cumulative effects of commodified music listening—a remaking of the relationships between listening and other musical behaviors, as well as those behaviors to each other—were played out over many decades, with fits and starts, and steps backwards as well as forwards.

Several scholars, for example, have noted the increasing fragmentation of American culture into categories of high and low in the latter half of the nineteenth century, with order and sacrelization increasingly imposed by cultural elites on uneducated audiences.[14] There has been substantial criticism about the details of this historical shift, some of which I agree with (and will discuss in Chapter 5), but from the perspective of listeners, I think it is most important to recognize the messiness and complexity of the shift at a national level. Between 1860 and 1880, the behaviors of concert going were debated, modified, and remade, even as the phenomenon as a whole seemed to grow. Middle-class concert-goers, who initially made music listening primary in their lives by yearning for a culture of refinement and European-style "gentility," created the foundation for long-term changes in America's musical life. However, they also sometimes found themselves at odds, even marginalized, by ministers, educators, and critics—guardians of cultural power—in nineteenth-century American society.

As with most cultural histories, then, telling the story of music listening in the nineteenth-century United States depends on accurate generalization, or at least on an awareness of how generalization works as a tool for narrative understanding. Generalization in history can be useful for making comparisons and summarizing arguments, but the rhetorical frames in which generalizations operate are sometimes discarded or lost, leaving only distortions and reifications. Obviously, in this study, I make some simplifications for the purposes of narrowing my subject and creating a resonant narrative.

I focus on the United States, for instance, which—as any American studies professor will tell you—is a handy political category, but, given the cultural, economic, geographic, and social connections between the American nation and the rest of the world, is always otherwise problematic. I focus on "urbanization" as a central force in the development of music consumerism, something which is useful for understanding the general growth of major antebellum cities like Boston, Philadelphia, and New York but which was invented by the surveying perspective of scholars rather than by those in the midst of such change, and which also is an historical abstraction that glosses over the different experiences of urban life across regions, cities, neighborhoods, families, and individuals. I also make conclusions about the shared experiences of those who might be described retrospectively as "middle class," even though the nature of middle-class status in the nineteenth century was complex and remains a debated and unevenly employed concept among historians.

I discuss each of these descriptive categories further in the text that follows, but I have also sought to keep such generalizations in check by drawing my argumentative conclusions primarily from the evidence left by actual concert-goers. The tendency in previous studies of music reception has been to consult existing archives of music journalism—particularly reviews—to understand how music had meaning for listeners and consumers.[15] While such evidence is vital for piecing together the circumstances of public musical events, journalism does not necessarily capture the experiences of ordinary people, for whom a concert may have had far different significance than it did for a professional and literate expert.[16] Indeed, as William Weber has noted, "Histories of Victorian society have taken the moralists of the time a great deal too seriously, simply because they were so vocal and articulate."[17] While journalists' descriptions of specific performances are sometimes the only sources remaining for making sense of the musical past, I have sought whenever possible to account for experiences of hearing by starting with the people who actually had those experiences.

Is it possible to locate existing sources for the experiences of listeners in the nineteenth century? As I mentioned already, part of the neglect of actual hearers is due to assumptions that the experience of hearing music is "interior" and not something about which people tend to leave records. As Richard Butsch noted about abandoning a project on the change from music making to music listening: "After some preliminary explorations of dusty archives and old books, I concluded it would be difficult to document such private practices."[18] But theorists of hearing have been less hesitant, borrowing creative methods from ethnography, archeology, social history, and the history of the book to reveal the everyday experiences of listeners.

Dena Epstein's seminal book, *Sinful Tunes and Spirituals*, while addressing a different group of people in American society than I do here, broke new methodological ground in 1977 by carefully documenting the musical lives of African Americans through the use of missionary accounts, letters, autobiographies, novels, and other untapped archival sources.[19] As I have mentioned, a small number of cultural historians have written about changes in audience behavior, especially the emergence of "silent" listening in European classical music performances and the "pacifying" of American concert and theater audiences in the mid-nineteenth century.[20] Such work does not specifically address music listening broadly across genres or time periods and tends to rely on limited textual evidence, but it nevertheless offers important background. Other scholars have written works about the development of radio and recording technologies[21] as well as "acoustic histories" of the United States;[22] neither group addresses behaviors of *music* listening directly, but each provides a vision of how the perceptions of music audiences may have been shaped in different ways over time.

In addition, to meet the challenges of locating evidence of actual people's responses to music in the past, I have turned to the work of a number of reception theorists in non-musical disciplines. Literary historians, especially, have studied personal reading through book marginalia, diaries, and autobiographies and have examined changing literary attitudes through etiquette guidebooks, advertisements, prints, and paintings.[23] I have successfully located similar items for nineteenth-century music lovers about what they have heard and how they experienced changes in musical life. In particular, I have relied on the scores of unpublished nineteenth-century diaries and scrapbooks located in both local and state archives. Diaries are not typically catalogued for music, and often require spending days reading material that might contain only one or two fragmentary references to a concert or singing lesson. But piecing such fragments together slowly builds a fuller "emic" or "experience-near" understanding of nineteenth-century Americans' musical lives and provides a rich glimpse of how music consumption developed and how it had profound meaning for individuals and for communities.

Diaries are flawed historical sources, of course. They represent a peculiar species of writing that gained enormous currency in the mid-nineteenth-century United States, as part of what Scott Casper has called the country's "biographical mania."[24] Still, diary writing found the most currency among those young adult members of the middle class who were most self-consciously seeking their way in the world and, on finding themselves without parental and household obligations, had the time to write; and likewise among the literate, who were comfortable using written expression and reading as a basis of daily reflection, memory, and learning. While archived diaries may be an appropriate source for learning about nineteenth-century concert-listeners, who were also generally young and middle class, they do not readily or fully illuminate the role or impact of music listening among others in American society, including the poor, African Americans, immigrants, or members of the urban working class.

In addition, the information offered by diaries is not simply straightforward or uniform. While diaries are today considered documents of secret and private thoughts, hidden away in dresser drawers and not to be violated by prying eyes, in the nineteenth century they had different meanings that had more to do with changing notions of self, literacy, and society. Marilyn Motz, for example, has contrasted more urbanized "introspective" diaries, which looked inward at one's personal and spiritual growth through educated reflection, with rural diaries that looked outward and chronicled community events and the physical environment without commentary or emotion. Even then, such functions were not resolute.

While introspective diaries may have helped literate adults to develop a stronger narrative of themselves either as persons of moral character or as unique individuals, they could also operate more immediately as a record or memory aid for the writers as they negotiated the fraught terrain of social obligation and tried to remember whom they had met and the nature of the interaction. The diary writing of middle-class Victorian girls, in particular, was generally framed as a tool for establishing self-autonomy, but employed in prescribed social contexts in which diaries were often shared with peers, controlled by parental expectations, and which served as an escape valve for emotions and thoughts considered potentially disruptive or dangerous. Ultimately, diaries in the nineteenth century offered a certain spontaneity and immediacy that today convey entrance into the private realm but remain structured by an artful self-consciousness that might be described as semi-public.[25]

Diaries may provide as incomplete an historical record of nineteenth-century musical life as journalistic accounts but, even with such biases and problems, I believe they offer a greater possibility than newspaper reviews for understanding the phenomenological aspects of human avidity. Relying on diaries, in fact, helped me to focus on people rather than the details of musical performances and works; in the past, the latter focus has helped to erase listeners from history. I would even go so far as to say that I have purposefully resisted any privileging of musical works or styles in order to move my thinking away from the analytical frame of "composer/text/performance" so entrenched in academic music studies. I did go out and find some recordings of the operas that music lovers mentioned in their diaries, but I saw such texts as only part of the many details that made up any event of reception. In fact, initially, I preferred *not* knowing what symphony or song was being referenced by an auditor or an artifact. That ignorance allowed me, for a brief moment, to explore audiencing in a more open-ended way before my own musicological knowledge and associations narrowed my thinking. The suspension of knowing also got me psychologically closer to the "newness" of the musical works that music lovers themselves were experiencing.

My historical research for this project was necessarily informed by my previous training in anthropology and ethnomusicology. Such an intersection of history and anthropology is not new, of course; in fact, there is a long-standing interdisciplinary tradition that links the two disciplines variously in terms of topic and method.[26] In this book, I have been most interested in what might be called "ethnographic history." As explained by historian Rhys Isaac: "The direct observation and interrogation methods of anthropology cannot be applied to social worlds long vanished, but there is an approach by which the historian can approximate, albeit fragmentarily, the notebook of the field ethnographer."[27] I saw the past as a "field" and derived meaning by "entering" its environs, interacting with people, examining my own assumptions, and through that whole process trying to build a deeper understanding of a culture different from my own. In the archives, I "met" all sorts of people and had numerous experiences—through diaries, images, even objects. I tried to make sense not only of the historical content of such evidence but also to learn from the process of encounter itself, which often contained the familiar but also things that I didn't understand: odd language or design, misplaced emphasis, or, as Robert Darnton pointed out in *The Great Cat Massacre*, jokes that weren't funny.[28] I couldn't ask questions and receive answers from informants; but I nevertheless pursued questions and expected answers from people and, in general, valued the paths opened up to me as I moved from diary to diary, object to object, experience to experience.[29]

More specifically, after some background reading on music in the antebellum era, I travelled to nearby archives (the Boston Public Library and the American Antiquarian Society) and began looking for "informants" in the collections. I knew of diarists that had been mentioned in other books, which provided me with a start.[30] After exhausting such known sources, I started to read additional diaries "blind," with the hope that I might stumble upon a chance mention of listening experiences; most offered very little about music, but a few turned out to be unexpected gems. In addition to diaries, I studied concert programs, prints, letters, published memoirs, local histories, and other primary and secondary sources to deepen my understanding about diarists' references, comments, and experiences, and I pursued further biographical information about specific diarists who seemed particularly intriguing.[31] I even tried to visit the actual places they mentioned.[32] After several years, many archives, and roughly fifty good diary-finds, two things happened: I felt like I "knew" some people, as well as I might, and I started to recognize repetitions and patterns across their actions and experiences. Those repetitions and patterns formed the initial hypotheses that inform this narrative.

In the end, this book is only a beginning. I make no attempt to exhaustively chronicle the cultures of music listening, past and present, and I see enormous potential for further curatorial and analytical work by others on musical listening practices, or their impact, in other specific time periods and places or among other social groups in the nineteenth century. My goal, at this stage in the topic's development, has been to create a coherent narrative of the *emergence* of music listening in the United States, from its early stages in the antebellum era, when entrepreneurs first packaged and sold the experience of hearing musical performance to urban consumers, to the 1880s, when genteel critics began to successfully reframe and more narrowly define the value of listening in terms of cultural refinement and spiritual fulfillment. My narrative includes a variety of interconnected stories, including the role of hearing in shaping an understanding of the rapidly growing urban environment, the complex and differing meanings of public entertainment across groups defined by gender, race, and class, the creation of new kinds of social connections and community through regular audiencing, and debates among musicians, educators, and audiences about how to value listening as a musical—and cultural—behavior. Throughout, I have attempted to address the broader historical forces of industrialization, urbanization, and commercialization in shaping musical audiences in America, while seeking to derive historical insight from the perceptions and understandings of literate middle-class urban listeners, as they experimented with, and eventually embraced, new ways of acting musically.

I open, in Chapter 1, by describing the growing commercialization of urban culture in the United States during the antebellum era, which generated new and multiple means for hearing music, including parades, museum exhibitions, pleasure gardens, band performances, and concerts. This provides a broad setting for the developments I discuss in subsequent chapters. Chapters 2 and 3 describe the rise of commercialized, public, concert listening between, roughly, 1840 and 1860. In Chapter 2, I probe auditory literacy in the "non-musical" realms of nature, theater, church, and oratory and showing how urban concert listening borrowed from, and extended, those more established practices of reception and consumption. In Chapter 3, I address the ways that participation in commercialized concert culture— "audiencing," to put it broadly—gave white urbanites of the period a means to more clearly define middle-class culture. My discussion draws on diary evidence to investigate new groups of avid and devoted listeners in the late 1840s and 1850s, who, for the first time in history, were able to shape their musical experiences entirely around commercial entertainments; in particular, I address the role of commercial music and celebrity in the urban middle-class practices of "self-making" that developed in the period.

Chapters 4 and 5 analyze how a culture of music loving grew out of these developments, from the late 1850s to the early 1880s. First, in Chapter 4, I explore the shared practices of "music lovers," who, before and after the Civil War, creatively imbued participation in musical life with a visceral excitement that both paralleled evangelical religious enthusiasm and confronted the behavioral strictures of middle-class Victorian culture. In Chapter 5, I loop back over the same period, addressing the meanings of and debates about this new culture. In particular, I address how elite and upper middle-class guardians of gentility attempted to redefine music listening in narrower terms, first using the language of disease and mania to denigrate the most publicly enthusiastic and commercially driven audience practices in the 1850s, and then, after the Civil War, explicitly identifying vulgar forms of audiencing associated with mass culture, passivity, femininity, and manipulation. While this Gilded Age social fragmentation has already been studied by American historians, the evidence I present, as well as the particular focus on music listening, may offer new perspectives on the matter.

Overall, I argue that the rise of consumer listening in the nineteenth century gave urban, white, middle-class Americans new, significant means of acting musically, and profoundly shaped subsequent debates about modernity and musicality. I hope, at least, that starting a conversation about the history of music listening will help readers, critics, and music fans today to better appreciate the ideologies that have shaped their individual musical lives and, too, will give those involved in public debates about music— including everything from how best to teach music to children to the definitions of "music piracy"—an informed understanding of how we got here and what, exactly, is at stake.

CHAPTER ONE

"P. T. Barnum, Introducing Madelle. Jenny Lind to Ossian E. Dodge"

Capitalizing on Music in the Antebellum Era

+{≡}+

Dodge's Bid

At the end of September 1850, Ossian E. Dodge, a writer of comic songs and sketches, attended a ticket auction in Boston for an upcoming concert series featuring the Swedish opera singer Jenny Lind. One can only imagine the scene: the auction, devised by famed impresario P. T. Barnum, took place at Tremont Temple, an old theater that had been purchased by a group of Free Baptists several years earlier and was still rented out for public events.[1] Its large rectangular hall was necessary to accommodate the gathered crowd of merchants, speculators, clerks, lawyers, writers, teachers and music lovers, all of whom were humming with excitement about the possibility of hearing Lind and, even more, about personally participating in the public sensation swirling around her impending appearance. Only weeks earlier, in New York City, a hatter named John Genin had bid $225 for a ticket in a similar auction; the story of his bid had become the latest sensation in cities up and down the East Coast. For the citizens of Boston, who were always suspicious of the outrageous ambitions of New Yorkers, it was a matter of civic pride that they best Genin's bid and thereby demonstrate their own appreciation for "the Swedish Nightingale."

Bidding started high—at fifty dollars for what would have been a three- or four-dollar ticket. At a time when the average worker made seven dollars a week, even a one-dollar ticket was beyond the reach of many. Dodge had earlier told an acquaintance that he was interested in the auction merely out of curiosity; he sat quietly, scanning the crowd, as if mentally composing a sketch for *The Literary Museum*, a small-circulation magazine he wrote and edited. A boisterous crowd of top-hatted men lunging up into the air with urgent bids during a public auction was not altogether unusual in a northern antebellum city, but this auction was tied not to a banking venture but to a musical event, as well as to a female performer whose blemish-less Christian character had been exceedingly advertised in the national press. Dodge would likely have much fun poking at the contradictions in a short observational piece. When the bidding reached seventy-five dollars, however, Dodge—either stirred by the competitive atmosphere or acting on a hidden plan—suddenly took off his top hat and lurched up onto the seat next to him. To everyone's surprise, he shouted "Two hundred and twenty-five dollars!" to the auctioneer, a bid that outdid all the rest and precisely matched Genin's amount in New York. The crowd turned toward Dodge with a murmur. After a pause in which they assessed his sincerity, everyone again began to bid furiously, with rivals, including Dodge, moving the amounts upward by leaps of fifty dollars. Before long, the top bid had moved past five hundred dollars.

While major cities of the United States had hosted tours of European performers before Lind's, the announcement of her American tour had been met with unprecedented enthusiasm. During her premiere in New York City, weeks earlier, she was cheered in the streets by thousands of onlookers, and her concerts, held on multiple nights to overflowing audiences, were the news of the day, attracting immense, roaming crowds outside of the Castle Garden venue and inviting intense press coverage. Lind was, by most accounts, a gifted singer who radiated a "sweetness" and "purity" that differed starkly with the day's cut-throat business competition and scheming. But the extent of her notoriety came from a campaign orchestrated by her tour manager, Phineas T. Barnum. Barnum was well known by the 1850s for his sideshow antics—exhibiting an old African American woman as George Washington's nurse and running a museum of curiosities in New York City. By the time he arranged Lind's tour, he had developed an array of sophisticated promotional maneuvers, all designed to use the expanding communication networks of the time to create a public "sensation." In addition to auctions, like the ones in New York and Boston, the arrival of Lind in America had already been "puffed" for months, by means of seemingly ubiquitous editorials and biographical sketches of Lind and Barnum, as well as endless testimony from those who knew her (or claimed to know her). Barnum arranged song-writing contests, held massive public rallies, and secured Lind's endorsement for products in local shops. "We had Jenny Lind gloves, Jenny Lind bonnets, Jenny Lind riding hats, Jenny Lind shawls, mantillas, robes, chairs, sofas, pianos—in fact, every thing was Jenny Lind," Barnum wrote later.[2]

The Boston auction itself was rapidly taken over by Lindmania as soon as the bidding started. As if watching a parade from the side of the street, people lifted themselves on top of one another, craning their necks to get a view of the top bidders, turning their heads side to side as offers were shouted to the auctioneer onstage. When the price passed $225, the crowd knew that Boston would be forever remembered as part of Lind's historic visit to the United States, and that Ossian Dodge—"Is he from Boston originally?" "He's a penny writer of some sort." "Didn't he put on a vocal exhibition a few months ago?"—would serve as its representative. People became more and more agitated as they waited to see whether the cheerful, now-hatless Ossian Dodge, still standing above them on his seat, would best the latest bid.

"Five hundred fifty dollars!" a man cried. A groan issued from the crowd. "Five hundred and seventy-five!" answered Dodge.

They clapped and shouted wildly at each of his bids, releasing the tension created when the men paused and weighed their options. When Dodge's main competitor suddenly froze at the bid of $575, they thought, with some relief that the duel was over, but the competitor failed to sit down. After a moment rather too long, his challenge went out, annunciated carefully, hinting at both a reluctance to go further and a bristled sense of pride: "Six hundred dollars."

The crowd turned to Dodge and waited, tense, hopeful. Dodge just smiled calmly. He sensed his competitor's limits and looked out over the faces of the crowd, savoring their anticipation. Then, with a triumphant crescendo, he responded, "Six hundred and TWENTY-FIVE dollars!"

With relief and astonishment, the crowd exploded with a howling, uproarious applause. Ossian Dodge had pledged nearly two years of what would have been someone's annual salary for a chance to see Jenny Lind perform, on one night, and from the seat of his choosing. Dodge reached down for his hat, waved it triumphantly above his head, and, with a slightly embarrassed smile that was meant to exhibit his humility and gratitude for such a response, formally bowed to the cheering audience.

The ensuing events were fairly bizarre, even for those fully caught up in the humbug and hysteria for Jenny Lind. Over the next week, Dodge worked hard to make certain that everyone remembered his winning bid. In particular, he commissioned a lithograph from Boston's James H. Bufford and Co. that depicted Barnum humbly introducing "Mademoiselle Jenny Lind" to him in a well-furnished parlor. It was an event that had not, to anyone's knowledge, actually occurred, something that allowed Dodge to play around with the facts of the situation. In particular, Dodge placed himself in an imaginary world of refinement and respectability: he is dressed in a suit coat with tails and an elaborately ornamented waistcoat; on the table behind him is a top hat, which he presumably had just placed there. Barnum and Lind are elegantly dressed; Lind, especially so, attired in an off-the-shoulder, multi-layered gown and white gloves. The room in which they are shown appears to be an expensive parlor: the figures stand on a detailed oriental rug, corners of large and highly ornamented furniture just into the picture, and scrolls—indicating the ornate edges of mirror or painting frames[3]—contain the figures at shoulder level.[4] In addition, the image implausibly depicts Dodge, leaning patiently on the table behind him, looking confidently—even smirking—at his companions, waiting for them to come to *him*. While Barnum humbly gestures Lind toward Dodge, Lind herself is clearly bowing, with downcast eyes. Indeed, the caption reverses the protocol one would expect in the circumstance of an unknown audience member being introduced to a star: "P. T. Barnum, introducing Mad-elle Jenny Lind to Ossian E. Dodge, The 'Boston vocalist,' & purchaser of the $625 Ticket for the first Concert of the Sweedish [*sic*] Nightingale in Boston."

All of this was fantasy, but it was plausible enough and worked as a brilliant stroke of advertising. It built on Dodge's word-of-mouth reputation as a slightly crazed highest ticket bidder and transformed it into something bigger and more important—that he was on personal terms with both Barnum and Jenny Lind. By capturing that fiction visually, he enabled its quick apprehension even by those who did not know of, or understand, the circumstances on which he had based the portrait in the first place. If anyone missed the message, Dodge also appeared in an advertisment on the inside front-cover of Lind's 1850 Boston concert program, titled "That First Ticket," which read:

As the sum of SIX HUNDRED AND TWENTY-FIVE DOLLARS premium was paid for the first choice of a seat to this Concert, and as it is a higher one than was *ever* before paid upon any like occasion in the world, it is with pleasure that we announce the name of the purchaser to be OSSIAN E. DODGE, a vocalist and musical composer of much celebrity and worth. It is believed that he paid this sum in order to show respect to JENNY LIND, who is justly regarded as being at the head of the profession to which Mr. D. belongs.[5]

Shortly after the appearance of the advertisement, Dodge's ultimate goal became clear: to become as successful a musical performer as Lind herself. Indeed, in the month following the ticket auction, Dodge featured the lithograph in advertisements for a newly announced concert tour in which he planned to sing his own vocal repertoire, accompanying himself on guitar. Not only that, but he reproduced the print as the cover illustration for a re-

Cover of "Ossian's Serenade." Boston: Oliver Ditson, 1850. *Lester S. Levy Collection of Sheet Music, Sheridan Libraries, The Johns Hopkins University.*

issued edition of the sheet music for "Ossian's Serenade," a song he had published only a year before, in 1849. The image of him meeting Lind seemed to be everywhere; soon after the ticket auction, stand-alone versions of the lithograph festooned walls, shop windows, and billboards all over the Boston area, helping to cultivate Dodge as a celebrity, "The Boston Vocalist." Believing that he, in some way, had to be a musical peer, or at least an acquaintance, of Lind's, the music-loving public of New England flocked to his vocal concerts in the winter of 1850 and 1851, forcing him sometimes to put on two shows a night to handle the demand and enabling him to make enormous profits (some estimates put his take as high as $11,000).[6]

Dodge didn't remain in Boston for long; in the wake of his concert tour, he was made a delegate to the "World's Peace Congress" in London in 1851, and then he worked as a roving correspondent and editor for his own publication, *The Boston Museum*, until 1858, when he left to open a music store in Cleveland. In the 1860s, he invested in real estate in St. Paul, Minnesota, where he settled into a life as a wealthy gentleman. Dodge's successes, though, all stemmed from that one moment in Boston, in 1850, when his bid to acquire a seat for a Jenny Lind concert launched him into the world of musical celebrity. As late as 1859, almost a decade after the Lind ticket auction, famed writer Oliver Wendell Holmes, Sr., in an *Atlantic Monthly* short story, described several unframed prints pinned up on the wall of the apartment of one his characters, familiarly referring to one of them as "that grand national portrait-piece—P. T. Barnum presenting Ossian E. Dodge to Jenny Lind."[7]

Dealing Music, Making Markets

Dodge's actions and success seem curious today. What did his fellow Bostonians think about his audacious use of the Lind ticket auction to advance his own singing career? Clearly, Dodge's fictional lithograph had appeal long after his brief foray into the world of concert performance had ended — Holmes even referred to it as a "national portrait-piece." But why? To understand the meanings of Dodge's bid, we have to examine more closely the historical circumstances of public music performance before 1850. A concert, featuring a program of music, was not new at that time, of course; it was an event in which members of the elite in the United States had had the leisure to indulge since before the American Revolution. Tradesmen, mechanics, and artisans, too, generally had been able to hear shorter performances of music, as paying audience members in urban theaters since the early 1800s. And music was present more generally at church services, singing schools, parades, and dances, all of which enjoyed widespread participation in the national era.[8]

Much of this activity, however, was local and ephemeral. Urban theater was the most professionally oriented, regularly offering plays and music to a range of social classes.[9] Still, only major cities like Boston, New York, and Philadelphia had standing theaters in the early 1800s. And before the 1820s, such theaters relied on stock companies of local actors and singers to fill most parts and support the occasional traveling star in a production. Even when touring troupes became more prevalent, staying at a theater for an "engagement," there was no regional or national booking system; individual theater owners contracted with troupes directly, something that maintained the localism of any production.[10]

Outside of the world of musical theater, most musicians performing before an audience in American cities of the early 1800s were groups of devoted local amateurs. Many formed music clubs and societies, which enabled interested members in a community to gather regularly to make music; they occasionally opened such performances to non-members as well. Church choirs and sacred music societies sometimes offered one-time concerts and festivals.[11] Or a wealthy patron might arrange for an itinerant teacher/instrumentalist to perform in a private residence for those in society, either at a party or to commemorate a special occasion.[12] Such performances were not part of a sustained commercial enterprise, open to all, as we understand it today. Most concerts were one-time happenings, offered by invitation-only, or through costly subscription prices that severely limited the social breadth of the audience. Indeed, Kenneth Silverman summed up concerts in the early Republic as "little more than social gatherings for the eligible followed by dancing."[13]

For a majority of Americans living in smaller towns and rural communities in the early 1800s, attending a commercial public performance was more than likely a special, marked occasion. Military-inspired bands could be heard periodically in local parades; singers and minstrels might be seen in the circuses or traveling shows that might occasionally roll through town, and one might watch the musicians at a community dance. While instrumental concerts of music had connotations of aristocratic excess and elite sociability, vocal performances, which were more in line with religious traditions of hymnody, generally enjoyed more widespread support. In particular, singing schools, offered by itinerant teachers once or twice a year, created highly anticipated exhibitions. But most American communities simply did not have the musical and physical resources to maintain a regular series of music and theatre productions. Besides, many Americans believed that regular attendance at public amusements was dangerous since it appealed to uncontrollable emotions. Theater, especially, which was associated with numerous vices from simple deception to prostitution, challenged deeply held religious and moral principles. In general, those outside of elite social circles believed that music could be made more respectably, regularly, and easily in the privacy of one's home, as a pleasant pastime among friends and family.

Even for those who did have the means to attend concerts regularly, attendance had more to do with the wider ritual of coming together in a shared space rather than purposely witnessing the presentation of a work; concerts were not considered exclusively musical as much as social, an opportunity for the fashionable members of society to see and be seen in order to affirm the symbolic contours of the local community. Audiences' attention to such performances could best be described as distracted. Eliza Quincy, a young member of one of Boston's most prominent nineteenth-century families, humorously described an 1816 Handel and Haydn Society concert at King's Chapel solely in terms of her curiosity about the audience:

During the performance my mother's attention was attracted by the appearance of a gentleman standing in the broad aisle. Calling my father to her in an interval of the music she said, "Can you tell me who that man is in the broad aisle. His head is very fine, he must be something remarkable." Mr. Quincy looked sharply at the lady. "Now are you certain you do not know who that man is?" "No, I never saw that gentleman before. I have no idea who he is, but I am sure he is a remarkable man from the shape of his head." "To be sure he is very remarkable," said Mr. Quincy, "that man is Nathaniel Bowditch, the eminent astronomer, the author of the 'Practical navigator,' the translator of La Place's 'Mecanique Celeste.' I am surprised you never saw him before, as he is a favorite friend of mine but he lives in Salem & is now in town as a member of the Council."[14]

Even as late as 1843, George Templeton Strong, attending a New York Philharmonic concert, noted in his diary: "I selected the little side gallery, where I could look down in a calm and philosophical manner on the splendors below, and especially upon George C. Anthon making very strong love apparently to one of the——s! and upon Schermerhorn making himself generally ornamental, and Fanning C. Tucker trying to devise outlets for his legs and barking his knees on the bench next in front of him, and Mr. Lucius Wilmerding dozing off regularly at the soft passages and waking up with a jump, at the loud ones, and so forth."[15]

By the mid-1840s, the local and ephemeral nature of concert going had noticeably started to change. In the mid-1830s, small but steady numbers of professional virtuosos and opera companies began to visit East Coast cities and perform limited runs before curious—and soon enthralled—audiences. In the early 1840s, a vogue for blackface minstrelsy transformed the world of musical theater, and increasing numbers of traveling minstrel companies delighted northern theater audiences with dancing, music, and outrageous satire. Unlike earlier benefit or subscription concerts, these performances were unabashed commercial events, arranged by professional promoters, where relatively large numbers of people in a metropolis, often not known to each other, were asked to come together, not for light socializing or to affirm community but to seize an opportunity to exchange their accumulated cash for the experience of witnessing something novel and amusing.

Offered at the height of the first wave of industrialization in the United States, when young people were, for the first time, leaving behind farm work, bartering, and church fairs in exchange for factory work, cash wages, and self-improvement, new kinds of urban music performance heightened the importance of audiencing. People thrilled at the opportunity to listen to others perform and to witness astonishing feats of technique that they could not perform themselves. The novel talent of the new performers directed the attention of previous, elite concert-goers toward what was happening onstage rather than toward fellow audience members; for new audience members, access to the performances for the first time freed them from having to create their own music.

The arts need not be commodified at all, of course, and in many cultures and regions of the United States music was shared without the exchange of money. But between 1815 and 1840 Americans experienced a social change that was as momentous as the earlier struggle to establish a democratic republic: an economic revolution that weakened the self-sufficiency of family farms and local communities by fostering individual competition for wealth in national industrial "markets." America's burgeoning market economy was voracious, expanding rapidly in the 1820s and 1830s thanks to a combination of political hubris, vast resources, and technological ingenuity, from canal and railroad boosterism in an expanding western frontier to new divisions of labor in mechanized factories. In cities, in particular, an artisanal economy began to yield to a new system in which people did not work to make whole products as much as work to earn a wage for assembling parts. They could then use their accumulated wages to buy fully manufactured products in a commercial sphere. This shift toward commercialization left very little of everyday life untouched by the second half of the nineteenth century.[16] The transformation was chaotic, one that unfolded irregularly and left many without access to its opportunities and benefits. However, in general, even those who remained outside of the new wage economy began to accept the ideological wedding of democracy and market capitalism. As Alexis de Tocqueville noted about America in the 1830s, "Nothing is greater or more brilliant than commerce; it attracts the attention of the public and fills the imagination of the multitude; all energetic passions are directed towards it."[17]

Music and other aesthetic endeavors were not the most immediately obvious sources of capital, but they were not immune to commercial exploitation.[18] By the end of the eighteenth century, a new species of American entrepreneur, the jack-of-all-music-trades known as the "music dealer," had started to explore ways to profit from music. Music dealers first sought to capitalize on already existing practices of home music making by selling instruments and repair services, as well as offering extended lessons on those instruments, for a fee. Such instrument instruction required knowledge of the latest published music from Europe, and the use of distributable scores that students could study and practice; the same dealers soon began to print music to meet that demand, something that turned into a major business by mid-century.

Benjamin Carr, for example, started his career in the 1794 by offering pianofortes, assorted other musical instruments, and printed music, some of which he had composed, at his "Musical Repository" in Philadelphia. Carr also actively played piano and served as a vocalist in local theater productions. Around the same time, in New York City, James Hewitt worked as the house composer at St. John's Street Theater, while in the off-season also performing as a musician, composing songs, teaching pupils in music theory, and running a New York branch of Benjamin Carr's Philadelphia-based store. He later moved to Boston, where, in addition to being the organist for Trinity Church, he published music, started a music academy, and opened a rental music library out of his home.[19] Probably the most famous promoter of such music commerce was Gottlieb Graupner, a German immigrant and accomplished player of both double bass and oboe, who had played under famed composer and conductor Joseph Hayden. He arrived in Boston in 1795, and, after working in the orchestra at the Federal Theatre, started a music academy, a music printing office, and music instrument shop, founded the city's Philharmonic Society in 1810, and began offering several subscription concerts given by himself and his wife, an operatic singer.

Very few of these early ventures to commercialize music were uniformly successful. Most dealers could not avoid, in the words of Philadelphia music publisher James Moller, "laboring under some pecuniary embarrassment."[20] Precipitous expansion of one's business was a risky move that often revealed the limits of public interest in music. Ferdinand Palmo, for instance, the founder of Palmo's Opera House in New York City, boldly attempted to offer full Italian opera productions in 1844 and 1845, but his inability to make a profit quickly drove him to bankruptcy; he ended his days as a hotel cook.[21] Historian Russell Sanjek notes that "throughout the series of three-year economic depressions that burdened Americans at regular intervals, music dealers were continually obliged to add different lines of merchandise," including show blacking, stationery, cigars, billiard balls, combs, glassware, dry goods, engravings, mending glue, and short fiction.

Hewitt's music-lending library, in addition to musical scores, incongruously offered "Spanish cigars, in boxes of 250 each." Most dealers had to take day jobs in the theater, or in churches as music directors or organists; many moved between Boston, New York, Baltimore, and Philadelphia to stay afloat financially.

It is also notable that early music entrepreneurs did not attempt, in any sustained way, to commercialize public music performance. Through the early decades of the nineteenth century in the United States, the heart of the music trade remained home music making; for dealers, performances were tangential events, aimed at creating interest in the other branches of the business. The main reason was that public concerts of music faced a number of difficult obstacles. The presence of capable musicians was not a given, nor was a program of music they could actually play together. A hall large enough to accommodate a sizable audience yet cheap enough to rent was absent in many communities. Most importantly, the financial success of any public concert depended on the unpredictable net profits gained through door ticket sales or pre-concert subscriptions, and audience demand in most places simply wasn't large enough to sustain the effort. The small numbers of concert rooms and theaters that did exist in cities and towns before the 1840s generally represented the number that could be sustained by the size and needs of a local population, and, more than likely, were the net result of many previous experiments, bankruptcies, and closings. To venture beyond that number was often an act of optimistic folly, and successful additions to the concert scene were the exception rather than the norm. As Joseph Sill ironically enthused in 1840 about the entertainments in his city: "it is not wonderful when I remember that there are now 4 Theatres open every night—and 1 Equestrian Circus! Rather too much for Philadelphia!"[22]

Urban Concert Culture and Middle-Class Urbanity

Concerts became viable as a regular for-profit business only after the sweeping social transformations wrought by urbanization. While antebellum urbanization was not on the scale of postbellum growth, between 1820 and 1850, the nation's five largest cities grew significantly.[23] Originally, American cities were notable for their compactness—most historians call them "walking cities." Located near harbors or river junctions, which allowed access for goods, the settled areas of even the largest cities, such as New York, Boston, and Philadelphia, rarely extended beyond two miles from their geographical centers—the average distance a person could walk in half an hour. Wharves, warehouses, mercantile offices, and small manufacturing establishments were built together; public buildings, churches, hotels, and residential areas were nearby. But new transportation networks in the 1820s and 1830s, including better roads, canal projects, and railroads, enabled merchants to look toward the interior for markets and trade and enabled different classes of people to spread themselves out across a wider and wider area.

Indeed, an important element of the expansion of capitalist markets in the United States during the antebellum era was a kind of social unification that political institutions had only tentatively enacted. Cities, towns, and even rural areas became networked to each other and to the world like never before; innovations in transportation, particularly the canal and the railroad, made cities newly accessible for potential labor and for expanding markets. As de Tocqueville explained, "They have already changed the whole order of nature for their own advantage. They have joined the Hudson to the Mississippi and made the Atlantic Ocean communicate with the Gulf of Mexico, across a continent of more than five hundred leagues in extent which separates the two seas."[24]

In terms of music, access to long-distance travel was necessary for delivering building supplies and workers to build theaters, halls, shops, and schools; for opening up national markets for musical goods like instruments and sheet music; and for enabling the congregation of musicians, managers, dealers, teachers, and audiences. Karen Alquist has shown how the development of opera in New York City was directly linked to the opening of the Erie Canal in 1825, which enhanced New York's status as the country's biggest Atlantic port by also making it the economic—and cultural—gateway to America's western frontier.[25] Likewise, both R. Allen Lott and Arthur Loesser have attributed the increase in piano making and performing in the antebellum period to the advent of the Atlantic steam ship.[26]

Cities not only enhanced their own markets for music but helped to promote and spread that culture outward, as well. Katherine Preston has argued that opera performance reached the town halls and churches of smaller localities like Worcester, Massachusetts, or Ann Arbor, Michigan, as soon as canals and railroads made the trip possible and profitable.[27] And the importance of the railroad to an expanding concert business became increasingly important during and after the Civil War, as is clear from even a cursory glance at pianist Louis Moreau Gottschalk's daily journal in the 1860s, where he is constantly shuttling himself and several grand pianos from city to village to town, sometimes giving concerts in two different places in a day.[28]

This expansion of urban infrastructure was enhanced by a parallel shift in attitude about the role of concerts in society. Such a shift was precipitated by the rise of an urban middle-class in the 1830s and 1840s, the group, in the words of Katherine Preston, "most likely to attend performances, purchase sheet music, buy instruments from the ever-growing numbers of American instruments builders, or hire musicians to teach their sons and (in particular) their daughters."[29] The middle class has always been a complex social category in the United States. While there was a "middling" class in eighteenth-century Europe, which indicated a fixed position between gentry and peasant, American leaders rejected such Old World social hierarchy as being opposed to ideologies of equality and liberty, and instead promoted social class as an ideology to be learned rather than a condition fixed by birth or occupation. Thomas Jefferson's ideal citizen, for example, was a "gentlemen farmer," a somewhat bizarre (at least to European observers) melding of existing categories of social status.

In the antebellum era, then, middle class-ness might be most accurately described in terms of an emerging *class consciousness* rather than a concrete social group.[30] Middle-class status in America was institutionalized as a desirable goal for all; even those who were economically poor, or culturally marginalized, like free blacks, sought to acquire goods and practice behaviors that might display a certain level of middle-class respectability.[31] Bustling port cities in the early 1800s, especially, became associated with such class experimentation. Immigrants from Ireland and Germany, along with native migrants from more rural areas, arrived daily, seeking livelihoods from the unprecedented levels of building, trade, and manufacturing. A new ideal of the "self-made" man, profiting from his own ingenuity, transformed older frameworks of business.

Problems arose, however. While public discourse promoted the erasure of class hierarchy, something that initially created a sense of pride and possibility, it also very quickly created a growing sense of anxiety. Especially to those aspiring to middle-class respectability, it became clear that one could easily move down, as well as up, the social ladder. Middling young white males who served as store clerks, for instance, a class position that was ostensibly "white collar" and involved "headwork," also found that, in the eyes of proprietors and customers, they easily slipped into the realm of porters, typically Irish or African American laborers who performed any firm's daily "handwork" of clearing, moving, and stocking.[32] Indeed, many of the young clerks who signed up for membership every year in urban mercantile libraries, a public step toward middle-class status, often "vanished with the shifting tides of economic fortune."[33]

De Tocqueville noted also that the fungible demarcations of class in the United States created confusion in daily social interaction. "True dignity in manners consists in always taking one's proper station," he wrote. "In democracies all stations appear doubtful."[34] A young Lucy Emerson expressed such confusion in her diary, after encountering a stranger who nevertheless greeted her familiarly: "As I was coming home through Washington Street, just at the corner of Bromfield Street, I met two gentlemen as I supposed from their appearance. One of them when I looked up, had his eyeglass in his eye, looked down in my face & said, oh you darling! I was so provoked I did not know what to do & he passed on."[35] In the presumed absence of "proper stations," social interaction had to be remade anew. In cities, where social change was most acute, the necessity of remaking manners became an urgent project. Karen Halttunen explains, "In what was believed to be a fluid social world, where no one occupied a fixed social position, the question, 'Who am I?' loomed large; and in an urban social world where many of the people who met face-to-face each day were strangers, the question, 'Who are you really?' assumed even greater significance."[36]

In order to more satisfactorily address doubts about one's own success and identity, aspirants to the middle class refashioned European ideas of gentility to the new market-driven, urban context of Jacksonian America. Gentility was a centuries-old code of civility and learning among the upper classes of Europe; it involved a wide range of behaviors and norms that sought to create a "polite society" that existed on a different realm than that of "common" people. Middle-class Americans in the antebellum era similarly came to distinguish themselves as a group, first, by promoting "a meritocratic social logic" or what we would today call professionalism—the acquisition of specialized skills through non-manual labor.[37] Related to this professionalism was the acquisition of proper education and taste. Despite their embrace of the rewards of capitalist competition and commerce, new generations of genteel Americans actively sought to distinguish themselves from singularly-driven "getters"—or worse, wily confidence men—by their moral sense and European-style cultural refinement, derived through appreciation for fine arts like painting, music, and literature. Finally, both professionalism and taste were displayed through personal grooming and social etiquette. Middle-class ideology made crucial associations between inner truth and outer display, locating the most meaningful aspects of one's character in the private sphere while relying on careful public display as a means of confirmation.[38]

Concert promoters very quickly learned to exploit these concerns and thereby transform the appeal of musical performances. Middle-class valuing of competitive specialization and expertise was a move that opened the door to virtuoso performers onstage.[39] As already mentioned, before the 1840s, musicians onstage were typically local amateurs, playing privately, or semi-privately, for peers in an audience. Middle-class emphasis on individual achievement and talent, as well as studied appreciation of the fine arts, moved amateurs toward a more exclusive standard however. New York critic Henry Watson explained: "Why should tradesmen, tailors, and others . . . be allowed to occupy situations to the exclusion of professional gentlemen who, having studied hard, and having expended money to acquire the knowledge of their art, are now denied the benefits which should accrue from its possession, by these interlopers, these would-be musicians?"[40] Middle-class attitudes toward music making were best exemplified by European musical virtuosos who were starting to test the market for public performance and tour major cities in the United States in the 1830s. Virtuosos were rooted in the grand art traditions of Europe, promoted the elevation of technical skill and, in their professional status as touring performers who were unanchored by local ties and political favors, captured the meritocratic ethos of genteel urbanites.

At the same time, concert promoters were careful to address middle-class ideas about public and private spheres. Linked to the growing middle-class ideology of professionalization was the increasing role of the family and its private "domestic sphere." The family had functioned as a public economic and religious institution throughout the colonial period, but middle-class ideology resituated the family as a private emotional haven, overseen by women, that could provide moral development and psychological well-being for its individual members. Music mirrored this division. While the masculine, competitive, and professionalized public sphere outside the home was represented by the virtuoso performer, the feminized domestic ideal was represented by the musicking of mothers and daughters, typically involving private lessons in singing and piano, as well as parlor performances that emphasized the intimacies of family relations and courtship.[41]

The promotion of urban concerts explicitly supported existing networks of private musical instruction with new public performance events. Private music teachers were sure to "assist" at evening concert events to attain public credentials; piano manufacturers advertised that one could play on the very same Chickering grand at home as a virtuoso had on stage;[42] sheet music publishers marketed pieces not in terms of their composers or subject matter but rather as they had been performed by particular stars or at particular events. These moves dialectically linked public and private musical realms: repeated encounters with touring opera and instrumental virtuosos provided businessmen and their families knowledge of cultural forms normally associated with Europe and fetishized skill and technique, which effectively "raised the bar" for home-performance and created the need for further private instruction. Proper home instruction and performance then necessitated further exploration of concert life to keep up with trends, and so on.

In fact, concert entrepreneurs found their first widespread success among middle-class audiences by featuring singing families, like the Cheney Family, the Rogers Family, the Baker Family, the Wright Family, and the Hutchinson Family, all of which toured the country during the late 1830s and early 1840s.[43] The "family" tag signified familiar and wholesome entertainment— a public reproduction of what, ostensibly, genteel American families had gaily performed for each other, privately, in their own parlors and drawing rooms. As Walt Whitman explained, contrasting the elaborate culture of European opera with the "heart music" of singing families:

Elegant simplicity in manner is more judicious than the dancing school bows and curtsies, and inane smiles, and kissing of the tips of a kid glove a la Pico. Songs whose words you can hear and understand are preferable to a mass of unintelligible stuff (for who makes out even the libretto of English opera, as now given on the stage?) which for all the sense you get out of it, might as well be in Arabic. Sensible sweetness is better than all distorted by unnatural nonsense.[44]

Entrepreneurs' modestly successful efforts at exploiting middle-class values and desires through musical performance were enhanced even further by unforeseen economic circumstances. In 1837, the United States suffered a devastating economic depression, which hit all realms of urban life, especially the market for theater, where much public music was found. Nineteenth-century theater historian William Clapp, for example, noted that at the Boston Theatre "the season of 1838–9 was almost devoid of interest. The fortunes of the drama were so desperate, that the curtains went up some nights to less than $90 in the house. Mr. Barry, under this state of affairs, allowed the No-haired Horse to appear, and also permitted one Shales, an amateur, to astonish the modern Athenians with his impersonation of *Richard III*."

Contemporary commentators in Boston, New York, and Philadelphia all noted a steady decline in competition from older national-era theaters after 1838. Many were simply unable to recover from their business losses; others simply tried business as usual once things improved, which did not appeal to a public wary of returning to the conditions that had precipitated the depression. As Van Wyck Brooks characterized those coming of age during the time: "The more sensitive minds of the younger generation, the imaginative, the impressionable, the perceptive, those who characterize a generation . . . were thoroughly disaffected."[45]

The breakdown of the traditional theater-based entertainment system for music opened up opportunities for a business more singularly dedicated to public music performance. New York editorialists talked about music performance—which included productions at pleasure gardens, "opera" houses (often featuring minstrel acts), small concert saloons, and larger concert halls—as being lighter in content, relatively less-expensive to produce (the salaries required by star actors, at least at first, could be avoided), and more "American" and forward-looking than European-style musical theater.[46] This was true not only of New York City; the 1837 Depression affected places as diverse as Boston, New Haven, Philadelphia, Lexington (Kentucky), and Charleston, and *all* saw a significant increase in new establishments for commercial musical entertainment between 1840 and 1860.[47]

Boston, for instance, which had long survived on only a handful of theaters and museums, saw new venues like the Vaudeville Saloon, the Olympic Saloon, the Boston Museum, the Howard Athenaeum, Graham's Olympic Saloon, the Boston Adelphi, and the Lyceum Theatre all open between 1840 and 1848. Such growth was symbiotically linked to the development of the omnibus and train lines between 1833 and 1845, which linked Boston neighborhoods and opened up the city to more and more outsiders, including daily visitors from New England towns, as well as more permanent migrants wishing to try their luck in the city's growing economy. Beginning with a visit by ballet star Fanny Ellsler in 1840, performers flocked to the city; commercial concerts included those by John Braham, the Hutchinson Family, Signor Marti, Anna Bishop, the Moravian Singers, the Lehmann Family, the Ravels, the Germania Musical Society, the Boston Philharmonic Society, and Thomas Rice. Performances by traveling opera troupes became the latest rage among audiences. As William Clapp explained at the appearance of the Seguins at the Howard Athenaeum in 1845: "So potent was the spell that bound old Boston to English opera then, that almost every performance had a good house, and many were honored with overflows. Two benefits were awarded to Mrs. Seguin, and both had 1400 auditors within the walls, beside many hundreds unable to obtain admission, that remained upon the side-walks content with catching a strain at intervals."[48]

Spectacle, Competition, and Magniloquence

In retrospect, the recovery years of 1838–40 might be understood as a dividing line for the business of musical entertainment in the United States. The momentous economic and social changes of the Jacksonian era, from a new transportation infrastructure to the development of a middle-class "genteel" culture, seemed to have finally converged on the world of music; concert entrepreneurs and performers especially gained a new dominance in the wider world of urban popular entertainment. As the *New York World* noted about the concert business in 1843: "Every soul—every heart—every being [is] getting madder and madder after music."[49]

New urban venues, performers, and events significantly increased available opportunities to hear musical entertainment, which, in turn, started a fierce competition for audiences. The period between 1840 and 1845 marked an increasing acceptance of a level of outrageousness and one-upping that would have been scandalous just years before. Musical offerings tended more and more toward the exotic and reintroduced the theatrical to musical performance: multi-instrumentalists, singing Chinese families, blackface minstrels, dancing Quakers, Alpine bell ringers, a three-year-old "cantatrice," "invisible musicians," and musical automatons, including a fully mechanical, round-the-clock-performing minstrel troupe at Peale's Museum in New York. Sales gimmicks abounded. While the harmonicon, a multi-reed instrument (similar to an organ), was fairly familiar to Americans, for example, soon performers were unveiling grand harmonicons, pan-harmonicons, orchestrions, even a "rock harmonicon." In 1841, a New York "hornist" by the name of Mr. Aupick, announced that he would distribute his collection of sixty well-framed paintings by lottery with the purchase of a ticket to his concert. In 1845, Leopold de Meyer circulated his own biography in advance of his tour and offered a private "preview soiree" as a way to generate audience anticipation.[50]

Touring European virtuosos outdid everyone else in creating concert spectacle. Niccolò Paganini and Franz Liszt, among others, had been performing mind-bending displays of technique and showmanship for European audiences throughout the early decades of the nineteenth century; this approach found great success in the music market of the United States.[51] Ole Bull, a Norwegian violinist who visited the United States in 1843, startled audiences with his crowd-pleasing showmanship and emotional polyphonic playing, which he performed on a modified instrument. At one poorly attended performance by The Havana Opera Troupe in Boston, in 1846, Giovanni Bottesini, the troupe's orchestra leader, and known as the "Paganini of the double bass," "astonished the musicians by his converting a three stringed double bass into a violin, and the prodigies of execution he brought from an instrument so unwieldy to others." Henri Kowalski noted that "Leopold de Meyer played fantasias for the left hand while he ate vanilla ice-cream with his right; Wehli played a military piece; when he wished to imitate the cannons, he sat down on the keys in the lowest bass." Joseph Gungl, the German conductor, reported that "J. L. Hatton, the pianist and composer, at a concert appear[ed] with sleigh bells fastened to his right leg. When he came to the proper place in the piece he was playing, something about a sleigh ride, he shook this leg violently while an assistant made a noise like the cracking of whip."[52]

Behind the scenes, promoters were hard at work too, creating hype, or what Arthur Loesser called "magniloquence."[53] It used to be that concert promoters, in the course of arranging a performance, might provide limited advertising for upcoming events. As H. Earle Johnson hints in his description of concerts in Boston as early as the 1820s:

The routine of arranging a concert is plain. Out of the void an itinerant musician reached Boston, having stopped on the way to undertake a concert in the smaller hamlets; after a few days of friendly intercourse with the musicians of the town . . . he would enlist cooperation for an evening of music at Concert Hall or the Exchange Coffee House. "Communications" would forthwith appear in the paper, attesting to the abilities of the visiting artist and coyly announcing a remarkable exhibition of vocal or instrumental powers such as had never been heard in that metropolis, assisted by the leading musicians of the town.[54]

Public concerts in major American cities, by the 1850s, however, became utterly dependent, like popular exhibitions, on large amounts of press attention and "puffery" to generate curiosity. Concerts were never simply announced but always heightened by being "an unrivalled entertainment," "a grand entertainment," "of unusual attraction," "performed on newly improved instruments," or advertising repeatedly over weeks that the performance night in question was the "positively last night." Reputation was built by sheer assertion and association. A favorite device, for example, was to refer to Paganini (who had died in 1840). Like the "new Bob Dylan" label that hampered many folk singers in the 1960s, almost every instrumental soloist in the 1840s became "the Paganini of" his or her instrument—there were Paganinis of violin, piano, flute, harp, and accordion. Guilt worked as well as humbug. Bernard Ullman, who managed the tours of Henri Herz and Sigismund Thalberg, frequently played on Americans' self-defensiveness about their level of refinement, suggesting that if Americans did not adequately patronize Thalberg's concerts, then European stereotypes of them as cultural poseurs must be true.[55] Another common promotion practice was "deadheading," which was a means of ensuring demand for a concert ticket by actually making tickets unavailable for the first show; theater managers would fill out a house at a concert through free passes to friends, journalists, and even strangers, with the hope that, in R. Allen Lott's words, "a crowded hall would encourage people to investigate—with the help of cold hard cash."[56]

In the end, no one was immune. While singing families and opera were swept into the marketplace for entertainment along with magicians, dancers, automatons, and ventriloquists, older, more isolated forms of private musical performance supported by small groups of subscribing elites, church congregations, and devoted middle-class amateurs faced pressures to "spectacularize." This was a bitter pill, since many of those groups had actively resisted simple and unabashed commercialism in favor of cultivating a more discriminating "taste." However, the goal of refining public musical taste had long suffered under high overheads and fickle audiences; the numbers of failed urban music societies with good intentions were numerous.

Some elite performers, conductors, and concert organizations began to test new models of public interaction. For example, Michael Broyles has shown that such experiments with spectacle were a source of great tension between Boston's two largest music performance societies in the late 1830s—the Boston Academy of Music and the Boston Philharmonic Society. The Academy was founded by Boston's older elite residents and saw itself as deeply concerned with the public good and the education of musical taste in the city. The Philharmonic, in contrast, was founded by businessmen, music dealers, and band musicians, and was solely for the purpose of offering more concert entertainment in the city. The Philharmonic drew far larger crowds at its events. In fact, thanks to its success, the Society was able to engage virtuosos like Ole Bull, to hire acclaimed violinist Leopold Herwig to head its orchestra in 1844, and even to reduce its standard ticket price to fifty cents (rather than the Academy's one dollar). The Philharmonic's Herwig then negotiated with the Academy of Music to alternate their concerts on different nights, something that further eroded the Academy's ability to compete with the Philharmonic and weakened its ability to espouse widespread public musical refinement.[57]

Dodge's Dodge

Barnum's handling of Lind's 1850 concert tour of the United States, mentioned at the opening to this chapter, represented a culmination of these developments. There was no doubt that the tour was a commercial venture. Lind's concert programs included typical advertisements indicating "Jenny Lind music available at the door," or that one might obtain an "authorized edition of Jenny Lind's Music" from a New York publisher. A program for her 10 October 1850 concert at Tremont Temple in Boston included ads for "White & Potter" (the local publishers of the program), "Merriam & Baker Gentlemen's Furnishing Store," and an announcement for "Whipple's Grand Original Exhibition of Dissolving Views":

Now open at the Tremont Temple, and will continue for two weeks, every evening, except the nights of Jenny Lind's Concerts, commencing with the Scenery of the White Mountains; the Floome, Lincoln, N.H.; the Basin; Nacier's Bridge; . . .

etc. . . . The Drummond Light will be exhibited, and its formation explained. . . .
The Oxhydrogen Microscope will reveal the wonders of the Insect world, showing
the wonderful formation of objects too small to be seen with the naked eye. . . . The
exhibition to close with a grand display of Pyramic Fires. Music by Frank Howard.
Tickets 25 cts.[58]

Indeed, despite Lind's much ballyhooed "purity," she was a shrewd busi-
nesswoman who was savvy enough to renegotiate her terms once she realized the demand for her concerts in the United States. And Barnum's description of the tour in his autobiography focuses heavily on the contractual
arrangements, including a reproduction of the lengthy contract between
them, as well as the various ways in which he went about marketing her
talent.[59]

Lind's appearances were calculated to attract the widest possible interest,
especially from audience members who had not participated in music culture before. Barnum expanded opportunities for participation beyond simply witnessing Lind's singing, both in time (before and after concerts) and
in kind. Specifically, for those who could not afford a ticket or did not have
physical access to her shows, he created a host of associated activities: pre-
show songwriting contests, ticket auctions, arrival parades, merchandising,
and press coverage. Barnum's particular creation of "spectacle" included
both onstage antics and offstage attractions.

Even more calculated was Barnum's exploitation of class ideology to appeal to new audiences. Lind was well known for her moral propriety and
Christian faith, in addition to her extraordinary talent as a singer. She later
became a symbol for middle-class refinement, reflecting the spirit of female
gentility not only for her audiences but also for the public generally in
the 1850s.[60] She was perfect for helping Barnum, a grizzled veteran of the
popular exhibition business and the inventor of "humbug," or commercial
fraud, to shed the more unsavory aspects of his reputation and more fully
embrace the refinement—and wealth—of the emerging urban middle class.
As Barnum explained: "Inasmuch as my name has long been associated
with 'humbug,' and the American public suspect that my capacities do not
extend beyond the power to exhibit a stuffed monkey-skin or a dead mermaid, I can afford to lose fifty thousand dollars in such an enterprise as
bringing to this country, in the zenith of her life and celebrity, the greatest
musical wonder in the world, provided the engagement is carried out with
credit to the management."[61]

This intent is clear in the program designs for shows in Boston, New
York, and Buffalo, which all emphasize decorum. Unlike Barnum's usual
attention-getting entertainment bills, which ignored coherent design for
grandiose and multiple typefaces punctuated with pointing fingers and

other informational marks, Lind's program covers were sparse, featuring plain brown paper on which were printed four small portraits of the relevant players in the event (Lind, Barnum, conductor Julius Benedict, and accompanist Giovanni Belletti), each bordered by scrolling vines. Inside, the programs contained a detailed list of the orchestra's individual members, as well as the songs Lind would sing, followed by a lengthy "Sketch of the Life" of each player, emphasizing his or her education and achievements. Some included frameable engravings of Lind. The programs themselves were weighty—for her Buffalo appearances, each of her songs in the program had a full-page spread, with Italian, German, and Swedish verses next to English translations, and amounted to thirty-eight pages in total.

At the same time that Barnum promoted middle-class ideals and their attraction for most Americans, he was careful not to exclude anyone based on class status. It was no coincidence that she did not sing in drawing rooms of the elite, or even in the city theaters that typically featured opera productions; instead, she appeared in the largest possible venues in a given place, from the Castle Garden pavilion in New York City to the "Great Hall" of the newly built Fitchburg Railroad Depot, west of Boston, an appearance Barnum touted "at Reduced Prices, in order to give all classes who are desirous of hearing her an opportunity of doing so."[62] In all, what was being promoted, here, was a celebration of a special occasion; this was not merely a show, but a grand, national reception of an artist of significance.

A Jenny Lind concert, as managed by Barnum, did not simply offer a performance of *music*; through its multiple events and diverse appeal, it offered a more complex and layered performance of *America's commercial music culture*. Jenny Lind, Barnum, the diverse audience, the financial details of the tour, the class aspirations of Americans in general—all were all put on public view and offered up as part of the experience. Indeed, like a magician playfully teasing his audience with behind-the-scenes glimpses or the involvement of audience members in his tricks, Barnum was inviting Americans to examine—and enjoy—their own participation in Lind's tour. In this way, despite his own public avowal of his old ways of profiting through confidence games that encouraged people to discover his own deceitfulness, he in fact managed Lind in a way that produced the same feelings of curiosity. He made participation in commercial exchange an exciting opportunity to be "in" on something. In the past it was the "truth" of artful deceptions like the "Feejee Mermaid"; this time it was the "purity" and "artistry" of the Swedish Nightingale.[63]

Ossian Dodge, who, as introduced at the beginning of this chapter, flamboyantly bid for a Jenny Lind ticket at Tremont Temple in September 1850, seemed to understand this playfulness. From a business standpoint,

Dodge's actions echoed the devices of publicity commonly used by Barnum to drum up interest in his curiosities. Barnum later admitted that he had encouraged the hatter John Genin, his friend and business neighbor along New York City's Broadway Avenue, to bid on the first ticket at New York's auction as a way to achieve notoriety and profits.[64] As writer J. T. Trowbridge wrote about the incident: "Genin was neither a musical enthusiast nor a millionaire, but a man of business . . . who had been shrewd enough to foresee the value of such an advertisement."[65] While there is no evidence that Dodge similarly communicated with Barnum before the ticket auction in Boston, Dodge nevertheless appeared to have understood Barnum's tricks of the trade. Dodge shared Genin's motives but took them a step farther. He saw that the temporary and abstract business relationship he established with Barnum and Lind made it plausible that he might enjoy the social intimacy of two of the most famous people in America. That would be his mark on the world.

On a broader cultural level, Dodge's bid and his portrait of meeting Lind was not atypical for a young man trying to make it in the rapidly changing and competitive environment of the antebellum American city. Born in Cayuga County, New York, in 1820, Ossian Euclid Dodge worked at a variety of jobs up until Jenny Lind's arrival in 1850: apprentice cabinet maker, ornamental painter, wax flower maker, itinerant teacher, comic singer, sketch writer, and finally editor and publisher of *The Literary Museum*, which he purchased as it was going under financially in 1849. Like George Washington Dixon, P. T. Barnum, and many other young men in that period, however, Dodge found most success in the fast-growing world of entertainment, where public exhibitions, panoramas, shows, concerts, museums, novels, and newspapers all proved quite lucrative, particularly when promoted with both a flash of outrageousness and a comforting wink, indicating that all was in good fun.[66]

Dodge was especially skilled at self-promotion, crafting a persona that tapped into the public's concern for public morality while often playfully expanding the boundaries of that morality in the service of making money. Indeed, his autobiography, published in 1860 when he was forty years old, was an outrageous compendium of practical jokes and sketches, intermixed with accounts of selfless moral acts promoted a bit too much as such. In the descriptions of his many early jobs, for example, he doesn't simply teach the art of making wax fruit and flowers but does so as a master artist. He doesn't simply sing comic songs, but sings original "moral" comic songs that provide a much-needed antidote to the vulgarity of popular tunes. He isn't simply a teetotaler but a teetotaler that, through wit and steadfast conviction, commands the respect of Senator (and wine drinker) Henry Clay.[67] In many ways, its style and structure copied Barnum's own 1855 bestseller, *The Life of P. T. Barnum, Written by Himself.*

Some saw him as an out-and-out charlatan. J. T. Trowbridge, the nineteenth-century Boston writer, knew Dodge personally and character- ized his performances as consisting "largely in grotesque grimaces, and the feats of a voice that could go down and down into the very sepul- chres and catacombs of basso profundo, until the hearer wondered in what ventriloquial caverns it would lose itself and become a ghost of sound."[68] Trowbridge based a character in his novel *Martin Merrivale* on Dodge; the character, newspaper editor Mr. Killings, comes off as a humorously double-talking self-promoter, paying his writers in cash with antiquated small change ("fourpence" and "ninepence") and supplementing his day job by staging panoramas, featuring himself as a hero.[69] C. F. Martin, the American guitar maker, formed a similar opinion after Dodge—with ob- noxious self-importance—pestered Martin with requests for a particular guitar that had been displayed at the Crystal Palace Exhibition in 1851.[70]

And there was something less than respectable about some of Dodge's accomplishments. Trowbridge claimed that Dodge took the author credit for lyrics and music written by others, and that "all the songs he claimed as his own were produced in this vicarious manner." Additional evidence indi- cates that his fame was not exactly laudatory: some dictionaries of the pe- riod trace the contemporary meaning of the word "dodge"—as an artifice or strategem for the purpose of deception—to Ossian Dodge himself, or at least recognize the irony of the man's name. A volume of the *Literary World* in the 1850s contained what appears to be a direct reference: "We may well admire the cleverness displayed by this would-be Chatterton, in his attempt to sell the unwary with an Ossian dodge."[71]

Even if Dodge was humbugging the people of Boston, however, the suc- cess of his publicity stunt indicated a lot about the changing musical envi- ronment of the urban United States in the 1850s. "Dodge's dodge," as one publication put it, worked because it exploited people's expectations and depended on social structures that were vital for understanding how musi- cal institutions of the time worked. For example, Dodge clearly tapped into the class desires of middle-class Bostonians, both in the face of cultural competition from New Yorkers and from the snobbish dismissals of Euro- pean elites. Accounts of Dodge's ticket bid in newspapers make it clear that it likely signified self-congratulation at the fact that the audiences of Boston were capable of recognizing and generously supporting a sophisticated art- ist like Lind. The imagined scene of Dodge's lithograph print takes place in a Victorian parlor, instead of a back room at Tremont Temple or in front of Lind's steamship docked in Boston Harbor, because the parlor was a site where class identity in this period was negotiated and displayed. One detail in the carefully refined scene of Dodge's lithograph is that Barnum's figure has a purse, clearly marked with $625, half-stuffed into his coat pocket. Those caught up in Lindmania at the time would have known that Genin the Hatter had bid only $225 in the previous New York auction, and thus they may have understood Dodge's bid as a statement of regional pride. More broadly, Neil Harris has argued that the hysteria over Jenny Lind must be understood in the wider context of cultural anxiety in the United States, where Americans were trying to visibly demonstrate that "finer values, which Europeans had insisted were swamped by money-getting and chicanery, still ruled the New World."[72]

At the same time, however, while Dodge's ruse points to middle-class anxieties about America's musical life and how it compared to that of Europe, it also highlights that America's musical life was of a different order. Part of the excitement of Dodge's ticket bid was the extent to which he openly embraced the commercial foundation of the event; he didn't have elite pretensions about Lind or opera in general but rather promoted his investment in a ticket as a legitimate mode of participation in a musical event. Buying and selling were, actually, what was being promoted here. Interestingly, in the days following the auction, Dodge was not widely excoriated for using the public ticket auction as a springboard for his personal career; rather he was celebrated as someone who had acted boldly, who dared to bid on the Lind ticket at levels no other individual would match. Charles G. Rosenberg, a contemporary biographer of Lind who was present at the auction, described the bid as an "investment" and wrote that Dodge, "like a sensible and skilfull husbandman, he had known where to scatter [his crop of dollars]."[73] An article in *The Musical World*, of London, commented: "Dodge, the vocalist, has, by this dodge, become immortal. By this sudden jerk he has shot himself out of nothing into entity. Henceforth, Dodge will be as a standing synonyme [sic] for done. Well done, Dodge."[74] And, in fact, Dodge made no attempt to hide the self-aggrandizing motivation behind his bid. As his anonymous biographers wrote, "Mr. Dodge attended this auction with the intention of paying $2,000 for a choice seat, if it could not be purchased for a less sum—knowing the great advantage that a reputation of this kind would prove to a man in the concert business."[75] The message was clear: music had joined the market revolution.

But it couldn't have been only someone's personal success that created the lasting appeal of Dodge's portrait throughout the decade after his winning bid. While Dodge's ruse of attaining celebrity as both audience member and performer depended on a commercialized environment in which audience members and performers were institutionally separated, his crossing over from one role to the other was what was most unexpected. In fact, there was great irony in his attaining celebrity as an audience member. While Dodge was clearly a businessman striving for a music career, he simultaneously suggested new possibilities for musical participation. In his portrait, a performer, a manager, and an audience member equally occupied the visual space as distinct and notable figures, realizing a deal with one another. Unlike the previous decades, in which a theater audience typically expressed its will by collectively interrupting the actors onstage during a performance, this image implied a different kind of audience power. Explicitly backstage and more personal, this power derived from the commodification of music: formalized display of a star performer in the marketplace cultivated the thrill of individual choice, encounter, connection, and knowing.

We do not know if Ossian Dodge actually attended the first Lind concert. In fact, his personal experiences as an audience member remain unarticulated. All we really have to contemplate, much like the people of the 1850s, is his public image as an audience member. In the end, perhaps, one might argue that that image had an even wider, more lasting historical effect than his more immediate career goals. While Dodge seemed intent on moving quickly from the role of audience member to that of performer in order to gain notice in the newspapers and make a quick profit, the legions of new concert-goers who were deeply affected by Jenny Lind's tour, and who contemplated Dodge's lithograph in public store windows and on their apartment walls, were beginning to realize a lasting and significant transformation in America's musical life. They did not as easily leave behind their positions in the parquet and balcony, nor did they want to. Dodge, the hustling "Boston vocalist," was part of a passing generation, but Dodge, the music-loving ticket bidder, was a symbol of the future.

CHAPTER TWO

"I Think I Will Do Nothing . . . But Listen"
Forming a New Urban Ear

+{⚬}+

What Do You Hear, Walt Whitman?

In the mid-1840s, around the time that Ossian Dodge first began hustling for renown in Boston, another young man on-the-make was working furiously as an editor, writer, and printer for a variety of newspapers in New York City. Walt Whitman was an aspiring novelist and poet from Brooklyn, New York, who had lived in and around Long Island, Brooklyn, and New York City since his youth. Working for the *Aurora*, the *Statesman*, the *Democratic Review*, the *Brooklyn Evening Star*, the *Brooklyn Eagle*, and other papers, he wrote hundreds of sketches commenting on the day's politics, as well as the changing and chaotic life of New York's streets.

He would linger on corners, observing and listening to firemen, fruit peddlers, omnibus drivers, and sailors. He covered political rallies and parades, the arrival of goods at the wharves, and what it was like to bunk for a night at the police station. On any given day, he might visit a gymnasium or a fortune teller, catch the latest exhibit at a dime museum, and then attend an evening lecture on phrenology or wander the gardens at Niblo's. He often played roles: he was as thrilled to join in a drinking song with the boisterous "mechanics" in the Bowery, as he was promenading up and down Park Avenue in his dandyish clothes and mingling with the fashionable.[1] In all, Whitman saw it as his job to absorb as much as he could. As he later said about his masterwork, *Leaves of Grass*, "the book arose out of my life in Brooklyn and New York from 1838 to 1853, absorbing a million people, for fifteen years, with an intimacy, an eagerness, an abandon, probably never equalled."[2]

New York was the epicenter of commercial amusements in America, and

Whitman was an especially active participant in the city's rapidly growing number of theaters, lectures, exhibitions, and concerts in the 1840s. He was a regular at the Bowery Theater, for instance, savoring the intense emotionalism of actors like Junius Brutus Booth and Edwin Forrest. He was an enthusiastic follower of oratory, attending lectures by Brooklyn preacher Henry Ward Beecher or temperance speaker John Gough. In his early years, he even considered becoming a lecturer himself, and he attended political rallies and abolitionist meetings at Broadway Tabernacle to study the fiery rhetoric of reformers. Perhaps most of all, Whitman discovered music. At first, he was ambivalent about the virtuosos starting to trickle into America, like Ole Bull and Leopold de Meyer; he outright resisted the Italian opera as unsuited for common Americans with whom he identified. His nativist politics in his editorials in the early 1840s fed these initial impressions, and the music he preferred was that of homegrown singing families, Dodworth's Brass Band, or the comic songs of blackface minstrels. However, by 1847, with the opening of the Astor Place Opera House, Whitman was converted. With his status as a journalist on the "free-list" for concerts in the city, he heard most of the major virtuosos that passed through in the late 1840s and early 1850s, including favorites like the Italian baritone Cesare Badiali and contralto Marietta Alboni.[3]

Many have talked about Whitman's appreciation for music, locating the influences of opera and its various singers on his own singing. Indeed, Whitman is popularly called "the bard of democracy," someone whose voice was emblematic of the nation and its people.[4] David Reynolds has gone so far as to juxtapose Whitman's "participatory, dialogic spirit" to a current United States shaped by "passive spectatorship and the mass media."[5] Few, however, have given attention to Whitman's formative role not as a singer but as an extraordinary *listener*. Whitman was constantly practicing and refining his skills as a listener as he walked the streets, attended lectures, and reviewed concerts. His journalistic attention to the vibrant cultural world of New York was not so much through detached observation, as one might expect of a journalist today, nor of the "passive spectatorship" Reynolds points to, but rather through more immediate, transformative hearing. There was both a physical and spiritual intimacy inherent in his "taking-in" of sounds. As he wrote, "I have instant conductors all over me whether I pass or stop / They seize every object and lead it harmlessly through me."[6]

The intimate power of the human voice moved him deeply, and he developed a sophisticated ear for different styles, favoring speakers who were broad-minded, clear and direct, but also who could rouse audiences with careful flourishes of repetition and rhythm—"to make people rage, weep, hate, desire."[7] Despite never having had any formal musical training (he never even learned to play an instrument), music affected him with such force that he described his listening to it in terms of being conveyed physically. He frequently connected the act of listening to the feeling of movement, employing the metaphor of being carried away by ocean waves and using verbs like ascending, winding, surging. As he wrote about a band concert he attended in the foyer of the opera house in Philadelphia:

I was carried away, seeing, absorbing many wonders. Dainty abandon, sometimes as if Nature laughing on a hillside in the sunshine; serious and firm monotonies, as of winds; a horn sounding through the tangle of the forest, and the dying echoes; soothing floating of waves, but presently rising in surges, angrily lashing, muttering, heavy, piercing peals of laughter, for interstices; now and then weird, as Nature herself is in certain moods—but mainly spontaneous, easy, careless.[8]

Hearing and its basic principles of reception, absorption, and resonance was an especially fundamental theme in his first book of poetry in 1855, *Leaves of Grass*. The clearest moment comes when, after describing his own compulsion toward "writing and talk," he suggests that just being aware, in the moment, is enough. Moreover, he proposes, "I think I will do nothing for a long time but listen / And accrue what I hear into myself. . . . and let sounds contribute toward me." He begins with a "sound I love," the human voice, and then attends to sounds "tuned to their uses":

I hear the sound of the human voice. . . . a sound I love, I hear all sounds as they are tuned to their uses. . . . sounds of the city and sounds out of the city, sounds of the day and night;
Talkative young ones to those that like them. . . . the recitative of fish-pedlars and fruit-pedlars . . . the loud laugh of workpeople at their meals,
The angry base of disjointed friendship. . . . the faint tones of the sick,
The judge with hands tight to the desk, his shaky lips pronouncing a death-sentence,
The heave-e-yo of stevedores unlading ships by the wharves. . . . the refrain of the anchor-lifters;
The ring of alarm-bells. . . . the cry of fire. . . . the whirr of swift-streaking engines and hose-carts with premonitory tinkles and colored lights,
The steam-whistle. . . . the solid roll of the train of approaching cars;
The slow-march played at night at the head of the association,
They go to guard some corpse. . . . the flag-tops are draped with black muslin.

He ends with a rapturous description of the opera.[9]

This sequence of listening to the sounds around him would be significantly expanded in future editions of *Leaves of Grass*, eventually becoming stanza 26 of the "Song of Myself." Beginning with the 1860 edition of the book, he also started to include other, similar poetic experiments in listening. He listed examples of carpenters, masons, shoemakers, and mothers engaging in song while working in "I Hear America Singing," indicating the positive strength of everyday Americans. In "I Heard You Solemn-Sweet Pipes of the Organ," he marveled at the rich world of sound, from the loudest to the most intimate, each encounter of hearing functioning as an experience of the stages of life:

> I heard you solemn-sweet pipes of the organ as last Sunday morn I pass'd the church,
> Winds of autumn, as I walk'd the woods at dusk I heard your long-stretch'd sighs up above so mournful,
> I heard the perfect Italian tenor singing at the opera, I heard the soprano in the midst of the quartet singing;
> Heart of my love! you too I heard murmuring low through one of the wrists around my head,
> Heard the pulse of you when all was still ringing little bells last night under my ear.[10]

He would often start poems by describing his encounter with a particular sound (the wind, a canary, a tenor, a locomotive), which would then launch him into reverie. This framework appears in "Out of the Cradle Endlessly Rocking," prompted by the chanting of a mocking-bird; in "As Consequent, Etc.," in which the narrator hears the "whisper'd reverberations" of war and history in beach shells; and in "The Singer in Prison," whose song makes "the hearer's pulses stop for ecstasy and awe." At the opening of "Italian Music in Dakota," he riffs on the juxtaposition of a disciplined regimental band playing in the "gnarl'd realm" of the prairie. In "Proud Music of the Storm," the roar of a storm causes him to outline similarly moving acoustic moments from across the world and in history, declaring: "Such led to thee O soul / All senses, shows and objects, lead to thee / but now it seems to me sound leads o'er all the rest."

In all of this, Whitman moved hearing to the foreground of his readers' attention, using meta-language to point to it. When he wrote "I Hear America Singing" he was ostensibly celebrating the musical vibrancy of ordinary Americans, but the emphasis in the poem is also on the fact that he, Whitman, is stopping to listen to it. In "Vocalism," he asks pointedly, "O what is it in me that makes me tremble so at voices?" In the poem "Salut Au Monde," he asks simply, "What do you hear Walt Whitman?" In a move reminiscent of "Ossian Dodge's dodge," his answer cleverly shifts the roles of singer and listener, simultaneously relating his experience of hearing while also asking readers to reproduce that action in their encounter with his poem. Whitman celebrated his own listening as a means to self-realization, but he was hoping, too, to create a nation of readers/listeners that would hear *him*.[11]

In this circular rhetorical framework—asking people to listen to him sing about listening to Americans sing—Whitman surrounded the multiple roles inherent in performance and attempted to collapse them together. As David Reynolds explained, this was an ideal of oratory at the time: "Absorbed into poetry, the antebellum personal style erased the boundary between performer and listener, between writer and reader."[12] By emphasizing the equality of seeming opposites like speaking and listening, assertion and acceptance, Whitman-the-narrator was (as with all instances of opposition in *Leaves of Grass*) seeking to erase such dualities and create moments of direct connection with all readers, all circumstances.

Commercial concert entrepreneurs were as equally intent on building a connection with diverse audiences as Whitman was, but with the aim of reproducibility and profit rather than democracy and evocation. They were asking people to appreciate and even enthuse about the music making of others—in this case, professional singers and instrumentalists—and to express that appreciation not by explicit empathy, emulation, or joining in, but rather by a more narrowly defined and exclusive engagement of listening and observation. In non-commercialized events, musical actions were more varied, open-ended, and "unmarked"; the most important thing was participating in the singularity of the occasion. In commercial concert culture, musical actions were rigidly segregated and specific; the most important thing was the predictable enactment of a narrow range of actions—performing and listening—in a reproducible framework of musical experience.

This was, in many ways, an experiment in listening as radical as Whitman's. In early nineteenth-century Europe, where musical performance was a significant part of the cultures of Paris, Vienna, and London, audience culture was well developed. And as I have suggested, for the wealthier members of the American middle class, witnessing European stars onstage fit the new ideology of professionalism, as well as their own desires for cultural capital. But for non-elite Americans or those living outside major East Coast cities, who did not have wide access to such experiences, appropriate concert-going behavior was not necessarily intuitive. As pianist Louis Moreau Gottschalk complained from Indianapolis, while on tour in 1862:

What singular audiences I meet with! . . . The other evening an honest farmer asked me, before the concert, pointing to my piano, what that "big accordeon was." He had seen square pianos, upright pianos, but the tail bothered him. Eight or ten days since, at Zanesville, a charming young girl, and her honourable mamma, passed the whole of the concert in watching my feet. They did not know the use of the pedals, and saw in my movements only a kind of queer trembling, and odd and rudimentary steps in dancing which, for two hours and a quarter, afforded them an inexhaustible source of amusement. They were on the front benches, and greatly annoyed me.[13]

In a world based primarily on singing lessons, church choirs, watching parades, playing instruments with friends, and dancing, how did people learn to properly engage in the occasion of commercial performance, to sit and listen? How did they make sense of music from within the prescribed audience role that concert entrepreneurs were asking them to assume?

The act of audiencing, itself, was not exactly foreign to new audience members; it just had not been fully defined for them in the context of music. While Gottschalk exasperatingly perceived untutored audience members as merely bumbling their way through concerts, they were nevertheless paying close attention. They were studying his "big accordeon" and finding amusement in what he was doing to the foot pedals of his piano. They clapped and whistled to show appreciation and demanded an encore if pleased with the performance. This was not behavior of which Gottschalk approved, but rather than dismiss it as ignorant I think it is more useful to consider that his audiences in Indianapolis, Litchfield, Buffalo, and other smaller cities and towns were simply doing what they felt was appropriate for the occasion.

The behaviors of new concert-goers suggests that most aspiring middle-class Americans were relying on the particular cultures of audiencing—both musical and non-musical—that existed in the colonial and postcolonial period. If relatively few people in the United States had had the opportunity to attend concerts regularly before 1850, most members of communities, large and small, had heard a sermon. Many had had the opportunity to watch a dance or circus show. Urban antebellum Americans, in particular, lived in a rich and changing world of sound; like Whitman, they were "just listening," all the time—to preachers, actors, orators, politicians, and salesmen; to minstrels and bands and virtuoso musicians; and, sometimes against their will, to the street vendors, carriage traffic, and foreign tongues of the city. Concert listening was exciting because it redirected and augmented familiar practices. Everyone could do it, and yet it felt exceptional. Whitman's own development, from an initial, broad, fascination with the sounds of the urban environment to his later, detailed knowledge and enthusiasm for Italian opera, is emblematic of how participation in concert culture drew on broader experiences of sound and aurality.

The history of concert audiences, and the struggle to institutionalize listening as a heightened form of consumption, then, must be understood in the broader context of listening's history. The recognition of the sense of hearing as a historically and culturally situated action is indebted to the field of "sensory history."[14] Growing research indicates that while there are many important events in the history of human listening before the nineteenth century, and while older practices of hearing certainly persisted in the period, the Western Industrial Revolution of the late eighteenth and early nineteenth centuries is a watershed moment, when attentive hearing became a newly marked practice. Protestantism had long emphasized the significance of hearing the word of God, for instance, but the fervor and intensity of the religious revivals that swept through the United States in the early 1800s, as well as competition from secular orators and other voices in the marketplace, made that hearing even more important to those involved in such movements. Scientists' objectification of the ear and reformulation of listening as a professional skill, something that began with the invention of the stethoscope in the late 1700s, was further transformed in nineteenth-century England and the United States, where one's ability to distinguish good from bad sound was directly related to social class, morality, and character.[15]

It is in this context that new forms of urban concert listening developed. While intense listening to virtuoso performers at commercial events eventually became an unremarkable way for members of the urban middle class to spend their time, that naturalization was the result of public debate on the part of entrepreneurs, critics, and cultural leaders, as well as personal learning and adjustment on the part of early concert-goers, all of which took place in particular historical contexts punctuated by train whistles, populist poetry, born-again cries, and stump speeches. As John Picker put it, "The subjective nature of sensation was of central interest to the Victorians."[16]

In this chapter, I will address the listening practices of the antebellum era by first examining the politics of listening created by new urban sound environments. The richness of urban sound environments was both enticing and disorienting for many Americans and precipitated a wide range of experimentation in how best to control sound and its meanings. Second, I will outline the more established modes of hearing in the church, theater, and lecture hall, which, over the course of the antebellum era, were increasingly woven together as part of a secularized, cosmopolitan culture. Both situations significantly shaped the auditory literacy required of consumers in the concert hall.

Disruption and Attention: The Politics of Antebellum Soundscapes

When seventeen-year-old Francis Bennett arrived in Boston at the end of August 1854 in order to take a job at the new dry-goods store owned by Charles Fox Hovey and Company, he found himself in a world much different than his hometown of Gloucester, Massachusetts. On his first evening in the city, for instance, he and his friend Charles acquired their first taste of anti-Irish sentiment when a crowd hissed at a performance of "St. Patrick's Day in the Morning" at a band concert.[17] He also had his first sustained encounter with a "Negro meeting house," from which he heard the lively cries of the congregation in the midst of worship: "Of the screeching and yelling I ever heard I <u>never heard</u> any [that] beat those negroes."[18] Most of all, however, Bennett found himself fascinated by his repeated surprise encounters with "bands of music," marching in formation up and down the city streets.

Frequently, when he left home for work or an errand, the tumult of a rally or parade—streaming flags and banners, cries and speeches, and especially drum and fife music—would interrupt his path and draw him away from his intended destination or purpose. While visiting Court Street "to look through Parker's telescope," for instance, he reported in his diary: "As I was studying them [stars and moons], I heard a band of music in Court Square. I immediately ran up there. It was the New York Baxter Light Guard in citizens dress going to the National Theater. I followed them down. As I was coming up I met the North End Free Blues with a band at the head of Hanover Street. I followed them down as far as the East Boston Ferry."[19]

Later in October, he admitted being sidetracked once again: "After I had left my valise, I went down to the union. I had been there but a few moments when I heard a band of music coming down Washington Street. I went out and followed them as far as [unintelligible] St."[20] Two weeks later, he was diverted from an errand by not one but *three* separate bands, marching in support of the new, nativist, political party, the Know Nothings: "After tea I started to go down in Hanover Street on errand. As I was going by Brimfield St., on Tremont St. I heard a drum and fife. I immediately ran down Brimfield into Washington St. and found it to be a company of Know Nothings. I followed them as far as Dover St." After he stopped home briefly, he heard more music. "Just as I was coming out I heard a band of music. I found it was another company of Know Nothings with a burial. I followed on. They proceeded as far as Williams Market when they met another company of the same sort with a band. The other company turned round and took the lead. I followed them up as far as Blackstone Sq."[21]

For a contemporary listener, with access to the world's musics at the click of button, Bennett's excitement about these encounters might seem somewhat foreign. In fact, he appears haplessly instinctive as he follows one band and then just as quickly changes course to follow another, like Buster Keaton in a slapstick street chase. But one of the most common characteristics of everyday antebellum musical experience was that much of it was, by definition, unplanned and uncontrolled. The infrequency and inaccessibility of professional concerts before the mid-1850s meant that heard music was frequently not a matter of personal selection as local happenstance—a passing marching band, echoes of evening choir practice at a nearby church, an impromptu singing performance at a party. Such experiences were marked by the momentary thrill of spontaneity and discovery rather than the studied appreciation of familiarity; in any moment of hearing, it was difficult to know how long the encounter might be, or even what sounds, exactly, were being heard.

The city was especially rich with such surprise encounters with music; in fact, urban areas, filled indoors with the muffled movements and chatter of close neighbors and outdoors with the rattling of horses and carriages on cobblestones, the drone of machinery, and the punctuations of street vendors, presented hearers with a wide, dynamic world of sound, of which music was only a piece. Traditionally, the noisiest times in American towns and cities were always holidays and other ceremonial public occasions; an event was not official if it was not marked with the ringing of church bells or the firing of cannons. However, growing antebellum cities presented a more continuous level of sound than had been encountered before. R. Murray Shafer has written of the ways in which urbanization in the nineteenth century shifted the soundscape from a "hi-fi" orientation, in which "discrete sounds can be heard clearly because of the low ambient noise level," to a "lo-fi" orientation, in which "individual acoustic signals are obscured in an overdense population of sounds . . . there is no distance, only presence."[22] In an expanding urban sphere, filled with people, building projects, and technologies, public places—like squares and parks, docks and urban throughways, open to all—became saturated with continuous, overlapping, or simultaneous sounds from a variety of disconnected sources.

New York had the greatest reputation for street sounds, notably captured for posterity in Samuel Wood's 1808 book, *The Cries of New York*, which featured woodcut vignettes of twenty-six different street vendors advertising their wares with vocal calls, bells, and other noise.[23] The Hutchinson Family Singers, who first arrived in New York in 1843, were thoroughly taken aback by the sheer volume:

The peculiarities of the New Yorkers are very different from the Bostonians. The blowing of horns by the fisherman Hawkers every morning is truly interesting which is followed by their loud course [sic] voices, appealing to the Sympathies of the Citizens to buy their Loading. Then the cry of the chimney sweep is highly gratifying. The music of Bells attached to some old rag cart which is toted about town by some poor menial through the streets. Then the Charcoal seller has confined to the lowest part of his charcoal-carts a Triangle that by the furious driving of the cart through the streets the Triangle is made to ring most furiously and if any one wishes to buy Charcoal they have to be on hand when the Triangle rings!!²⁴

Or, as Edgar Allen Poe explained more irritably: "How often does it happen that where two individuals are transacting business of vital importance, where fate hangs upon every syllable and upon every moment—how frequently does it occur that all conversation is delayed, for five or even ten minutes at a time, until these devils'-triangles [charcoal wagons] have got out of hearing, or until the leathern throats of the clam-and-cat-fish vendors have been hallooed, and shrieked, and yelled, into a temporary hoarseness and silence!"[25]

In addition to street vendors, there were numerous other environmental sounds, many of which are lost to hearers today. Joseph Sill reported that during winter in Philadelphia, "We can hear the tinkling of the Sleigh-Bells at almost any hour of the night."[26] Graham and Shane White report that, in 1815, New Yorkers complained about "black women on the streets using 'obscene and infamous language,' particularly 'profane oaths and vulgar epithets,' and the aggressive way they conducted themselves, 'crowding and jostling' white citizens."[27] Nathan Webb, a young man in Boston in the late 1780s, used to walk the town at night, listening for illicit conversation: "Return'd home ½ past 10 o'clock. At this hour of the night 'tis not a little curious to patrol the streets for an hour or so & view the night walkers— hear them chatt &c."[28]

Diarists also frequently noted the sounds accompanying a fire, a common occurrence in antebellum cities. Arriving in Philadelphia in 1844, the Hutchinsons talked about being awakened in the middle of the night by an alarm:

Just now, a loud alarm of fire and we had the pleasure of listening to the horrid cries of the unprincipled, immoral fireman. Philadelphia has a large circle of Moral people, but the firemen are the most outrageous persons that are known in this republic. How heart-rending it is to hear their unhallowed cries as they pass by our room in a *fiendish* manner, profane and uncalled for expressions continually escaping their lips. Oh! It is frightful indeed.[29]

William Clapp explained that fire bells sometimes interrupted his productions at the Boston Theatre, as occurred memorably during one staging of Romeo and Juliet:

The play had reached the fifth act, and the noble Montague lay dead, the fair Juliet weeping over him. At this point the Old South bell began to toll out alarming peals, and with such vehemence did the bell-puller do his work, that the audience began to fear that even the theatre was in flames, and some movement occurred in the dress circle. Poor Cleveland, dead as Romeo, but still alive as the Apologist, could not resist the ruling passion. He immediately, in the midst of Juliet's lamentations, set up and said: "Ladies and Gentlemen, I beg you not to be alarmed. It is only the Old South bell, I assure you," and before the fair Capulet had time to recover from her astonishment, Romeo again lay dead before her.[30]

Music, while folded into these lively urban soundscapes, was often marked as special, a set of organized melodious sounds which, when encountered, needed to be recognized and savored, perhaps as a balance to the din of everyday life. Anna Cushing and her friends, for instance, traveling in Springfield, Massachusetts, were rudely awakened by music, but nevertheless found the experience pleasurable:

As we had made a zealous determination to compose ourselves to slumber, we were again aroused by the sound of music—up rose we instantly and with alacrity, and, standing at the window, listened with much pleasure to eight or nine songs from some gentlemen, who seemed to be singing for their own amusement, at some distance from the house—"The Post Bellou," "Young Agnes," "The Gondolier," "To Greece We Give Our Shicking Blades," "Here's to You From Browne" &c. &c. After all this, we really did go to sleep at last, in rather an [?] state of mind.[31]

William Hoffman recounted a quiet evening in Albany in 1848 where he and his fellow clerks, closing up their store for the day, enjoyed a dessert and caught a strain of music from down the street: "After the closing of the Store Roger and myself—with James McCaw, enjoyed a good Apple Pie. I bought it—he takes leave—Roger is now standing in the Door listening to very enchanting music—oh it is melodious. Retire at 10 with Roger."[32]

More often than not, however, music encountered in the city was assertive rather than relaxing, meant to grab one's attention. Parades, for instance, the most frequent and potent sources of musical sound, were not only loud and visually stimulating; they *moved*, filling large swaths of the city with music and inviting citizens to join in and spontaneously knit themselves together in ways that marked or re-marked territory. Unlike the silent promenading popular among more elite citizens, which sought to reinforce social boundaries through "the performative utterance of gentility," the relentless, interpenetrating sounds of the street band were more insistently "trying to convince others of the rightness of a particular program to change or defend ways of life."[33]

Parade music was often used purposefully by various political factions to make unavoidable public statements. As Francis Bennett's experiences show, the Know Nothings were quite adept at this tactic. However, so were their competitors, the Whigs. As Edmund Quincy, Jr., once reported in his diary, "As I was returning from my resitation the sound of marshall [martial] music reached my ears. It proved to be the Scot Whigs marching to Rights big tent pitched on the common above our house."[34] While not every presidential campaign included widespread parading, the election of 1860 fostered the formation of paramilitary "marching clubs," known as the "Wide-Awakes," who would beat drums and play music as they marched in the streets in support of candidates.[35]

In addition to political parties, African Americans staged similar parades throughout American cities in the early nineteenth century, often against the wishes of white leaders. In New York,

most of the parades they organized would be loud and lengthy affairs—the annual parades celebrating the end of slavery took at least three or four hours—traversing all the major and many of the minor streets of the city. Bands usually accompanied the marchers; in the case of the first parade to celebrate the end of New York slavery in 1827, there were, according to the New York American, as many as "four or five bands, comprising a great variety of instruments, played with much skill."[36]

Otherwise, military companies that regularly mustered in communities almost always were accompanied by a band. William Smith reported in 1843: "The new military company that is forming was out in South Street to night about 12 of them bad music dull nothing new."[37] Seventeen-year-old Thomas Whitaker of Waltham, Massachusetts, witnessed a more exciting muster: "This day as [sic] been a special day in Waltham. The grand army—and music bands of different places—met here. The mill stopped. And this morning the soldiers and the bands marched on the streets. I walked round with them in the morning. There was about 7 o[r] 8 different bands and a great many soldiers. It was interesting to watch them."[38]

At times, public music could be a source of real social tension. In fact, any unintended and unwanted hearing of music (as with urban sound generally) was a common subject of complaint in the antebellum era. Young law student George Templeton Strong, for example, was almost constantly at odds with his neighbors over their music making.

I was aroused by a fearful yelling, which I took at first for the cry of murder and then for the last dying speech and confession of some hopeless cat in the agonies of strangulation. But on going to the window I found that the unearthly noises in question proceeded from a "feminine," or, as Tom Cringle calls it, a "young female lady," at a house a considerable of a way off, yelling forth "the Mellow Horn" at the top of her voice, with a running accompaniment of what had once been (probably) a piano, but now sounded more like a band of marrow bones and cleavers, or Oky's "Chorus of Coffee Mills and Scissors Grinders." Some boarding school miss, probably. She's at it still, and some one of her beaux has just joined in the second verse at the full stretch of his lungs, like a chimney sweeper or Stentor himself. Horrible! What a noise![39]

A poem appearing in an 1852 issue of Ossian Dodge's *The Literary Museum*, titled "A Musical Bore," registered a similar complaint:

Just over the way
We hear every day
A fellow who's learning the bugle to play;
Or it may be a horn, of that sort, perchance,
Called the 'French,' because '*twasn't* invented in France.
It must be a horn, and we're rather inclined
To think it is one of the very same kind
Whose music brought down old Jericho's wall.
To *this* horn, that job would be nothing at all!
The fellow that blows it,
(And O! how he goes it!)
Has lungs like a double-deck bellows, and ears
Like a jackass's own, for it can't be he hears;
And he ought to be chartered, *he* had, to blow
Rocks—
Gun-cotton itself could not equal his shocks![40]

There is a clear strain of class prejudice in these complaints; identification of which sounds were pleasing and desired and which sounds were a nuisance was not necessarily a scientific process and tended to rely on growing middle-class ideologies of "proper" decorum and social interaction. In fact, both in the North and the South, genteel people came to value the quietude of silent reading and listening as a form of "productive leisure" that was explicitly opposed to the louder, more boisterous pastimes of slaves, immigrants, and workers. As in the days when European colonists and Native Americans struggled to understand each other's sound worlds, aural difference now became a wedge that allowed those in power to place certain social groups figuratively and literally outside the bounds of civilization.[41]

Racial and ethnic prejudice abounded in published descriptions of the music of lower-class blacks and immigrants. Black church worship was uniformly described by middle-class observers in terms of shrieking and yelling. As one Presbyterian minister wrote in 1859:

I was much interested, and yet at the same time shocked, by a spectacle which I witnessed two nights ago. Hearing singing in the neighborhood church—It belongs to the white congregation of a Cumberland Presbyterian Church—I stood at the door and looked in—and such confusion of sights and sounds! The Negroes were holding a revival meeting. Some were standing, others sitting, others moving from one seat to another, several exhorting along the aisles. The whole congregation kept up one loud monotonous strain, interrupted by various sounds: groans and screams and clapping of hands. . . . I was astonished that such proceedings were countenanced in even a Cumberland church.[42]

Immigrants did not fare much better. In 1853, for example, *The Literary Museum* included a news item on the rash of Italian "hand-organists" apparently plaguing Boston:

This city is swarming with itinerating musicians of both sexes and all sizes, with their various instruments and accompanying circumstances in the shape of monkeys, tamborines, and fantoccini. The reporter of the *Boston Herald* has explored the locality where these active nuisances "most do congregate." They are Italians by birth or parentage, and their residence is just out of Ann street near Cross street in a place called Fulton court, in a building which has been divided into four dwellings and each house into six rooms, beside garret and cellar. Into this old building, subdivided as above, nightly congregate about two hundred souls, besides some forty or fifty monkeys in assorted toggery, a large number of hand-organs of different degrees of harmony, according to age and use, many of them accompanied with varied and curious fantoccini, also a host of tamborines, and some few other instruments called musical, from which they grind and force sounds harmonious or otherwise.[43]

As a reporter for the *Boston Post* more succinctly summed up middle-class attitudes about the music of the lower classes in 1838: "The poor can but share / A crack'd fiddle in the air, / Which offends all sound morality."[44]

Overall, the middle-class response to such "noise" was to retreat, after the Civil War, along new trolley lines to quieter suburbs, with tree-lined streets and free-standing single-family homes. Indeed, the preferred decor of the middle class—what we would now label as "Victorian"—was one that purposefully emphasized silence. As Mark M. Smith notes, "Although antebellum architects were sometimes only dimly aware of the absorptive tendencies of different materials, it seems probable that the northern middle class stumbled on and became appreciative of materials that absorbed sound in their efforts to keep homes warm."[45]

Still, leaders felt compelled to legislate against unnecessary noise. Public regulation of unwanted music and related sounds—or "noise"—was not a new concept. The South Carolina Slave Code of 1740 banned "using and keeping of drums, horns, or other loud instruments, which may call together or give sign or notice to one another of their wicked designs and purposes." Singing during worship had long been policed by authorities, including Puritan attacks on singing Quakers, or Ranters, in the late seventeenth century; the push for "regular singing" in New England churches during the 1730s; and middle-class complaints about the clapping, shrieking, and unruly singing of evangelical revival meetings during the Second Great Awakening. However, noise legislation became more precise and specific over the course of the nineteenth century, as it was recognized as a key tool for creating the ideal of civil, orderly conduct. Boston, for instance, passed a law that stated "No person shall ring or cause to be rung any bell, or blow or cause to be blown any horn or other instrument, in notice of the sale of any article, or for any other purpose, in the said streets or elsewhere, unless duly licensed by the Mayor and Aldermen."[46] This criminalization of noise was significantly mirrored in the enforcement of silence as a key element of discipline in antebellum northern prisons.[47]

The control of sound in society was never easy, however, and city leaders' attempts to create "sound morality" sometimes backfired. Henry Clay Southworth reported that Independence Day in New York City was almost unbearable, even *with* laws against fireworks. "This being the night previous to the fourth," he wrote in 1850, "We have nothing but the firing of guns and all kinds of fire arms the cracking of fire crackers the explosion of rockets all night long until late to morrow night. Now while I am writing this there is an endless din—it is against the laws of the City but still they are totally disregarded."[48] Susan Davis explains that in Philadelphia, "City councils attempted to suppress street vendors' cries, bells, and horns as early as the 1830s. Others, typically radical artisans, defended the rights of perambulating sellers, asserting that tradesmen's noise was a kind of public information."[49] In 1838, after the Boston Common Council banned the ringing of dinner bells, a group called the Anti-Bell-Ringing Society was formed in protest. They brought frivolous noise suits to the police court and generally ridiculed the "spirit of ultraism in legislation" by sarcastically taking anti-sound laws to their extreme; their officers included a "Confabulator, to do all the Society's Unnecessary Talking."[50]

Those affected by noise legislation quickly learned to use sound purposefully to irritate and disrupt the social order. On Christmas Eve in Philadelphia during the antebellum era, roving processions of young working-class men, known as "fantasticals" or "Callithumpians," challenged middle-class leaders by collecting free drinks in neighborhood taverns, blocking streets, and carousing in main business and theater districts of the city. Davis notes in particular that "Callithumpians made charivari-like rough music, taking the conventions of marching bands and fife and drum corps and turning them inside out. Dressed in burlesque, they mocked real music with cracked pots, cowbells, kitchen utensils, bent horns, cow horns, fake trumpets, and the whole folk repertoire of homemade and pretend instruments."[51] The first staged blackface performances clearly aimed at up-ending middle-class ideas by featuring unruly sounds, including, for instance, "dat terror to all pianos, harps, and organs, de BANJO."[52] George W. Dixon, one of the earliest blackface stage performers, called his 1830 book of songs and sketches *Dixon's Oddities: A Glorious Collection of Nerve-Working, Side-Cracking, Care-Destroying, Mouth-Tormenting Songs.*

Whatever the success of antebellum sound legislation, the very acts of establishing and breaking such laws brought concentrated attention to sound and its effects on the part of both makers and hearers. In particular, battles between different groups in society about their participation in and experience of the sonic environment began to shape collective values about ideal soundscapes and the nature and role of listening in society. Mark M. Smith has suggested, in fact, that the alleged production of noise on the part of lower and working classes led to an increased attention to the cultivated reception of sound among the aspiring middle class as a mark of aesthetic superiority.[53]

Sensory attention was especially foregrounded in a new wave of sentiment for "plain living" among middle-class reformers, who sought to diminish the effects of rapid commercialization in American life in the 1840s and 1850s.[54] Guidebooks for women raising children and running a genteel household specifically stressed habits of attention as a means to efficiency. Lydia Child, for example, wrote to mothers in 1831 that

Why is it that a botanist will see hundreds of plants in a field, which the careless stroller may pass again and again without perceiving? It is because his *attention* has been fixed upon plants. How is the great novelist enabled to give you such natural pictures of life and manners? A close *attention* to all the varieties of human character, enables him to represent them as they are. You will find that a smart, notable housewife is always an "*observing* woman."[55]

In the arts, attentive observation was also valued, but new writers like Henry David Thoreau and Walt Whitman seized on the physical immediacy of listening, in particular, as a powerful means of making sense of circumstances. Thoreau was influenced by the Transcendentalism of his mentor, Ralph Waldo Emerson, who took contemplative walks in the meadows and woods of Concord every day in order to discover inner harmony and moral strength.[56] Thoreau took this philosophy to the extreme by living alone in a cabin for a year and a half along Concord's Walden Pond. Thoreau resisted prescribing any particular philosophy for his readers, but he did demonstrate the utility of *focus*. As he put it, "My purpose in going to Walden Pond was not to live cheaply nor to live dearly there, but to transact some private business with the fewest obstacles."[57] In his most famous passage from the account of his experiment, *Walden*, published in 1854, Thoreau urges his readers toward "Simplicity, simplicity, simplicity! I say, let your affairs be as two or three, and not a hundred or a thousand; instead of a million count half a dozen, and keep your accounts on your thumb-nail."[58]

Thoreau followed his own advice, at least in his writing, offering chapters in *Walden* that focus on the meanings found in, or prompted by, discrete, singular experiences: reading, sounds, the bean-field, the pond in winter. His chapter titled "Sounds," notably, revels in "the bloom of the present moment," accounting for the sounds he hears as he sits at the door of his cabin, from the falling of a "fresh and tender bough" from the sumac tree nearby to the "distant rumbling of wagons over bridges." With patience and wit, he ruminates on the meaning and feelings he experiences upon hearing each single sound: a train whistle, whip-poor-wills, cows, owls, and the "tr-r-r-oonk!" of frogs.[59]

At the same time as sensory attention was being promoted by domestic guidebooks and transcendentalist philosophers, others were beginning to develop what Jonathan Stern has called "audile technique," a means of separating listening from the other senses and approaching it as a rational skill.[60] While the science of acoustics and the study of the phenomenon of listening was still very young in the antebellum period (pioneers of the science of acoustics, like Hermann Helmholtz, Walter Sabine, and Alexander Graham Bell, would not publish their initial, ground-breaking work until after 1865), techniques of listening were developed nevertheless by various professionals for whom sound figured in their work: antebellum doctors, for example, who had started to identify symptoms by selectively listening to the body through a new device called the stethoscope; miners, who were reporting ways of hearing the substance into which they were boring; and sound telegraphers, who had developed a kind of heightened interpretive-listening while on the job.[61]

For many aspiring members of the middle class, listening to music in concerts provided their own professional standard. Properly hearing and responding to the carefully crafted sounds of music—or, having a "musical ear"—was an object of meticulous study among those aspiring to society. As early as 1831, for example, an essay in *The New England Magazine* asserted "we may hence with confidence maintain, that the first steps of the human race in the path of civilization and intellectual culture, are to be referred . . . to the power of music over the human soul."[62] In 1834, William S. Porter, principal of Monson Academy in Massachusetts and a friend of music educator Lowell Mason, published the more extensive *The Musical Cyclopedia, or the Principles of Music Considered as a Science and an Art, Embracing a Complete Musical Dictionary*, in which he stated:

To have an ear for music, is to have a delicate sense of hearing, so that the ear becomes annoyed by faults, either of tone or measure, and struck with the beauties of the art, when they are heard. A musical ear is chiefly the result of cultivation, and depends mainly on early impressions. . . . By practice alone can the discriminating powers of the ear be carried to the highest point of perfection. To accustom ourselves to listen with attention, is the first step to improvement.[63]

Additional publications in this genre included regular essays and editorials in magazines like *Littell's Living Age, Putnam's Monthly Magazine* and *Harper's Weekly*, praising "civilized" hearing and response at concerts, as well as book-length treatments like Francis James Fetis's *Music Explained to the World: Or, How to Understand Music and Enjoy Its Performance* (sponsored by the Boston Academy of Music), William Mullinger Higgins's *The Philosophy of Sound and History of Music*, and Joseph Bird's *Gleanings from the History of Music*.[64]

The valuing of the "musical ear" in elite circles became so ubiquitous that it became the subject of comedic ridicule. In "The Man With the Musical Ear," an 1853 sketch in *Arthur's Home Magazine*, a man describing himself as "the victim of a fine ear" is tortured as he makes his way through the streets and parlors of the city. Finding himself fleeing a soirée after being asked to follow a Beethoven sonata with the more popular piece by Frantisek Kotzwara, "The Battle of Prague," which "goes on and will go on to the end of time, murdering the peace of mind of every luckless owner of an ear such as mine," the man attends the soirée of Professor Millefiori, "the fashionable Italian vocal teacher." There he is forced to endure "a dozen or more of soprani, mezzo-soprani, contralti, baratoni, and bassi," of whose performance he has "a dim, obscure recollection as of so many contests for the palm of superior noise." Vowing that it is his final soirée, he spills onto the street, where he suffers the greatest agony, "the oyster and the apple-men; the strawberry and the shad-women—what are they to me but so many liberated fiends, placed on earth to persecute the owners of ears!" In the end, he embarks on a project "for the correction of these street evils": a series of music manuscripts—"The Shad-woman's Complete Musical Instructor," "The Oysterman's Apollo," and the "News-Boys' Guide to Parnassus"—all of which provide new musical arrangements for street-sellers' cries, adapting them to the "most beautiful melodies."[65]

Jonathan Sterne has pointed out that widespread application of the principles of audile technique "came to music rather late," not until the latter half of the nineteenth century.[66] And as the final joke in "The Man With the Musical Ear" acknowledged, it was well understood that books of musical instruction and improvement did not necessarily reach those for whom they were intended. For the most part, the music appreciation valued by the middle class remained in the domain of aesthetics, to be expounded on and shared by philosophers and critics. Those not firmly in the circles of respectable society instead relied on themselves. In their diaries they wrote about the sounds they heard in the city, noted the acoustics of concert halls, described when they were moved by preaching and other kinds of oratory, and systematically developed their own knowledge of how to hear music

"Man with the Musical Ear." *Arthur's Home Magazine* (September 1853), 167.

meaningfully. Many early urban concert-goers were, in effect, vocational listeners, more like doctors, miners, and telegraphers than the aesthetes writing books of music instruction. As Walt Whitman said, "I looked upon these concerts in the open air—the nights often so beautiful, calm—as bright gleams athwart the sad history of the harrowing city and time. Yet my enjoyment was altogether untechnical: I knew nothing about music: simply took it in, enjoyed it, from the human side: had a good ear—did not trouble myself to explain or analyze."[67]

Of course, there is a difference between explaining technique and employing it; while Whitman attributed his having "a good ear" to the luck of human genetics, he—along with most of his contemporaries—likely did not simply hear music with a blank slate. Particular cultures of hearing—especially tied to various kinds of oratory and ritual—had long existed in American society and were highly influential in people's daily lives; in fact, they had become so familiar as to be entirely natural, almost invisible. We need to uncover those cultures of hearing in order to make full sense of how people approached the prospect of concert audiencing.

Cultures of Hearing: Church, Theater, and Oratory

Until the Civil War, the place where the majority of Americans listened most was in church. In fact, listening in church had been a key aspect of daily life in many localities since the founding of North America's first European colonies. Roman Catholic and Anglican worship in Europe for centuries had offered an immersive experience of sound, enhanced by everything from the use of organs as part of religious ritual to the resonant qualities of cathedral architecture.[68] Protestant religious worship also valued listening, but excised much of the perceived pageantry of the Roman Catholic service and instead placed heavy emphasis on the simple act of apprehending God's Word in the Bible. While this included learning to read scripture on one's own, it also meant earnestly listening to ministers preach in accordance with the Bible's statement that "faith cometh by hearing."[69]

This was a serious matter for both preachers and congregants, since any sermon could be critical in affecting one's realization of faith. In Puritan New England, everyone in a settlement was expected to attend all services. In the words of historian Ola Winslow, it meant that the devout listened to: "Sermons, thousands of them. Two per week, one hundred and four per annum from every minister until his last earthly Sunday. No sermon was less than two hours long and usually it was longer. . . . In every New England town 'pious, plaine-hearted Christians' spent weeks of their waking lives, year after year, seated in the pew, listening. The obligation was largely self-imposed; they wished to listen."[70]

With preaching so crucial for the souls of any congregation, seating was altered from the inward-facing boxes of Anglican-style churches to rows of benches angled toward the preacher in an amphitheater arrangement. Additionally, many congregations paid for large sounding boards over the pulpit. A sounding board helped to increase the clarity and range of a minister's voice and direct it out over the pews, allowing congregants to better hear him articulate God's Word.[71]

Over time, the doctrinaire Puritanism of the first generation of settlers weakened by the late 1600s under increasing secularism. To some extent, in all denominations, the simple role of hearing God's Word became less intense, and other standards, like social standing and family membership, became influential in the practical matters of congregations, from seating to voting power.[72] Not surprisingly, the revivals of the Great Awakening, in the 1740s and after, involved a reclaiming of the power and immediacy of listening in one's faith. Early Great Awakening preachers like Jonathan Edwards and George Whitefield were specifically concerned with developing a "prophetic mode" of preaching that sought to emotionally move hearers toward critical self-examination and renewed commitment to the Christian faith.

Whitefield went so far as to publish a sermon in 1740 called "Directions How to Hear Sermons," in which he articulated the qualities of "qualified hearers." Beginning with a lament that "out of those thousands that flock to hear sermons, but few, comparatively speaking, are effectually influenced by them," he sought to remind people, quoting Jesus, to "take heed how you hear." For Whitefield, this entailed, first, a proper expectation, not for pleasure but for learning; hearers must be neither too prejudiced against or toward any preacher as a person, but remain in a "teachable disposition." In particular, hearers must maintain an urgent focus on a preacher's words, as if their lives depended on them, since "Whilst Christ was Himself on earth, it is said, that the people hung upon Him to hear the gracious words that proceeded out of His mouth. And if we looked on ministers as we ought, as the sent of Jesus Christ, we should hang upon them to hear their words also." In fact, indicating its unfortunate regularity, he specifically criticized those "unhappy men" who "instead of hanging on the preacher to hear Him, doze or sleep whilst He is speaking to them from God." In the end, following these prescriptions would allow God's Word to "be delivered to [hearers'] own hearts," and with, proper prayer and self-examination, enable them to live as "perfect men in Christ Jesus."[73]

This renewed interest in the power of hearing God's Word was explosive. Not only did sermons become catalysts for conversion, but also for other kinds of listening. Those who had never studied theology, nor shown any proclivity for public speaking, claimed that they were "called" to preach through heard instructions from God. Soundless, "interior" hearing became an important factor in conversion stories, often acting as the catalyst for the dramatic "turning" that precipitated being "born again." Sounds of thunder, bells, and birds were all carefully examined for evidence of either God's grace or Satan's temptation. By the start of the nineteenth century, Leigh Eric Schmidt explains, "The devout—Quakers, Baptists, Moravians, Methodists, evangelical Congregationalists and Presbyterians, among them— heard with an acuteness that was often overwhelming."[74]

While the church provided the primary framework of listening for them, antebellum Americans were also learning to hear while at the theater. Theater was considered representative of English decadence and had been banned by Congress for much of the American Revolution, but in the 1790s, it rebounded even stronger than before, with a wave of theater building in Boston, New York, and Philadelphia. Often financed by local elites as stockholders, most theaters were built with generous "pits"—an open floor area before the stage, and with reduced ticket prices, both of which attracted artisans and other workers to an amusement typically patronized by the gentry. Even with continued opposition from religious groups, theater became one of the most important forms of popular culture in cities.

The content of "theater" in the early 1800s did not focus on the production of whole plays but rather featured, on any given night, a variety of acts across the categories of "overture," "main piece," and "afterpiece." As Karen Alquist notes, "In one evening they could be moved to tears by tragedy or melodrama, dazzled by spectacle, kept laughing by comedy, amazed by athletic feats of dance or acrobatics, swept up by the power of a piece of music, and comforted by an old-favorite song."[75] Audience members engaged such varied programming with participatory enthusiasm. Theater spectating was not an act of receiving or witnessing stagecraft, as much as creating a simultaneous, responsive performance. Theater audiences were well known for engaging in rowdy interaction with the action onstage. They stopped actors and forced them to repeat lines; burst into applause or catcalls at any moment, when so moved; and generally moved about the theater without particular regard for the coherence or sanctity of the staged narrative.

Theater in the early 1800s was more like a rock concert today, at least in terms of audience interaction. It was not necessarily that audiences were simply *not* listening, as some critics would charge at mid-century, but rather that audiences listened in such a way that freely expressed their own concerns and needs.[76] In the 1790s, for example, when political debates between Federalists and Democratic-Republicans were at their height, audiences tended to understand what they saw and heard in the context of partisanship. Any reference that might be interpreted as favoring one side or another could spark cheers, hissing, and, sometimes, even rioting. Along the same lines, class worked as another filter for understanding; artisans and mechanics tended to react enthusiastically to dramas that highlighted characters or situations from their own lives. In general, melodramas that offered simple character types encouraged such identification, as actor Frank Chanfrau discovered when his character Mose, a representation of the New York City Bowery b'hoy, became a sensation for working-class audiences throughout the 1850s.[77]

Identification with characters was further heightened by the promotion of "stars" after the 1820s. The star system featured the presence of famous actors in the lead parts of a production. While audiences had previously identified with character types, they soon came to identify with the person of the actor, which superseded any one role he or she might be playing. Such identification continued traditions which were often disruptive of the stage action, since audiences expected—and demanded, through non-staged contact in encores, curtain speeches, and the like—stars to cater to popular will.[78] Richard Butsch explains, "In live theater the meanings from the text (the play) and from social interaction (performers with audience) merged, since audiences interacted with actors as both text (the characters) and as social beings (actors). There was no separation here of text from context."[79]

Related to both church and theater was the world of antebellum rhetorical culture. Oratory was a key tool in American democratic life, and had been a mainstay of election campaigning, both at the national and local levels, since the founding of the Republic. In the 1840s, many of America's best-known politicians were also its best orators, including Daniel Webster, Henry Clay, and John Calhoun. Social reformers, including temperance and anti-slavery advocates like Wendell Phillips, Ralph Waldo Emerson, Henry Ward Beecher, Frederick Douglass, and Cassius Clay, used the power of oratory to great advantage. Popular, too, was the American lyceum movement, developed in the 1820s as a means to coordinate public education in the arts, sciences, religion, philosophy, and literature. By the mid-1840s, 4,000 communities in the United States had a lyceum or similar society for sponsoring public lectures. As Van Wyck Brooks commented: "There were constant courses in every town and village . . . on chemistry, botany, history, on literature and philosophy; and almost every eminent man in New England joined in the general effort to propagate knowledge. . . . It was quite the rage."[80]

In reform oratory, which often took place amidst audiences who were ill-disposed toward the speaker's message, moral elevation of the audience and redirection of their emotions were key. This was typically achieved through evocative stories and imagery. As Terry Baxter explains, "American reform oratory was . . . characterized by the arousal of strong emotions. Often this served to ingratiate the orator to the audience by replacing any anger or resentment they may have felt at the rebukes of the orator with terror, pity, or delight. The contradicting emotion was yet one more part of the 'power' the orator was allowed to assert over his audiences."[81]

Important, too, was creating an intimacy that fostered identification, especially since most of the listeners at lectures might not know a traveling lecturer personally. For some lecturers, this meant using "folksy" language; for others, it meant physical proximity. Whig senator Henry Clay, for example, always made a point of standing as near as possible to his auditors; others followed suit, leaning out toward audiences while speaking or leaving the safety of the podium in order to convey a sense of democratic openness and even vulnerability. The key was for speakers to come across as representative; listeners had to see some version of themselves on stage even as they admired the special rhetorical skills of any speaker.[82]

Despite dire warnings from people like George Whitefield about the dangers of inappropriate or wrongly motivated hearing, Americans, as a whole, never fully separated their moments of listening in church, lecture hall, and theater from, respectively, salvation, education, or pleasure. The diarists I have studied frequently attended theater, lectures, church, and concerts as part of their weekly routine, and naturally wove such events together in the continuity of their daily experience. But this was aided by the erosion of structural divisions between the cultural realms of religion, oratory, and theater, thanks to the rapid expansion of cities, communications, and markets in the growing country of the 1820s and 1830s. A social movement toward "democratization," unleashed by the populist tone of the Jackson campaign in 1825, helped to weaken institutional authority and encouraged new vernacular forms of expression that borrowed from a range of cultural sources. In addition, there was increasing pressure on all public cultural institutions to appeal to new generations of potential participants to compete in a broad marketplace of culture. As a result, the kinds of hearing expected in church, theater, and lecture hall—urgent listening to preachers, expressive reaction to plays, and strong identification with orators—began to significantly influence one another.

Crossover between cultures of hearing occurred first out of necessity. In a rapidly growing society, there often was not time or immediate resources to construct buildings dedicated to specific uses; instead, existing structures served mixed uses. In 1832, for instance, when Free Church Presbyterians in New York City were searching for a space for their expanding congregation, they obtained a ten-year lease on the Chatham Theater. While it was not unheard of for a congregation to rent a commercial space for services, that they did so in a theater "plunged the enterprise into the center of the heterogeneous public," as Jeanne Kilde put it, and opened up services to theatrical associations like staging, drama, and personality.[83] The Free Church Presbyterians actually precipitated a wider trend among evangelists of all denominations, who attempted to actively "convert" theaters, opera houses, and saloons by bringing religion to the heart of what was perceived as commercial, non-religious territory.[84]

Churches, in turn, operated as theaters and concert halls; some of the institutions that had been initially converted from theaters were returned to secular use over time. The 1836 Free-Presbyterian Broadway Tabernacle was frequented by George Strong in the 1840s for a variety of secular lectures and concerts. The Millerite "Old Tabernacle" in Boston became the Howard Athenaeum, a venue for variety acts, plays, and opera, in 1845. Tremont Theater in Boston, built in 1827, became Tremont Temple in 1843; after a fire in 1852, it was rebuilt and used for a variety of public events, including auctions, lectures, and concerts. Kilde states that after the Civil War, "architects generally found little need to distinguish between requirements for secular and religious auditoriums" and new construction of both sacred and secular auditoriums included curvilinear seating, proscenium arches, staged places for speakers/preachers and choruses/choirs as standard in any auditorium space.[85]

This "mixed-use" of buildings was reinforced by hearers, who often engaged in their own "mixed-use" understandings of what they heard, bringing together ideologies and practices from one cultural form to another. Theater, for instance, whose rowdiness and illicit behavior made it off-limits for most Christian families for much of the colonial period, was transformed by a concerted effort on the part of theater owners in the 1840s and 1850s to present a more controlled atmosphere suitable for genteel audiences.[86] Conversely, oratory, initially considered by some to be a "moral entertainment" that offered an alternative to the dangers of the theater, became decidedly more theatrical. As theater became more "disciplined," the contrasting "moral entertainment" of lectures became less of a unique draw and antebellum orators found themselves raising the bar of spectacle and rhetorical flash, in an effort to compete with each other and against other forms of spectacular public amusement. As Baxter said, "orators were not infrequently compared to actors, and their platforms to stages.[87]

While oratory became more theatrical, so did preaching. Evangelical revival meetings, unlike previous forms of congregational worship limited to a selected group within a local community, were large, public events, open to all believers—and, especially, non-believers. In such a context of unknown audiences, a speaker's authority derived not from erudition or social connections, as they had previously, but solely from charismatic presentation. Charles Finney was characteristically direct about revivalism's theatrical connections. While he believed that theater was immoral, he nevertheless advocated that preachers adopt the "practiced spontaneity" of stage-acting as a viable method for reaching non-believers and skeptics.[88] Indeed, general adoption of a plain-spoken yet highly demonstrative and emotional delivery helped to make several preachers, including Henry Ward Beecher, Lorenzo Dow, and Charles Finney, household names, more like celebrity lecturers than ministers.

The result was that sermons, previously considered even by the most devout as events to be endured out of religious duty, became freely chosen as a form of amusement. Walt Whitman, for example, attended multiple churches less for personal worship than to hear the preachers in action. William Hoffman, another young New Yorker, regularly spent the "hour for Meeting" by splitting his time between several churches across denominations; he identified each church in his diary by the particular preacher he went to hear. Henry Clay Southworth attended a variety of churches every Sunday, including Baptist, Episcopal, Free, and Dutch Reformed, often with friends or women of interest. His diary entry for one Sunday in July 1850 was typical: "In the morning attend church at the 'Church of the Messiah' Mr. Osgood preached, dined with Lucy, attend Trinity Church at Brooklyn in the afternoon, and in the evening went to Church at Dr. Beecher's in company with Miss Strong."[89] In general, Southworth and others viewed preachers critically, as one might treat a lecturer. As Caroline Dall wrote in her diary about a visiting preacher: "I closed my eyes and listened to him with great delight. I am sorry that he is either thoughtless or conceited."[90]

Along the same lines, camp meetings and other revival meetings, according to R. Laurence Moore, became "arguably the first large-scale popular entertainments in the United States" in which people combined a serious interest in salvation with "comraderie, diversion from routine, and relaxation from labor. . . . People looked forward to revivals in the same way they looked forward to a 'mammoth picnic'; campsites came complete with concession stands selling gingerbread, lemonade, and, in the days before temperance took over, liquor."[91] For more traditional ministers in established denominations, revivals were not only offensive in content, dispensing with centuries of Calvinist doctrine, but were offensive in style, offering spectacle over piety, surface over depth.

Experiencing worship as a pleasurable occasion for audiencing was an ongoing problem in Protestant ecclesiasticism, one that had cropped up in earlier decades as churches attempted to refine their worship practices. Protestant churches in New England, for instance, had long resisted the introduction of instruments in services because the presence of musicians directed one's attention to the quality of the music rather than "making a joyful noise unto the Lord." In the 1730s, some Congregational church leaders called for "regular singing" rather than the harsh cacophony created by individualized singing. Newly published hymnals distributed the music widely in the 1760s, and singing schools, offered seasonally in local communities by visiting teachers, were formed as a means to enable congregants to learn how to read music.

This was a tricky business, however. The point was to regularize singing not make it into concert performance. The advent of a new, more complex sacred music known as "fuguing," led by composer William Billings, did not please conservative members of the church. And singing schools developed not simply as supportive enterprises for church worship but established institutions in themselves, ones that proved a powerful attraction for young people, who used the occasion of classes as an opportunity to socialize away from the strict oversight of their parents. Moreover, singing-school classes often held their own "exhibitions" to show off their new choral skills, and, eventually, by the beginning of the nineteenth century, singing-school students began to insist on sitting together as a choir during services. Such choirs initially led the congregation in singing from the rear of the church, but over time they had become the sole source of music for services: they sang from a gallery in the front of the church, located behind the minister's pulpit, and the rest of the congregation became an audience and listened. This gradual separation of one group of skilled performers from the rest of the congregation not only confronted Calvinist traditions but also introduced new frameworks of performing and listening that intensified the connections between Christian worship and secular forms like theater.[92]

The parallels between worship and theater or concert culture were not lost on participants. Samuel Gilman, for example, wrote a memoir in 1829 of his experiences in a New England church choir in which he took pride in the work involved:

It is impossible to look back without some of the animation of triumph upon those golden hours of my early manhood, when I stood among friends and acquaintances, and we all started off with the keenest alacrity in some favorite air, that made the roof of our native church resound, and caused the distant, though unfrequent traveller to pause upon his way, for the purpose of more distinctly catching the swelling and dying sounds that waved over the hills and reverberated from wood to wood.

However, at the same time, Gilman recognized that this pride was not exactly in the spirit of worship:

And yet, when I remember how little we kept in view the main and real object of sacred music—when I think how much we sang to the praise and honor and glory of our inflated selves alone—when I reflect that the majority of us absolutely did not intend that any other ear in the universe should listen to our performances, save those of the admiring human audience below and around us—I am inclined to feel more shame and regret than pleasure at these youthful recollections.[93]

Nathaniel Gould was far more critical. In his 1853 history, *Church Music in America*, whose subtitle included *With Cursory Remarks on Its Legiti-*

mate Use and Its Abuse, he called the period between 1770 and 1806 the "dark ages of psalmody," criticizing fuguing as nothing more than "bewitching jingles," condemning the behavior of choir members (who, in unguarded moments in the choir loft were known to take a nap or enjoy a glass of lemonade), and in general pointing to the growing perversion of worship practices. As he imagined a foreign visitor to an American church:

He goes to church,—sees the man of God in his place, who reads the Scriptures,—prays. All is solemn and appropriate. The psalm or hymn is to be announced, and he says, "Let us continue the worship of God by singing." The hymn is read. The stranger expects, and has a right to expect, the same solemnity, in this performance, as in that which has preceded. He looks where other eyes are directed, and there sees a number of young persons, apparently in confusion, partly hidden by a curtain, preparing for some exploit. By and by he hears, perhaps, the sound of instruments similar to those he had heard before at the theatre,—if he had ever been there. The singers catch the sound,—they rise, and thoughtlessly commence, and continue the exercises as directed. Nothing in the air of the performers or in the style of performance gives any indication of solemnity, that can, in his mind, possibly connect this service to what he has heard before.[94]

Despite such criticism, however, the practice of choir singing continued, enjoying great appeal throughout the nineteenth century. As Gould acidly noted, choral composer William Billings even had what we would today call fans: "At his rehearsals his room was crowded, inside and out, with listeners, like the hearers of Jenny Lind, or the Germania Band."[95] The performative aspects of church music were especially exploited during a highly successful tour during the 1860s of a group known as Father Kemp and His Old Folks, in which people dressed up in vintage Puritan clothes and fugued tunes. Father Kemp playfully trod the line between sacred music performance and more secularized humor. As he joked in his memoir about one performance as part of a service in a New Bedford church:

The house was packed long before the time of commencement, and it is believed not a pew-owner got into the building. The audience was evidently composed mostly of those who had never been to church before. My choir sung one tune. When it was concluded, the "most enthusiastic applause," as the theatrical critics say, followed; the spectators (not worshippers) clapped hands and stamped feet, while the "peanut brigade" in the galleries whistled and hooted with double their usual zeal. The situation was painful and ridiculous. After a few vain attempts to calm the storm, the minister dismissed the congregation, and the "Old Folks" were ever afterwards found "at home" on Sunday evenings.[96]

In the end, the focus on "good" music in church was not simply to create more opportunities for entertaining experiences, but rather followed the logic of professionalism that was transforming middle-class society at large. It was clear that many middle-class families in Protestant churches wanted all music they heard to be of a certain quality, and if that necessitated "professionalizing" the performance of church music, then so be it. As Gilman explained, "The extensive cultivation of secular music in private families may render very many ears so fastidious, as absolutely to frustrate the object of sacred music at church, since the tasteless and indiscriminate clamour necessarily produced by the voices of a mixed congregation, must tend to excite in the more refined classes a disgusted and indevout spirit, rather than the sweet and lofty aspirations of choral praise."[97]

In fact, this general trend toward professionalism in all realms of middle-class experience culminated in the presence of events that subtly—and to some, confusingly—combined the sacred and the secular. Ralph Waldo Emerson, a former minister, became immensely popular in the United States during the 1840s as a lecturer, educating ordinary Americans about the theories and values of his brand of Transcendentalism. When people went to hear Emerson speak in the 1840s, were they listening to a preacher or an orator? In the late 1810s, the Handel and Haydn Society in Boston began producing a series of sacred music concerts that featured Handel's *Messiah*, performed in a secular concert hall. People attended and listened with appropriate solemnity. Were they worshiping or attending a concert, acting according to the efficacy of ritual or the pleasures of entertainment? When singer John Braham gave a concert at the "Exchange Saloon" in New Haven in 1842 and then, a little later, offered a "Sacred Concert" at the Church Street Church, were the citizens troubled by the apparent moral discrepancy?[98] It simply wasn't clear, and few listeners fussed with the distinction. As Moore commented about Emerson: "His hearers correctly understood that his advice for living fit comfortably within a Christian moral framework" and that his success "indicated how little distinction many Americans made between religious and secular teaching."[99]

In other words, people were beginning to listen all the same. Listening was becoming a generalized skill that people learned, interiorized, and could apply to very different situations across previously separated realms. Nathaniel Gould feared that in America's churches "there are many performers and hearers striving rather to tickle, and have their ears tickled, than their hearts improved."[100] But in a culture in which preachers were entertaining and lecturers were inspiring—and music was somehow both—he was tilting at windmills. All public performance was inevitably commodified to some extent; preachers, actors, lecturers, and musicians were in competition for ears *and* hearts.

Concert going expanded beyond its elite origins in the United States amid this context of convergent listening. At least from the perspective of urban middle-class auditors, concerts were to be heard like other performance events in the marketplace of culture—with both the pleasure afforded by entertainment and the seriousness accorded to self-improvement. That the act of listening to music had become a form of economic consumption at all, however, was not necessarily a logical equation. While it is commonplace to associate the act of *making* with production and the act of *receiving* with consumption, the concepts of "production" and "consumption" actually derive meaning from the contexts in which they are used.[101]

In the antebellum era a significant segment of the American music market was centered on music publishing and instrument manufacturing, which eventually came together to create the extraordinary popularity of the home piano at mid-century. Middle-class families made the piano a central fixture of the parlor in the antebellum era, with both musical and extramusical meanings: it was specifically feminized as a means for young middle-class women to display their individual education and refinement, and, additionally, it served as a piece of formal decoration that indicated a family's class prestige.[102] Based on the piano's success, one might say that the realm of "production" in the antebellum period consisted of the craftsmen, businessmen, and educators who made and distributed the tools of making music: instruments, music, and lessons.[103] Buyers could use, or "consume," those goods in a number of ways, including displaying them in the home or employing them—through playing or singing—in the act of making musical sound. Of course, the playing of instruments or the singing of songs was itself "producerly," as Roland Barthes might say: it required productive and physical work on the part of the consumer to wrest sound from an instrument or to decipher and correctly render the latest song.[104] But both these primary and secondary modes of production fit well with the work ethic of middle-class America, since they all depended on talent, application of skill, and personal achievement.

Increasing opportunities to consume music through listening at public concerts complicated this economic and cultural framework. While the sales of instruments and sheet music continued to support home-musicking throughout the nineteenth century, the public concert or show in the 1840s presented a different object of exchange, or musical commodity: not the tools of making music but musical performance itself. In other words, potential buyers were asked not to purchase the means for *creating* a shared musical event but instead were asked to purchase an opportunity to *witness* a musical event. In fact, commercial concerts narrowed musical experience by highlighting an intense relationship between listener and performer and placing all others that may have been involved in making music—directors, composers, critics, instrument manufacturers, retailers, promoters, designers, and so forth—backstage, invisible in the shadows. In the wit of Arthur Loesser: "In general . . . we may say that ordinary song consumers of 1820, and long after, were inclined to assume vaguely that music was generated anonymously by a kind of spontaneous combustion."[105]

While such listening was shaped, as I have suggested, by traditions in religion, oratory, and theater, its first direct manifestation in the United States was in the "exhibitions of music" that musicians offered to elite audiences in the late eighteenth century. An "exhibition," a noun stemming from the Latin "exhibere," or "to hold out," attained its modern meaning of a public display of works of art, manufactured articles, natural productions, and so forth, in the mid-eighteenth century.[106] It was closely aligned with the curiosities of early museums, in which "show-rooms" were filled with animal skeletons, undetermined artifacts from archeological digs, paintings, statuary, humans of freakish size or deformity, and native peoples in tableau recreations of their exotic home habitats.[107]

In general, musical exhibitions could be associated with *both* the superficial flashiness of entertainment and the mundane seriousness of lectures. On the one hand, for instance, *exhibition* was a term used by religious leaders to condemn the theatricality of church choirs. (As one booklet on church music warned: "Remember that singing in a religious assembly, is not of the nature of a musical exhibition, but is a serious and important part of the worship of God"[108]). At the same time, however, the term *exhibition* was employed to indicate theatrical performances that were not dramatic *enough*. As George Hogarth commented in 1838 about Mozart's alleged inability to create effective opera: "Their great length brings the action of the drama to a stand as often as they occur, while their artificial structure, and the elaborate style of singing which they require, render their performance a musical exhibition, rather than the expression of the feelings and passions of a dramatic personage."[109]

While perhaps confusing to us today, a musical exhibition was thus perfect for potential middle-class audiences in search of diversion because it was understood as strictly neither an immoral performance like a stage play nor a dry and intellectual sermon, devoid of modern sensibility. It was, rather, a kind of useful demonstration; it represented a "safe" or moral way for people to engage in an event of performance. As already discussed, antebellum theater did not have the "fourth wall" that it has today, in which the action on stage occurs as if the audience is not there. Audiences and performers regularly interacted with one another, trading insults, receiving requests, and repeating favorite passages, without any pretense to the "realism" of the narrative's internal time or to the scenery of the work being performed. Of course, this could lead to possibly chaotic situations, including riots, which, in part, made the theater unrefined and dangerous for potential middle-class audience members. In exhibitions, however, a kind of fourth wall *did* exist. Unlike a play, whose meaning was centered in the socialized moment of its creation, an exhibition was a virtual capsule of another world; its meaning and appeal lay in the metonymic connection between its showing and its previous natural state.

An exhibition's display for an audience was always a heightened signifier for another reality, somewhere else. Audiences were expected not necessarily to join in the exhibited music as listening participants as much as simply *listen in* on the situation publicly put before them.[110] Music exhibitions, then, were not concerts, as we understand them today, but rather American versions of a unique eighteenth-century European phenomenon that Paul Metzner has labeled "publicization," a public display of private activity for the entertainment of others.[111] There was an element of *revelation* involved in such events (which might be understood by the current term *exhibitionist*). School music exhibitions, for example, regularly held at the end of the academic year, were events where students would "show off" their otherwise unheard learning. Music societies and clubs, too, would hold periodic exhibitions to make known their otherwise private and friendly music making. Often, the excuse for such exhibitions, which, according to social protocol, would be grossly presumptuous otherwise, would be to benefit one of its ailing members or a local institution in need.

In the 1830s, such exhibitions became more widely commercialized as stand-alone events, targeted toward the burgeoning middle class. Igor Kopytoff has described the ways in which objects can move in and out of "commodity status," and this is a clear example of such a juncture for musical performance.[112] As I mentioned earlier, among the first performers in the United States to engage in such commercial displays were singing families, who essentially commodified their private music making for public consumption. The rage for such families was short-lived, but the virtuoso concert culture that took its place in the following decade encouraged a similar exploration of public and private realms, as well as the power of revelation and display.

There was more than simple economic "demand" at work here. Iwan Rhys Morus, who has written about the appeal of the industrial exhibitions of London in the first half of the nineteenth century, explains the ways in which exhibition audiences "were being taught to see machines as consumer goods, to be admired, fetishized and desired."[113] The same was true of music. Participating in a concert as a listener, for example, reproduced the prestige of European art culture, something that enabled many of the earliest aspirants to the middle class in antebellum America not only to experience iconic works of musical taste but to promote and celebrate such taste itself. John Evelev explains, "Listening to Jenny Lind sing, or watching 'The Drunkard' at the Lecture Room, or listening to Emerson lecture at the Lyceum Hall, the antebellum urban middle class could see their values performed on stage and their collective identity embodied by their fellow audience members, reassuring them of their prominence in American life."[114]

In addition, the act of listening itself worked as a privately held and developed skill, potentially exhibiting levels of virtuosity normally associated with singing or playing an instrument. Indeed, there was a proud independence wrought by repeated listening to concerts and developing opinions about performers that corresponded to growing middle-class ideals of individuality.[115] Music listening was not only an acquirable skill, but a skill that marked character—after all, any gentlemen of standing had to have cultivated a "musical ear."

The skill of listening was also a practical means to negotiate the antebellum economy. In the volatile retail market of early American industrial capitalism, there was little governmental regulation of commercial exchanges; the watchword was "buyer beware." Language—indicated by the new terms of *humbug*, *ballyhoo*, and *puffery*, as well as the vogue for ventriloquism— was especially pernicious: the sounds and words of salesmen were thought to be dangerously influential forces of duplicity. As P. T. Barnum explained, in his early days as a goods merchant: "Each party expected to be cheated, if it was possible. . . . We must believe little that we saw, and less that we heard."[116] While this could create anxiety among budding middle-class consumers, many also worked to develop an ability to hear sales pitches in a way that would accurately gauge the worth of suspect goods and services.

Interest in concerts, plays, and shows, in particular, drew on the implicit relationship between stage acting and wider cultural anxieties about performance, masks, and facades that palpably shaped behaviors in the streets, markets, and parlors of antebellum cities. Not only were public performances places of seduction for the naive, but they were also places of heightened awareness for the informed. Consumers were always playing the game of figuring out the nature of their transactions with merchants, who, like the duplicitous villains of melodrama—and actors themselves— were never what they seemed. Buying a performance of music necessitated a heightened attention to its tangible qualities, and just as a consumer might examine the shape of a hat at a store or the condition of a crop at market.[117]

Almost every diarist I encountered noted the amounts spent on concert experiences, and some followed notes about ticket amounts and other entertainment transactions with comments about the quality of the experience, as if there was a one-to-one correspondence. Unfortunately, for many, that was hardly ever the case. As George Strong succinctly complained after one purchase: "I went to a fifty-cent Sacred Music concert, and a great bore it was."[118] Pianist Louis Moreau Gottschalk complained bitterly about the constant attention his audiences paid to ticket prices. "They are furious at the price for admission—one dollar," he wrote. "A singular American characteristic! They insult us as if we forced them to pay."[119]

Despite skepticism about what exactly they were purchasing, people still attended concerts, if the increasing numbers of concert venues in the 1840s are any indication. Listening to commercial music performance today is often interpreted as "passive," a mindless acceptance of works already manufactured and with pre-determined meanings. But in the 1840s and into the 1850s, participation in commercial music entertainment as a listener arguably represented a *widening* of musical possibility. Certainly, similar complaints about puffery, manipulation, and other promotional "dodges" that put audiences at the mercy of powerful concert impresarios were voiced throughout the antebellum period. But before 1855 or so, such distinctions about the specific action of music listening were not yet fully formed. As I showed at the beginning of the chapter, Whitman's engagement with the popular culture of New York City and his ongoing experimentation with hearing and listening—as that of other contemporaries—suggest that the role of "audience" in the 1840s and 1850s was still open and undetermined, still pregnant with meaningful possibility for all involved.

As I mentioned in the Introduction, consumer "revolutions" in history can be overstated; in terms of commodification, Igor Kopytoff echoes this sentiment by writing that "commoditization is best looked upon as a process of becoming rather than as an all-or-nothing state of being."[120] The commercialization of music listening was not a simple evolution in mentality, nor was it met without resistance from various quarters. For people who had not, or could not, embrace the culture of East Coast urban concert going, musical practices continued to emphasize the making of sound and movement through singing, playing, and dance. Rural whites, for instance, tended to make music variously as part of worship services, during communal social occasions. Enslaved African Americans in the South, men and women, managed to sing while working, in funerals, at church services, and in brief moments of rest; free blacks in New York arranged their own balls, sang at community church services, and also gathered at temporary, all-night, dance cellars.[121] Northern, urban, male workers—both native and immigrant—ate, drank, gambled, socialized, and, especially, sang in neighborhood saloons.[122]

Nevertheless, I think one *can* point to a gradual shift in the ways in which commercial concert listening began to alter the trajectory of amateur musical life. Ideologically, the expansion of public concert going presented new means of "being musical." It tapped into a desire somewhat different from that created in amateur musicking: not for making music but for hearing music made. For a segment of northern, middle-class, white urbanites, musical performance came to function less as an organic result of everyday human engagement and more as a possible consumer experience among many, a commodity that could be bought for a price. Along with that change was a wider redefinition of what it meant to produce and consume music. As audiencing became more significant in the everyday lives of white, urban, middle-class Americans over the course of the nineteenth century, it became possible to speak of a new kind of audience for whom the marketplace of music was a primary influence in shaping their understanding of how to interact with others, demarcating work and leisure, and providing frameworks of social and personal identity. In the world of genteel Americans, professional musicians did not simply make music but shared social prestige; concert-goers did not only listen to music but cultivated aesthetic sensibility and knowledge; amateur musicians did not simply socialize through music but sought to copy and display staged virtuosity.[123]

How the wider population of Americans made sense of this new middle-class musicality depended somewhat on the circumstances of various social groups. If urban middle-class families privileged concert going as part of an ideology of professionalism and self-achievement, others, for example those usually living outside but within reach of large cities, interpreted concert going as a temporary but exciting opportunity to "take in" a show as part of their experience of the city. But to the extent that middle-class values shaped the broader commercialization of the United States by the late nineteenth century, regular audiencing became a wider cultural trend. As Peter G. Buckley observed, the changing popularity of antebellum singing families: "By the late nineteenth century, most entertainments were provided for families rather than by them."[124] To most fully understand the complexities of this change, we need to consider the experiences of younger members of the middle class as they transformed their purchase of a mere opportunity to hear music into a wider, more entrenched consumer culture.

CHAPTER THREE

"Music Is What Awakens in You When You Are Reminded by the Instruments"
Hearing a New Life at Mid-Century

Song of Myself

In the exploding urban concert market of the 1840s and 1850s, those interested in music found themselves having to actively manage their leisure
time. Nathan Beekley, for example, a young clerk in Philadelphia, wrote in
his diary of 1849 about regularly attending shows and concerts across several different establishments, including Philadelphia's Musical Fund Hall,
Chestnut Street Theatre, the Walnut Street Theatre, the National Theatre,
McGuires's Dancing Rooms, and the local Barnum's Museum. As was
appropriate for the time period, he did not distinguish between types of
musical performance; he enjoyed the musical burlesque of The Virginia
Serenaders' minstrel shows as much as the serious dramatic productions of
the Seguin Opera Company. Beekley was not wealthy—he mentioned making $500 a year, which put him just above the average worker—and he
regularly chastised himself in the diary about the money he was spending
on his pursuit of amusements, which, at one dollar for some of the performances, was "too salty." As he wrote, "It won't do—must stop going
to places of amusement—it don't pay—particularly since losing so much
money."[1] But he was always back again after several days.

By the end of the year, he shifted his attention to more refined venues.
As he wrote, "To keep out of the broils, I went to the opera again this evening."[2] It was clearly an effort to better himself, since he had come to worry
more and more about the presence of "rowdies" at minstrel shows and,
recognizing his own inclinations, he wished to avoid the jeopardy they

posed to his character. Overall, while he sometimes played his violin at home on nights when he was tired, audiencing was a wider behavioral pattern in his life. In fact, outside of his job, which he rarely described in any detail, most of his off-hours were occupied with music. He continued to go to commercial musical performances at least once a week, and sometimes as often as six nights a week during the height of the concert season. In addition to his concert going, he found time to attend firemen's parades, noting only that "the music was not as good as it might have been."[3] When he called on a young woman, more often than not he proposed to take her to a concert. On Sundays, he attended multiple Episcopalian, German Reformed, and Dutch Reformed churches; he did so simply to hear the organ or the choirs, and not to worship.

While Beekley might appear overly fascinated with urban musical entertainment, he was not alone. Henry Clay Southworth, a young clerk in New York during 1850 and 1851, likewise wrote about regularly attending a variety of commercial entertainment venues. Not fond of dancing, nor inclined to play an instrument, he instead attended lectures, walked on Broadway "to view the beauty and the fashion," and made regular visits to Niblo's Garden (Monday evenings) and to burlesques and minstrel shows at theaters like Burton's and Brougham's Lyceum.[4] Charles Tracy, a young man from a wealthy New York family that regularly attended concert and opera performances, reported in his diary during the 1850s that he was mostly bored by concerts and, instead, found himself "tempted" by the burlesques at Laura Keene's Variety Theater or the "Ethiopian entertainments" at the Olympic. Though he attended such shows alone, without friends or family, he described them enthusiastically, coming home "perfectly satisfied."[5] George Templeton Strong, a young lawyer in New York City at mid-century, left an extraordinarily detailed diary that indicated what he described as his "musical mania." He maintained a strong fascination with the city's musical environment, from military bands and amateur-musician neighbors (which mostly annoyed him) to popular singers like Henry Russell, from the rehearsals and concerts of private music societies like the New York Philharmonic and opera at the exclusive Astor Place to hugely popular events by traveling virtuosos.[6]

Why did these young men embrace the musical entertainments of the city so enthusiastically? What did the act of listening to musical performance mean, or do, for them? Beekley seemed to be seeking the right kinds of social associations—all while keeping a careful eye on his expenses. Southworth associated concert experiences specifically with the fraternity of urban bachelor culture. Tracy sought to escape the boredom he felt among his elite peers at refined concerts and to sample another kind of life in minstrelsy and burlesque. Strong seemed inclined to judge the musical life of the city itself, accumulating varied musical experiences and measuring their worth. Participating in musical amusements was not simply "entertaining" for these young men. Each of the diaries of Beekley, Southworth, Tracy, and Strong represents a powerful reflection of a different identity. Indeed, by repeatedly describing and thinking about concert going in their autobiographical writing, these young men were indicating the deeper pull and significance of musical behavior for self-construction.

While it is notoriously difficult to locate an historical trajectory for something as nebulous as "the self," many Americans living in the early 1800s reported a new sense of individual autonomy: a shift in the ways in which they were conceiving of possibilities for action in their own lives, including their relationships with others and their commitments and responsibilities as human beings. The Enlightenment concept of political autonomy, introduced to the United States during the American Revolution, had first enacted the potential power of the self for ordinary people: Republican philosophy conceived of government in the terms of a social contract entered into by sovereign, property-owning individuals. The Second Great Awakening, a religious revival that swept the United States from the 1820s to the Civil War, called greater attention to the self, not simply in the limited terms of civil rights but rather as an open-ended project of spiritual and moral conviction. Preachers fostered an intensely personal version of Protestantism that encouraged believers to become "born again" through conversion, something that Daniel Walker Howe has called "the first form of conscious self-reconstruction that many Americans encountered."[7]

Religious notions of individual autonomy were simultaneously echoed by the new opportunities provided by the market economies of burgeoning American cities. Cities contained a chaotic and shifting web of populations and cultures: migrants from the rural countryside; increasing numbers of immigrant families, especially from Ireland and Germany; older native elites; newer middle-class merchants and entrepreneurs, free blacks and slaves. As these people sought to live together, they tended to sort themselves out along new class, ethnic, and gender lines that upset older, established communal standards of mutual dependence. James A. Henretta has pointed to a general shift from vertical social interaction, where the top-down authority of parents, community, and church dictated people's actions and shaped ideas, to horizontal social interaction, where authority was more leveled out in a complex web of influences that had to do with individual initiative, economic class, and social status.[8] In many ways, social interaction in capitalist society was equally top-down in terms of its power relations: urban economic elites had as much control of workers and lower classes as family and church leaders had had in rural areas. The difference, however, was that the new market reality was inflected by public rhetoric asserting that top-down control was less pervasive or, at least, potentially could be overcome. If, previously, a person's life-course was determined in predictable ways by shared traditions and institutions, new arrivals in cities were eager to embrace an ideology that emphasized a different process of "economic individualism," that involved attaining an "occupation," enduring trials in the marketplace, and achieving individual success.

For many, life in this new, larger urban environment encouraged an intense, self-examination and questioning. How do I live here? Can I be the same person that I was before? As Thomas Augst has written,

Like Ulysses anticipating the disordering of his rational sense by the Sirens, individuals coming off of farms to bustling commercial centers such as New York or Philadelphia in the decades before the Civil War found themselves facing a challenge of self-command—the need to engage not merely in "self-control" but to compose themselves in the midst of an unpredictable and dangerous world, to commit themselves to a vision of the future despite their limited experience, despite uncertainty about their own natures and capacities.[9]

As the nineteenth century progressed, urban-based economic individualism was increasingly complicated by additional conceptions of the "self." English and German Romanticism, for example, promoting a deep inner "psyche" that was linked to Nature and the divine, was especially influential on those hesitant to embrace the worldliness of commerce. The Romantic self helped to shape the ideas of writers as diverse as Margaret Fuller, Horace Bushnell, and Frederick Douglass, but it was most famously articulated by essayist and lecturer Ralph Waldo Emerson, who, in the 1840s, urged Americans to realize their inner, transcendent selves—linked together as a kind of collective soul—as an alternative to the more competitive and superficial individualism assumed in liberal capitalism.[10]

The extent to which antebellum concerns with the self ought to be defined in terms of religious independence, political autonomy, economic individualism, or Romantic/Transcendental humanism is a matter of debate among historians. In particular, the extent to which the general ideal of self-making in the urban market economy was limited to aspiring middle-class males, or actually democratized to include those marginalized in American society, remains in dispute.[11] However, it is clear that much of the public and private rhetoric in the antebellum era revolved around the problem of defining and practicing individual autonomy in a context of rapid social, political and economic reorganization. In speeches, in etiquette books, and in their own diaries and conversations, Americans of the antebellum era developed a collective "self culture" that probed and explored the very implications of "constructing" the self. As E. Anthony Rotundo explains, "The dominant concerns were the concerns of the self—self-improvement, self-control, self-interest, self-advancement. Passions like personal ambition and aggression—though not seen as virtues—were allowed free passage in society. And the important bonds between people were now fastened by individual preference more than birth or social duty."[12]

How did music figure into this exploration of the self? Howe has declared that "urban life in the nineteenth century provided greater variety in available recreations, and these . . . both the new mass culture and the new high culture, offered opportunities for self-definition to consumers." Likewise, Jackson Lears has suggested that "by the 1840s and 1850s, a crucial dimension of consumer goods' emotional pull in American culture involved a carnivalization of the psyche—a brief entry into a world brimming with possibilities for self-transformation."[13] Neither offers much detail to back up such claims, and the extent to which commercial forms of leisure figured in self-culture remains an understudied area of academic history.[14] Literary scholars, instead, have done the most to address the cultural history of self-making, exploring the engagement and development of individual sensibilities through reading, autobiographical writing, and education-fouca. Augst, especially, has built on Michel Foucault's notion that writing can operate as a "technology of the self," enhancing one's ability to examine and shape one's own identity; in his work on the lives of nineteenth-century clerks, Augst has made the case for lectures, conduct books, songs, penmanship instruction, phrenology and physiognomy, and didactic stories as important forms of "moral knowledge" made available to ordinary Americans in the antebellum marketplace.[15]

In this chapter, I will argue that urban concert going functioned for many middle-class urbanites as a tool for self-transformation. It is clear from the diaries of the period that the dreamworld of commercial music entertainment—with its spectacle, virtuosity, and intense emotions—especially embodied for many the city's overwhelming power and capability for self-renewal. As Walt Whitman noted, "Music is what awakens in you when you are reminded by the instruments." First, I will discuss selfhood among young males migrating to the city; they left the most diary evidence for exploring this phenomenon and were the public archetype in the 1840s and 1850s for new conceptions of selfhood. To offer a slightly different perspective, however, I will also discuss music and self-making among other specific groups for which there is historical evidence, namely middle-class white women and middle-class African American men and women, and, that is, other members of the middling class who, thanks to subordinate positions in the political and economic frameworks of American society, experienced associations of music and selfhood with slightly different emphases and meanings.[16]

The Musical Explorations of Self-Made White Men

The personal growth of young men in the city was a common theme in the antebellum era. Beginning with Benjamin Franklin, who in 1805 described himself arriving in Philadelphia with nothing more than enthusiasm and three loaves of bread under his arm, accounts of naive migrants undergoing trials of manhood in the big city abounded in the literature of the early nineteenth century, to the point that such encounters were already clichéd by the 1840s.[17] But the stereotype was nevertheless rooted in historical reality. In the preceding colonial era, roughly up until 1815, manhood was primarily defined by one's role in a family and in a community. One moved from boyhood to manhood primarily through the inheritance of family property or through the process of apprenticeship, which entailed learning a trade under the careful guidance of the community. By the 1820s, however, such social models of manhood had become untenable. After the War of 1812, rapid population growth and technological advancements reduced the need for agricultural labor. Sons that would have inherited land from their fathers or been apprenticed to another family in the community suddenly found themselves without an economic future, and, as Karen Halttunen explains, "thousands of young men swarmed into cities such as Boston, New York, Philadelphia, Rochester, New Haven, and Lowell to work as insurance clerks and brokers, storekeepers and traders, skilled and semi-skilled artisans, merchants, professional men, innkeepers, drivers, stablers, and dockhands."[18]

Young white men migrating from a rural area to a city understood such a movement as literally from one world to another. For those used to the numbing and repetitive labor of farm-work or the social restrictions imposed by small-town life, the openness, anonymity, and variety of city life could be literally magical, a way to try out new roles and goals, to erase old wounds and mistakes and start anew. Indeed, ideas about the urban environment—based on vague impressions of physical size, exotic peoples, even noise—created enthusiastic, if naive, expectations. As a young J. T. Trowbridge recalled his arrival in New York City at daybreak on 15 May 1847, after traveling on the Erie Canal from Rochester and then by steamboat down the Hudson River:

And what a daybreak it was! The great river, the shipping, the mast-fringed wharves, the misty morning light, the silent streets of the hardly yet awakening city, the vastness and strangeness and mystery of it all, kindled my enthusiasm and made me glad I had come. In all that mighty metropolis I knew not a single soul; I brought no message to any one, not a letter of introduction; I knew no more what was before me than if I had dropped upon Mars or the Moon; but what of that? Here was life, and I was young![19]

When the Hutchinson Family Singers first left their rural New Hampshire home in 1843 for engagements in New York and Boston they were equally awestruck. Asa Hutchinson enthused:

O! New York is all that I have had it represented to be! Boston does not compare with it for life and business. The splendid Street "Broad Way" is the most Splendid Street that I ever saw, and then the Grand Park, and the Splendid water works where the water is thrown into the air to the height of 25 or 30 feet and then falls in to the Pool again in the most majestic Style. Then the Splendid "Niblos Garden" is worth a journey of 50 miles to see the fine flowers & plants. O New York is the place for me.[20]

Throughout the 1830s and 1840s, there were increasing numbers of protests from religious leaders and frequent disruptions to urban commerce due to labor strikes and demonstrations. And as more and more migrants arrived in the city, they found that their dreams would have to fit into a context of fierce competition and sometimes brutal suffering. However, despite evidence that a majority of urban citizens never fully realized capitalism's benefits, the city's commercial environment remained an experiment—dangerous and thrilling—in individual male agency. Continued rhapsody about the city reflected excitement simply over the very *potential* for individual liberty and advancement.

Tied to the pronouncements of America's economic independence and perpetual "progress" in ubiquitous groundbreaking ceremonies for new buildings and public works, the mythology of the "self-made man" had a certain logic as both a national and personal creed: as the canal and the railroad had given young white men a chance to embark in new directions, the anonymity of the urban free market gave every individual a chance to reorient his identity. In particular, the mythology was adopted and actively promoted by members of the urban middle class and became a powerful ideology in the context of the postcolonial, rapidly expanding United States. Economic individualism appealed to anyone seeking to differentiate themselves from both weakening power of the older colonial gentry and the disempowerment increasingly experienced by manual laborers.[21] It also presented a powerful appeal to gender generally: as the role of women became increasingly associated with care and protection of the home in the postcolonial era, the idea of leaving home for the world of commerce became sharply significant—young men were leaving not simply to find work, but they were embarking on a discovery of their manhood, away from female influence.[22]

Music was very much a part of this process. In 1802, future senator Daniel Webster saw fit to describe his experience as a young man in terms of a communal country dance: "The world is nothing but a contra-dance, and everyone, volens, nolens [willingly, unwillingly], has a part in it. Some are sinking, others rising, others balancing, some gradually ascending towards the top, others flamingly leading down, some cast off from Fame and Fortune, and some again in comfortable allemande with both."[23] But by the 1840s, the connectedness of the communal "contra-dance," in which "everyone, volens, nolens, has a part in it," made little sense as a metaphor for young men's development. The urban world of commercial concerts and shows offered a starkly different kind of system in which individual choice was an opportunity to creatively and idiosyncratically construct one's self. As Ralph Waldo Emerson, living in Concord, west of Boston, yearned: "I think sometimes—could I only have music on my own terms—could I live in a great city, and know where I could go whenever I wished the ablution and inundation of music waves—that were a bath and a medicine."[24] Philadelphia businessman Joseph Sill put it more bluntly in a reflection about the concert and theater season in 1840, saying, "I certainly enjoy these opportunities and often think I should sadly miss them, if any accident should compel me to pass my time in the Country, or in towns where these resources were not to be found."[25]

The life stories of some young migrants to the city feature music quite prominently. Trowbridge, for example, was first introduced to the city through theater going, since he happened to find lodging in an apartment house that was owned by none other than the conductor of the orchestra at Niblo's Garden, an outdoor venue that offered light music, short dramatic acts, and fireworks on summer nights. Trowbridge described his wonder at accepting an invitation to the Garden's theater from the conductor, M. Perrault:

Well I remember the awesome mystery of the dim stage entrance,—his violin preceding him, as we passed the obliging doorkeeper, and I following, fast held by his other hand;—then the tortuous way behind the scenes and under the stage, to a seat in the front row, near the orchestra (there were no orchestra stalls in those days). The house was filling rapidly; the musicians took their places; quiet succeeded the rustle of music leaves and the tuning of instruments, and suddenly, in an instant, what there was of me was converted into a bundle of thrills from head to foot, my joy in the music quickened by the novelty of the situation and the pride I felt in Perrault's leadership.[26]

The transformative effects of the entertainment are interestingly described in terms of self-development: "what there was of me" is a line that indicates an only partially formed self that is then "converted into a bundle of thrills." Trowbridge's "joy in the music" is especially "quickened" by its association with the new, strange, urbane father figure, or role model, of Perrault. Over time, his growing knowledge of urban entertainment culture, and the many pleasures it afforded, made the act of listening to music as an audience member a sign of maturity, and it became more important to Trowbridge than learning how to play an instrument, which was what he knew from his boyhood. At one point, when he ran out of money, he sold his old flute to a pawn shop, justifying the sale with his new urban identity: "I parted with a flute that I had paid two dollars and a half for when I had boyish ambition to become a player, and which I was glad to pledge for the cost of a dinner when I had given up the practice and didn't expect ever to resume it."[27]

Otherwise, he rhapsodized in his autobiography about the hold that New York's musical life had on him and the ways in which he associated it with his adventures as a young man:

Opposite my room, but a block or two farther down Broadway, was the Café des Mille Colonnes, a brilliant house of entertainment, with a balcony on which an orchestra used to play, on summer evenings, the popular airs of the period, to which I listened many a lonely hour, sitting by the window of my unlighted chamber, "thinking—thinking—thinking!" [a reference to comments made to him during a recent phrenology exam]. The throngs of pedestrians mingled below, moving (marvelous to conceive) each to his or her "separate business and desire"; the Omnibuses and carriages rumbled and rattled past; while, over all, those strains of sonorous brass built their bridge of music, from the high café balcony to my still higher window ledge, spanning joy and woe, sin and sorrow, past and future, all the mysteries of the dark river of life. Night after night were played the same pieces, which became so interwoven with the thoughts of my solitary hours, with all my hopes and doubts, longings and aspirations, that for years afterward I could never hear one of those mellow, martial, or pensive strains without being immediately transported back to my garret and my crust.[28]

Clearly, in Trowbridge's story, learning about the city and its entertainments is a part of his growing up; geographical change is mirrored by life change. In particular, the interweaving of particular "strains of sonorous brass" and his "hopes and doubts" in his memory help him to craft a lasting sense of self.

The migration of another young man, William Hoffman, even more directly demonstrates the ways in which participation in urban leisure aided his transformation to adulthood. In the late 1840s, William lived on his family farm in Claverack, New York, describing in his diary his life there as tedious and back-breaking: piling wood, cutting trees, plowing, repairing fences, planting. He was not really interested in music; he refused, for example, to contribute a "small sum for the support of a 'singing school,'" one of the main musical activities in his community. And when he did engage in amusements, he did so socially, attending a circus with friends (an event he did not at all enjoy) or, with fellow farm hands, prevailing upon a "Darky who happened along with a Violin" to "play several airs," for which Hoffman offered a glass of cider in return.

His first taste of urban life came in April 1848, when he left for Albany, New York. It was a move about which he afterward indicated a certain unhappiness, including dozing at church services and complaining about his job as a clerk, and writing frequently, for instance, "Today has been very dull indeed." He soon, however, started to participate in the events of the city with his fellow clerks: hanging out and listening to the "spouting barnburners" outside the capitol building, attending political rallies, and becoming interested in the gang-like culture of local fire-fighting units (without actually joining one). Significantly, he also began to notice popular amusements, writing that his boss went to see the Hutchinsons, making a trip to a performance at the local museum, and listening to "bands of music" in the street.

In October 1848, after a fire in his neighborhood that almost killed him, he departed Albany for New York City, where he deepened his acquaintance with public amusements and embraced the urban life of a bachelor, keeping up with the latest scandals and news items in the local papers, drumming up customers for trade during the work week, and engaging in "sin" at local saloons in the evenings, while still attending church every Sunday. Even after contracting cholera and having to make several extended trips back home to recuperate, he found himself yearning for the city. In one telling instance, William arranged a successful "cotillion ball" for twenty-five young couples with a local friend George. But when George, in a flush of excitement over the event, urged a repeat of the experience, William could only awkwardly demur, writing in his diary, "I do not much favor the idea as I shall be too soon compelled to return to New York."

Notably, one of the crowning events of his bachelorhood, and which ends his diary, was his witnessing of the arrival of Jenny Lind in New York in September 1850. From August 1850, when P. T. Barnum first hyped Lind's arrival, to 1 November, at the end of her run in New York City, Hoffman took a keen interest in the goings-on: copying newspaper reports about Lind verbatim into his diary; waiting with the crowd at the wharf on the day of her arrival; trying to catch a glimpse of her as she passed in her carriage; noting the announcements of the new hall that was to be built for her concerts; commenting on the reviews for her initial performances. At the beginning of November, he decided to end his diary, citing not having time to write because of his duties at work. Nevertheless, his final passage was a reference to Lind: "Jenny still continues to draw a large concourse of people at her evening concerts. Tickets now $3. & less where procured from speculators." That his story of his transition to urban life ends with details about procuring concert tickets suggests the centrality of commercial entertainment in his maturation.[29]

The effects of urban entertainments were not, of course, limited to the physical boundaries of cities. As I discussed in Chapter 1, antebellum opera companies and pianists had discovered, by the 1850s, the wide-open markets for their music in the smaller towns of the East coast, as well as the growing communities of the American West. After the Civil War, in particular, the binary of rural/urban worked more as an ideological association in the experience of some town dwellers rather than a stark geographical division. Urban musical entertainment became a realm of participation through which they might move temporarily, either through a "night at the museum" among friends or through attendance at a performance as it passed through their own town or village. The effects were often the same: even temporary participation in a commercial musical entertainment was marked as a challenge to older, traditional values and, especially for the young, was thus a potent means for staking out one's independence and adulthood.

Otis Oakman, for example, a sixteen-year-old resident of Marshfield, south of Boston, had a fairly typical musical life for a young man living in a small New England town in the 1850s. In his diary, between manual farm chores of turning the rye, hoeing fields, or digging ditches, he wrote about playing fiddle and attending singing school every two or three days when a teacher was in town, usually in fall and winter. He went to several concerts by a local singer at the town's South Meetinghouse, but the girls in attendance held more interest for him than the music; infrequent temperance meetings engaged him more seriously.

Later, however, at age nineteen, he started work at the family store and was soon spending his money on various amusements, for which he made careful accounting: On 11 October 1853, for example, he wrote simply: "12 ½ cents at the Indian exhibition." On 17 September 1854, he saw "Harrington's Ventriloquism exhibition . . . 15 cts." At the beginning of the next month, he noted, "I went to work at South Weymouth every day this week. Went to a fire Monday night, to a lecture Tues. night, and to a show Thurs. night. 15 cts. Fri. night spent 10 cts. 5cts. for a song & 5 for perfection." Not every entertainment was to his liking (he complained, for instance, on 2 November 1854: "Thurs. night paid 13 cts. to a fool of a so called phrenological for poking on my head"), but overall, he seemed to reorient his spare time toward a wider orbit of opportunities, especially those connected to commercial performances.

The following year, in October 1855, Oakman started going into Boston for the first time, attending several promenades and concerts and buying music for his violin: "Went in for Concert—15 cts. Bought a song 25 cts.," he wrote on Tuesday, 2 October. Two nights later, he "went to a little show. Expended about 9 cts. Besides the passage which was 50 cts." After attending a local dancing school to prepare for the "Leap Year Ball" in February, his attention turned to work until the summer. During July and August of 1856, he regularly went into Boston by boat to "have a 'squeal,'" including attending the circus, seeing the Bunker Hill Monument, and enjoying a performance at the Boston Museum with friends. Oakman's concert attendance was not as extensive as those actually living in cities, like Nathan Beekley or Henry Southworth, and he continued to play the violin and attend singing school. But his increasing participation in Boston's amusements had enough meaning (monetary and otherwise) for him to note the performances in his diary, and they became part of the memories of his boyhood life.[30]

The 1876 diary of Loyed Chamberlain, a nineteen-year-old lawyer's apprentice in Brockton, Massachusetts, though much later than the diary account of Oakham, indicates the lasting incidence of this pattern. While working in the law offices of "White and Sumner" during the winter months, Chamberlain initially spent his evenings engaged in "sings" with his church choir. In March, he noted that he attended a performance by the Bay State Opera one evening and "had a splendid entertainment." He also started attending lectures and local concerts, sometimes escaping during court recess to hear a passing parade band play, or paying fifty cents for admittance to Boston's Barnum's Museum. The following year, in 1877, his priorities seemed to change, along with his work duties: while he still attended choir sings in Brockton, he was required to sometimes travel to Boston and, while there, he attended lectures, plays, and opera performances. First, he saw a performance of *Faust*, and then notes on 16 February 1877:

Mr. McElroy & I went to Boston in the 9.33 train went up to the [Boston] Athaneum where his sister works & then tromped round until 12.30—took dinner in the E. Q. Building. . . . In the afternoon went on to the Back bay & then to the Tabernacle—heard Moody & Sanky preach & sing—Had a nice [unintelligible words] at Caleg's Warward in [?] "Yanky Dudle" & in [?] some of M. Pickin galleries. Cam out at 7—.[31]

Throughout the spring, the gravitational center of his participation in music seemed to shift from the suburb of Brockton to somewhere closer to

"Auditorium of the Boston Theatre, 1854." Frontispiece to Eugene Tompkins, *The History of the Boston Theatre, 1854–1901*. Boston: Houghton, Mifflin, 1908.

Boston. While he started singing lessons with his friend James and sometimes "had music" at home, he recorded more frequent experiences in Boston: hearing lectures, attending the opera *Martha*, seeing another Moody and Sankey song-meeting, and hearing an unnamed "Grand Concert" (all duly noted in a list at the back of his diary, with the amounts expended for tickets—none over fifty cents). Like Oakham and other young bachelors with intermittent business in the city, Chamberlain was reorienting his taste, and beginning to craft an independent self, through his musical choices.

The Musical Negotiations of Middle-Class White Women

Young men exploring the city, of course, offer the simplest picture of the ways in which popular musical entertainments symbolized urban culture. On the whole, Trowbridge, Hoffman, Oakham, and Chamberlain were all striving to become successful adults in the market-based capitalist culture by engaging in activities they perceived as more cosmopolitan or "urbane." Together, they point to the ways in which the middle-class mythology of "self-making" had come to dominate urban culture, and even broader American ideals of freedom and equality, by mid-century. However, one must also keep in mind that their excitement about the novelty of concert going depended on the fact that they had the ability to purchase a concert ticket in the first place. If they had enough money, no one prevented them from exploring new opera houses and theaters or indicated how they were to respond to their experiences. For others, this was not necessarily the case. Especially for those who regularly faced social barriers that prevented, limited, or policed their participation in the public sphere, the connections between commercial musical entertainment, urbanity, and self-construction were far more complex.

African Americans, women, and immigrants were all limited in their participation in the market economy and therefore also were denied the kind of selfhood afforded to young white men. The linking of freedom, choice, and self-making made male selfhood attractive nonetheless; as Jean Matthews explains, "it took men and women who had a burning awareness of themselves as individuals unjustly cramped, thwarted, and humiliated because of their membership in a subordinate group to demand that the logic of liberal individualism be applied without consideration of race or sex."[32] However, the push for universalizing male versions of individualism also had complications. The collective oppression of such groups required its members not only to unite in order to survive but also often to interpret injustice against one member as an injustice against the entire group, something that worked against the very idea of individualism for which they were striving. The catch-22 of the situation carried over into all aspects of life. While such groups eagerly participated in commercial amusements, for example, any excitement about individually "moving up" in society through concert going was always tempered by the fact that "moving out" in society grossly magnified any individual action—or, especially, any misstep—as typical of one's race, ethnicity, or sex.

Selfhood for women, for example, was consistently defined by the limited roles allotted to them in a patriarchal society. Up until the 1830s, in most states, for example, married women abdicated their legal autonomy to their husbands; they could neither vote nor own property. The inability of women to participate, even partially, in the public sphere was a huge obstacle to realizing the self-making of their male counterparts. During the early years of the Republic, "republican motherhood" arose as a new role for women that was meant to complement that of men: women were defined as mothers whose purpose was to use their "natural" capacities for feeling and morality to raise virtuous sons. Women's development in this model was, as before, rather static—women filled a pre-determined role rather than grew in an open-ended and exploratory way. To become an adult woman in society meant marrying and having children, and thus much of young women's lives were focused on locating and arranging to marry the right suitor.

Some white middle-class women in the antebellum era started to organize themselves to push for greater equality. As Matthews has pointed out, the 1848 Seneca Falls Women's Rights *Declaration of Sentiments*, one of the key documents of the women's suffrage movement, cites one of the principal sins of Man as closing to women "all avenues to wealth and distinction which he considers most honorable to himself." Matthews explains, "Feminists in particular were drawn to the Romantic versions of individualism which conceived of the individual less as a finished unit than as a bundle of potentialities which required freedom as their essential medium of growth. To deprive the individual of the necessary scope for development was thus the ultimate injustice because it violated the essence of human nature."[33] However, most white middle-class women were not involved in the feminist movement. They more commonly carved out a version of self-making in the 1840s and 1850s that took place in the private realms that were most under their control—friendship and the home. Reading, for instance, was one activity that they used for the purpose of developing individual identity. Mary Kelley notes: "Immersing themselves in a variety of ideas and personae, reading women explored a world of possible selves. . . . They rehearsed, they interpreted, they negotiated different selves, fashioning identities that were distinctively their own."[34]

Music worked similarly. In white middle-class culture, women were understood as "creatures of the heart," whose natural inclination toward "sensibility" helped to cultivate the sincerity and moral character lacking in the utilitarian business world of males. The ability to appreciate music's emotional qualities was thought to be part of that sincerity, and any woman of good standing was expected to have musical training and knowledge among her "accomplishments." While some women, like Lucy Lowell (discussed in detail in Chapter 4), derided voice lessons and enforced performances before young men at parties, others used such learning to assert and construct unique selves.[35]

This is quite clear from the evidence in sheet music binders from the time period. Many young women paid to have their collections of sheet music, acquired from years of lessons, bound in leather and personalized with their names embossed in gold on the front. The binders purposefully indicated the individual preferences of their owners through idiosyncratic variations in content and organization; each sheet music binder became a representation of its owner.[36] Indexes, created by hand and inserted at the beginning, were often quite elaborate, with schemes that variously grouped music by genre, composer, or order of receipt. Much of the music was given to the women by friends or male suitors, something that was formally indicated in handwriting on the covers ("To Miss Harriet Bullock with the Compliments of Webster Moran, Cadet, U. S. M. T."), and which located the music in each individual's encounters and experiences.

Marginal comments, especially, indicated personal taste and directly incorporated the music into the lives of the women. One girl, named Nettie, for example, annotated much of her music with comments like "My decided favorite 1854" at the top of a Meyerbeer's "Valse des Démons," or the words "Cousin Joe" on the figure of a mustachioed man wearing a red cape and black mask on the cover lithograph of another piece. In response to "Brilliant Variations for the Piano Forte on Von Weber's Last Waltz, Composed by Henri Herz," she entered something closer to a diary entry: "Von Weber must have had in mind our melancholy clergyman's love when he wrote this. Why? Oh, it sounds that way—a kind of subdued breathing of sanctified Affliction. Like the sermon he preached from Thil. 4:11 'I have learned, &.'" Another girl, Minna Brooker, of Virginia, wrote at the top of her copy of "The Celebrated Ethiopian Song and Chorus: Emma Snow" that it was "The ugliest piece in the book—so say Miss Minna Brooker." In fact, Minna, like many young women who kept binders, regularly signed much of her sheet music, as if she was not only indicating possession but purposefully thinking about herself in the third person. On the lithograph for one piece, "Pleasant Memories, a Vocal Work," which featured mythical scenes of medieval castles, she even wrote her name next to an angel floating over a fallen knight, inserting herself into the fantasy.[37]

Besides private music lessons, public concerts were also expected as a means for young antebellum women to develop a genteel sensibility. Opera and instrumental performances, at least in major cities like New York and Philadelphia, had been adopted by late eighteenth-century elites as sites of refinement and sociability; they were events that enabled the wealthy— both men and women—to distinguish themselves from the masses. There one could formally display one's etiquette, knowledge, and social status and even safely flirt with members of the opposite sex in the presence of a controlled community of peers. The democratization of commercial musical entertainments in the 1840s weakened older elite audiences' emphasis on supercilious fashion and worldly display, both of which were anathema to middle-class sensibility. Instead, going to the opera or a concert could serve as a way to associate oneself with the highest aesthetic achievements of Europe. This reframing of the concert world made such public events far more palatable to the middle class and, especially, a virtuous woman's sensibility.

However, for respectable women, simply going out to a musical performance remained a weighted proposition. First, even reformed concert going retained, in general, associations of fashion and display. The very ritualistic social context of the concert hall, as well as the fact that it offered a form of staged performance, worked against genteel ideas of sincerity. As Karen Halttunen explains, "For nineteenth-century sentimentalists the dangers presented by fashionable hypocrisy were incalculable. The life of fashion, in destroying personal sincerity, threatened to reduce middle-class 'society,' and by implication American society, to complete chaos."[38] Second, the belief in a women's delicate nature dictated that women should generally avoid the chaos of the public sphere, where access to events and institutions was relatively open and where interaction with others was frequently unexpected and uncontrolled. Women's movements outside of the home, even to exclusive concerts, were thus carefully restricted to avoid moments where they might lose their dignity.[39] Even the circumstances of popular virtuoso concerts in the 1850s exacerbated women's perceived vulnerabilities. Such events were held in large halls before thousands of people, supported by waves of puffery and ballyhoo, resulting in crowds of riotous onlookers—all such conditions were a clear affront to sensibility. If the whole point of the domestic sphere was to cultivate a private haven away from the vulgarity and competition of the marketplace, democratized, commercial concert events were, for genteel women, not only inappropriate but also potentially dangerous.

Overall, then, the place of concerts in white middle-class women's self-making was more complicated because women's participation was always under the gaze of the community, and any woman had to work through all of these dilemmas before she could purchase a ticket. How was one to judge the nature of a public music event? "Theater" had the reputation of being a place where prostitutes did business, and was therefore to be avoided at all costs. However, in a time when traditional theaters were regularly used as venues for concert events, and theatricality was woven into musical performance, assessing an event was difficult. Was opera "theater"? Was a particular performer sincere in his or her intentions?

These were questions faced by twenty-year-old Anna Thaxter of Boston, who, in 1846, had extensive discussions with friends about whether to attend a performance by the Seguins:

We talked about the propriety of going to the theatre and the opera, a subject in which we are quite interested, as Susan and I particularly long to hear the Seguins. Charlotte has not so many scruples as we have—but we are inclined to think, that the effect upon the actors and actresses themselves cannot be very good, and if not, that we ought not to give our countenance to the performance by attending. What will be our final conclusion, I do not know; I am only very certain that we should like to think it is right to go, if feasible, but hope that inclination will not give too strong a bias to our minds, in the forming of an opinion.[40]

Three days later, when a certain Mr. Peters arrived and invited her to see *The Bohemian Girl*, she quickly accepted, only to report: "Went to the opera. I enjoyed it very much but not so much as I anticipated, from description. The acting seemed ridiculous, and I was ready to laugh in the most affecting parts; the music, much of it, was fine, of course, as Mr. and Mrs. Seguin and Mrs. Frazer were the performers."

Most public music performances were acceptable for white middle-class women, as long as men, able to protect their reputations from harm, accompanied them. Indeed, until the advent of the afternoon matinee in the 1870s, a woman of good standing could not even go out at night alone without inviting devastating speculation about her character.[41] Caroline White, for example, a twenty-three-year-old newlywed living in Brookline, Massachusetts, wrote in her diary about having to wait for her husband to come home from business trips so that he could take her out. After attending her first opera performance in 1851, and especially after seeing Jenny Lind a few months later, her periods of waiting for her husband's return became more and more frustrating. She wrote in her diary with some humor about the situation, but there was still an undercurrent of resentment about the differences between what men and women could do: "Oh! Dear me! What a great pity that I should be tied to such a donkey—this is written from Frank's dictation. 'Le bon homme' came home late last night—stopped in town to see and hear Madame Thillon at the 'Howard.' I did not see him till today."

Even when male escorts were available, concert attendance was often wrapped up in social obligations or the rituals of courtship that made full participation in the event difficult. Anna Thaxter, for example, who did return to opera going, was able to do so only after a suitor, Ben, formally invited her. And despite her own inherent interest in the productions, he worked to frame those experiences as having the most meaning in terms of their courtship. Specifically, as a token of his affection, he sometimes returned the day after with a gift of sheet music that enabled them to "revive" the performance, and, of course, see her again. Her feelings about opera, as a consequence, are often inflected by her feelings about him. Ellen Ruggles, an accomplished singer who first came to the attention of George Strong at the opera, found herself changing her musical inclinations to please her new husband; because he hated the polka, for example, she ceased waltzing, and her participation in opera became centered around the box seats she shared with her husband. While she eventually started going to the opera without him, when he was too busy at work, she spent the first seven years of her marriage abiding by her husband's inclinations. In fact, what is quite remarkable about Strong's diary is the absence of his wife's opinions on the many performances they attended in that period.

Of course, as Kathy Peiss argues, while today we understand leisure "as a realm of autonomy and choice, a sphere of life separate from the obligations of the workplace," for women in the nineteenth and early twentieth centuries, this was simply not true, because leisure was more "intertwined with the rhythms of household labor and the relations of kinship."[42] Several women in the mid-nineteenth century, for instance, kept diaries that indicated how little they were able to enjoy "leisure time," let alone music concerts. Adelaide Burr, a farmer's wife outside of Worcester, Massachusetts, for example, indicated that in the year of 1867, she spent most of her time baking, ironing, and cleaning, attending only a visiting "Caravan Circus" in June, and then two local school concerts in the late fall.[43] And, overall, even many women with the interest and the means to go to concerts simply stayed home. After the death of her sister in 1848, Anna Thaxter Cushing stopped going to public concerts for a while, yet continued to record the concert-going activities of her husband: "Ben has not been very well, today, but has gone out this evening to a concert at the Hall, which I suppose will be a very fine one."[44] Caroline White likewise seemed to live vicariously through her husband's public activities:

> Dec. 9: "Frank has gone into Boston to hear Maberlini, if he can get a ticket. She gives her first concert this evening."
> Feb. 3: "Frank is away this evening—gone to hear the 'Black Swan.'"
> Feb. 4: "Dear Frank is away again this eve—He heard Mad. Thillon in the 'Black Domino' tonight."[45]

Some feminists demanded the Romantic ideal of selfhood through participation in public performances of music. Margaret Fuller, especially, promoted the Transcendentalist ideal of realizing one's true natural self as a means for women to realize, autonomously, their own natures. In particular, she dismissed the attainment of political or economic power equal to men (which she saw as simply an initial obstacle) and instead understood women's potential as a higher spiritual fulfillment, which women alone had the capacity to cultivate. As a result, she promoted concert music, which she thought communicated universal spiritual truths. While writing regularly about literature and music in New York City's *Herald Tribune* between 1844 and 1846, she became an especially enthusiastic listener of Beethoven's work, linking her own feelings of self-expansion and kinship with Beethoven's "genius" to her ideas about women's selfhood. As she said after hearing Beethoven's *Symphony No. 7*: "When I heard this symphony, I said 'I will triumph.'"[46]

Fuller, however, was extraordinary. Only over the course of the nineteenth century is there evidence that women may have started to realize Fuller's version of musical self-construction when, instead of independent attendance at concert events, they turned to private music societies and increasing behind-the-scenes patronage of the arts, something I address in the next chapter. At mid-century, concerts tended to function for white middle-class women as a means to reinforce genteel notions of women's identity, that is, a shared identity equated with and defined by courtship and marriage. The extent that women were able to realize the culture of the self through concert going with their suitors and husbands depended, mostly, on the nature of their romantic relationships.

The Musical Frustrations of the Black Middle Class

Besides white middle-class women, no other social group in the nineteenth century experienced the complexities of crafting selfhood in the public cultural sphere more profoundly than middle-class African American men and women. In the late eighteenth century, free blacks in northern cities, especially Philadelphia and New York, even while facing ongoing economic and political oppression from the dominant white majority, developed their own community institutions, services, and class hierarchy. Occupational opportunities for free black men and women in cities tended toward manual labor, though there were a small proportion of African Americans in almost every major city that also worked in non-manual occupations. To the surprise of foreign visitors and the consternation of white leaders, some free blacks attained economic success and publicly adopted the refined values and behaviors of white elite culture, something that was most evident among the fashionable African American patrons of the African Grove Theater in New York City, or the gentlemanly wealth of Philadelphia inventor and businessman James Forten.[47] By the 1840s and 1850s, free black communities in Philadelphia and New York were large enough to accommodate a small number of African Americans who occupied middling status. They were small shopkeepers and merchants, as well as professionals such as teachers, lawyers, or dentists; they sought and promoted nineteenth-century middle-class ideology, including professionalism, gentility, and education as a form of racial "uplift," or, a means "to serve and sustain black people."[48]

Gender distinctions among middle-class blacks were, in some ways, similar to that among middle-class whites; as historian R. J. Young notes, "many Northern African American males subscribed to the separate spheres' philosophy of the middle class. Rarely were women thought of as friends and colleagues."[49] The notions of elevation and self-worth in the middle-class ideal of self-making had special resonance for African American men in the context of legal slavery in the South and racist oppression in the North. The phrase "We are men!," which appeared frequently in newspapers, speeches, and anti-slavery convention documents, was not only a testament to African Americans' freedom in the personal sense but also freedom in the social sense, from the bonds of slavery.[50] However, even in northern cities with the largest free black communities—namely, Philadelphia and New York City—African American male selfhood had to be constructed against a social system in which such selfhood was routinely and explicitly denied. That African Americans in the antebellum era could be classified as property was a condition that, by definition, prevented African American men from participating in a selfhood that staked itself, at least in part, on property ownership.[51] Thus Carla Peterson has argued that African Americans ended up searching for answers to questions that most whites of the period might have found existentially twisted: "How can I escape being a commodity? How can I own myself? How can I possess property? And, more abstractly, How can I achieve and maintain self-possession?"[52]

African American women experienced the double-bind of having to negotiate both the prescriptions put upon them for their race and for their sex. Still, the middle-class female members of free black society aspired to the wider "cult of true womanhood" as a means to create wider racial uplift. Of course, this meant deemphasizing the fragility and submissiveness that the ideal ascribed to women and emphasizing instead the possibilities of a "cultivated sensibility" through education. As the preamble to the constitution of the Female Literary Association of Philadelphia declared, "[It is our] duty . . . as daughters of a despised race, to use our utmost endeavors to enlighten the understanding, to cultivate the talents entrusted to our keeping, that by so doing, we may in a great measure, break down the strong barrier of prejudice, and raise ourselves to an equality with those of our fellow beings, who differ from us in complexion."[53] Such aims were not easy. The public activity of education and uplift, while encouraged by some men in the free black community, also seemed to others a violation of gender roles.[54] And while embrace of a modified role of "bourgeois woman" was possible, that role was, more often, simply beyond the daily experiences of most African American women, who worked out of economic necessity and faced persistent gender and racial stereotypes that directly worked against idealized notions of female purity, piety, and submissiveness.[55]

The white, evangelical, anti-slavery movement, which developed in earnest in the North during the 1830s, helped to foster white sympathy for African American selfhood generally by promoting a legal ideal of "bodily autonomy," that is, the individual right to occupy an existence free from pain.[56] Slave narratives, often funded and promoted by abolitionists, were crucial in cultivating, both for their writers and their audiences, a sense of slaves as unique, individual human beings, with experiences, desires, and needs. But white involvement in helping African Americans to realize self-hood was always distorted by what Carla Peterson calls "the context of black underdevelopment." While slave autobiographies may have given their writers stronger senses of self, she argues, "in writing their lives they often found that they had created alienated images of themselves. And, in agreeing to sell their life experiences in the marketplace, they further exposed themselves to the gaze of an alien audience."[57] Even white benevolent societies, which became quite active in the 1830s and 1840s in helping the poor in America's cities, including free blacks, inadvertently reinforced the absence of individual selfhood and liberty among African Americans by offering aid to them as a group.

Overall, the participation of African Americans in the musical entertainment of cities has to be understood in terms of these complexities. At one level, the lure of antebellum cities for young African Americans, men and women, was as strong as that for whites. Maryland slave Frederick Douglass, for instance, marveled at the "Great House" of his plantation but even then it was nothing compared to the stories he heard about Baltimore:

I had something of the feeling about Baltimore that is expressed in the proverb, that "being hanged in England is preferable to dying a natural death in Ireland." I had the strongest desire to see Baltimore. Cousin Tom, though not fluent in speech, had inspired me with that desire by his eloquent description of the place. I could never point out any thing at the Great House, no matter how beautiful or powerful, but that he had seen something at Baltimore far exceeding, both in beauty and strength, the object which I pointed out to him.[58]

But, of course, going to the city represented a far different kind of escape for Douglass than, say, Trowbridge—it was not from lack of economic opportunity but from the brutal conditions of plantation slavery, not toward open-ended exploration but, as he suggests himself, "a different kind of death." This desire for the city was signified especially by the tendency for free blacks to congregate in urban areas, where bustling streets offered an additional sense of distance and freedom from the powerlessness of slavery. As Barbara Fields explains, "The city had very particular advantages for a free black person in a slave society. For the manumitted slave, it offered greater independence and a greater sense of responsibility for his own life than the rural community, where the round of work, leisure, and associations remained closely encircled by the regime of slavery."[59] Even Douglass, a slave, eventually did make it to Baltimore, where he was forced to work for temporary owners; there he learned to read, became a boat caulker, and experienced an increasing sense of his own dignity.

Music was, not always by choice, very much part of the northern urban life for African Americans. Racial assumptions about the "natural" musicality of blacks, in particular, created a prevalence of musical work: as musicians and bandsmen, music teachers, and sometimes concert performers and composers. Eileen Southern notes that 32 out of 9,076 blacks in Philadelphia in 1849 were musicians, a larger proportion than among the wider population.[60] Some of the most notable black performers in the antebellum era, for example, were Francis (Frank) Johnson, who led a band in Philadelphia and introduced the "promenade" concert to the United States after a tour of France in the 1830s; Elizabeth Taylor Greenfield, "The Black Swan," America's first black concert singer, who toured eastern and midwestern cities between 1851 and 1853; and the Luca Family, a singing family of brothers who toured in the 1850s and sang with the Hutchinsons in 1859. In addition, amateur and professional bands were quite active for both white and black audiences at dances, parties, events, and parades.[61]

Beyond performance, however, middle-class blacks, men and women, embraced participation as audience members in the wider urban culture of public concerts and exhibitions. Juanita Karpf explains, "Enthusiasm for at least one component of 'European culture'—art music—was evident among the free black population beginning in the early decades of the nineteenth century. Middle-class black communities in large urban areas such as Boston, New York, Philadelphia, and Washington, DC, readily supported busy schedules of concerts and musical soirées."[62] In general, middle-class blacks took it upon themselves, as had whites, to create an assortment of societies and concert organizations. The Philadelphia Library Company of Colored Persons of Philadelphia, founded in 1833, for instance, offered concerts, lectures, and debates to its members. Amateur societies, including Philomathean and Phoenixonian Institutes in New York City and the Demosthenian Institute and Minerva Literary Association in Philadelphia featured performing musicians at lectures and other events. The many black churches in Philadelphia, New York, Baltimore, and Boston were also supporters of public musical performance. Sacred music concerts were regularly offered at St. Philips and the First Presbyterian Church in New York City, St. Thomas and First and Second Presbyterian Churches in Philadelphia, and Belknap Baptist Church in Boston.[63]

Just as whites incorporated commercial music entertainment into their sense of self-development, free blacks in northern cities used the world of musical entertainment for the purpose of advancement, both personal and social. Joseph Willson described his own experience of free black society in Philadelphia in the 1840s by declaring that "the love of music is universal; it is cultivated to some extent—vocal or instrumental—by all; so that it is almost impossible to enter a parlor where the ear of the visitor is not, in some sort or other, greeted therewith. It is consequently made a prominent part of the amusements on all occasions of social meeting together of friends."[64] Charlotte Forten, daughter of wealthy African American businessman James Forten, was raised in material comfort in Philadelphia and then in Salem, Massachusetts, where she studied in public school, took music lessons, and attended concerts (including an 1854 appearance by Thalberg), a background that inspired her to become a teacher and work in the abolitionist movement.[65] By mid-century, Philadelphia's African American gentry had successfully adopted more conventional signifiers of middle-class individual selfhood, including, in the words of David McBride, "secular imagination, widening one's private space, sentimentality, reaffirmation of Victorian ideals and classical intellectualism."[66]

In general, however, the black middle-class men and women encountered barriers when trying to enjoy musical life on the same ground as their white counterparts. While blacks in both southern and northern cities after 1840 were allowed to attend public theaters and concert halls, they were typically relegated to the "gallery," a section of the balcony furthest from the stage and also the place where prostitutes traditionally plied their trade. This segregation was most galling to middle-class blacks; such treatment exposed the hypocrisies of urban "freedom" and the developing racial order. Attempts to physically relocate to more respectable parts of the theater were almost always rebuffed, sometimes violently. James O. Horton and Lois E. Horton reported:

In 1847, Julian McCrae purchased tickets to a Boston theater but was forcibly excluded because of his color. When he sought redress through the courts, the judge ruled only that McCrae be reimbursed for the price of the tickets. In a similar case of discrimination, William C. Nell, Sarah Parker, and Caroline E. Putnam were denied their reserved seats at a Howard Theater performance. Nell protested when theater manager Palmer ordered them to the gallery, a section reserved for blacks. Police officer Philbrick then tried to eject the party from the theater.[67]

James Trotter noted that the Luca Family, when appearing with the Hutchinson Family Singers in Fremont, Ohio, on 25 February 1859, were reviewed in the local newspaper with dismay: "How woefully we were disappointed! . . . We have, perhaps, a stronger feeling of prejudice than we should have felt under other circumstances, had their abolition proclivities been less startling; but to see respectable white persons (we presume they are such) traveling hand in hand with a party of negroes, and eating at the same table with them, is rather too strong a pill to be gulped down by a democratic community." Eventually, by 1855, most public notices for theaters and concerts across the country warned that "Negroes will not be admitted."

W. E. B. DuBois noted at the end of the century that middle-class blacks may have "reached the full measure of the best type of modern European culture," but it became clear that this measure took place in an ideological context of racial difference and associated social power that forcibly remade the meanings of black cultural participation. Specifically, Juanita Karpf explains, despite middle-class black achievements, "the dominant white culture continued to exercise its prerogative of exclusive entitlement to art music and its insistence that the majority of black Americans were incapable of comprehending and interpreting that tradition."[68] As Frederick Douglass once commented about getting stares from white fellow audience members at a concert, "Too bad that colored folks should dare to love music and to have the same emotion common to white folks."[69]

Indeed, the popularity of blackface minstrelsy after the mid-1840s, which became increasingly focused on the racial stereotypes of Jim Crow and Zip Coon by the Civil War,[70] placed *any* black musicking—including more refined concert performance—into an ideological apparatus that was white-defined and controlled. Ronald Radano has thus argued that, in the wake of minstrelsy, black musical achievement could only function as a definitional element of white middle-class self-making, thus defeating, from the start, middle-class black aspirations:

For those white agrarians and capitalists finding virtue in the ethos (if not always the actuality) of nose-to-the-grindstone hard work, the difference of blackness was particularly well demonstrated as a form of play acted out in the many varieties of slave performance. If whiteness claimed its character in the labors of capitalists, blackness expressed its opposite, reflected in the putative natural musicality, feeling manner, and childlike demeanor of the docile slave. Play lay at the heart of the entertaining, performative character of authentic "Negroes singing," an image made increasingly popular in the new inventions of blackface that began to circulate across the states from the mid-1840s.[71]

Radano does not take into account the presence of "non-slave" black musicking, or at least does not give it much weight; still his point is that free blacks, after 1845, were forced to either work within "the sound logic of racial signification" or retreat to their own, isolated institutions of musical entertainment.

Stars, Celebrity, and the Self

Despite different conceptions of the self and varying degrees of success in realizing individual autonomy, the ideal of selfhood was a driving force in antebellum American society. During this period of confusing change, the rules by which one defined and measured individual agency seemed unclear; personally achieving a sense of autonomy was a meaningful recovery of the moral dignity previously conferred by communal and social institutions. Character, until the 1820s, had been based on one's public reputation; outward actions during interactions with others were the means by which people were measured, and thus cultivating proper habits in the presence of others was paramount. But in the 1840s, the increasing anonymity of the urban environment, growing middle-class preoccupation with one's "true self," evangelical emphasis on one's individual path toward salvation, and increasing exposure to Romantic ideas of the "psyche" created a different kind of intense interest on *inner* character rather than *outward* deeds. In the words of Jeffrey Sklansky, there was a shift from "material self rule" to "psychic self-development."[72]

Despite the rhetoric to the contrary, many middle-class Americans found that psychic self-development required the support and encouragement of social institutions. In particular, middle-class men and women, white and black, turned to their new modern surroundings—the marketplace of culture—to shape identity. From the American Revolution to the 1830s, representative men had been marketed as a means by which to provide useful examples for republican virtue, to be studied and emulated. George Washington, for example, became an icon of democratic self-sacrifice and national unity through the circulation of his life story and of his image on lamps, plates, cups, and rugs in the early 1800s. But in the 1840s, the performance of self became its own end, giving birth to a huge industry that offered young men and women, across social categories, a chance to explore what a modern "self" might be and how they might share in it. Biographies and memoirs became best-sellers, lecturers like Ralph Waldo Emerson philosophized about self-reliance, the new technology of photography enabled entrepreneurs like Matthew Brady to make a living selling portraits of individuals at his New York studio, and even autograph-collecting came into vogue.[73] According to Thomas Augst, "wisdom was realized by seeing Emerson speak in the company of a larger community, by speaking aloud to one's diary, and through the many other means by which nineteenth-century Americans learned to quote from their own experience, to become familiar with the natural grammar of democratic civic life."[74]

Most important was the growing culture of celebrity, in which individuals, with the help of rapidly growing numbers of newspapers and magazines, began to market themselves rather than their achievements or products. In particular, those who were typically "invisible" to the public, except through their products, began to relish and court public attention. Walt Whitman, for example, purposefully included his own image (along with an autograph) in his 1855 book of poems, *Leaves of Grass,* creating intense interest in his identity. N. P. Willis likewise developed a style of journalism that was based as much on personal anecdotes about his experiences among writers, artists, and musicians, as on reasoned analysis of their works. Overall, the names of writers started to appear on front-page bylines and became an important means to advertise and sell any publication.[75]

Even those who were, by profession, more publicly visible, found that promoting their own personal lives in addition to their work could be a valuable means for survival. Actors like Edwin Forrest, who was renowned for playing outsized, heroic roles on stage, became even more widely known for his volatile personality, professional rivalries, and marriage troubles. Jenny Lind, as I have already discussed, attracted unprecedented public interest for her Christian character and charity work as much as her vocal talent. Circulating images of George Washington in the early Republic was primarily a public educational effort, meant to unite the country, but the promotions of Whitman, Willis, Forrest, and Lind operated differently, blurring the public function of news and education with the private allure of entertainment; their self-display was, in the words of David Blake "a collective performance of celebrity." Not surprisingly, it was the promotional gimmicks of commercial theater not politics that provided the framework for America's larger culture of celebrity in the 1830s.[76]

While it is impossible to weigh the social influence of one cultural form against another in this (or any) time period, it is safe to say that music provided a rich repository of stars at mid-century. Critic John S. Dwight reported that just in the 1850s alone, virtuoso appearances in Boston included

Jenny Lind (1850), pianists Alfred Jaell (1851–1854), Scharfenberg of New York, Louis Moreau Gottschalk (1853), Robert Heller (1854), Satter (1855 and later), and Thalberg (1857); organist G. W. Morgan of New York (1856); violinists Ole Bull (second visit (1853), Paul Julien and Camilla Urso (about 1852); and singers, Mdm. Thillon (1851), Mme. Alboni and Mme. Sontag (1852), Mme. Lagrange (1855), Mme. Johannsen (1857), and Carl Formes (1858); opera singers Marietta Alboni and Henriette Sontag (1853), Maretzek, Baiali, Brignoli (1855), Nantier-Didiee, Hensler, Salviani, Morelli (1856).[77]

Even then, Dwight failed to mention the many minstrel and band performers that filled the pages of local newspapers, as well as the wide array of opera singers performing with troupes.

Such a parade of music stars provided their eager audience members with various opportunities to think about themselves. One part of the appeal of the seemingly endless stream of virtuosos after 1850, for example, was the extent to which each performer surpassed expectations about individual achievement and capability. Joseph Sill, for example, attending a performance of singer John Braham in 1840, realized that even ordinary-looking people could express unique talent: "Many were disappointed at first sight by his diminutive stature, and plain physiognomy; but he had scarcely sung a few bars when their attention became riveted by the expressive manner in which he sung Handel's music and during the whole of his performance one might have heard a pin drop, so great was the hush!"[78] William Cullen Bryant noted that the achievements of a performer could even surprise the most jaded of audience members, as happened during a concert by pianist Leopold de Meyer in 1846:

A veteran teacher of music in Buffalo, famous for being hard to be pleased by any public musical entertainment, found himself unable to sit still during the first piece played by De Meyer, but rose, in the fullness of his delight, and continued standing. When the music ceased, he ran to him and shook both of his hands, again and again, with most uncomfortable energy. At the end of the next performance he sprang again on the platform and hugged the artist so rapturously that the room rang with laughter.[79]

Audiences were not interested in emulating the specific, virtuous characteristics of performers, as they might have been with Washington and other representatives of Republicanism, nor did people themselves express the desire to be music stars. Instead, they wrote and thought about stars more simply as fellow human beings, with admirable personal qualities. Stars proved the very existence and power of individual achievement; they were each a testament to a shared American culture of possibility in which everybody could be somebody. As historian Leo Braudy quipped: "In a self-made country, who had not the potential to be self-made himself, with the help of an equally self-made audience?"[80]

In fact, the most powerful and alluring stars were thought to overcome the "artifice" of performance. The word "star" itself captures this attitude. A star was not just a famous actor or a singer but a unique person whose presence transcended any one role, burning brightly through the artificial masks of the stage.[81] As Walt Whitman wrote about Allesandro Bettini:

The fresh vigorous tones of Bettini! I have often wished to know this man, for a minute, that I might tell him how much of the highest order of pleasure he has conferred upon me. His voice has often affected me to tears. Its clear, firm, wonderfully exalting notes, filling and expanding away; dwelling like a poised lark up in heaven; have made my very soul tremble. Critics talk of others who are more perfectly artistical. But the singing of this man has breathing blood within it; the living soul, of which the lower stage they call art, is but the shell and the sham.[82]

As late as the 1880s Lucy Lowell of Boston, who had became fascinated by opera singer Etelka Gerster, was writing in her diary not about what Gerster performed (which included a host of Italian and German operas) but about how she transcended her roles: "In the mad scene she was perfect, never forgetting herself for an instant, even when she received flowers. . . . She is altogether, as I have said, many times, a perfectly charming, attractive, loveable woman, you feel all the time a strong affection for her. Should like to know her, I'm sure she is charming, she must be, with her face & whole manner and bearing."[83]

Of course, while audience members watched for hints of the underlying personalities of performers onstage, most also appreciated additional backstage knowledge, which helped them to assess a given star's personal qualities. Such knowledge about the intimate lives of stars was amply supplied by burgeoning newspapers and magazines of the time; some audience members sought out information themselves. Lucy Emerson, for instance, wrote extensively about actors Charles and Ellen Kean, after seeing them twice in Shakespeare's *Twelfth Night* production in Boston in 1845. After declaring in her diary that "He was charming, handsome, gentlemanly, & modest, & all together I was almost out of my senses with delight," she confirmed that impression with additional information two nights later:

Mary Greenwood told me, while I was walking with Maria Hall, something that was very provoking. Susie Smith told Alice Haskell & Fanny Whitney that the Keans were going away at little before four yesterday afternoon, from the back door of the Tremont so they went down there & waited some time & at last they came with Mrs. Kean's maid & a young gentleman. Mr. Kean said "Here we are going out of the back door as quietly as possible" "yes" said she "just like a dog—" & that just as they had got into the carriage Mr. Kean saw the girls, leant forward & said something to his wife, & then they both looked back at them. I would have given anything to have seen them, but next year when they come I declare I will. They said that they both looked just as well as they did on the stage, & that the beautiful black hair of Clifford's is his natural hair.

It should be said that backstage knowledge was not always positive, especially when it did not match a star's public persona. Given the investment of audiences in stars' personal characteristics, that situation could be a bitter pill. Painter Sarah Gooll Putnam, for example, did not know quite what to make of her meeting with acclaimed author Harriet Beecher Stowe in 1882: "I went to a little music (with John) at Dr. Harris'[s]. He had been having several festivities, this Summer. Mrs. Harriet Beecher Stowe was there &

her manners were most weird—most unpleasing, and nightmarish. It is very well to be celebrated, but it is just as well to treat other folks as if they were human beings & not foot stools, or coat hooks."[84] Overall, however, whether with positive or negative results, the search for the true self of a star remained a central approach to audiencing at mid-century and fit with larger ideas about personal performance in Victorian culture.[85]

The first and most notable nineteenth-century music star to evoke intense interest in his or her backstage qualities was Jenny Lind. Barnum intentionally manipulated audiences in 1850 to focus on Lind's personal character, but at the same time, he seemed to have tapped emotions not even he expected. Barnum shrewdly hyped her simplicity, innocence, and humility as a contrast to the alleged immorality of the theater, but those qualities also worked to heighten the effect of her own, otherworldly, singing talent. As John Dizekes put it, "People searched her appearance and especially her face for clues to that inner person . . . she would begin hesitantly, nervously, and then: her talent would come to the rescue, her voice, almost as though it existed independently of the body which contained it, would gush out in crystalline splendor and convert a precarious moment into an ecstatic one."[86] One audience member, in a reminiscence solicited by opera singer Frieda Hempel in the 1920s, said, "Nothing could have been more naïve and charming than her manner on the stage. She would trip on and off, as if in an ecstasy of delight at the opportunity of singing, bowing and smiling to her audience, and giving everyone present a flattering sense in contributing in measure to the success of the evening."[87]

In diaries and letters, Lind's audience members repeatedly emphasized Lind's personal character. William Hoffman, who showed up several times with the crowds outside Castle Garden, hoping to get inside but stymied by the high ticket prices, took to repeatedly copying newspaper reports about her personal qualities in his diary, concluding that "her great powers of benevolence speak for her the most enviable qualities of soul that any being ever could possess."[88] Henry Southworth, the twenty-year-old New York City store clerk mentioned at the beginning of this chapter, also participated in the welcoming crowds for Lind and sought to get a glimpse of her at her hotel. He described his experience of hearing her sing in concert not in terms of her music program but rather her personality: "I cannot express my delight and wonder in words, she is indeed a wonderful woman, she sings with perfect ear and is at home, in everything she does."[89] Lind even seemed to heighten auditors' awareness of their own selves. Caroline White, in response to hearing Jenny Lind in Boston, wrote in her diary: "I have heard her! The wonderful Jenny! And though language itself has been exhausted in her praise—it seems to me too much cannot be said, such a volume of <u>such sounds</u>—singing, clear melodious—can any one listen to them and not feel one's aspirations glow warmer, loftier, holier, than ever before?"[90]

Especially after repeated encounters with the same performer, audience members often began to feel a strong and uniquely charged connection to what they perceived as the performer's "inner" self. In a time when people were striving to achieve what Lucia McMahon has called an intense "sharing of selfhood" in both friendships and romantic relationships, concert audiences often idealized a "bond of feeling" with performers, similar to the communion nineteenth-century romance readers often felt with characters and with authors.[91] Many stars of the nineteenth century inspired music lovers to understand their listening experiences as part of a continuing and reciprocal relationship. Walt Whitman, for example, idolized opera contralto Marietta Alboni. He saw her every time she appeared in New York City; knew her body, her facial expressions, and physical movements by heart; and addressed her by name in *Leaves of Grass*, the only person to receive such an honor: "The teeming lady comes! / The lustrious orb—Venus contralto—the blooming mother, / Sister of loftiest gods—Alboni's self I hear." Later, he would reminisce, "Seems to me now when I look back, the Italian contralto Marietta Alboni . . . and the Italian singer Bettini, have had the greatest and most lasting effect upon me. I should like very well if Madame Alboni and the old composer Verdi . . . could know how much noble pleasure and happiness they gave me and how deeply I always remember them and thank them to this day."[92]

Poet Anne Lynch had similar feelings for violinist Ole Bull, recognizing in his playing an explosion of feeling that mimicked her own desires. She was even moved to write directly to him:

I have never found one to love with my whole soul, and perhaps it is well, for I should die and be consumed with the intensity of that passion, but friendship is as beautiful as love and that I cannot live without, though even here I have never been satisfied. I have never met a nature who could return to me the half of what I could give, and so my life has been one long famine and my heart the cannibal of itself. If I seem to you too enthusiastic in my expressions of friendship for you, remember that my heart has been frozen for a whole lifetime and it must naturally overflow on meeting one so large and so noble as your own. Ah, Ole Bull! If I could tell you the history of my life, so cold, so barren without and so volcanic within![93]

The ultimate example of sharing selfhood with music stars might be Lowell Patton, the son of prominent New York minister William Patton and an admirer of a young Abby Hutchinson of the Hutchinson Family Singers. "His infatuation with the group, and with Abby in particular, bordered on mania," Scott Gac explains. "Starting in the early 1840s and continuing for more than fifty years, Patton clipped every newspaper article on the group that he could find . . . the persistent young admirer, no doubt spared the status of a crazed groupie by virtue of his wealth, eventually married Abby Hutchinson."[94]

Music was especially suited for the purpose of self-making, since it represented an intensely emotional and sensual experience that could create a heightened, vaguely erotic, intimacy with another. By attending a public concert, people could easily experience an intense emotional bond with another person, something that they could only find otherwise through chance and the labor of courtship. Heightening that bond was its contrary elusiveness: it was always temporary and, to some extent, illusory—audiences did not actually know Ole Bull, or Jenny Lind, personally and probably never would. Indeed, that each star existed as both a humble ordinary person *and* a worldwide concert phenomenon was an intense and irresistible mystery.

Even if audience members never became actual friends with (or spouses of) the stars they admired, their recognition of kindred selves on stage operated like a spiritual revelation, inspiring an outpouring of personal empathy and goodwill that often spilled over from a star to one's fellow audience members. As another of Bull's admirers explained after witnessing one of his first American concerts:

Ole Bull has certainly impressed me as no man ever impressed me before. The most glorious sensation I ever had was to sit in one of his audiences, and feel that all were elevated to the same pitch with myself. My impulse was to speak to every one as to an intimate friend. The most indifferent person was a living soul to me. The most remote or proud I did not fear or despise. In that element they were all accessible, nay, all worth reaching. This surely was the highest testimony to his great art and his great soul.[95]

Toward the end of the 1850s, this depth of feeling experienced by some concert-goers would lead them toward new urban subcultures, based not so much on ethnicity or class or race, but on participation in commercial music entertainments. They believed that the soaring feelings of discovery and ambition that emerged at public concerts could not only serve as tools for self-understanding but also more fully occupy one's daily life and define the most cherished friendships.

CHAPTER FOUR

"How I Should Like to Hear It All Over Again & Again"

Loving Music, 1850–1885

+{⚙}+

The Passion of Lucy Lowell

On 14 April 1884, twenty-four-year-old Lucy Lowell attended the opening of a Wagner festival at Boston's Mechanics Hall, sponsored by famed conductor Theodore Thomas and his Orchestra. The festival was opening its national tour in Boston, and it featured some of the greatest Wagnerian opera singers of the time, several of whom were performers in the annual Wagner Festival in Bayreuth, Germany. While Lowell had heard Wagner's music before and was able to recognize some of the excerpts from *Tann-häuser* and *Die Walküre*, the five concerts of the festival would give her the opportunity to hear his operas in a full and intense dose. Her reaction to the first night's concert was close to awe. "I never imagined anything so beautiful," she rhapsodized in her diary. "Altogether it was the most interesting & delightful performance I ever heard. Crowds of people. I should like to hear just the same thing over again every week for months, so as to get familiar with it, & then perhaps I might"—she wrote "get" but then crossed the word out—"somewhere nearly appreciate it."[1]

The following night, she witnessed the same solo singers, as well as several choral pieces from *Die Meistersinger*, which she found "lively, jolly, and beautiful." However, Lowell was most taken with tenor Walter Winkel-mann, and spent much of her diary recollection of the concert contemplating his explosive style, which she found bewitching:

Then Walter sings his prize song, & never in my life was I so perfectly carried away, excited, overcome as by Winkelmann's singing of that song, it was perfectly superb, people can criticize his way of singing if they like, but I say they might as well keep still when a man gets up and sings like an inspired creature as he did. Winkelmann sits all the time perfectly unmoved & as tho' in a dream (almost) & then sings—well, it would be worth going to Germany just to hear him sing that song. He is fascinating, I think, & the only thing that reconciles me to not going to the Festival tomorrow P.M. is that he's not going to sing.[2]

Even though she couldn't attend the third afternoon of the Festival, she met with her friend Edith in the early evening, and they "talked Wagner." As she wrote, "She'd been last night & this P.M. & was as wild as I, so we just raved & enjoyed it tremendously." That night she returned to Mechanics Hall with her cousin Lewis to witness the third concert of performances. She described the trip in her diary in unusually clipped phrases, as if impatiently trying to get to her seat: "In at 5, to Cousin Lewis,' he & I to Wagner, it rained hard on the way up." Perhaps the excitement of the previous two days had raised her expectations too high, however, for halfway into the program of *Tristan und Isolde*, she found that "it didn't excite me at all" and, with some regret, she wrote that she was "terribly disappointed."[3]

Working through the experience, she never once doubted the abilities of the performers in whom she had invested so much enthusiasm but instead suspected Mechanics Hall itself. It was not, after all, the first time she'd had a bad listening experience there. Two years before, in 1882, after seeing Adelina Patti perform in *La Traviata* at the Hall, she had complained, "it is so vast a place that the whole thing was vague and unsatisfactory." Soon after, on 13 May 1882, she marveled that singer Etelka Gerster, appearing in *La Sonnambula*, was actually able to reach her entire audience: "I never heard such enthusiasm (in Boston) in my life. And this in that barn where I thought it was impossible to get an audience excited."[4] In fact, learning afterward that her mother and sister, seated closer to the stage, "were perfectly wild," her suspicions were confirmed. She wrote, "I was disgusted for it must have been cousin L's seats wh' [which] were in [section] M., our own in F. The orchestra magnificent from M., but the solos seemed far away."[5]

On the fourth day of the Wagner festival, Thursday, 17 May 1884, Lowell attended the 2 P.M. matinee performance, this time sitting with her mother in section F and finding the performances "perfectly overwhelming." After dinner and visits with friends in Boston, she went back yet again, with Cousin Lewis and her father, for the farewell performance. Even though she detected a weariness in Winkelmann's voice, which was sometimes "flat," she became swept up in the Thomas Orchestra's opening performance of the "Andante" to Beethoven's *Symphony No. 5*, which she noted was "the most heavenly, exquisite, perfectly beautiful thing I ever heard. . . .

I never had any idea before how an orchestra could play. It would have been worthwhile to go to stupid performances every night to end up with that symphony so played." Her enthusiasm carried through a subsequent performance of the *Götterdämmerung*, after which she wrote: "Such a scene of wild enthusiasm I've never seen. Amalie Materna, Winkelmann & Thomas were called back over & over again, the audience was all standing & they just shouted & cheered, stamped, waved handkerchiefs & were actually beside themselves. Cousin Lewis & I rushed forward so that we were close to them as they went up & down fr. The stage & they (especially Materna) were tremendously excited & pleased."[6]

Lowell would repeat the experience when the singers returned briefly on a repeat swing in May 1884, before moving on to their final North American performances in Montreal. A year later, in another Wagner Festival directed by a young Walter Damrosch, Lucy attended two, full, four-hour performances of *Die Walküre* within five days, reading the text in German beforehand so as to better appreciate the music. In September, Lowell finally made a pilgrimage to Vienna, Austria, to see Winkelmann and Materna perform before a home audience, and in 1888 she would finally travel to what Mark Twain called the "Shrine of St. Wagner," the composer's own opera house that he had built in Bayreuth, Germany.

Even though she was deeply moved by such experiences, it was those first, naive encounters with Theodore Thomas's Orchestra in Section F of Mechanics Hall that always stood out the most, for it was in those moments that she seemed truly to learn about the potential power of aural experience. Like many young people, she was prone to hyperbole, but her descriptions of the 1884 Wagner Festival concerts took up a greater proportion of her diary (over ten pages) than any other concert she would experience, and it was something that would help define the rest of her adult life. Indeed, she seemed to realize the significance of the Festival. As if astonished, the usually loquacious Lowell wrote nothing at all in her diary on Friday, 18 April 1884, the day after the first week of performances. Instead, on Saturday, she managed only to briefly comment: "Head washed, read. Utterly unsettled by excitement of the Wagner concerts." Then, with a dash of sarcasm, she added, "I suppose it can't be good for a person to go to things that excite her so that she can't fix her mind on anything for days afterwards."[7]

While clerks and other aspirants to the middle-class at mid-century may have been attracted by the sheer novelty of urban concerts and the opportunities such events provided for self-making, more established members of the middle class in the ensuing decades began to define more fully the audience practices that would support their pursuit of music. Such concert-goers, or "music lovers," as they became known, developed strong opinions about performer expressiveness, new works, effective concert hall construction, and applause. They continually experimented with various ways of incorporating musical experience in everyday life, from making pilgrimages and compiling scrapbooks. Some began to build cadres of regular concert-going companions, with whom they could discuss favorite composers and experiences. By the 1880s, new generations of concert-goers had constructed an experiential, insider's knowledge about performance that, in turn, helped to cultivate new understandings of "good" audiencing.

The building of such knowledge wasn't simply cumulative. The Civil War and its aftermath, for example, halted the development of America's burgeoning concert culture of the 1850s by profoundly disrupting transportation and funding, as well as removing personnel.[8] In general, the tumult of war forced many northern middle-class Americans to retreat to the "private sphere" for their musicking, a move that had long-term effects, including enlarging the market for sheet music and parlor pianos.[9] At the same time, however, there were continuities with pre-War concert culture. In the late 1860s, northern entrepreneurs, music societies, and music lovers, filled with new energy, were eager to revive public concerts in America's cities. As critic John S. Dwight simply declared, "The war is over! There is now time to think again of music."[10] In 1865, Theodore Thomas began a series of summer concerts in New York City with his Orchestra, something that would launch his career over the next several decades as America's most famous conductor.[11] Six music conservatories were established between 1865 and 1868, and permanent orchestras were established in New York, Boston, Chicago, Cincinnati, and Philadelphia between 1878 and 1900.[12] Otherwise, decommissioned military bands, amateur and professional, catered to a popular demand for instrumental music, and blackface minstrelsy, primarily an East Coast urban style before the war, gained wide influence among white middle-class Americans as it moved away from its rebellious working-class origins and toward more explicitly racist content and a standardized variety format.

In all, postwar generations of urban music lovers were born into a more accessible but more complicated musical world. In particular, the relationship between culture and commerce became newly significant in such a context, as increasing numbers of middle-class educators and critics argued for specific parameters of value that separated out acceptable and unacceptable cultural participation. While self-making continued to be a central theme in middle-class ideology, how the self was made—and with which activities and skills—became more and more debated, making any individual's audiencing a series of weighted choices. By Lucy Lowell's time in the early 1880s, a middle-class young person could not simply consume music as a listener, but had to somehow demonstrate that he or she was a *discerning* listener, concentrating on, in Matthew Arnold's famous phrase, "The best that has been thought and known in the world."[13] Learning how to "love music" in the latter half of the nineteenth century was thus a process of not only engaging in available musical resources and figuring out how to incorporate them into one's daily life, but also negotiating the wider cultural meanings of that participation.

Of course, for young Lucy Lowell, discernment was not a quality she necessarily needed to demonstrate; the prestige of her family name alone evoked a certain level of refinement. The Lowells of Boston were one of the most distinguished families in the United States, with Puritan New England roots and a rich lineage of talented and successful businessmen, jurists, and poets. Lucy was part of a particular branch of the family that moved more quietly through the world than some of the others; even then, her parents negotiated Boston society with relative ease.

Rather than starting industrialization in the United States or becoming a national literary figure like other Lowells, Lucy's father, John Lowell, was a respected federal judge. "Judge John," as he was known, was a long-bearded, amiable character, who started his career with a published criticism of the 1857 Dred Scott decision and who was appointed by Abraham Lincoln in 1865 to the Circuit Court, where he ruled on maritime disputes, patent cases, and other topics of the day until his retirement in 1884. Humbly studious, and an avid gardener, he was known as much for his aptitude for growing roses as for his thoughtful legal decisions.

Lucy's mother, whom John married in 1853, was Lucy Buckminster Emerson, member of another famous Boston family, the Emersons. Her father, George B. Emerson, was Ralph Waldo Emerson's cousin and founder of a prestigious girls' school in Boston. Lucy Emerson's diary, kept in the mid-1840s before her marriage to Judge John, indicates a proper young woman, quick with condescension (she called Edgar Allen Poe, for instance, "a ridiculous looking man" and was easily offended by over-stepping suitors) but who also enthused about theater and enjoyed the seasonal concerts of the Academy of Music.[14]

Lucy (her mother's namesake and called "Lulu" by some of her family members) was the fourth of seven children born between 1854 and 1869. She was close with her mother, and her mother's friend Mamie, with whom she regularly attended concerts and shows. The family lived in the peaceful suburb of Chestnut Hill in Newton, just a short train (or horse carriage) ride west of Boston, a situation that must have been a rather idyllic escape from both the dirt and noise of the city, as well as its busy social schedule.

What we know of Lucy's life comes primarily from her diary, the first volume of which was given to her in 1880, when she was twenty years old, by her best friend, Edith Annie Fiske.

Like many young women in the nineteenth century, Lucy began her diary as a mnemonic device, noting people that she had met or accounting for daily events. She did not pour her heart and soul into its pages—when she experienced serious losses, for example, such as the death of her sister, Mary Lothrop Lowell, in 1882 (when Lucy was twenty-two), or her older brother George, who died just two years later, she did not detail those events but simply stopped writing and grieved in silence. However she did occasionally use her diary as a means for reflecting on (and improving) her immediate behavior and outlook. Lucy was independent, intelligent, and often irascible, which was not a combination that predicted smooth relations with others. She often noted, for example, regretting her behavior after a party or gathering. In fact, she opened her diary by recounting a testy exchange with her mother, and vowing to "try to be more good-natured and less cantankerous" toward members of her family.[15]

Of course, being good-natured could be taxing for anyone living according to the strict social requirements of a single, young lady in Boston society. In the first year of her diary, 1880, Lowell mentioned being flattered at the attention she received from young men at parties and dances, and was quietly pleased at being serenaded by four young men one spring evening, including a boy named John Putnam, who showed up later to sing duets with her. However, by 1882, she wrote, "I find myself getting more and more unsociable & think I've quite got over my excitement over boys which I used to feel 2 years ago. One reason may be that no one but people who bore or are quite uninteresting to me ever come here (except some of the little boys) & the people whom I should like to see never come here by any chance! Such is life!"[16] Her disdain for the conventions of courtship became sharp and incisive from then on. For example, when her parents tried to introduce her to a young gentleman whom Lucy thought a "bore," and he had the temerity to ask for a picture so he could remember her, she bristled at the intimacy of the request, writing, "I wouldn't have him have a picture of me!"[17]

Instead, over time, Lowell shifted her attention toward music. Like any young genteel woman in the nineteenth century, Lowell worked at cultivating her artistic sensibility, which included making a trip from her home in Newton into the city of Boston for singing lessons, usually every Monday and Thursday. However, in the seven volumes she completed over the course of the 1880s, she never once described the content of those lessons or expressed any real interest in them. Perhaps that was because of what singing represented for her; while she reported enjoying moments in which she privately sang with close friends, she openly disdained the idea of singing in front of groups of strangers at parties: "Had a dinner party for Miss Tweedy. Mabel & Hattie were the other girls, John Howard Messers, G. D. Chapin, L. Pierce & R. Loug, gentlemen," she wrote in 1880. "I had to sing in eve'g. Bah!"[18]

Instead, for Lucy, music meant the sound and spectacle on the stages of Boston's increasing number of concert halls and opera houses. She attended performances by almost every touring opera and symphonic star that passed through Boston, as well as the opera, symphony concerts, musical society benefits, the theatre, the circus, exhibitions, amateur performances, and dances, a rate of attendance that was certainly greater than that of most people her age. A telling example of her fascination was her twenty-seventh birthday, in 1887. She received a number of thoughtful gifts from her parents and siblings, including money, a "very pretty" inkstand and a tray of silver, a penhandle, a buttoner, and a letter-weigher, but wrote in her diary that while she was grateful for such gifts, the most meaningful was something her mother had thrown in with the inkstand as an extra: a season ticket to the rehearsals of the Boston Symphony, which began the next day.[19]

Concert going became a serious occupation for Lucy. Missing any part of a performance made her annoyed. She loathed leaving concerts early, for instance, which was sometimes required by tram schedules or her less-invested concert-going companions. She was highly "disgusted" when, from time to time, the trains did not run on time from Brookline to Boston and forced her to miss the first act of an opera production.[20] Once, when her parents insisted that she go to Buffalo with them one winter to visit relatives, she regretted agreeing, because she would miss her routine, including performances by the Boston Symphony Orchestra conducted by George Henschel:

I'm going to miss lots of things that I hate to lose, do no good & just go to Buffalo to be asked round to all sorts of parties &c. that I don't want to go to. I've got to lose—a Henschel rehearsal, Mrs. Hall's lunch, spending the night at the Bryants,' church at Mr. Brooks,' a history lesson, a sewing circle (Ethel's last), a singing lesson, a Henschel recital. I'm mad, but, now I've written it all down, it's worked off a little steam & I feel a trifle better.[21]

Even at performances she attended, Lucy could become quite frustrated when her seating was bad or the sound of the hall was distorted. She thus noted the quality of the sound for various seating positions in a given hall, to be used for future reference. She also found it hard to tolerate non-musical distractions. When fellow audience members at a performance of Wagner's *Die Walküre* were too vocal in their enthusiasm, she wrote, "The audience was large and enthusiastic tho' not appreciative or intelligent for they would talk thro' the music before the curtain rose and applauded in the middle."[22] Even onstage distractions were bothersome. When eminent Boston publisher Mr. Ticknor agreed to read the "connecting poem" to Beethoven's Egmont Overture on 11 December 1885, she complained, "I hate reading with music . . . especially where the reading went on at the same time with slow music, I then wanted to throttle Mr. T or do something to stop him so that I could listen to the music." Though she loved the opera, she admitted that, in the presence of mediocre singers, "I would go for the orchestra only, in fact I sometimes wish I could listen to that alone without any tho't of the stage."[23]

Overall, she lamented the Victorian restrictions for women attending public concerts, saying "If I were only a man, or, next best, had a musical man at my beck & call, how I would go to hear music."[24] To overcome this restriction, she went to concerts with various combinations of family members, friends, and acquaintances, taking advantage of whomever might be available to escort her. But still, the hardest month of each year was March, when the concert season in Boston typically ended. It was something she counted down mournfully in her diary, and then mourned afterward as well, writing: "Well, it's over and now come 4½ months without any music to speak of!"[25] Periods of dormancy in Boston's musical life were especially difficult, since even during the concert season she lamented not having enough music to hear.

As if to capture and hold on to performances, Lowell began to write about them in her diary. While she wrote merrily of sing-alongs with friends at parties, dancing at balls, and shrieking with laughter at burlesque plays at the Boston Museum or Union Hall, and sometimes noted a musician at a party or in the pit "playing wonderfully well" at such events, her diary descriptions of such events were brief, generalized, and mostly about enjoying time with friends. In her writing about concert events, her tone was far more self-aware. She paid careful attention to her listening, recording the names of each of the performers and their instruments, and then writing pages of play-by-play reactions to the unfolding segments of the production. Rarely did she elaborate about those with whom she attended or describe her interactions with them. Her diary entries about concerts had a crystal clear focus on the stage, nothing else. Implicit in her focus was that she would see and hear well, and also that she might be moved—even transported—by the music she would encounter.

She was a demanding listener. Even though she sometimes said in her diary that she knew little about instrumental "execution," over the course of her early twenties, from 1880 to 1884, she cultivated an extraordinary knowledge of key opera productions and their characters, the emotional arcs of various symphonies, as well as the capabilities of various players, conductors, and impresarios. By 1882, she often sounded more like a seasoned journalist than a shy debutante, as she showed in a critical response to a production of *Faust*:

We were much disappointed that Rossini didn't sing Marguerite, Vachon took her place suddenly & sang execrably, but was pretty & attractive looking. She hadn't rehearsed so she did well considering, but she did sing terribly out, she sang in French. Campanini was fine as Faust, but did not do as well as he would have done if he hadn't had to sing with a Marguerite, who didn't know what to do. Novara was <u>splendid</u> as Mephistopheles, acting in a very diabolical way & singing well. Galassi (as Valentino) was, as always, magnificent, his voice is perfectly superb. Orchestra & chorus admirable.[26]

Indeed, in some parts of her diary, she switched from the first-person singular to the second person, as if trying to make her assessments more objectively convincing. As she wrote about Etelka Gerster in an Italian production of the *Barber of Seville*: "Gerster was utterly, entirely & perfectly bewitching . . . You get a good idea of her genius by seeing her first in 'Lucia' & then in 'The Barber,' for two more different parts can't be imagined & when you see how exquisitely she does them both, you appreciate her power."[27]

Even though she could be demanding of performers, Lowell was surprisingly open to new musical experiences. Unlike some of her peers, who were becoming more and more conservative in their tastes during the 1880s, she preferred to give unfamiliar music a chance by really listening to it and responding in the moment without reference to "expert" reviews or expectations. Of course, Lucy had certain preferences: she liked the "Andante" of Beethoven's *Symphony No. 5* so much that she mentioned it enthusiastically whenever she encountered it. After 1882, she didn't even refer to Beethoven by name, using only the numbers or titles of his symphonies, as if having to identify his genius was to state the obvious. Sometimes, too, one concert experience could obliterate another. When she had the opportunity to attend a conventional performance by pianist Carl Baermann, for example, a week after the 1885 Wagner Festival, she wrote in her diary that she and her friends "weren't excited about it at all" and gave her tickets away. The reverberations of Wagner were too strong.

However, Lowell rarely accepted or rejected anything wholesale and she often seemed pleasantly surprised at her reactions: she found Berlioz's *Sym-*

phonie Fantastique "very weird and interesting", found herself liking new music by Delibes, and noted hearing a Svendson's Symphony, calling it "strange but interesting and parts of it lovely."[28] While she initially resisted an excerpt of Brahms's music upon first hearing in 1882, she admitted two years later being surprised with herself for actually *liking* a performance of a Brahms symphony.[29] In 1886, she wrote about the *Siegfried Idyll*: "I don't understand how I could have not liked it the first time I heard it."[30]

Focusing attention on the *performance* of a work rather than the work itself made her listening emotionally dynamic and always in-the-moment; ultimately, she conceived of performance and listening as means of human engagement, actions that she expected to be mutually meaningful. According to Lucy, for example, the worst thing any player could do was to play "mechanically," that is, to have "brilliant execution but no feeling." As she negatively mentioned about Patti in *Lucia*: "Patti's singing of the great flute song was wonderful, but not, to me, in the least moving."[31] Or as she wrote about a chamber concert: "Piano by Mr. Carl Faelton, who plays well but without feeling or soul."[32] Feeling or soul could even carry music that was not up to par. In February 1882, when she and her mother went to a Philharmonic concert, she noted, "It wasn't particularly interesting, except for Carl Baermann's playing which was exquisite. He played a Rheinberger concerto wh' wasn't much, but his playing was wonderful, his touch delicious."[33]

Her idea of "expression" was complex. She valued not simply abstract "beauty" or simple aural pleasure—those were important qualities, to be sure (and a designation of a performer's voice as "harsh and disagreeable" meant, for Lucy, no further engagement)—but for Lowell a truly outstanding performance, one that would move her with passion and power, had to involve communion with the inner life of another human being. As she explained about seeing Theodore Thomas conduct Wagner's *Tannhäuser*: "That orchestra always excites me tremendously, how <u>can</u> any one say they play mechanically? To me there is a life & spirit wh' carries me right along & I feel the same magnetic influence which Thomas evidently places on his musicians to a man. They respond to his slightest gesture & produce an effect wh' is absolutely electric."[34]

This direct, personal connection was also important in her feelings for the various singers she encountered over the years. She always described Etelka Gerster, for example, in affectionate, loving terms that emphasized her demeanor and true character:

Her simplicity & sweetness all through were irresistible. In the music lesson scene she sang a pretty thing, encored, sang "Carnival of Venice," encored, sang Faubert's

"In the Mch Night," a sweet little laughing song, in wh' her pronunciation of the German and her whole manner fascinating, then encored again & she sang "Old Folks at Home" & oh, the delicious sweetness & purity of her notes in that & the feeling she put into it, her cunning broken English & her sweet & lovely expression of face were so exquisite, can't express it, that's all, the darling.[35]

Sometimes, Lucy even felt that slight flaws in execution enhanced her ability to perceive and be moved by a singer's personality. As she demonstrated in her description of Materna:

Her voice is by no means perfect, some of the notes are rough & almost harsh, she uses the tremolo a great deal & sometimes sings out of tune, but the power of all her notes, the beauty of some of them, the spirit & intensity, sympathy, & soul of her singing make her more grand a singer than any one I ever heard. She is large, very stout & very plain, but you never think of the woman [her appearance] in listening to her wonderful singing.[36]

At a cultural level, being emotionally moved by a performer could be especially meaningful for women in a society that actively controlled women's emotional lives. As Peter J. Rabinowitz writes about the phenomenon of women crying at Louis Moreau Gottschalk's piano concerts: "Tears were not a simple, involuntary acquiescence on the part of naive listeners, but were rather part of a complex interpretive system through which nineteenth-century women processed the sounds they heard in order to serve a variety of social and cultural needs." A concert was reframed by many women patrons as an "occasion for tears," which created a collective space where women could express their emotions and desires more freely and openly than they could anywhere else.[37]

Wagner, in fact, became significant as a cultural force in the United States for this very reason. While he had become associated with various radical social and political movements in Europe, the appeal of his operas in the United States was primarily due to the highly intense, emotional, even erotic, release it provided its listeners, many of them women. Willa Cather powerfully dramatized such a release in her 1904 story, "A Wagner Matinee," in which an older pioneer-wife from Nebraska, visiting her nephew in Boston, thrillingly attends the opera for the first time in thirty years and refuses to leave. "For her, just outside the door of the concert hall, lay the black pond with the cattle-tracked bluffs; the tall, unpainted house, with weather-curled boards; naked as a tower, the crook-backed ash seedlings where the dish-cloths hung to dry; the gaunt, moulting turkeys picking up refuse about the kitchen door."[38] Music historian Joseph Horowitz characterized Wagner's appeal a bit more sensationally: "The disappointing effects of husband and bedroom were silenced by a musical-dramatic orgasm as explicit and complete as any mortal intercourse."[39]

The emotional appeal of Wagner could be a delicate matter for a woman in polite society, something that Lucy recognized. When she took her first trip to Europe in 1885 and obtained tickets to see some of her favorite Wagnerian singers, including Emil Scaria and Hermann Winkelmann, on their home stage of the famed Vienna Opera House, she was overcome with the magnitude of where she was and what she was doing, writing in her diary, simply: "In eve'g we went to the Opera, what would our Puritan ancestors say!"[40] Otherwise, after experiencing the second Wagner Festival in Boston, she noted that her friends worried a bit about the effects of Wagner's music: "Isa & Edith had a long discussion about the effect of the Walkure, whether it is demoralizing or elevating, & which Wagner in general is, whether the tremendous effect that he undoubtedly has on the emotions is only br't about by the effect on the senses or whether his poetry & imagination make the feeling something higher than merely sensuous (awful word)."[41]

For the most part, however, Lucy didn't seem to have been bothered much by Wagner's hold on her. Just as she "got over" her "excitement over boys," Lowell similarly embraced the opera and concert life of Boston with few apologies.

It is tempting to speculate how Lowell's highly charged emotional experiences with music may have fit into the rest of her personal and public life, but her diary does not offer access to the intimate details of her personal connections and needs. Indeed, after two travel diaries, the last covering a trip to Europe in 1890, she stopped writing. The public record indicates that she went on to lead the life of a socially active, elite, Boston woman. Remaining single, she eventually moved away from her father's estate at Chestnut Hill, settling in a house on St. James Avenue in the heart of Boston. She became a leader in civic organizations, like many of the woman of her social standing in the Progressive Era. She was a trustee of Boston's Museum of Fine Arts, on the board of the Perkins Institution and Massachusetts School for the Blind, and President of the American Unitarian Association from 1920 to 1921. Until her death, in 1946, she played recurring roles in Boston's cultural life as a patron and participant, while managing the legacy of her parents.

As if shaping her own legacy, Lowell's diary offers not necessarily what we might like to know about her life but what *she* felt was important: a youthful expression of musical passion and a glimpse of a life profoundly shaped by the act of listening to music. While certainly a member of America's elite in the latter nineteenth century, her experience and her opinions in many ways represent the culmination of a developing culture after the Civil War in which auditory enthusiasm could organize one's daily activity, orient personal values, cultivate a sense of belonging, and shape new kinds of shared knowledge. This was a culture that deeply affected the lives of individuals who participated; it also reflected wider social changes under-foot in the post–Civil War era, a time shaped by increased immigration, significant labor unrest, and increasingly pronounced divisions between so-cial classes.

Over the next two chapters, I will explore the development of "music loving" as an identifiable set of practices and ideologies. First, in this chap-ter, I will explore the several decades before Lowell's time, to explain how various music lovers themselves explored and developed a shared under-standing of audiencing. Then, in Chapter 5, I will go back over this period to address more directly some of the ways in which critics and reformers, reacting to broader forces of industrialization and class division, sparked efforts to reform audiencing and its nascent meanings. In moving across the period between 1850 and 1885, in both of these chapters, my aim is not to collapse or minimize historical differences between the mid-nineteenth century and the late nineteenth century, but rather to survey and bring to-gether evidence that might suggest the complex ways music loving co-alesced as a set of behaviors and ideas.

Public Concerts and the Search for Musical Sensation

Music festivals, like the ones Lucy Lowell attended in Boston in 1884 and 1885, were outgrowths of the "monster" concert format that became in-creasingly popular after the Civil War. Instead of single touring engage-ments by a star, which dominated in the 1840s and 1850s, entrepreneurs arranged ever bigger, longer, and more sensational performances, with multiple artists over days and sometimes weeks, eventually reaching pro-portions that stretched even the most outrageous conventions of the Amer-ican concert business. The term *monster concert* was invented by French con-ductor Louis Jullien who, in 1853, arrived to great fanfare in the United States and promptly put together one of the largest orchestras on record for a series of two hundred New York City concerts that he dubbed "Monster Concerts for the Masses." After 1860, the race was on among entrepreneurs to top one another's efforts; they sought to make concerts even bigger and more spectacular, putting literally thousands of performers onstage at once and erecting huge, temporary performance halls, the size of several contem-porary football fields, to accommodate their grandiose ambitions. Urban boosters often supported such schemes, seeing monster concert events as a way to promote the cultural sophistication of a locality and attract business. It was the logical endgame of mass entertainment before the rise of electronic media.

The most notable of these concerts was the 1869 National Peace Jubilee and Grand Music Festival in Boston. Conceived by Union Army bandleader Patrick Gilmore, it featured 1,000 performers and 10,000 choral singers (including 7,000 local-area school children), performing for an audience of 30,000 in a temporary wood-and-plaster "coliseum" built on the then-empty lot of what is now Copley Square. Given that most concert venues at the time averaged a capacity of approximately 1,200 people (the largest venue at the time, the Boston Theatre, held 3,000), and that the population in Boston at the time was around 250,000, the numbers were extraordinary. It didn't stop there, however. Gilmore's sequel, the 1872 World Peace Jubilee, held in the same spot, featured performers from Europe and the United States and accommodated even *more* people: 2,000 orchestra performers, 20,000 choral members, and a coliseum that could hold 100,000 audience members.

It is easy to gloss over such large numbers, especially from our modern perspective where sports arenas and stadiums holding 60,000 or more people are commonplace. From a performance perspective, however, such events were mind-boggling. As composer Johann Strauss, who appeared as a guest conductor at the World Peace Jubilee, explained:

On the musicians' tribune there were twenty thousand singers; in front of them the members of the orchestra—and these were the people I was to conduct. A hundred assistant conductors had been placed at my disposal to control these gigantic masses, but I was only able to recognize those nearest to me, and though we had rehearsals there was no possibility of giving an artistic performance, a proper production. . . . Now just conceive of my position face to face with a public of four hundred thousand Americans. There I stood at the raised desk, high above all the others. How would the business start, how would it end? Suddenly a cannon-shot rang out, a gentle hint for us twenty thousand to begin playing The Blue Danube. I gave the signal, my hundred assistant conductors followed me as quickly and as well as they could, and then there broke out an unholy row such as I shall never forget.[42]

Editorials of the time confirmed Strauss's characterization of an "unholy row": John S. Dwight characterized the jubilee as a "racket." However, while Strauss was facing a conducting nightmare, auditors felt that they were participating in something historic. Fifteen-year-old Helen Atkins, for example, wrote about her excitement: "We all went in to the jubilee and enjoyed it ever so much," Helen wrote in 1872. "Strauss played 'The Blue Danube' perfectly mag[nificent]—!!!!!! All went off very finely . . . a very full house."[43]

"View of the interior of the Coliseum, St. James Park—The Scene on the Opening Day, June 15." From Patrick Gilmore, *History of the National Peace Jubilee and Great Music Festival*. Boston: By the author, 1871, 442.

For audience members, such concerts did not offer a radical new vision for music in America but rather calculatedly enhanced specific qualities of established public music performance in order to arouse specific feelings of excitement and pleasure. For one, the jubilee concerts were marked by social events that invited a large slice of Boston's population—from wealthy elites to workers and blacks—to congregate in a single place and thereby put a rapidly growing society on display for itself. These events took place at a time when "masses" of people were still a novelty in everyday life and reserved for battlefields and ritual public events like parades or inaugurations. As the *Boston Herald* put it:

Whoever was fortunate enough to secure a position within the Coliseum yesterday where a bird's eye view could be had of the vast multitude there congregated had the pleasure of looking upon an assembly of not less than FIFTY THOUSAND PEOPLE. For two full hours did we survey this sea of humanity, visiting every part of the building where man or woman could secure a position either to see or hear, noting carefully, as the engineer would his topography, every feature that could possibly be of worth in working out our estimate of the congregated thousands.[44]

Second, they exploited the engineering and technological know-how feeding the construction boom in cities and mimicked urbanization's transformation of the landscape by creating, almost overnight, some of the biggest interior spaces in the country at that time. Having a ticket to sit in the

Coliseum, and experience the dynamics of the place itself, was almost as important as hearing the music performed. Indeed, artist renderings of the event were almost always in a bird's-eye or landscape format, not available to ordinary people, and dramatized the expanse of the space; *Frank Leslie's Illustrated* included a four page fold-out image of the inside of the Coliseum, drawn from the perspective of the upper rear balcony and emphasizing the stage as a very distant vanishing point.[45] As Mary Atkins enthused, somewhat alarmed, "The Coliseum was packed. Men & boys hung upon the beams."[46]

And third, they enabled people to experience unprecedented sensations of sound. In Mansfield, Massachusetts, twenty-six miles outside of Boston, one resident reported that "he knew just what time each day the Anvil chorus was played, and on the days when he stayed at home, he watch the clock, and by listening, could hear the detonations of the Boston cannon."[47] One must remember, of course, that this was a time before electric amplification had made bone-tingling volume commonplace. Oddly enough, while the 1,000 musicians onstage playing a single note must have been impressive, many reported that the music was not as loud as expected and that it was actually the roar of the audience that was startling:

Not the least moral feature of the Festival is the applause,—so overwhelming in its demonstration that timid souls have said their prayers and trusted blindly in the stability of wooden rafters. The Anvil Chorus gives one a shake both bodily and morally, and there follows no "soft collision of applauding gloves," but a tempestuous storm of stamping, cheering, waving hats and handkerchiefs, that gives such a start to the blood it rings louder in people's ears than the chorus itself.[48]

In the end, the jubilee concerts in Boston were temporary. After the World Peace Jubilee of 1872 was over, the Coliseum was dismantled to make way for Boston's new Museum of Fine Arts. The crowds of people went back to the regular entertainment of local museums, minstrel halls, and opera houses and their enthusiasm about hearing a 1,000-person chorus, or of seeing Strauss conduct, likely also faded into memory. However, the jubilee concerts are important for understanding music loving, because in their very extravagance they dramatized the nature of music's appeal and power for nineteenth-century urban audiences. Their most thrilling qualities—like mass gatherings of people, an emphasis on performance space, and the physical experience of sound—were qualities that music lovers *always* attended to, regularly and systematically, in the course of their participation in concert culture. While ordinary audience members at the peace jubilees required the extravagant artifice of a coliseum and an unprecedented number of musicians onstage in order to become excited by the novelty and power of auditory experience, music lovers brought that sense of excitement to every concert, big or small, simply as part of their drive and inner passion for public musical performance.

Music lovers were not simply lovers of music but also connoisseurs of the practice of "audiencing," more generally. Due to the relative novelty of regular concert going and the unpredictable quality of both venues and performances, they were always quite aware of the conditions around them. For example, music-loving diarists frequently commented on the fullness (or emptiness) of the house at a performance. While part of the excitement of attending concerts was experiencing music with a mass of people, music lovers' attention mostly had to do with measuring the health of a given city's concert-life; the fullness or thinness of a house was also an indicator of a population's refinement and sophistication and, more selfishly, the extent to which one's habitual attendance at concerts could continue unabated. As an editorialist for *Putnam's Monthly Magazine* noted about a Sigismund Thalberg concert in 1856: "Many cities of men and women M. Thalberg has seen and conquered—but we are sure that he never saw an audience better worth conquering than this which New York offered him, and that he never won a victory more complete, or more flattering."[49] Henry Clay Southworth worried that an 1851 "Promenade concert" at New York's Tripler Hall was "very thinly attended, being only 200 persons present," which was significant given the "immense orchestra of about 100 persons."[50]

Not only were music lovers aware of an audience's size but also its specific behaviors. American theater audiences had long been used to a degree of sovereignty: they regularly engaged in socializing which was oblivious to the stage action, or made interruptive demands that paused and startled productions with applause, stomping, and catcalls. Even rioting was not uncommon if a promoter or performer failed to please. This kind of sovereignty began to have class overtones in cities like New York and Philadelphia by the 1830s, pitting rowdier working-class men in the "pit," against the elite men and women in the upper boxes. This sort of division would come to a head in New York in the famous Astor Place Riot of 1849 in which a rivalry between upper-class English actor William Charles Macready and working-class American actor Edwin Forrest turned into open class warfare when supporters of Forrest, attempting to disrupt a performance by Macready at the elite Astor Place Opera House, clashed with police and national guardsmen, killing twenty-five of the protesters.[51]

Public concerts were not immune to these convulsions. When Italian opera was introduced to New York and Philadelphia in the 1830s and 1840s, elites in those cities seized on the form as an opportunity for exclusive, refined socializing, something resisted by the working classes in those cities, who insisted on their own means of rowdy, participatory engagement. Some New York journalists like Walt Whitman mocked the ritualized fashion and display at foreign-language opera in favor of older forms of spontaneous, boisterous appreciation at "American" music theater.[52] While the reverent silence that we know today at formal concerts would not actually become an ideal behavior among music lovers until the end of the nineteenth century (something I discuss in more detail in the next chapter), there were indications even before the Civil War that interruptions of appreciation during a performance could destroy the spell of the music of the performer for some upper class members of the audience. Caroline Healey Dall, a Boston painter, complained about rowdy behavior at a Henry Russell concert in 1840 because it inhibited her concentration on the music: "Bit my lip during all the hissings clappings and screamings—hoping that the time is yet to come when a really well behaved audience will allow me to enjoy music without these at-present inseparable adjuncts."[53] When Joseph and Mary Anne Wood were engaged for a Philadelphia production of *Norma* in 1841, the performance was halted by members of the audience who were upset about Wood pulling out of a competing benefit performance, a disruption that outraged Joseph Sill, who was just there for the music:

The opera went off delightfully, and gave great pleasure to the entire audience, until the final Scene, when just as Mr. Wood began to sing his part in the beautiful Duett with Mrs. Wood, commencing 'Oh dread reflection!,' two or three pieces of Coin were thrown from the upper Boxes close to Mr. Wood, which startled them both, & stopped the Duett. The Audience broke out in loud plaudits, & beg'd them to go on, and they again began, but were immediatley assail'd by loud hisses from a few voices, & the discharge of more coin in the direction of Mr. Wood. Mrs. Wood now became much agitated, and nearly fainted—when Mr. Fry jump'd up from the middle of the Pit, and beg'd that the persons who had thus interrupted the harmony of the Evening should desist, and permit the opera to proceed. The tumult still however continued, and there being no Police present to seize the offenders, the stage manager, Mr. Murdock, then came forward, and said 'that whatever disapprobation anyone might wish to show to Mr. Wood, this was neither the time or place for its exhibition—that the management could settle their differences with Mr. Wood privately, as it was a mere question of Dollars & Cents, and he besought the audience to permit the piece to be concluded &c. &c. . . . The opera was then permitted to proceed, and the Drop soon after descended, to the great relief of the Audience, who were much incensed at the wanton attack that had been permitted. The whole disorder was kept up by about a dozen individuals, who ought to have been apprehended at once, and who would have been, in any other City than this; in which the Police is a mere dead Letter.[54]

Some middle-class music lovers and critics embraced these elite attitudes toward "disorder" after mid-century, but more often they also sought alternative modes of expression that privileged their own kind of devoted engagement. It did not mean that enthusiastic appreciation was to be avoided; many music lovers mentioned that thunderous applause and crying out at the end of a performance could be exciting. Lowell, for instance, frequently noted pleasure at noisy applause and relished demanded encores as a means to keep a performer in sight and on stage—as she wrote about Materna: "She was called back several times & I (for one) couldn't bear to have her go & know that we should not hear her anymore."[55] But, for her, the applause had to come from a spontaneous feeling of gratitude and enjoyment. She had nothing but scorn, for instance, for new audiences at rehearsals for the Boston Symphony Orchestra, who either applauded emptily or not at all— they were clearly ignorant. "To the last rehearsal," she once wrote. "I was furious with the stupid old audience for giving no applause & apparently quite oblivious of the fact that it was the end of the season."[56] Whether approving or not, music lovers were studying their fellow audience members, individually measuring their own participation and developing conclusions about what they felt to be the appropriate expression of enthusiasm for music.

Along with developing knowledge about audience participation, music lovers were interested in the opportunity to hear someone confidently project his or her voice or the sound of his or her instrument into the large open space of an auditorium. As already mentioned, in a time before electric amplification, this was a unique situation that combined sheer, physical power of the performer or performers with experiential knowledge about the utilitarian aspects of building materials and design. Many concerts halls in America, for example, were built to mimic "good" concert halls in Europe. As Michael Forsyth writes, "With little knowledge of room acoustics, the early concert hall architect was unable to predict the sound quality and the effect of different shapes and materials in a hall. He could only observe existing buildings and then speculate, sometimes by analogy with music musical instruments."[57]

The science of concert-hall acoustics had some early progenitors. English composer William Gardiner, writing in 1833, noted the problem of a drummer in the American Revolutionary War who could not be heard owing to newly fallen snow; he used the example to talk about the bad effects of drapery in concert halls which he argued "utterly destroys the reverberation of sound by absorbing it." Otherwise, he suggested that "The best figure for a concert-room is a parallelogram, or long square, in which the sounds are equally diffused. Our cathedrals partake of this form, and are the finest buildings in the country for the display of musical effects."[58] One of the major changes in concert-hall design in the nineteenth century was a gradual shift from opera-style balcony seating, in which audience members faced each other and had to turn to see the stage, to forum seating in which the stage became the main focus of everyone in the room. As historian Alan Durant notes, "Throughout the eighteenth and nineteenth centuries, it is arguably this accentuation of the forum or arena of performance (as object of admiration and concentrated attention) which is the most consistent trajectory of concert development."[59]

Lucy Lowell was certainly not the only concert-goer to note the qualities of various concert halls. Thirty years earlier, William Hoffman, after finally attending a Jenny Lind concert in 1850, wrote in his diary about the "size and finish" of New York's Tripler Hall.[60] Likewise, Henry Southworth visited Brougham's Lyceum, another new New York City theater, to check it out; he reported simply, "quite pretty theatre but small."[61] From mid-century, concert halls were often large civic projects that were built for both capacity and for sound. Even though designs drew mostly on anecdotal evidence, the structure and resonance of halls became selling points for potential audiences. Business directories for cities like Boston and New York touted the magnificence of their halls for audiences. One Boston directory for 1860–61 glowingly described the city's Music Hall, built just six years earlier, in terms of its structural characteristics, including its ceiling "45 feet above the upper balcony," the seventeen, unique, semi-circular windows "that light the hall by day," the hall's capacity of 1,500 people on the floor, and that "the whole has been constructed with special reference to the science of acoustics,—a consideration of the utmost importance in a building intended as a music hall."[62]

In general, the rule of thumb among music lovers was that conditions had to be such that they did not distract from experiencing the music. That included not only the direction of the seating but also the environment; auditoriums that were too dark, malodorous, crowded, cold, or hot were all to be avoided. Lucy Buckminster Emerson Lowell, for example, testily noted the "intense perfume" of the straw-filled seats in Boston's new Howard Athenaeum in 1845.[63] Charles Pelham Curtis, like many others, reported difficult conditions for listening, writing in his diary: "Last evening we went to hear the opera of Lohengrin . . . but the theatre was so hot that Margaret nearly fainted and left with her mother."[64] George Templeton Strong likewise complained: "The Tabernacle is the worst possible room for an orchestra . . . the reverberation from the absurd little dome and skylight muddles everything up." Conversely, Anna Thaxter, attending Boston's new Music Hall in 1851, reported that she was quite delighted. "The seats are very comfortable, and the hall is lighted by [illegible] of gas, four or five hundred in number, all around the [edge] of the walls—a great benefit to the eyes."[65]

Indeed, as Lowell was discovering the benefits of Section F in Boston's Mechanics Hall, music lovers were learning the acoustic properties of various halls so as to position themselves to best hear the music coming from the stage. Joseph Sill was thrilled in 1840 when he was able to obtain a box where, as he commented, "we were so close to him that his softest tones were heard."[66] Much later, in 1905, Henry Van Dyke summed up the ways in which an imagined music lover might think of his seat, chosen explicitly for its acoustic properties, as a secret treasure:

The Lover of Music had come to his favorite seat. It was in the front row of the balcony, just where the curve reaches its outermost point, and, like a rounded headland, meets the unbroken flow of the long-rolling, invisible waves or rhythmical sound. The value of that chosen place did not seem to be known to the world, else there would have been a higher price demanded for the privilege of occupying it. People were willing to pay far more to get into the boxes, or even to have a chair reserved on the crowded level of the parquet.[67]

Awareness of the properties of sound in different environments often encouraged music lovers to measure and experiment with their own hearing. It had long been understood that musical sound directly evoked emotional responses. In 1838, Gardiner outlined the emotional effects of all sorts of musical structures, including the cadenza, the arpeggio, legato, portamento, and crescendo and diminuendo:

What is more alarming than the gradual increase of a mighty sound, when it pours upon the ear from a distance; whether it proceeds from the roar of a multitude, or the raging of a storm, the *auditory sense* is overwhelmed, and the mind is filled with imaginary danger! When the increasing force accumulates to excessive loudness, the vibrations become too great for the soul to bear. There is also a sublimity in the gradual decrease of sounds. What filled the mind of the Greeks with more terror, than the dying accents of the gladiators, or the roar of the battle, falling into silence and death![68]

But nineteenth-century listeners talked about hearing a musical performance as an astonishingly physical experience. Some reported being fascinated by the bodily presence of the virtuosos who performed onstage, ranging from the dexterity of their limbs as they manipulated instruments to the relationship between singers' looks and their voices. As Walt Whitman wrote in his journal: "It did me good even to watch the violinists drawing their bows so masterly—every motion a study."[69] Otherwise, music lovers were attuned to the power and quality of performed sound at a visceral, almost intuitive, level. Voices had to "strike" or "move" them to be important. As Sarah Putnam put her dislike of Patti: "I was not overwhelmed by Patti's voice. It does not go to one's heart."[70] Composer and pianist Gottschalk articulated such beliefs in the physical qualities of music by citing examples of invisible sounds creating concrete effects—an organ causing the flames of church candles to waver, an orchestra rippling the surface of water, minor keys affecting the behavior of dogs. As he explained, "musical sound, rhythmical or not rhythmical, influences our whole being; it quickens the pulse, slightly excites perspiration, and produces a species of voluptuous and transient irritation in our nervous system."[71]

Of course, music lovers' knowledge of the physicality of listening must be understood within the behavioral strictures of middle-class Victorian culture, where physical restraint was directly tied to emotional control and sensation-focused listening was bound to produce a highly charged psychological response. Witnessing the extravagant audio-visual productions and violently fluctuating dynamics of opera, especially, music lovers often expressed overwhelming visceral ecstasy, imagining music "filling their souls" to the point of losing composure, something that was experienced as excitingly dangerous and quite cathartic.[72] Walt Whitman, in *Leaves of Grass*, drawing on his own fascination with New York opera in the 1840s, described music listening as a kind of sexual communion: "A tenor large and fresh as the creation fills me/The orbic flex of his mouth is pouring and filling me full." Music "convulses" him, "whirls" him, "throbs" him, "sails" him, and "wrenches unnamable ardors" from him. He is "licked" "exposed," "cut," and "squeezed" by waves of orchestral sound.[73] Jackson Lears reports a similar reaction from poet Ella Wheeler Wilcox, in response to Wagner's *Tristan und Isolde*: "A clamorous sea of chords swept o'er my soul/submerging reason. Mutinous desire/Stood at the helm; the stars were in eclipse;/I heard wild billows beat, and thunders roll;/And as the universe flamed into fire,/I swooned upon the reef of coral lips."[74]

Not all music lovers were always thrilled with being so affected. George Strong complained of the volume of a New York Vocal Society rehearsal: "I feel a sensation of noise all over when I think of it. It made me fairly dizzy—stunned me for the time being."[75] Sarah Putnam, the Boston painter, noted that her second-row seats at a Wagner concert were too close for the "tremendous" solos of Materna and Scaria and quoted her friend, Mrs. Sargent, who had wryly remarked that "Sitting so near them was like sitting under Niagara Falls."[76] But, on the whole, the sound of public concerts, with their full orchestras and magnificent halls, created a powerful yearning for sensation. William Foster Apthorp, a music critic for the *Atlantic Monthly*, explained:

I think that sheer quality of sound has, in general, a much greater power over the emotions of the music-loving public than melody pure and simple. And be it remembered that this power is wholly physical. A grand and imposing sonority, a well-timed crescendo or diminuendo, have such command over the nervous excitability of most persons as often completely to silence their habitual demand for purely melodious effects. The choruses "Crucify him" in Mendelssohn's *Christus*, with their overwhelming effects of sonority, and their total lack of what is commonly called melody, have many more sincere admirers than the corresponding choruses in Bach's *St. Matthew-Passion*, in which the dramatic effect is almost wholly dependent upon the intrinsic character of the melody itself.[77]

Lengthening the Enjoyment: Sustaining Enthusiasm in Daily Life

Some scholars have argued that concert culture in the nineteenth century functioned as an escape from everyday life, a way of temporarily shutting out the noise of the industrial environment. As R. Murray Schafer observed, "Music moves into concert halls when it can no longer be effectively heard out of doors . . . the string quartet and urban pandemonium are historically contemporaneous."[78] However, this was not entirely true in the United States until the end of the nineteenth century; the diaries of music lovers in the middle fifty years of the century indicate that, even if their participation in concert culture was about contrast and escape, it was mixed with contrary feelings of continuity and desire, not about simply shutting out the city as much as using the cultural opportunities the city provided to shape an aestheticized life. In other words, concerts made sense not as fleeting diversions but as cosmopolitan rituals to be savored, reproduced, remembered, and connected.

At one level, commercialization made this process easy. Divorced from the logistical and social complexities of making music communally, in the traditions of ritual or ceremonial occasion, commodified musical texts and practices instead operated as abstract "products" that could be acquired, arranged, and incorporated into individual lives. The increased presence of commercial amusements in American life at mid-century (through many more performances, numerous and larger concert halls, voluminous press coverage, and advertising) enabled musical performance to serve independently as one of the many building blocks of middle-class selfhood. It was not rooted in particular social occasions of performance but rather in the air, freely available to those with access to urban culture and otherwise aware of their surroundings.

Popular secular tunes and revival hymns, especially, led the way, seeping into the everyday consciousness of Americans, often appearing—in brief turns of phrase or subtle gestures—in realms that were typically thought of as isolated from such cultural currents. Many diarists, including both enthusiasts and the indifferent, complained that popular tunes and dances could become stuck in one's head. Strong, the New York City lawyer, frequently found himself walking the streets or lying in his bed, tortured by a popular song in his head that he could not shake: "didn't get asleep at all the rest of the night. An abominable, wooden kind of cadence upside down in one of those polka tunes haunted me like an evil spirit, and came jerking and creaking into my head whenever I began to subside into a doze."[79] Song lyrics seemed to infiltrate the thinking and even speech of individuals as they went about daily lives seemingly far-removed from the hustle and bustle of urban nightlife. When a friend of Otis Oakham went to sea, he quoted a lyric from a well-known revival hymn in his diary: "'When shall we meet again/Meet never to sever/When shall peace wreath her chain/Round us forever."[80] Likewise, Charles Parker, who lived a quiet life in central New York town as a clerk in his father's dry-goods store and, in the evenings, avidly played guitar with friends in a back room, nevertheless provided evidence that a new railroad station in town had brought more than travelers to the streets. At one point in his diary, he copied the entire lyrics to a minstrel song titled "Shoo Fly," which he called "a great favorite with young America now," and otherwise began quoting snippets of lyrics from songs to express his tempestuous romance with a local girl, Belle (whom he called "Belle zebub").[81]

Concert-music performance similarly infiltrated the daily lives of middle-class concert-goers. Amateur performances at parties and family gatherings were increasingly inflected by references to concert experiences and behaviors. In 1846, Anna Thaxter and her friends, for instance, tried a concert and a dance to relieve their discomfort one hot afternoon:

What a warm afternoon! We did nothing but try to keep cool, sprinkling ourselves with water, fanning &c. were resorted to, but with no very great success. We, at length, descended to the parlor, to try the effect of music, if the sounds proceeding from a distressed, old, and shattered piano, could be dignified with that name; and wonderful to relate, having barred the door against all intruders, we got up a dance![82]

Kenneth Allen, a seventeen-year-old student living in West Newton, Massachusetts, just west of Boston, in the late 1850s, and a serious student of the flute, reported mimicking opera audience practices at a family party: "In the evening, the girls had a 'soiree,' that is, they played several pieces on the piano and sang, and Cousin Harriet gave us bouquets to throw at them."[83] Charles Tracy and the friends he was visiting created their own operatics: "Willy and John Clarke favored us with their version of the grand challenging duet in 'Lucia' between Ashton & Elgardo. And so the evening passed away very pleasantly in music, laughing, talking, &c. &c."[84] Likewise, Lucy

Lowell reported participating in a mock symphony performance with friends in a sleigh on the way home from the theater: "I went to Fiske's at 6.30, with Hattie & Tapp. White rose club of York! Jolly time. Duchess as kilingly funny as last year & we played the sleigh ride symphony, Hattie & Mamie F. piano, Edith comb & glasses, Ned drum, Rob nightingale & whip, Bess sleigh bells, Dr. Stackpole tamborine, I triangle, Mr. E. Hubbard leader. Afterwards danced. I with Ned &c."[85]

In general, however, evocations of concert performances were simply not the same as the intense and direct experience of performed music in the concert hall. Ardent concert-goers, perhaps unlike ordinary participants in music culture, were painfully aware of the ephemeral nature of musical performance. In an age without the convenience of electronic recordings of favorite performances, one frequently had to wait to hear music. Thus William Hoffman wrote wistfully in his diary after hearing a young woman sing at a party in 1850, "Her singing entertained me much as I have not heard much good singing for a long time."[86] Frustratingly, the memories of musical experiences, however intense or moving, often seemed to recede and disappear after only one hearing. As Joseph Sill studiously noted in his diary, "It is perhaps the greatest proof of ability to say that a Man is possess'd of a Good memory, or a power of retaining in his own mind a recollection of what he has either seen, heard, or read. . . . These observations have arisen from a review of my own particular deficiency in the powers of Memory."[87] How could one sustain the memory of music—and the feelings created by it—over time?

Whenever possible, repeated hearings of the same piece could help to fix the music in one's mind. In the 1850s, it was customary for touring performers to complete a "run" of shows in the places they visited as long as audiences kept coming, so as to accommodate all that wished to see them and to increase profits. And it was common for audiences to attend multiple (and often all) performances in the same run, especially if the music was complex enough to merit such attention.[88] George Strong regularly attended every performance of pieces that he liked, commenting "I never can satisfy myself about music till I have heard it more than once and have ruminated on it, marked, learned, and inwardly digested it."[89] Music lovers engaged in these practices enthusiastically and often lamented in their diaries that they could not hear a piece *more* often than a run of performances allowed. As Lucy Lowell opined about Wagner's "The Ring Trilogy": "O dear how I should like to hear it all over again & again & go to Bayreuth! I wish I could spend next winter in Vienna & go every night anything of Wagner's is given."[90]

Otherwise, a longing for music was satisfied, in part, by seeking out as many musical performances as possible. The number of musical experiences one could have in any given week depended on many factors, including the number of theaters and halls in the vicinity, and, of course, the availability of cash needed to purchase tickets or subscriptions. But many music lovers, even without money, found ways to experience music. Walt Whitman, when not at the opera, lingered outside churches and halls, listening to the music from the street. Nathan Beekley of Philadelphia sought out music four or more nights a week in 1849, spending a large percentage of his income on music. As I have mentioned, he even attended multiple church services on Sundays—across denominations—in order to hear music. Likewise, Strong would sometimes roam the streets in search of a music fix: "Walked downtown this morning, stopping at three Papistical churches on my way (St. Patrick's, Canal Street, and Barclay Street) in hope of hearing some good music. Disappointed. Best thing I heard was the Canal Street *Gloria*, which may have been one of Cherubini's."[91]

In addition to searching for additional performances, many music lovers worked to *extend* audience experiences they had already had. In other words, they acted like audience members long after performances were over, reviving in everyday life not only specific performances of music but also their identities as "audience members." This extension of the audience role could become, for some music lovers, a continuous project of engagement. In the 1850s and 1860s, as performers started to be perceived and promoted as unique individuals, offstage engagement became an important means for enhancing and sustaining music lovers' feelings of connection to the musical world. Those caught up in the "Lindmania" of the 1850s, for example, vied to capture glimpses of Lind not simply in performance but also outside of performance, both before and after her concerts: arriving in a steamship at the wharf, on the balcony of her hotel room, travelling through the streets in her carriage. As already discussed, Lind enthusiasts had the opportunity to purchase all sorts of Lind images and other artifacts; for many, these could serve as souvenirs, a way to literally carry the concert experience into one's own home. Indeed, such items sometimes functioned not as souvenirs but as objects of musical interest in their own right. One woman, for example, mentioned that she had only discovered Lind because of the encouragement of a friend, who "had been a great admirer of her singing and had a large bust in white marble of her, in his front hall."[92]

In the post–Civil War period, engagement offstage sometimes also took on the more explicit form of pilgrimage, in which music lovers would travel to sites associated with various performers and composers. Pilgrimages were often wrapped up with a "Grand Tour" of Europe, a requisite coming-of-age event for wealthy Americans in which they traveled to perceived centers of civilization in Europe, particularly Italy and Germany, for the purposes of recreation and education. For music lovers, the Grand Tour often turned into a much-saved-for pilgrimage to significant sites such as Paris, Salzburg, and Vienna.[93] Similar to Lucy Lowell's trip to Vienna in 1885, Alice Drake, a young piano student from Colorado, made a voyage to Weimar, Germany, in the 1890s and promptly sought out the house of the recently deceased Franz Liszt, quizzing the house's caretaker, and playing on Liszt's pianos, a thrill she recounts by exclaiming, "I never tho't I would ever do that!!" Later, in Salzburg, she and her friends searched for Mozart's house:

The first thing we did, of course, was to find Mozart's house. It is in a narrow, crooked street, at first we couldn't find it, we thought the neighborhood was rather dubious. We first climbed up to the third floor and found we were in the wrong house, so piled down and tried it in the next house which proved to be the right one. The stairs were of stone and so old, they were all worn, we could hardly realize that Mozart really lived here.[94]

In the late nineteenth century, the notion of musical pilgrimage was even institutionalized by composer Richard Wagner, who welcomed eager listeners worldwide to his concert hall at Bayreuth. As Mark Twain, who traveled to Bayreuth to see the phenomenon for himself, wryly remarked, "I came home wondering why people should come from all corners of America to hear these operas, when we have lately had a season or two of them in New York with these same singers in the several parts, and possibly this same orchestra." The joke, of course, was that such repetition was the point.[95]

Another way to keep the music alive between performances was to literally reproduce music events through publishing and amateur performance. At mid-century, concert-goers often turned to the piano to reproduce the pieces they had heard and amateur performers found themselves drawn, as audience members, to the virtuosity of the professional stage. As I have already discussed, this was a phenomenon that instrument and sheet music entrepreneurs knew well. Advertisements for sheet music, appearing in concert programs regularly during the 1850s, clearly emphasized this relationship, as demonstrated by the following blurb in a program to a Henriette Sontag performance at Boston's Music Hall:

Just published the new American book of the Concert, containing full translations of all the pieces performed at this or any Concert given by other artists. With every Book will be given a copy of the SONTAG GEMS, Containing the SWISS SONG, the POLKA ARIA, the RICCI WALTZ, and the LINDA ARIA, arranged for the Pianoforte, making ten pages of Music. Price for the Concert Book, including the Sontag Gems, 25 cts. To be had at the Ticket Office and at the Hall.[96]

In 1849, the Germania Society even distributed the sheet music to one of their original pieces, arranged for piano, to the women in their audiences, with the implication that they would use the music to remember the performance. It was appropriately called "Ladies Souvenir Pollka."[97]

Even those who could not play an instrument used sheet music as a means to remember concert experiences. In 1843, George Strong protested his induction into the New York Vocal Society as "injudicious" because he was unable "to recall the circumstance of my ever having attempted a recitative, aria, bravura, Punchlied, comic song, or any other kind of musical composition, or, in fact, sung a note, in tune or out of tune, on any occasion whatever."[98] Nevertheless, by 1846, he reported that he had purchased the sheet music to Beethoven's *Orpheus* for the purposes of musical study. As he explained:

Not that I am, or expect to be, able to perform or execute the same, but there's much satisfaction in investigating a production that one has enjoyed so much, and in seeing exactly how effects were produced, the recollections of which haunt one so long. This and the memorable C-Minor Symphony (to be repeated next Saturday night, I'm happy to say) have been floating about in my head in a fragmentary kind of way for the past year or so, and keeping their place in my memory with marvelous pertinacity—fragments of them in some distorted shape or other running in my head in season and out of season, and with such a vivid remembrance that when I shut my eyes and think of the first crescendo in the Andante of the latter symphony, or of its astounding finale, it seems as if I could almost hear them in full blast from the Philharmonic orchestra.[99]

This use of published music to mark moments of concert going dropped off over the course of the nineteenth century, as the business of music publishing developed. If sheet music was marketed as a concert souvenir at mid-century, by the 1870s it was marketed more for the purpose of home music lessons, particularly for middle-class women learning piano. This domestication of music publishing can be seen especially in publications like *The Musical and Sewing Machine Gazette* and in the presence of song-sheets in other "domestic periodicals" of the post–Civil War period.[100] Participation in public concert experiences continued to be a part of middle-class life, of course, but the private activity of amateur musicking in the 1870s was less about reproduction of one's own concert experiences than about reinforcing a broader public ideal of gentility centered on notions of shared taste and social class.[101] Still, piano manufacturers like Chickering, Steinway, and Weber continued to hire concert virtuosos to use their instruments for the purpose of increasing home sales from the 1860s well into the 1890s, something that maintained a semblance of the strong mid-century relationships between private amateur musicking and public concert going.[102]

While amateur playing could serve as a means to relive concert experiences, music lovers also experimented with more readily created forms of revival by creating meticulous descriptions of concerts in their personal diaries. The use of diaries as mnemonic devices was commonplace in Victorian society, especially when the protocols of social intercourse required careful attention to interaction, gifts, and obligations. Inscribing one's past interactions with others could help one to assess next moves and appropriate responses. In terms of music, however, there was a more specific and practical function of accurately recording one's sensory experiences. Music lovers used diaries not simply as tools, but as stand-ins, indices, for music performances themselves. Accounts of concerts were explicitly for the purpose of reproduction and were meant—sometimes desperately—to satisfy a longing for more music. Some music lovers attempted to fix on paper every moment, every feeling, during a concert. Thus Lowell could write in her diary after the last concert of the Boston Symphony in 1886: "I feel so desolate at thinking that this is the last, that I shall dwell on each detail, to lengthen out the enjoyment."[103] In this sense, they were acting more like the young antebellum clerks identified by historian Thomas Augst, who used diary writing to literally reproduce their new urban experiences and, by extension, their new modern selves. As he explained, "Writing in a diary not only records acts of meditation, reverie, and desire, but becomes the means for their ritual enactment."[104]

This required the development of a new descriptive vocabulary. Older generations of antebellum concert audiences had typically experienced music with a mild and intellectualized pleasure. "It was very satisfactory" or "we had a pleasant time" were common phrases for describing concert experiences. In fact, before 1850, people tended to describe their musical experiences with the phrase "we had some music," blandly lumping any sort of musical activity into a descriptive category not worthy of further comment, like the weather ("we had some rain").[105] But concert-goers after the 1850s often described their musical experiences with increasing subjectivity and specificity. In part, this is due to the greater variety of musical experiences available to people, something that naturally encouraged comparison. Nathan Beekley's accounts of his nightlife in 1849 Philadelphia, for instance, are initially made up of stock phrases like "heard splendid music," but he soon has brief comparisons in entries like: "Just come home from hearing that exceedingly popular singer, Madame Anna Bishop. Oh, she is a delightful singer, charming! In my humble opinion, she is superior to Madame Leaborde, who has created such a sensation recently," or "Went to hear the Virginia Serenaders . . . are really excellent—much better than last season."[106]

For others, comparative description could include rhapsodic passages that devotedly organized details about the conditions of a performance and closely analyzed the music's effects. Dedicated concert-goers like George Strong or Lucy Lowell could go on for three or more diary pages describing every moment in an opera and rendering judgments about each performance compared to others. This sort of description was not exactly like that of professional music critics in that it focused exclusively on a listener's personal and affective experience of the music and without much technical knowledge. At the same time, familiarity with the music and performers meant that music lovers were deeply engaged with every nuance of a performance in their writing. Lowell's brief account of a Boston chamber music concert in 1886, an event she wasn't even able to attend, gives just a hint of the combination of enthusiasm, longing, and specificity in the typical diary of a music lover:

Wish I'd been at the Sat. eve'g. concert to see Kneisel do a neat thing; Campanari was playing his solo when one of his strings broke & the thing would have had to stop (I suppose) if Kneisel had not (in a slight pause of the solo part) immediately given Campanari his violin so that it all went on without a break. A slight thing but showing both quickness & kindness, for the effects of Campanari's performance would have been hurt if the thing had been interrupted. Wish too that I could have heard whether Campanari got same kind of tone out of Kneisel's violin that Kneisel himself does, for certainly the tone of the 2 violins as played by their owners is quite different.[107]

In all, such recording encouraged self-conscious knowledge and comparison of how it felt to hear and see various performances and performers over time. One could, in effect, "collect" and arrange concerts just as one would collect and arrange phonograph records. As noted in Chapter 3, sheet music binders, personal collections of sheet music arranged and bound in leather, were a corollary to this sort of activity.

With the growth of the music press at mid-century, including regular reviews and the use of lithography and photography for circulating images of musical stars, scrapbooks supplanted diaries and sheet music binders as music lovers' most useful tool, able to contain both descriptive writing, clippings of reviews, and images. Even with its diversity, however, music lovers couldn't help but personally annotate the published pieces they clipped and pasted onto the pages of their books. Piano student Edith May Parks's scrapbook from the 1880s, for example, which contained clippings of reviews and the programs to every concert she attended, as well as clipped photographs and sketches of performers, featured a continuous run of comments and observations, written in pencil, next to the song titles listed on the programs. She noted instruments ("3 flutes, 13 clarion and oboes," and so forth), commented on the performers ("Mme. Levy's voice thin, poor star," "good-clean touch large hands"), rated the pieces she heard ("good song, not as good as Schubert," "The song that reached my heart"), and also noted encores and audience reactions. On the program to a Boston Symphony performance of Nicolai Rimsky-Korsakov's *Symphonic Suite*, she was moved to write a more extended description next to Part Two of the piece:

> The accompaniment has the bagpipe drone. The oboe then takes up the melody, then the strings with quickened pace, and at last the wind instruments, un poco piu animato. The chief motive of the first movement is heard in the basses. A trombone sounds a fanfare, which is answered by the trumpet; the first fundamental theme is heard, and an Allegro molto follows, derived from the preceding fanfare. . . . There are curious episodes in which all the strings repeat the same chord over and over again in rapid succession—very much like the responses of a congregation in church. I liked this it is so <u>amusing</u>.[108]

Just as they had with concerts themselves, music lovers found commercial print useful but wished to use it for their own purposes and meanings.

The Social Bonds of Enthusiasm

In 1846, thirty-four years before Lucy Lowell started her diary, twenty-year-old Anna Q. Thaxter [Cushing], of Dorchester, Massachusetts, likewise started a diary in which she noted an enthusiasm for concerts and lectures in the city of Boston. While Lowell was born into a life of comfortable wealth and never married, Thaxter was a single middle-class woman who had cared for her two siblings since the death of her parents when she was sixteen; at age twenty-one, she married her cousin and longtime suitor, Dr. Benjamin Cushing, with whom she had four children. Yet, despite their different circumstances, the women's musical lives were in many ways similar. They were both intelligent and independent-minded, developing a strong passion for music in their formative years. While they labored under the restrictive social norms for women in Victorian society, especially regarding participation in public life, they each developed relationships with friends and family members that enabled them to participate in Boston's thriving concert culture. And they thought deeply about the sounds they heard, noting performers and selections, and comparing their musical experiences.[109]

While comparing two people forty years apart may be complicated by changing historical circumstances, not to mention different personalities, thinking briefly about Thaxter and Lowell—one writing about her own musical life as concert culture in the United States was just emerging, and one writing as concert culture had become more fully formed—can suggest some of the ways in which music audiencing developed between the 1850s and the 1880s. When Anna Thaxter was exploring Boston in the late 1840s, the city's popular consumer culture of concerts, dime museums, exhibitions, and lectures constituted almost a grab-bag of public events, part of an entrepreneurial environment in which financial failure was as much a regular occurrence as success. Thaxter's experiences were rather limited, dependent on what was offered by theaters and producers—as well as nearby amateurs—at any given moment. In her diary, between 1846 and 1853, she describes hearing outdoor performances by brass bands, unexpectedly overhearing singing neighbors, and—after receiving invitations from male companions—attending single concerts by virtuosos such as Henri Herz, the Hutchinson Family Singers, Mr. and Mrs. Seguin, and Henriette Sontag. While she sometimes "longed" to go to performances, she enjoyed playing music at home as much as going out to hear it; she would often note enjoying a spontaneous performance at a gathering of friends or "getting up a little contradance."

Lowell's musical Boston consisted of less a grab-bag of events than a diverse world of choices. While she, too, longed to hear more of the music she loved, her listening experiences were relatively consistent, supported by the concert seasons and festivals of permanent orchestras and choral societies. In fact, the kind of music world Lowell encountered afforded her the ability to focus in a sustained way on particular composers and types of music—mostly Wagner's operas or Beethoven's symphonies. While Thaxter enjoyed amateur music making with her family as part of daily life, sparking memories and curiosity about works she had heard, Lowell downplayed the significance of amateur performance, regarding it as a tiresome social obligation. While Thaxter described her musical experiences, on the whole, with rather standard phrases that indicated pleasure or satisfaction ("The music was delightful. I enjoyed it highly"), Lowell wrote about music with a high level of descriptive detail that emphasized extraordinary moments of feeling. When Thaxter wrote at one point in her diary that a musician's violin-playing "quite carried me away," her expression of emotion stood out as quite special. Conversely, Lowell *expected* to be carried away at each performance and was critical of musicians or works she heard which did not reach her to the depths.

In all, Thaxter seemed content simply to be a participating member of concert culture in the late 1840s and early 1850s; audiencing in the city was new and thrilling, a satisfying way for her to form friendships and engage with the world outside her domestic duties. Lowell moved in a late nineteenth-century world where orchestras, minstrel troupes, bands, museums, theaters, and concert halls were more commonplace; she sought a different kind of experience that went beyond *the fact* of participation in public concerts toward achieving specific effects and meanings *through* that participation. Both were enthusiastic about music, but they practiced their enthusiasms in slightly different ways that reflect the maturation of music loving as a type of behavior in urban middle-class life.

While listening at public concerts increasingly influenced the lives of middle-class Americans in the latter half of the nineteenth century, "music lovers" were those who set themselves apart more and more from most concert-goers by demanding, seeking, and attempting to sustain particular kinds of musical experiences and feelings. The commercialization of concerts had brought extraordinary access to music for many Americans in the new wage economy and had woven music exhibitions and concerts more deeply into the middle-class social life of East Coast cities. However, such concerts, especially during the heyday of virtuoso performance at mid-century, were organized around the principle of audience anonymity (anyone with cash admitted) and ephemeral participation (a finite experience per ticket) that limited music's ability to signify continuing, deeply-felt values and experiences. Music lovers were those who refused to accept the limited and temporary musical participation afforded by the purchase of a concert ticket; they sought instead to creatively imbue their listening experiences with lasting personal connection and depth of feeling.

By doing so, music lovers had become not simply those taking advantage of urban commercial culture at large but rather were people consciously participating in a community of like-minded consumers. They were, like modern fans, both *a part* of the audience and increasingly *apart* from it.[110] While music lovers clearly embraced the opportunities of commercial concert culture, their contrariness was apparent again and again: when the star system unmoored performers from localities and exaggerated their professional skills in the 1840s, music lovers sought to understand stars as authentic people with whom they had a intimate bond. While audiences tended to manipulate performance with frequent encores and outbursts of pleasure or displeasure, music lovers willingly allowed *performances* to control *them*, paying close attention to the physical sensations of listening. While most people returned to their daily lives after concerts ended, music lovers actively extended their audience role beyond the purchased frame of performance by seeking out music in churches and homes, by attempting to see stars in the street, by making pilgrimages to significant sites, by performing their favorite pieces on home instruments, by collecting sheet music and meticulously recording descriptions of their listening experiences.

Music lovers were well aware that their engagement with music was different from that of other audience members. For many, their own peculiar

"The Box Circle." *Century Magazine* 69, no. 4 (February 1905): 593.

devotion to music was laid bare when sitting in the opera and theater, where audiences paid as much attention to each other as to the stage, and where display, as well as lively sociability, were paramount. Simply by becoming regular attendees of musical performances of specific forms or groups, or identifying favorite seats in concert halls and churches, music lovers began to distinguish themselves from others in the audience through their uniquely focused and comparative engagement with the music. George Strong, as early as the 1830s, was commenting that "it requires cultivation and practice to gain the power of enjoying [music], and it's natural that it should be so," with the implication that others in the audience were not so disposed to such work. In a satire of opera culture published in 1851, titled *The Lorgnette: Or, Studies of the Town. By an Opera Goer*, Donald Grant Mitchell sarcastically noted that "music, and the love of it, high as they seem to stand, are, I assure you, but secondary matters, and entirely subordinate to that higher culture of what is elegant in chit-chat, and striking in address, for which the Italian missionary house offers such wonderful facilities."[111] Gottschalk explained this distinction more thoroughly from his own perspective as a performer in 1862:

There is a class of individuals for whom the arts are only a fashionable luxury, and music, in particular, an agreeable noise and elegant superfluity that agreeably revives at a soirée the conversation when it languishes and commodiously serves to fill up the interval that separates the time for lemonade from the time for supper . . . but there are others, and it is to those that I address myself, who recognize in the artist the privileged instrument of a moral and civilizing influence, and who appreciate art because they draw from it pure and unspeakable enjoyment; who respect it, because it is the highest expression of human thought aspiring towards the Eternal Ideal, and love it as the friend into whose bosom they pour their joys and their griefs to find there a faithful echo of the emotions of their soul.[112]

Gottschalk points to differences between individuals who go to soirées and favor music as a "fashionable luxury" and individuals who see music as something deeper: an art that evokes enjoyment, high thought, the "Eternal Ideal," and passionate expression of joy and grief. He evokes a number of qualities, here—emotion and high thought, transcendence and enjoyment—which, later in the century, would become generally perceived as contradictory, but in the 1860s were perceived as various but related forms of deep engagement. Interestingly, he does not link such engagement with particular composers or styles of music—Gottschalk played "popular" tunes as well as excerpts from operas and concertos—but rather with a specific and active disposition on the part of some audience members that was based on recognition, appreciation, respect, and love. Most at stake for music lovers at mid-century, then, was a defense of aesthetic passion in the face of an ethic of refined socializing and distraction.

Aesthetic passion is not a phenomenon with a clear history, and scholars are only now beginning to explore some of its manifestations in various cultures over time. Modern "fandom" seems to offer the likeliest model for understanding the burgeoning culture of nineteenth-century music loving, and there are many parallels between music lovers and modern fans. For music lovers themselves, however, European audience practices may have been the most significant.

Love was a term that had been commonly used since at least the 1500s to describe a particular affinity for any pastime, including a love for theater or for music, and Western European countries had invented numerous terms to describe such enthusiasm. The French and the Italians led the way in the early eighteenth century with terms like *connoisseur*, which referred to someone (often a critic) who was well acquainted with one of the fine arts; and *dilletante*, which referred to someone who "delighted" in the arts, and which was propagated by the London-based gentlemen's club "The Society of Dilettanti," founded in 1733. Around mid-century, the French term *amateur*, meaning, literally, "lover," had also gained currency; Jean-Jacques Rousseau, in his *Dictionnaire de Musiques*, defined *amateur* as "Celui qui, sans etre Musicien de profession, fait la Partie dans un Concert pour son plaisir & par amour pour la Musique" [Someone who is not a musician by profession but participates in concerts for his own pleasure and for the love of music].[113]

By the late eighteenth century, however, such terms in English had taken on negative connotations. *Dilettante*, for example, began to refer to a person who, in the words of the *Oxford English Dictionary*, "interests himself in an art or science merely as a pastime and without serious aim or study ('a mere dilettante')."[114] Charles Burney, in a travel guide to France and Italy published in 1773, purposefully defined the terms *dilettante* and *amateur* as words English travelers needed to know, but he also noted that the word *amateur* "should be always translated a *dabbler*."[115]

The English term *music lover* started to appear in the early 1800s as a more neutral term that maintained the original, benign definitions of *dilettante* and *amateur*. The only difference was that while it was not incorrect to use *music lover* as a description for non-professional players, the phrase was used more frequently to refer to enthusiastic listeners. One of the earliest appearances of the term *music lover* was in Edward Holmes's 1828 travel guide, *A Ramble among the Musicians of Germany*, in which he notes, for instance, that "Every music lover who visits Vienna will like to know that Mozart lived in the Rauhenstein Gasse," or that

It is difficult for a music lover to pass a cathedral in which the organ is sounding, without stepping in for the sake of the plagal cadence, a piece of simple grandeur, which will always, while our nature remains, affect powerfully: but in Antwerp there is not only this attraction, but also the most inventive and florid compositions; and though the performance is a little rough, and the attention is much interrupted by the scuffling on the pavement of the cathedral, yet the matter is frequent, and is accomplished out of pure love, and not a job to be despatched.[116]

In fact, groups of enthusiastic audience members had begun to emerge in the concert life of London, Paris, and Vienna, by the end of the eighteenth century. James Johnson cites a growing "sentimental fraternity" among audiences at the opera in 1780s Paris, united by an ideology of individual, emotional engagement with music. He later describes the "habitués" of the 1820s Theatre Italien in Paris, who witnessed repeated performances and generally socialized with one another, and a new generation of dilettanti who sat in a special "loge de lions" to better see the lions of the stage performing at the French Opera in the 1830s.[117] Both Dana Gooley and Christopher Gibbs have discussed the various "absorbed spectators" of Franz Liszt in the 1830s.[118] William Weber has documented the emergence of popular music and classical music "taste publics" in the 1830s and 1840s in London and Vienna, each of which sought to "exorcise the demon of fashion from the world around them" and promote their own definition of music loving.[119]

American music lovers were not ignorant of such audience practices. Certainly, the various music magazines that popped up after the 1840s, which regularly covered the urban concert culture of East Coast cities, offered insights into the cultural life of European capitals, from performances of significant works to scientific lectures on sound and harmony. *Putnam's Monthly Magazine*, published in New York during the mid-1850s, had columns including "Art Matters" and "Editorial Notes" that surveyed "the foreign musical bulletins" for news of music in Europe. *The Musical Gazette*, a Boston-based magazine that first appeared in 1846 explicitly stated in an early issue that "we shall endeavor to keep our readers informed of all important musical movements in this and other countries. Having received a part of our musical education in Europe, and being in the constant receipt of the principal musical periodicals published in England, France, and Germany, we shall find no difficulty in supplying such intelligence."[120]

As previously mentioned, some American music lovers reproduced the British tradition of "educational" travel on the Continent, or the Grand Tour. Especially after the Civil War, American men and women of means made such travel a requisite badge of their class aspirations. For music lovers, such a trip always included careful attention to cosmopolitan musical life, especially fellow auditors at concerts. When Charles Pelham Curtis, traveling through London, Munich, and Paris in 1876 and 1877, attended the Grand Opera, he reported:

I went to a Bal masqué at the Gr[an]d Opera, which was very brilliant & gay. Strauss himself led the orchestra. The costumes were numerous & grotesque, but they are worn by people also are hired. I was sitting in a box looking at the crowd, when a gay masquée came & sat down next to me. She was attired in a pink satin waist & pink tights, pink boots—c'est tout.[121]

Sarah Spooner Bullard kept a similar record of her experiences in London and Paris in 1892, which included a trip to the Opera: "We went to the Opera to see [Wagner's] *Lohengrin* which was most beautifully upon the stage. I thoroughly enjoyed the evening. The audience was very brilliant most of the ladies being in full dress."[122] Alice Drake, mentioned earlier, devoted a whole diary notebook to her 1896 trip abroad, complete with sketches. By that point, traveling music lovers were more common; she met a fellow music lover on board her ship to Antwerp, and "both raved over Wagner and Ysaye [a Belgian composer] in turns." While in Berlin, she and her friends attended "a great deal of" concerts, studied "the motives" of Wagner in performance, and, like those who had gone before her, learned the ins-and-outs of various concert halls and their audiences:

I don't do anything but practice and rush around to numerous concerts. It is great fun to sit right next to some great artist and watch them. My first experience was in the Philharmonic. I had stehplatz [standing room], and as I was gazing around who should I see but Gabrilowitsch! I haven't heard him yet but they call him the second Rubenstein! He is a queer-looking chap.[123]

Overall, despite a circulating knowledge of European concert culture among American music lovers, there was always a sense that things in the United States would work a bit differently. (As Lowell commented about the Vienna Opera, "What would our Puritan ancestors say!"). European concert culture traditionally had had the support of royal government or the church; concerts took place in concerts halls that were built with several centuries-worth of accumulated wealth and were well known for their palatial opulence and emphasis on elite display, or "fashion." To invest one's emotions in the performances of such cities was, in part, to participate in the political institutions and class systems that enabled such experiences in the first place.

Conversely, American concert culture was supported by a different kind of class system, rooted locally in the form of commercial entrepreneurship or, more rarely, the patronage of businessmen. The very presence of public performers, orchestras, and productions—the existence of a "modern" music culture—was dependent on the vagaries of the market. Even after permanent symphony orchestras gained a foothold in most American cities after 1880, audience participation in public musical performance remained relatively new as a cultural practice, and, for the fifty preceding years, it had been shaped as much by promotional ballyhoo, weather, and economic circumstances (not to mention lingering religious and moral prescriptions *against* theater and entertainment) as by shared traditions of public ritual.

In addition, even though music lovers in various American cities were beginning to recognize themselves as different than ordinary audience members in the post–Civil War period, it would be a stretch to call them a unified community of listeners—at either the national or regional level—if by that one means a tightly-knit social group with common practices and beliefs. Participation in commercial concerts in the United States for much of the nineteenth century remained primarily an individual affair, governed by the practical matter of anonymously purchasing single seats in increasingly large concert halls. Music lovers did not knowingly sit together as a group, even if their search for the best sound in a hall may have placed them in close proximity. In general, the inner-directed and personal nature of music lovers' listening limited the extent to which the experience could be—and ought to be—shared. Social interaction with others always somehow represented a diminishing of the potential power of the listening experience. As George Strong wittily put it after sitting with a friend, "Concert last night. Sat with ——. Capital concert—Symphony well played—the Andante encored. Didn't hear much of the music, however."[124]

Of course, this is not to say that music lovers did not seek each other's company. While young men newly arrived in the city tended to engage in concert going as a solo activity, others also reported attending concerts with their friends and family members. Seventeen-year-old Francis Bennett of Gloucester, Massachusetts, for example, frequently sought out band concerts in town with his friends John Proctor and Charles Smith: "In the evening John Proctor and Charles Smith and I went up outside of the town style to hear the bell ringers . . . then we went over to the Pavillion to hear the music at the Loop."[125] William Hoffman's witnessing of Jenny Lind's arrival in New York notably involved his brother Daniel in most of the diary entries: "Daniel and myself were disappointed in our attempt to gaze upon the distinguished Lady . . . Daniel and myself were then standing directly opposite in Stewart's new building & had an excellent view."[126]

For women, concert-going companionship was, in part, out of necessity, but beyond that social requirement, many women reported a pleasurable sharing of their musical experiences. As already noted, Lucy Lowell had a deep relationship, in part based on shared experiences at concerts, with her sister Mary and her close friend Edith. Likewise, Anna Thaxter's musical experiences before her marriage almost always involved her sister Susan and friend Charlotte; not only did they have intense discussions about the propriety of opera but they also attended concerts together. A typical music-related diary entry from 3 November 1846 featured their delight at a Hutchinsons Family concert:

Susan went to Mr. Pope's this morning, and he invited her to go into town with Charlotte, Elizabeth, and himself to the concert. This afternoon sewed &c. Susan and I went to Charlotte's to tea, that one might be ready to go to town. It was a beautiful, warm, moonlit evening, and the music was delightful. Abby Hutchinson is as simple and natural as possible. We spent the night at Charlotte's.[127]

Even when music lovers were not concert going with friends, music still served to intensely evoke a sense of friendship, especially for those who had recently died. George Strong explained about his sister, "It's strange how completely, by listening to music that one hasn't heard much of since a certain period, one can bring back the thoughts and feelings of that period. Any of Eloise's old favorite songs, when I hear them or think over the tune, carry me back to the time when she first got them and used to practice them frequently, sooner than anything else can do."[128] For Caroline Dall, listening to music reminded her of a missing friend, Anna, something that caused her to lament her lack of singing proficiency:

Dear, dear Anna is going out of town for the season, what shall I do without her? I have heard the soft tones of her voice for the last time. "Oh not more dear, the horrid flowers, that bloom at noon—to sunny bee; Up to the garden—summer showers, Than thou my love, are dear to me!" I love that duet—it brings back, by-gone hours;—tears stood in my eyes, for the sweet melody moved my very soul. Oh what a shame it is, that loving music dearly as I do, I cannot become an adept in the science.[129]

There were hints, too, of a more communal approach to music loving at mid-century. Brook Farm was a utopian social experiment between 1844 and 1847 that included many of the leading lights of the transcendental movement, as well as a surplus of music lovers, including critic John S. Dwight and sometime resident Margaret Fuller. As John Van der Zee Sears remembered, "Music formed the principal feature of our entertainments. Vocal and instrumental music was thoroughly taught in the school, and, as nearly all the members of the community were music lovers, and many were singers and players, the place was melodious from morning until night."[130] Dwight, in particular, worked to cultivate a musical community at the Farm. As George Willis Cooke explained, "It was his own enthusiasm which kindled to a glow the musical interest of others. . . . His own ardor and persistence were so great as to arouse in others a like passionate love of music as an art and a means of true culture."[131] An often-told story was that the members of Brook Farm would occasionally leave the commune to take in concerts in nearby Boston: "Whenever such excursions were taken, the motive was usually something more serious than a search for pleasure. Nothing better evinces the fine zeal of these Brook Farmers—some of them simple folk enough—than their journeying to Boston to hear good music, and then walking back a good nine miles under the stars and in the middle of the night, with an early morning's work before them."[132]

Music magazines, too, were an important means for music lovers to learn about one another and about how to understand their own, sometimes disconcerting, passions; subscribers could imagine other subscribers reading the same articles and having similar feelings.[133] In fact, fostering a "music-loving public" as a single group was at the core of many magazines' missions. As *The Musical Gazette* explained, "We hope its tendency will be, to improve the knowledge and taste of its readers . . . it will be our aim to make it to those interested in music, what the various agricultural journals are, to those interested in agriculture."[134] Ossian Dodge's *The Literary Museum* functioned, even at an informal level, as an instrument of shared knowledge about music in the city; its familiar language and inside jokes pointed to a burgeoning community of listeners, or connoisseurs. The "Theatrical and Musical Information" from 24 July 1852, was typical of this style:

Harrington, the ventriloquist and unequalled necromancer in this country, is drawing crowded houses at Ordway's Hall, in this city. Harrington lives at north-Chelsea, in magnificent grandeur, and treats his friends to all the luxuries of the seasons. Didn't we enjoy those cherries? We "paws for a reply."

E. A. Carson is travelling with his Indians in Virginia.

Mrs. Bostwick, accompanied by Hoffman and Eben, have gone West to circulate musical notes.

Catherine Hayes is on her way East, from a successful tour through the Western cities.

The Germanians are at Newport, playing for the invalids.

Mr. Braham, the tenor, is in New-York city.

Alred Jaell is in Albany.

The Riley Family are concertizing in the New-York State.[135]

Another notable instance of music lovers forming a tightly knit social group was the presence of music societies or clubs that started to pop up in American cities and towns at mid-century. Singing societies and amateur orchestras were part of a long tradition of local music support in the United States. As early as the 1830s, organizations like Boston's Handel and Hayden Society, the Musical Fund Society of Philadelphia, and New York's Philharmonic Society were formed with the intent of themselves producing "high quality" performances and thereby cultivating a more refined public taste for music. In fact, many of the country's later nineteenth-century orchestral organizations grew out of such societies.

But clubs of *listeners*, focused on enthusing about public performances already offered in a locality, were rare until after the Civil War. Such clubs had origins in the activities of wealthy socialites like Ellen Ruggles, who transformed a tradition of "private" musical events among the upper tenth of New York city into semi-public activities that enabled networks of fellow wives and acquaintances to participate in concert life. In the 1850s, for example, she hosted several amateur benefit concerts for The Nursery for the Children of Poor Women, as well as whole "seasons" of "mass-meetings," during which she, her husband George Strong, and other couples would gather to perform sacred music. In the 1860s and 1870s, voluntary women's musical groups, sponsoring a mix of performances by local amateurs and contracted professional singers and virtuosos, became more and more prevalent in every town and city in the United States. These groups were places where white middle-class women were able to flourish as individuals with different talents and could express, openly, their different opinions and tastes. Indeed, genteel women's enthusiastic embrace of such semi-public activities would make them important patrons of American musical life and directly influence the meanings of public concert participation into the twentieth century.[136]

Even then, most were formed to focus local energies toward bringing professional performers and groups to a city; they functioned more like modern arts administration organizations than fan clubs. Such was the rationale, for example, behind the Tuesday Musicale, a group in Rochester, New York, started by several women in 1891:

With an enthusiastic body of workers in its thirty nine active members, encouraging in the many associates who look to it alone for a chance to hear a little music, and a hearty desire on the part of all together to keep up high ideals, the club should become the center from which shall proceed encouragement for all that is good in music, and in time a power to bring to Rochester the best from the outside world.[137]

While the secretary's notes from its initial meetings articulated the desire among its members for hearing music that they could not necessarily perform themselves, the Tuesday Musicale was not a means for its members to share their passions, except secondarily. In the Annual Report of the Musicale in 1893, several members' warned that the Musicale ought not to be seen as a social club but rather as a "power in the advancement and enlargement of the city's life."

Most music lovers were primarily focused on the transformational and sensual experience of music in their own lives in what historian Peter Gay has called the "ascent of inwardness in the Victorian age."[138] Some music lovers bonded strongly with family members and selected friends through shared enthusiasm for music, and slowly, through new publications and the work of various music activists, came to recognize shared proclivities for listening. But just as they started to come together in the post–Civil War period, the open "start-up" climate of commercial concerts—in which music loving was established—changed, becoming more fragmented and divisive. As I will discuss further in the next chapter, communities of music lovers were quickly caught up in the politics of musical taste that shaped public discourse in the post–Civil War era, especially after 1870, which pitted the defenders of "good music" against "music popularizers" and redefined the practices and meanings of music loving established in the antebellum period. Part of the reason why the first music lovers have never been adequately accounted for in American music history is that they never clearly defined themselves as a group—instead, others did that for them and not always based on the same experiences or with the same motivations.

"Attempering This Whole People to the Sentiment of Art"
Institutionalizing Musical Ecstasy

✦

The Varieties of Musical Skepticism

In a nation where the main preoccupations had always been politics and real estate, and where many remained skeptical of the grandeur of European performance culture, music lovers at mid-century were targets for ridicule. In fact, given the increasing spectacle surrounding urban concert life, music lovers were difficult to ignore. As the most peculiar behaviors of dedicated audiences—obsessively attending every performance on a tour, evaluating the acoustics of concert halls, collecting sheet music as souvenirs, or lingering outside hotels to catch a glimpse of touring stars—started to become more public, society wits and cultural critics discovered plenty of new material.

"Lind Mania" in the spring and summer of 1850 was an especially rich subject for social satire. While much of the general public seemed genuinely excited that a European opera star of Lind's stature would soon be gracing America's shores, the increasingly outlandish actions of her supporters— purposefully stoked by the elaborately staged promotions of her manager, P. T. Barnum—generated a veritable industry of jokes, parodies, and editorial cartoons. William Allen Butler, a New York City lawyer and part-time poet, for example, poked fun at one of Barnum's most popular schemes: an official competition to create a "national song" for Lind to sing during her tour. Noting the absurdity of calling on the nation's middle-class dilettante-poets (241 from Boston, 337 from New York City, and 3 from the "entire South, including 2 from Cuba") to celebrate Lind, Butler published a pamphlet called *Barnum's Parnassus: Being Confidential Disclosures of the Prize*

Committee on the Jenny Lind Song, with Specimens of the Leading American Poets in the Effulgence of Their Genius. Neither the judges nor Lind's fans escaped sarcasm:

Prize Committee man No. 2, proposed that a selection should be made of all the songs upon which *postage had been paid*, and that none others would be examined. Prize Committee man No. 3, hereupon rose to amend this proposition, and suggested that, on the contrary, only the *unpaid* songs should be opened, inasmuch as it was very evident that their authors were in need of the $200. Discussion on this amendment was becoming violent, when Prize Committee man No. 4, put a stop to it, by stating that he had been credibly informed, that the postage had not been paid *in a single instance*. The Committee was relieved.[1]

While the actual winner of the Lind song contest, novelist Bayard Taylor, crafted a sentimentally patriotic lyric that extolled a land where "song has a home in the hearts of the free," another song published at the same time by W. H. C. West more directly expressed the dismay of some observers at the extent to which Lind had taken over daily life:

If you step into a grocer's,
(Upon my word tis true!)
There is Jenny Lind's lump sugar,
And Jenny's cocoa too.
We shall all become great singers,
Tho' Jenny Lind pipes high;
At each snuff shop, in London,
Jenny Lind's pipes you may buy.
My wife has a Jenny Lind bonnet,
And a Jenny Lind visite;
With Jenny's portrait on it
My handkerchief looks neat.
My wife's a slave to fashion,
Against it never sinned;
Our baby and the kitten
Are call'd after Jenny Lind.[2]

The maniacal intensity of the American public was something that was not lost on New York City journalist Thomas W. Meaghan. Meaghan had made a living in the 1840s writing for salacious male weeklies like *The Sporting Whip*, *The Rake*, and other publications.[3] In 1850, calling himself "Asmodeus," he wrote a pamphlet called *The Jenny Lind Mania in Boston, or, the Sequel to Barnum's Parnassus.* The story starts with Asmodeus learning that Barnum has employed nearly the entire service industry of Boston, from bill-posters to steamboat runners, to help him orchestrate Lind's arrival. When he naively inquires with a friend whether he, too, might get in on the business, it becomes clear that this is no mere entrepreneurial venture:

For two long weeks, did I hear nought in my rambles, by night or day, in barber shops and work shops, in beer shops and stables, in hotels and private domicils, from Beacon Street to the Black Sea, all the cry was, Jenny Lind and Barnum, Barnum and Jenny Lind! Soon I met my ancient and respected friend Pearce, so full of madness and music that he rushed through the streets with the fearful velocity of an escaped locomotive.

   Hold worthy friend, quoth I, whither so fast? He gazed wildly at me for a moment, then shouted as he run—Jenny Lind and Barnum! Barnum and Jenny Lind![4]

Along the same lines, New York newspaper columnist Donald Grant Mitchell humorously compared the public's enthusiasm for Lind in 1850 to the Great Plague of the Middle Ages:

It has only been by dint of the most extreme caution, in avoiding contact with infected persons, that I have been able to preserve my usual state of health. It has even been a serious question with me if it were not worth my while to retire for a short time into the country, out of the reach of the contagion; but on second thought, a sense of duty prevailed over my fears, and has kept me firmly at my post. . . . It was really an awful exhibition to see thousands of these sufferers rushing along the streets, regardless of all ordinary proprieties, and sometimes screaming out at the very top of their voices. . . . Some carried huge bouquets of flowers, which they threw into the carriage of Miss Lind, and kissed their hands, and made all kinds of antics; after which they either grew melancholy, and slipped away through the back-streets, or quieted themselves with drink.[5]

   Editorial cartoons frequently portrayed audiences as anonymous dupes, playing right into Barnum's greedy hands. One image from 1850, for example, showed an eager young woman speaking to her dour and helpless father, above the caption: "A celebrated financier in Mount Vernon Street attempting to convince his beautiful daughter that Jenny Lind's Concert Tickets were not worth $10." In a lithograph titled "The Second Deluge," artist Franz Hinderoth showed the citizens of New York as sheep, turkeys, and donkeys being herded into Castle Garden (renamed "Modern Ark of Noah"), while Barnum, depicted as a mischievous saytr, sits in a tree thumbing his nose at the people lining his pockets.[6] Another image of Lind's audience depicted a brawl erupting during her arrival in New York City. The poem accompanying the woodcut described the disdain of New York City's Bowery b'hoys and g'hals for Lind's middle-class audience:

Corns were jam'd, and shins were skin'd,
To get a glimpse of Jenny Lind,
Many could'nt bear the shock,

Fell, pell-mell into the dock.
The fences broke, and there was Mose,
Giving a chap a bloody nose . . .
Perhaps you also will be a ninny,
For a Jackass is sure to run after a Jenny.[7]

Jenny Lind mania was certainly a unique phenomenon in American cultural history, but it marked the beginning of a public backlash against excess among concert audiences. No one in the press or politics cared so much about the music world as long as its excesses stayed within the parlors and exhibition rooms of Boston or New York. But as concert promoters competed more aggressively by staging greater and greater instances of public spectacle designed to disrupt everyday life and lure more and more people to sample public music entertainment, the peculiarities of concert audiencing literally spilled out into the city streets and became visible. "Monster" concerts, parades for European virtuosos, souvenirs, contests, more and more editorials and posters and poetry—all invited increased skepticism about public music and its ardent followers at mid-century.

The "monster" concert events of the 1869 and 1872 Peace Jubilees, organized in Boston by Patrick Gilmore, for example, easily lent themselves to caricature. While drawings in *Frank Leslie's Illustrated*, for example, carefully depicted the grandeur of the occupied Coliseum in Boston's St. James Park, with thousands of well-dressed auditors in their seats, artist C. G. Bush published several alternative views in *Harper's Weekly* that showed the cacophony and disorganization of the event. In one drawing, titled "Let Us Have Peace" (which was also the official title of the 1869 Jubilee, printed on all programs), the performers and audience are depicted as cacophonous, including rows of screaming babies, yowling local choirs (with wide, grotesquely open mouths), barking dogs, honking frogs, a cracked organ pipe, a minstrel band, hundreds of firemen hacking away at bells with sledge hammers, an entire section of organ grinders, and a double bass so big that it had to be held up by two people while two others used a two-man bow that looked like a tree saw.[8]

The absurd enormity of the event, especially as experienced by the tens of thousands of listeners attending the Coliseum in 1872, was satirized in a daily newspaper called *Jubilee Days*. Featuring humorous anecdotes and observations, as well as cartoon images of performers and audience members, the paper offered concert-goers the opportunity to laugh at themselves. The effects of intense and ardent listening were frequently noted. The 27 June issue, for example, published a sketch of a disheveled and exhausted man, holding a pair of binoculars, sprawled on seat, titled "A Faithful Listener, Who Has Not Lost a Single Rehearsal or Concert." Later issues poked

Images from *Jubilee Days, An Illustrated Daily Record of the World's Peace Jubilee*.
Boston, 1872.

fun at "types of listeners," in a series of images over the course of a week.
The first featured "The Hungry Amateur, Who Came by an Early Train;"
it gently mocked the notion that one might put music before food by de-
picting a single, skinny man leaning forward eagerly in his seat before the
stage, eating a sandwich he had hidden in his hat. The second image, titled
"The Man With a Musical Wife" showed a portly, sleeping gentleman, clearly
not enthused about having to attend the concerts, seated next to a finely
dressed woman, staring intently ahead at the stage. The nature of such a relationship was, evidently, widely recognizable. The third cartoon, "Startling
Effect on One of Our Fellow-Citizens of the 'Sprig of Shillalah,' as Played by
the Irish Band" was simply a caricature of an Irish immigrant, who had spontaneously jumped up amidst the staid audience and danced a jig, lending a
bigoted commentary on the different ways one might respond to music.[9]

While periodic waves of concert mania provided the subject of music
satire at mid-century, it was the growing presence of Wagnerians in the late
nineteenth century that finally presented critics of music loving with a uniform symbol for derision and ridicule. Wagnerians were known for their

devotion to operatic music that was text-heavy and which by all accounts was atonal and difficult; one had to learn to listen to Wagner, something that set his most ardent listeners clearly apart from the everyday audience member. After the work of Wagner was first performed before enthusiastic audiences in the United States in the 1880s, skeptics quickly seized on the excessive reverence accorded to the music. A letter to the New York journal *The Critic* in 1885 was typical:

An outsider is struck with their spectacular hankerings—their strange attire, their fantasticality of attitude and manner, their streaming locks and sibylline speech . . . there's your Wagnerian critic—mystic, positive, apostolic; a bandier of words which he generally does not understand; full of tall talk, musical mysticism, and metaphysical cant. Escaping from this Scylla, lo! yonder is the Charybdis of the Wagnerian *dilettante*, male or female as the case may be, who has been a pilgrim to Bayreuth, suffered a mortal bore there, endured the tyranny and rigors of an Arctic inn, just to do homage to principal and furnish a martyr to the new religion. And lastly—oh horrors! The Wagnerian woman. Is not she the woman who wanders to Concord, who edges in at philosophical conferences, who bristles with "lectures" and "papers" that have never been delivered, who burns with contempt for Italian "guitar-orchestras," and leans a lingering neck forward to catch the last vanishing echo of "The Flying Dutchman?"[10]

Mark Twain, visiting Wagner's concert hall in Bayreuth, Germany, was rather more subtle in his sarcasm:

I have seen all sorts of audiences—at theaters, operas, concerts, lectures, sermons, funerals—but none which was twin to the Wagner audience of Bayreuth for fixed and reverential attention, absolute attention and petrified retention to the end of an act of the attitude assumed at the beginning of it. You detect no movement in the solid mass of heads and shoulders. You seem to sit with the dead in the gloom of a tomb. You know that they are being stirred to their profoundest depths; that there are times when they want to rise and wave handkerchiefs and shout their approbation, and times when tears are running down their faces, and it would be a relief to free their pent emotions in sobs or screams; yet you hear not one utterance till the curtain swings together and the closing strains have slowly faded out and died; then the dead rise with one impulse and shake the building with their applause.[11]

Wagnerians were one of the important sources of the slang term *long-hair*, a characterization that came to refer generally to over-intellectual, bohemian lovers of classical music. Henry Heathcote Statham remembered the youths who worshiped Wagner, Schubert, and other German composers, saying,

It is the romanticism of that somewhat heavy, melancholy, semi-mystical type, which was peculiar to the Germany of a generation or two back, which would gaze with sentimental tears at the splendours of sunset, and sing passionate serenades

"Wagnerite." *Puck* 16, no. 404
(3 December 1884): 218.

to *die Treue*, with its long hair blowing wildly in the evening breeze, and then indulge itself with an orgy of beer and tobacco; which could be amused with schoolboy pranks, and was as innocent of soap and water as of many other niceties of civilization.[12]

Long hair was, in fact, a known characteristic of composer Franz Liszt, who was also Richard Wagner's father-in-law, something that only reinforced the stereotype. Thus a reviewer in *Century Illustrated Monthly* humorously compared Wagnerians with Liszt followers, explaining:

The genuine unalloyed Wagnerian wears long and rather matted locks, a long, spare, and untrimmed beard, and long untrimmed nails. The followers of Liszt, on the other hand, have their long hair carefully combed and brushed behind their ears, 'with a touch of vanity.' Moreover, these latter endeavor to remove every hair of beard from their faces, in order to do justice to the priestly connections of the illustrious abbé. . . . Liszt's worshipers also pay great attention to their hands, and, like the maestro, are fond of showing them, and from time to time raise them as if in blessing.[13]

If anything, all the jokes, parodies, and satiric jibes at music lovers in the latter half of the nineteenth century indicate that eager participation in the world of commercial entertainment remained questionable behavior. While it was true that developing one's emotional sensibility and becoming educated in the arts, including music, was generally regarded as a testament to one's refinement, there was, at the same time, something a little too uncontrolled and mystical about such sensibility. In the atmosphere of getting and contracts, profits and duty, people of artistic temperament were regularly met with ambivalence, if not outright resistance, among the urban middle-class.[14] It was why in 1850, for example, Nathaniel Hawthorne could only imagine with shame his Puritan ancestors' opinion of his chosen career: "'A writer of story-books! . . . Why, the degenerate fellow might as well have been a fiddler!'"[15]

Still, the changing tenor of criticism against music consumption seemed to have a direct relationship to its growing influence in the nineteenth century. Critics of the new world of commercial music culture at mid-century were not necessarily against the joys to be found in music but rather took exception with the extreme degree to which some people embraced music listening. Concert audiences' mass hysteria over music, and apparent ignorance of the manipulation involved in the marketing of music events, spoke directly to growing fears at the time about the anonymity, overcrowding, and confidence games of the city. Attacks on Wagnerians in the 1870s and 1880s were of a meaner, sharper sort than the satire about Lindmania in the 1850s. Longhairs like the Wagnerians were ridiculed as effeminate and overly concerned with art and ideas instead of practical matters, something that resonated in specific ways with a middle-class crisis of agency amidst the increasing bureaucratization of late nineteenth-century business life. As psychologist and philosopher William James wrote about the effects of the arts on his generation: "There is no more contemptible type of human character than that of the nerveless sentimentalist and dreamer, who spends his life in a weltering sea of sensibility, but never does a concrete manly deed."[16]

In the 1960s, sociologist Phillip Ennis wrote about the ways in which the condition of ecstasy or enthusiasm is threatening, arguing that "societies in general, and institutions sanctioning ecstatic experience in particular, are reluctant to lose control over their members and are especially ferocious toward anyone reaching directly for ecstasy by short-cutting the proper channels." While there are rules for how ecstatic emotion can be expressed in society, those seeking ecstasy tend to resist such prescriptions so that there is "a ceaseless battle of organized powers of society for control and monopoly over the means of ecstatic expression." Alongside the struggle for power—the primary focus of nineteenth- and twentieth-century sociology— Ennis suggestively called for the study of this struggle for the means of ecstatic expression to be seen as a way to more fully understand everyday life.[17]

In the same way, I contend that analyzing critical views of middle-class music lovers and their activities—what we might call "the struggle for musical feeling"—might tell us much about changing contexts of social life in America. What were the reactions to music lovers from different groups of people in society, or over time? More particularly, analyzing criticism of music lovers might indicate how the commodification of musical performance touched and affected other spheres of musical life. As I have suggested throughout previous chapters, the opportunity to purchase musical experience, whether or not one fully embraced it, created significant shifts in the musical ecology of the United States in this time period. What might criticisms of audiences, listeners, and concert-life tell us about how Americans grew to understand the proper role of music in society? In this chapter, I will outline three outsider perspectives on musical enthusiasm: as a mania, as social disorder, and as a gendered form of passivity. Such perspectives were not neatly chronological nor entirely separate, but they all posed music loving as a *problem*, something which would become one of the significant issues for defining musicality in the United States as it moved into the twentieth century.

Tarantism, Monomania, and Audience Pathology

In 1853, Boston Theatre owner and manager William Clapp looked back at ballerina Fanny Elssler's visit to Boston in 1840:

The announcement of her advent was hailed with joy, and our usually staid citizens indulged in various bursts of enthusiasm, and many actually walked before the Tremont House for hours, in hopes that the divinity would show herself at the window. . . . It was "Elssler" on every side. She was dreamed of, talked of, and idolized; and some wag having circulated a report that "Fanny" would take an airing in her barouche, quite a gathering took place on Tremont Street. Boston was not alone in this ovation, for the ladies from Boston to Philadelphia, all wore Elssler cuffs, made of velvet with bright buttons. In every store window articles were displayed flavoring of the mania. Elssler boot-jacks, Elssler bread, etc. etc., were to be seen, showing how violent was the attack of *Fannyelsslermaniaphobia*.[18]

It was clear that Clapp was not a physician, since "Fannyelsslermaniaphobia" made little medical sense. But the reference nevertheless suggested pathology as a way to summarize the intense sensation and the loss of control caused by public entertainment. Like an infection, the spectacle of commercial music, dance, and other forms of amusement could attack and easily overwhelm the public, temporarily forcing a whole city to suspend daily routine.

Such a use of medical discourse in relation to entertainment in the nineteenth century was not uncommon. *Mania*, the Greek word for madness, for example, was regularly used as a compound suffix to describe intense interests during that period. Not only was there Lindmania, but also balloonomania, railroad mania, Lisztmania, nymphomania, bibliomania, and tulip mania.[19] The metaphor of the epidemic was regularly employed to describe the latest steps that spread through the populace every several years, including the polka in 1844, which New York City columnist Donald Grant Mitchell reported as a kind of contagion: "The rage . . . for the whole family of polkas is most infectious; and not only has it taken educational possession of Misses who have not cast their nursery strings, but it has smitten men grown gouty."[20] Louisa May Alcott appropriately summed up the youthful fads of the antebellum era with metaphors of affliction:

Once upon a time there raged in a certain city one of those fashionable epidemics which occasionally attacked our youthful population. It wasn't the music mania, nor gymnastic convulsions, nor that wide-spread malady, croquet. Neither was it one of the new dances which, like a tarantula—bite, set every one a twirling, nor stage madness, nor yet that American lecturing influenza which yearly sweeps over the land. No, it was a new disease called the Art fever, and it attacked the young women of the community with great violence.[21]

Disease seemed particularly useful for thinking about music. It had been known for centuries that music could produce powerful psychological and physical effects. Greek musical philosophy associated musical modes with different emotions; Penelope Gouk reports that physicians in the Middle Ages drew on ancient authorities to use music therapeutically for both supernatural and natural purposes.[22] In the 1600s, Athanasius Kircher theorized a relationship between the "humours," fluids said to control the emotions, and aspects of musical sound, something that Franz Anton Mesmer took up in the late eighteenth century, as the basis for using piano or glass harmonica during his "magnetic" treatment sessions.[23] From that time and into the early nineteenth century, however, the heightened states created by music listening and dancing also took on more ominous implications.

At least since the fourteenth century, for example, women in parts of Spain and Italy had reported going into a state of coma after receiving a tarantula bite, only to be revived by music and uncontrollable dancing. Drawing on Kircher's popular theories on music and the humours, this "tarantism" had long been thought evidence of music's healing powers. But the phenomenon became a subject of renewed interest in the early nineteenth century as a clear example of the ways in which music could be linked to psychological disturbance.[24] Robley Dunglison, a leading American physician who had included Thomas Jefferson as one of his patients, explicitly interpreted tarantism as a psychological rather than a physiological disorder, calling it a "feigned or imaginary disease . . . characterized by excessive avidity for dancing at the sound of instruments." An 1845 encyclopedia of medicine, in a lengthy entry on chorea, specifically focused on "dancing diseases," suggesting that "the influence of music alone, independent of the measured efforts in dancing, ought not to be overlooked," noting that "in some of the diseases resembling the original St. Vitus's dance . . .

an extraordinary passion for music has been among the most prominent symptoms."[25]

Such association of a passion for music with medical pathology was even more strongly articulated in the developing concept of *monomania*. In 1810, drawing on the writings of Philippe Pinel, French physician Jean-Étienne Dominique Esquirol promoted a controversial but highly influential notion of "partial delirium," in which one of the alleged separate faculties of the brain could become diseased while the others remained intact, creating the possibility of abnormal obsessions or impulses in otherwise healthy people.[26] He argued that monomania was essentially "a disease of the sensibility" and thus located in a complex continuum from normal to abnormal:

The delirium of monomaniacs is exclusive, fixed, and permanent, like the ideas of a passionate man. Like the passions, monomania now manifests itself by joy, contentment, gayety, exaltation of the faculties, boldness, and transports of feeling; now, it is concentrated, sad, silent, timid and fearful. . . . Monomania is of all maladies, that which presents to the observer, phenomena the most strange and varied, and which offers, for our consideration, subjects the most numerous and profound. It embraces all the mysterious anomalies of sensibility, all the phenomena of the human understanding, all the consequences of the perversion of our natural inclinations, and all the errors of our passions.[27]

Esquirol identified a number of types of monomania, including "erotic," "homicidal," and "incendiary." In fact, Esquirol first made his public reputation by introducing the concept of criminal monomania into courts of law, something that laid the groundwork for what is today known as the "insanity defense."[28] Esquirol's original definition of monomania was far broader, however, emphasizing the pathological potential of all human inclinations and passions. For example, what he called "reasoning monomania" described a situation in which patients experienced a significant change in one set of "affections" while retaining logical reasoning and the ability to engage in "spirited and intellectual" discourse. The change was progressive: "In the first [period], the disposition and habits are changed; in the second, the affections are perverted; and at length, in the third, a maniacal excitement appears."[29] Esquirol clearly intended such "reasoning monomania" in a strictly clinical sense, focusing mostly on case studies of what we would now call obsessive/compulsive disorder. At the same time, however, such a progression of symptoms could easily fit the stories of music lovers, who, after encountering a work for the first time, became ardent concert-goers.

The parallel did not go unnoticed. The phrase *music-mania* actually had existed in English as a vernacular term for various music fads as early as the 1790s. However, Esquirol's work in the 1810s altered such usage, steering it more toward individual pathology, and giving birth to a parallel, new, compound word, *musicomania*. In an 1832 London publication, *The Cyclopaedia of Practical Medicine*, in a chapter on the "Diseases of Artisans," the editors linked the new term to occupational disease. "If cerebral congestions or aneurism of the heart are prevalent among orators . . . they are rather to be referred to the effect of the passions," they wrote. "M. Patissier has very properly remarked that the love of music may degenerate into a predominating passion. 'Musicians and painters,' he says 'are, in general, the most enthusiastic of all artists. We have seen musicians become deranged, and musicomania has been observed by many physicians.'"[30] Robley Dunglison's *New Dictionary of Medical Science and Literature*, published a year later in 1833, included a specific entry for *musicomania* (he listed *muso-mania* as a variant), describing the condition more broadly as "a variety of monomania in which the passion for music is carried to such an extent as to derange the intellectual faculties."[31] Dunglison's definition of musicomania left room for not only musicians but also listeners. Interestingly, in addition to being a physician, Dunglison was also president of Philadelphia's Musical Fund Society from 1853 to 1854 and from 1856 to his death in 1869, something that may have given him a first-hand appreciation of the disease's symptoms among the music-loving public.

It is unclear whether musicomania was widely accepted as a legitimate disease, at least in medical circles. Multiple reviewers of Dunglison's *New Dictionary* accused him of indiscriminately including non-medical or vernacular terms, something he changed in later editions,[32] and I could find no recorded medical case studies of musicomania in existence. In fact, the term—along with the more general "monomania"—fell out of favor in the medical establishment by 1900 and was listed in medical dictionaries as an "obsolete" condition until finally disappearing in the 1960s.[33] Nevertheless, the efforts of Esquirol, Dunglison, and others to humanize the treatment of the mentally ill had the unintended effect of popularizing medical terminology, and a generalized and non-clinical understanding of monomania soon became widespread in public discourse in both Europe and the United States.[34]

"Musical mania" was prevalent as a rather neutral description of a "love for music" in both English and American publications like *The Musical World*, *Putnam's Monthly Magazine*, *Harper's Monthly Magazine*, and *Dwight's Journal of Music*. As a Liverpool correspondent for *The Musical World* wrote under the heading of "The Musical Mania": "Who shall say that we are not a music loving people, on looking at the announcements in our present paper?"[35] As already discussed with reference to Jenny Lind, references to the medical meanings of musical mania were often used in jest to mockingly describe the extraordinary behaviors of audiences. Music lovers sometimes used it to indicate self-deprecating awareness of their own concert-hopping. "My musical mania is at its height just now," George Strong wrote in his diary, for example. "For after church I rushed down to St. Peter's, and I reached it just as Mozart's 'Number Twelve' was in full blast . . . I was just in a fit state to go into ecstasies at each individual note."[36]

In American literature, monomaniacs appeared frequently as characters, from the protagonist of Poe's "Tell-Tale Heart" to Melville's Ahab. Francesca Brittan explains a similar movement earlier in European literature, where "'fixated' protagonists proliferated through the 1820s and 1830s, as novelists and playwrights borrowed the scientific terminology associated with medical discourse to explore the aesthetic and dramatic potential of pathology. . . . These works established monomania as a quintessentially Romantic illness—an affliction not only of the hero, but of the creative and eccentric genius."[37]

The Romantic Movement also shaped an entire generation of eccentric "genius" composers in the latter half of the nineteenth century, from Beethoven to Wagner, who became known for their single-mindedness about music. In an 1887 profile of Richard Wagner in *Frank Leslie's Popular Monthly*, for example, one author argued for the significance of the "frenzy" of Wagner's work ethic and its relationship to both genius and monomania:

That Wagner was a genius may safely be acknowledged, even by those who dissent from his theories and deny their worth. The absolute frenzy with which he threw himself into his musical work, the uncompromising manner in which he defended every innovation which he made, the incredible labor he expended, not only on his works themselves, but upon making them intelligible to the world . . . all prove the truth of Carlyle's adage that genius is only a capacity for taking pains. In Wagner's case, because of early trials and neglect, because of subsequent opposition and abuse, genius became almost a monomania.[38]

French composer Hector Berlioz was the most directly vocal about the importance of monomania and its relationship to music. In a series of essays he first published in France in 1859, entitled "Musical Grotesques," he established the connections between musical passion and monomania:

The art of music is undeniably the one of all others which gives rise to the strangest passions, the absurdist ambitions. I will even say, to the most peculiar monomanias. Of the people who are shut up in insane asylums, those who think themselves Neptune or Jupiter are easily recognized as monomaniacs; but there are many others who enjoy entire freedom, whose relations have never dreamed of having recourse to the science of phrenology on their account, but whose madness is evident. Music has unsettled their brain.[39]

Yet he also argued for a more positive or practical reinterpretation of this sort of madness:

I have often asked myself: Is it because certain persons are mad, that they interest themselves in music, or is it that music has driven them mad? . . . The most impartial observation has led me to this conclusion: Music is a violent passion, like love; it can, without doubt, apparently deprive individuals who are possessed by it of their reason. But this derangement of the brain is only accidental, the reason of those persons soon regains its seat; it remains yet to be proved that this pretended derangement is not a sublime exaltation, an exceptional development of the intellect and sensibility.[40]

In other words, artists and other creative people were not deranged as much as eccentric, devoted, or inspired.

Key to this popular recognition of monomania among creative artists was a simultaneous embrace of the concept of enthusiasm, an older framework for understanding delirium that drew on religious discourse rather than science, but which also overlapped mania in its definition and connotations. In the twenty-first century, enthusiasm simply means excitement, but in the eighteenth and nineteenth centuries, it referred to a more powerful spiritual ecstasy or transcendence, a literal "taking in" of God (from the Greek *entheos*, or "God inside"). Plato, actually, had first articulated enthusiasm as a mental state of delirium, created in performance, through which ideas might pass from author to performer to hearer; he argued that while individual technique was important for the effects of poetry, even more important was inspiration, in its literal sense of the divine animating a person.

The idea of having "God inside" took on explicit religious connotations during the Middle Ages, and theologians during the Protestant Reformation condemned extreme instances of enthusiasm as heretical, particularly any report of direct communication with God. By the mid-eighteenth century, Enlightenment philosophers had begun to associate enthusiasm with derangement rather than heresy, but the resulting judgment of enthusiasts was similarly negative. As Jon Mee explains, what "Philosophical attacks on enthusiasm often had in common with older religious discourse was the suspicion of the passions intruding themselves on to the purity of rational discourse."[41]

Nevertheless, some writers and philosophers, including the Earl of Shaftesbury and the philosopher Immanuel Kant, tried to frame enthusiasm in more secular terms. Shaftesbury, in particular, differing with his teacher, John Locke, argued that enthusiasm, while sometimes dangerous, was a natural human passion, indicating a noble desire to join with others and with God. While the delirium of enthusiasm might make one unsociable, inside one's own head, so to speak, it could also represent the ultimate shared reality, when "ideas and images are too big for the narrow human vessel to contain" and thus express the divine.[42] At the end of the eighteenth century, writers and intellectuals in the Romantic movement in England, drawing on these insights, worked to recover and promote enthusiasm as a tool for creativity. As Wordsworth famously noted in 1802:

What is a Poet? . . . He is a man speaking to men: a man, it is true, endowed with more lively sensibility, more enthusiasm and tenderness, who has greater knowledge of human nature, and a more comprehensive soul . . . he has acquired a greater readiness and power in expressing what he thinks and feels, and especially those thoughts and feelings which, by his own choice, or from the structure of his own mind, arise in him without immediate external excitement.[43]

In the United States, Romantic enthusiasm inspired a host of writers, and their readers, in the 1840s. David Herd, for example, has argued that figures like Emerson, Whitman, and Thoreau offered the promise of "immediacy"—"between the individual and the divine originally, but subsequently between the creative person and the condition of inspiration, between readers and writers, teachers and students."[44] Enthusiasm also inspired music critics and composers to expound on the idea of "the sublime," or in the words of critic Friedrich Schlegel: "consciousness of the infinite in the individual."[45] As John Steinfort Kedney—using the hyperbole typical of the topic—wrote:

Music . . . furnishes symbols, not only for desires and aspirations which are precise or habitual, but for longings which are mysterious, and can not be put into words, whose genesis has become obliterated, and whose history is untraceable,—for vague solicitations of the perfect life, for the inexpressible sighs and the giddy joys of humanity. It supplies the wings upon which the soul seeks to fly back to the dim source whence it came, and whither it is going, to penetrate the darkness of its destiny, and to possess it before the time.[46]

The sublime was a reaction to the mid-eighteenth century Enlightenment emphasis on reasonable and pleasurable engagement with music. The "Longings . . . for vague solicitations of the perfect life" indicated by Kedney signaled reemphasis on the ineffable and the mysterious in music, states of wonder which were directly linked to religious enthusiasm and which he, and others, insisted had been lost.[47] When Walt Whitman described being literally swept away by music, when Lucy Lowell described vocal performances as "bewitching," when Caroline White rhapsodized about feelings of intimacy and friendship with "Jenny" [Lind], they all were pointing to the ways in which musical performance could dislodge rational convention and, more specifically, lead to altered states similar to ecstasy or enthusiasm.

On the whole, the attempt by Romantic artists and critics to co-opt contemporary thinking about delirium for their own purposes was not entirely successful. As Jon Mee comments, "If one is tempted to align enthusiasm with Romanticism as part of a binary opposition with, say, Reason and Enlightenment . . . one will miss the fact that, throughout the eighteenth century and beyond, enthusiasm remained as suspect as it had always been, if not properly regulated."[48] Indeed, open-ended enthusiasm remained on the outside of middle-class experience and was generally associated with the camp meetings of lower-class African Americans and whites. While people like George Templeton Strong might joke about his "musical mania," he was not actually inclined to pursue the loss of reason as a central framework for his engagement with concert performances. Such an approach simply flew in the face of middle-class values of discipline and order, and it could too easily be taken too far by those without the education and experience to balance it against the guidelines of Victorian propriety.[49]

Still, the attempt among middle-class doctors, philosophers, and artists to understand music loving in terms of psychology significantly located the power of music not in older conceptions of the mystical vibrations of musical sound, or the shared social circumstances of audiencing, but rather in an individual's private emotional and intellectual responses to any performance of a work. This new focus was clearly part of a wider ideological shift among the white middle class in the relationship between the self, the body, and affect. In the late eighteenth and early nineteenth centuries, Enlightenment thinkers moved away from a Christianized framework of emotion that focused on shared morality and spiritual passion, to a more secular, scientific conception that framed emotions in terms of bodily management and subjective agency. Martha Feldman has called this a "new subjectivity," featuring, at least in music, a movement from "a discourse on the passions, oriented to collective affect," to "a discourse on expression, oriented to the individual."[50] Such individualization of listening and response would have important ramifications in middle-class discussions about the arts, especially music and theater, after the Civil War, as social reformers attempted to educate the public about how to properly engage musical performance as a listener.

The Connoisseur and the Mob: Reforming Audience Excess

If enthusiasm could be understood as a psychological condition, it also had long-standing political meanings. Stemming mainly from the social upheaval of the Protestant Reformation, the nature of one's relationship to God could often serve as a means for defining status and power. Thus Martin Luther, in the 1520s, first identified a German version of enthusiasm, *Schwärmerei*, to disparage religious radicals fomenting a rebellion that threatened the Reformation.[51] Enthusiasm became especially politicized during the religious civil war in England in the mid 1600s, where it became a catch-all pejorative, used by Anglicans to smear Puritans and by Puritans to smear Quakers and Ranters. As Jon Mee explains, "For unbelievers and various kinds of freethinkers, as well as paradoxically enough for the dry men of the High Church tradition, just about any kind of overly demonstrative religious belief was enthusiasm."[52]

From the mid-seventeenth century, well into the eighteenth century, British writers, including Locke, Meric Casaubon, and Thomas More, contrasted enthusiasm with Enlightenment values of reason and civility; this distinction increasingly took on class overtones, pitting refined elites against unruly lower classes, outsiders, and agitators.[53] As Lawrence Klein and Anthony La Vopa point out:

> Although the enlightened might project an enthusiasm as a foil against which to define what constituted rational behavior in the public sphere, we can think of the enthusiasts themselves as trying to assert counter-publics, in defiance of a would-be rationalist hegemony. . . . The discourse of enthusiasm was repeatedly used to marginalize and thereby silence, according to class or gender or cognitive mode or religious affiliation. It was used to constitute authority against forms of power that were perceived as threatening.[54]

In fact, some have argued that the increasing "medicalizing" of enthusiasm as a form of mental distraction was itself political, since it enabled enthusiasm to become a general secular category, "free to be attached to any kind of socially disruptive mania."[55]

The politicization of enthusiasm as disruptive nonconformity can best be seen in the examples of those who actively *embraced* the label. Clement Hawes has written, for example, about a "manic style" in English literature during the late seventeenth century, in which marginalized writers like Abiezer Cope or Christopher Smart purposefully referenced the discourse of enthusiasm in order to create a "leveling" of the political and economic social order and to offer a space for class-based opposition and refusal.[56] Historian David Lovejoy notes that in the events leading up to the American Revolution, well-placed British loyalists in North America condescendingly compared the rebels to religious enthusiasts, since "all political enthusiasts were zealots, too . . . victims of false prophets, deceived by an ideological God." American patriots, however, embraced this insult as a way to proudly justify their social agitation, with John Adams favorably citing the work of the Earl of Shaftesbury.[57]

The class condescension implicit in the historical discourse of enthusiasm in the eighteenth century carried over into new contexts in the early decades of the nineteenth century. Especially in a rapidly urbanizing nation like the United States, the concept of enthusiasm was often used by those in power to malign the anonymous masses of immigrants from Ireland, Britain, and Germany, as well as thousands of new migrants from the countryside, whose crowding in the streets raised the threat of instinctual mob-rule over more traditional frameworks of virtuous leadership. As summarized later in the nineteenth century in the work of social psychologist Gustave Le Bon, crowds were devoid of individuality and reason and instead were susceptible to the "emotional contagion" of suggestion. In fact, Le Bon directly equated crowds with "religious sentiment," something he explained as a condition in which a person "puts all the resources of his mind, the complete submission of his will, and the whole-souled ardour of fanaticism at the service of a cause or an individual."[58] Le Bon proposed that this kind of susceptibility was specifically enhanced among certain "barbarian" races and classes, as well as in specific contexts of oratory or theater, where an audience's emotionally-heightened "crowd mind" might be manipulated easily by savvy performers.[59]

Characterizations of lower-class crowds acting with dangerous irrationality are plentiful in the nineteenth century. Camp meetings that started to rise up in New York State and then throughout the eastern seaboard during the Second Great Awakening in the 1820s and 1830s were, to upper- and middle-class commentators, a perfect representation of enthusiastic disorder and suggestibility among the poor. While R. Laurence Moore and other historians have argued that this was not in fact true, and that revivalist preachers were as concerned with order as much as ministers in established congregations, the reputation nevertheless caused policy changes in various evangelical denominations, particularly denominations hoping for more mainstream acceptance.[60] Images and descriptions of frontier camp meetings during the period emphasize what John Watson called the "unprofitable emotions of *screaming, hallooing* . . . and the *stepping and singing* of *senseless*, merry airs." Such complaints often pitted older, urban, wealthier congregants against younger, lower-class workers and immigrants, who were more interested in ecstatic redemption than social graces.[61] Before new rules were developed in the 1830s, Methodist camp meetings in Illinois and other frontier states had developed a reputation for carousing and disorder not dissimilar to perceptions of urban theaters.[62]

Depictions of theater and music crowds in the press, when not praising the beauty and refinement of elite attendees, tended to focus on disorder, with an emphasis on crowd violence, lack of control, and metaphors of savagery or animalism. Such characterizations fit with growing middle-class disdain for the social chaos created by immigration and urbanization. In a public letter written from a Leopold de Meyer piano concert in 1843, for example, William Cullen Bryant described a concert room as "crowded with people clinging to each other like bees when they swarm . . . the whole affair seemed an outbreak of popular enthusiasm."[63] Given the evangelical fervor sweeping the United States at the time, his reference to an audience as a "swarm," (a nod to Luther's *schwärmerei*), as well as his direct reference to social class in "*popular* enthusiasm," would have evoked, for his readers, images of poor folks at a raucous camp meeting.

Upper-class Bostonian Caroline Healy Dall described her experience of a Jenny Lind concert in 1850 as if she had just visited the cramped quarters of an inner-city tenement:

No one could conceive a more horrible crowd. Dark windows looked into the offices, and in no way could fresh air be obtained. We sat about 8 seats from the narrow. The gentleman who went with us, was not admitted with us—three weak women we were. When I heard the cry for water, air, open the windows &c.—who come as from desperate dying men—in choked voices—I felt what must come. I made several calm attempts to get out, but there was no possible means of egress, and a disappointed crowd were storming without.—The noise and tumult was now so great—windows breaking & panels giving way—that we heard not one syllable of the opening, Der Freschutz, not should we have known that the forty musicians were playing but for the motion of their hands. Jenny then sent forward an usher to say that if any gentle man wished to leave his place, she would be responsible for his ticket. But he could not be heard. The rush could be restrained no longer—and we fled for our lives, over settees & chair backs—from which the frightened occupants had risen. We saw bonnets torn off—women trampled on, men falling in tiers of five or six. I have seen crowds before, but I never imagined what a suffocating crowd would be. Police were rolled aside like marbles long before we quitted our seats.[64]

Editorial cartoons were similar. An image in London's *Punch* magazine in 1850 depicted the enthusiasm for the Jenny Lind tour in America with Lind sitting sheepishly on a stage, being crowned by a triumphant P. T. Barnum, as thousands of music lovers, looking like filthy, clownish peasants, climb on top of one another, cheer, bow, and gesticulate wildly. While it reflected nationalistic superiority, it also reflected the attitudes of many middle-class Americans.[65] Asmodeous, in his satire of the Jenny Lind mania in Boston, returned again and again to the motif of the uncontrollable crowd. He noted that Barnum had encouraged the "ugliest spirits in the city" who "did not content themselves with making a fiend-like noise, but displayed rowdyism of the most contemptible kind." But he also argued that Barnum had cleverly made everyone, including the elite, a part of the vulgar mass:

This tumultuous assemblage of jackasses and sheeps, to quote the words of Peter—otherwise Phineas—was almost exclusively native born and bred Bostonians, of all grades, classes, and conditions of life, from the newsboy to the merchant Prince, from the bar keeper to money changers, all and each putting up this hue and cry, braying and bleating for the good of Phineas, while he was keeping in the background, enjoying the joke and pulling at his wires, filling his pockets and twirling his fingers at the rabble he was using.[66]

The idea that enthusiasm for commercial music could lead to vulgarism was a very real anxiety, especially among those aspiring to the world of middle-class propriety. For many middle-class Americans after mid-century, the appreciation of the musical arts was a primary testament to one's refinement. "Sensibility," in particular, meaning the ability to experience every nuance of the world with feeling and intensity, was directed connected to one's social station; that one could be so affected day in and day out was the presumed indulgence of one who had the luxury, and the necessary cultivation of character, to do so. Music, in particular, was a potent source of such sensation. As a writer for the *New York Weekly Review* explained, "Music possesses elements and primary powers which, without the parade of external circumstances, without the medium of explanations, act directly, independently, immediately, upon our most hidden feelings, touch the most minute strings of sensibility, and cause our souls to vibrate with emotions of every variety and shade."[67]

Musical passion, however, raised difficult questions, especially for those trying to establish rules for behavior in middle-class society. While sensibility was important, another hallmark of a respectable person in the United States in the nineteenth century was his or her manners, or the ability to carefully control personal inclinations and impulses and thereby move among peers with polished grace and charm. Such standards of middle-class decorum were painstakingly laid out in the hundreds of etiquette manuals reprinted and published in the nineteenth century. As one writer gushed, "Oh, how beautiful is the youth who holds in check the impetuous forces within him, and makes them obedient to the calls of duty, propriety, and refinement! And indeed, this is refinement!"[68] But if it were true that music could "act directly, independently, immediately, upon our most hidden feelings," how would that power of direct sensation square, exactly, with genteel codes of restraint and graceful behavior? Theoretically, musical enthusiasm could be as much a threat to, as a component of, one's poise.[69]

Genteel manuals of behavior attempted to resolve the contradiction by

"Jenny Lind and the Americans." *Punch, or the London Charivari* 19 (5 October 1850): 146.

emphasizing a careful balance between musical sensation and decorum. As one explained: "Every approach to a rude, noisy, boisterous manner is reprehensible, for the obvious reason that it interferes with the comfort, and, consequently, with the rights of others; but this is at a wide remove from the ultra-modishness that requires the total suppression of every manifestation of natural emotion, and apparently, aims to convert beings influenced by the motives, feelings, and principles that constitute humanity, into a mere moving automata!"[70] Alfred Guillaume Gabriel d'Orsay offered a practical interpretation of the matter, citing the acceptability of musical enthusiasm in doses: "It is the misfortune of musical people generally to be such enthusiasts, that, once beginning, they seldom know when to leave off . . . a song *now* and *then* is very desirable, as it is a relief to conversation, but half a dozen consecutively, even from St. Cecilia in person, would become a bore."[71] Daniel Wise, in *The Young Lady's Counsellor*, suggested that quantity was not as significant as the *quality* of one's enthusiasm; the only genuine and acceptable enthusiasm came from deep within:

The everlasting chime of melody, which may charm the ear of her who listens aright to the voices of the visible world, originates in the soul of the listener. Whoso would draw a "concord of sweet sounds" from the world without, must carry music in her heart; just as the maiden, who sits before the richly-toned instrument, must first have the musical idea in herself, before she can call forth floods of melody from its obedient keys.[72]

Such answers were hardly satisfactory for every situation, however, especially in light of a deeper consideration of how exactly to value personal desire and social obligation in a society that often pitted one against the other. Historian Richard Bushman explains, "For all its sweetness and beauty, refinement troubled middle-class Americans. . . . They acknowledged the beauty of a refined life, but objected to its extravagance and vanity."[73] In addition, there were indications that sensibility was something hardwired into one's very nature, and might not be cultivated at all. As an 1853 book on music education asserted, the effects of music were not the same for everyone and "a delicate, sensitive ear is otherwise affected than that of a stronger, rougher nature. The tumult, the whistles, and the shrieks in which the latter delight, would throw the other into the highest state of alarm or discomfort."[74]

Because of this contradiction, music loving had always been an activity that, at some point, gave listeners pause. In their diaries, they struggled to balance their consciences and their desires. As I have already discussed, earlier in the century, concert-goers wrestled quite a bit with whether or not to attend something that might encourage excessive or immoral behavior. Thus Anna Thaxter Cushing in 1846 engaged in intense discussions with friends about the propriety of attending the opera; or Nathan Beekley of Philadelphia vowed repeatedly in his 1849 diary that he would "never again" attend "places of amusement" because of the money he was spending and the sometime presence of "rowdies;" or Lucy Lowell in 1884 suggested, only half-jokingly, that Wagner might not be good for her.

There is a slight shift in this commentary, however. While diarists before 1850 tended to wrestle with the morality of loving music itself, that is, engaging in the very behavior of concert going, diarists later in the century tended to assume that they would attend concerts but had conflicting feelings about *which* concerts to attend and *whose* music to love. Lowell, for instance, worried in 1887 that her liking of a Schubert symphony was not appropriate, writing after one performance, "I've never realized before how superb that Schubert symphony is. I like it better than any except Beethoven's 3rd, 5th, 7th, and 9th symphonies. It seems to me more interesting than Beethoven's others, tho' I suppose it's heresy to say so."[75] George Strong sinterestingly embodied these changed attitudes in his own diary over the course of ten or so years. As we have seen, in the 1840s, he was willing to make gentle fun of the informality of his fellow elites at concerts. By the 1850s, however, he was associating lack of serious engagement with the music in terms that were more clearly class-conscious, complaining not about chatting or sleeping among acquaintances but rather a degraded sense of taste among the anonymous "milliners' girls and their adorers, who look spoony and sentimental, and sigh out the aroma of shocking bad cigars by the hour together."[76]

Such shift in rhetoric was part of a wider social movement fostered by idealist middle-class reformers, who sought to introduce a new way to "love" music in the latter half of the century. Instead of passionate, enthusiastic attachment to a performance, they proposed what might be called a "classical" appreciation: ritualized, reverent, intellectual attention to the unfolding of a composition or work. As early as 1854, German composer Adolf Bernhard Marx, giving advice to those "whose object is to enjoy music without active participation . . . but to penetrate into its spiritual purport," warned:

The first and foremost advice to such would be not to surfeit themselves with music, after the manner of the enrages of our time; not to rush after all those operas, concerts, soirées, and every description of sing-song that is in vogue. All these only serve to nourish the music mania, this disease of our time, this longing to fly out of an universal emptiness and *ennui* into an universal weariness and sing-song, blunting and stupefying to the mind and enfeebling to the character; no susceptibility for art, or perception of it, can ever arise out of this turbid source.

In substituting the single-minded frenzy of musical mania for the older, superficial pleasures of elite concert going, Marx further argued, music lovers had missed the mark of true appreciation. "Susceptibility for art" had to be combined with careful education and modesty, for "love and devotion for art is already a definite activity."[77]

If antebellum music loving proposed focusing audience attention on performance as a way to challenge the informal socializing of theater culture, this new form of engagement proposed to refine music loving even further by removing the spontaneity and showmanship of live performance that might lead to obsession or spontaneous emotional display. Those promoting this reform found it entirely necessary in a culture that seemingly had been taken over by the excessive, superficial, and economically motivated spectacles of mass commercialism. True appreciation of art was not about purchasing tickets to see virtuosic curiosities but rather about hearing the timeless beauty of a composer's work. It was not about mysticism or possession, losing touch with the world, but rather about aestheticism or carefully controlled action in the world.[78]

Thus John S. Dwight, in establishing a magazine devoted to the movement, would write about the progression of music in American society: "It has taken the initiative, as the popular Art *par excellence*, in gradually attempering this whole people to the sentiment of Art. And whoever reflects upon it, must regard it as a most important saving influence in this rapid expansion of our democratic life." Dwight was an especially keen supporter of Beethoven in the United States and worked tirelessly to steer people away from spectacles like the 1,000-piece orchestra of the Peace Jubilee and more toward appreciation of "the master-works in symphony, concerto, overture."[79]

Social historians have noted that such a "disciplining of spectatorship," as John Kasson put it, is emblematic of postbellum ideologies of genteel refinement and taste and of the emergence of powerful class divisions in the United States after 1850.[80] And this shift can be seen in the approach of some critics. William Foster Apthorp, for example, in a long essay in the *Atlantic Monthly* in 1879, audaciously compared the approaches of "refined" musicians and "ordinary" music lovers:

A musician, after listening to a great work, does not, as a rule, care to have it immediately repeated. . . . But when the ordinary music-lover hears a piece of music that particularly pleases him, he generally wishes to hear it over again; he will listen to it day in and day out, until he gets thoroughly sick of it, and never wishes to hear it more. He sucks and sucks at his musical orange until there is nothing left but the dry peel, and then throws it away.[81]

In the same essay, he later uses intoxication as an analogy, something that would have had particularly alarming connotations for readers in an age where temperance had been recently at the center of urban and moral reform:

There is an enjoyment of wine which is not entirely sensual, for it calls into play the powers of comparison and judgment. The connoisseur and the boor enjoy it in very different ways. The one delights in the wine itself, the other in its effect, and the latter enjoyment to a certain extent precludes the possibility of the former. Substituting music for wine, we have a very good example of the relative points of view of the musician and the musical layman. The difference between them lies not so much in the class of music they enjoy as in the way in which they enjoy it.

Earlier criticisms of Ellsler or Lind "mania" identified temporarily excessive musical behavior as wildly inexplicable and in a way that left "normal" musical behavior unstated; it was simply understood how one should behave. But Apthorp was careful to associate excessive musical behavior with lack of discipline and education and to provide his readers with an alternative position, all through metaphorical language that supplied cues of social class. Even the title of his piece, "Musicians and Music Lovers," juxtaposes learned professionalism with ignorant amateurism; his text throughout associates the former with wine, connossieurship, deference, and judgment, and the latter with garbage, sensualism, immediate gratification, and boorishness. One listener is intellectually pleased, while the other engages in unrestrained bodily pleasure; one has taste and one does not.

Too much can be made, however, of the class motivations of musical reformers like Apthorp. Cultural historians like Lawrence Levine and Kasson have emphasized reform as a kind of social control, an instance of elites imposing their narrow values on ordinary concert-loving people. Such a view has received criticism elsewhere (especially for generalizing about reformers and ignoring both the aesthetic and populist impulses behind many reformers' efforts), but I would add that such scholars' singular emphasis on social change erases the connections and continuities between older and newer forms of music loving. It is true that nineteenth-century music classicists tended to be middle class, and they tended to equate the enthusiastic passion of virtuoso-inspired music loving with the excesses of "popular" or lower-class audience behavior. At the same time, they positioned themselves, as had older music lovers, against what they saw as a selfish upper class who used opera and concerts for a crass display of their wealth. Interpretations of classical reform as a *break* with more unruly and vibrant forms of audience participation also tend to gloss over the extent to which the reform movement depended on the already-established existence of devoted music listening, something to which the movement *added* new utopian ideas about the function of music loving in an increasingly anonymous and commercialized society.[82]

Both Kasson and Levine, for example, have talked about the "silence" that accompanied classical music appreciation, particularly how the imposition of new rules to keep audiences silent during performances were a means to overcome and control, in the words of Kasson, "boisterous informality and conviviality."[83] However, the evidence of audience behavior in the diaries of actual listeners indicates that silent listening is not the most accurate way to capture changing practices and aesthetic debates among post–Civil War music audiences. Antebellum music lovers valued silence as much as postbellum audiences; for the former, silence enabled them to fully experience the skills of virtuosos and was a sign of engagement and astonished appreciation. Instead of introducing the novelty of silence to a noisy environment, postbellum reformers changed the meanings and uses of silence according to new beliefs about the definition and function of music.[84]

Of course, music lovers did not necessarily abide by any reformers' prescriptions for how to listen to music. The sheer variety and fluidity of audiences in the nineteenth century made any attempt to control audience behavior difficult. As historian Peter G. Buckley has stated, "while there were growing divisions between socio-economic classes over the course of the nineteenth century, there were also "as many 'audiences' as there were theatres."[85] What is clear, however, is that after the Civil War, the critical discourse around music loving became far more complicated, employing not only *quantitative* terms of excess and disorder but also *qualitative* terms of taste and appreciation. If the initial criticism of popular music loving was simply about being *too invested* in music, by the close of the century accounts of audiences were more often about being *too invested in the wrong ways and for the wrong reasons.* The music listener-consumer had become a distinct and potentially acceptable musical role in middle-class American society, but only as far as it fit with prevailing ideologies of professionalism and taste. Competing forms of music loving meant that audiences could no longer simply enthuse about music; concert going involved more choices and negotiations about one's listening, each of which could reflect particular meanings about one's class, ambition, and education.

Feminine and Passive: Developing a Social Grammar of Audience

In order to appreciate the actions and attitudes of classical music reformers, one has to consider fully the direction and general environment of public musical life in America's cities during the 1860s and 1870s. While major East Coast cities had begun to build grand opera houses and concert halls, and hosted choral societies and small orchestras that strove to offer European music culture for upper- and middle-class audiences, much of the music offered for public listening in those cities could always be more easily and cheaply found in the vibrant marketplace of culture—minstrel houses, pleasure gardens, saloons, band pavilions, novelty theaters, and dime museums. As Dwight explained about the music boom of the early 1850s: "Very confused, crude, heterogeneous is this sudden musical activity in a young, utilitarian people. A thousand specious fashions too successfully dispute the place of true Art in the favor of each little public."[86]

It is not surprising, then, that in the hundreds of books and articles published in the second half of the century—often titled "how to listen to music"—the serious appreciation of music was almost always posed in opposition to indulgence in commercialized sensation. Reformers were trying not only to separate the superficial from the meaningful but also trying to recalibrate people's perception of musical entertainment. They understood enthusiasm not as a disciplined and active response to a work but rather as a thoughtless and manipulated response to a sensationalized event. Cultivating taste, most of all, involved cultivating understanding, so that whenever one encountered music in the public sphere, he or she could "properly" engage with it.[87] Music historian Edward Dickinson explained, for example, that to guard against "the enfeeblement which may result from over-indulgence in the sweets of this most intoxicating of aesthetic enjoyments" the cure is "more music of the highest order, together with a preparation of mind that enables one to discriminate between the qualities that fade and the qualities that endure, and an artistic conscience that refuses to find satisfaction in work that is not sincerely felt and skillfully wrought."[88]

Making the case for the reverent appreciation and understanding of works of musical art was not easy. While reform's moral mission may have been obvious to the reformers, it was not so clear to the public. The difficulty for reformers was typified by popular figures like bandleader Patrick Gilmore, who, in his ever-lengthy concert programs, linked the issue of public education to public gratification, which, at least for many classical music reformers, were not necessarily related:

In the preparation of his Programmes, Mr. Gilmore is governed by a two-fold motive—art and business. First, to do justice to the art by presenting some of the Standard Classical Compositions of the great masters in whole or in part, thus affording a rich treat to musical students and lovers of music in its highest form. Next, the gratification of the great public, who make no pretense to any knowledge or appreciation of "High-Art Music," but who become enraptured with the popular melody and the familiar strain, especially when rendered in the superb manner in which they will be at this Concert. To harmonize these extremes—the classical and the popular—requires that the educated musician and critical listener shall be of broad and generous spirit, and recognize the fact that the *first duty* of even the best military band in the world is, TO PLEASE THE PUBLIC, and this is the aim of GILMORE'S BAND.[89]

The reformist stance was also significantly complicated by shifts in the demographics of the concert world after the Civil War. When young Boston gentleman Nathan Webb helped to start an amateur music society in 1789, "a very desultory debate ensued . . . with respect to the manner of admitting female members."[90] But by the 1880s, white middle-class women, who had become the prime movers of amateur music clubs and societies in America, comprised a majority of the audience for recital and symphonic musical performance. Indeed in my own research, a majority of the diaries I found that discussed music before 1860 were by men; the majority of those after 1860 were by women. New York City opera manager Max Maretzek famously summed up this trend in 1855, when he declared that while members of the "gentlemanly section of New York Society" may like this or that artist, "beyond the principal cities, it is the ladies alone that patronize and love the arts."[91]

The efforts to democratize the value of good music became, in many ways, a women's movement. White middle-class women in large and small communities across the United States after the Civil War formed volunteer societies and clubs for the purpose of sponsoring public concerts and education. The Tuesday Musicale of Rochester, New York, for example, stated that after "encouraging the many associates who look to it alone for a chance to hear a little music, and a hearty desire on the part of all together to keep up high ideals, the club should become the center from which shall proceed encouragement for all that is good in music, and in time a power to bring to Rochester the best from the outside world."[92] Women's music clubs and societies specifically embraced many of the goals of reform, moving the public toward certain kinds of music and helping to foster education and appreciation. As the *New York Sun* proclaimed in 1904: "Without this guarantee and the influence of the club members many small towns would never hear the well known artists. . . . All over the country these clubs have done a wonderful missionary work in bringing to people of the smaller cities the best of the virtuosos."[93]

Musicologist Ruth Solie has argued that both nineteenth-century male reformers and women patrons were part of a "form of romanticism that idealized and sentimentalized women at the same time that it idealized and sentimentalized the aesthetic experience, creating a natural link between them."[94] Women patronizing musical performance could be interpreted as, in Maretzek's words, an extension of any American woman's "natural appreciation for the grand and the beautiful, which would seem to be born actually in her nature."[95] Women's role in helping to foster reform and civic awareness of art, however, had unforeseen and significant consequences. As white elite and middle-class women worked to manage clubs and arrange appearances by touring stars, they became savvy business entrepreneurs—a realm previously controlled by New York-based male agents and managers—and thus cultivated a new source of power and visibility outside of the home.[96] The advent of matinee and rehearsal performances during the day, a time that appealed to far more women than men, was an important innovation that erased the more salacious "nightlife" aspects of concert going but also enabled women to gather together in public and develop their own culture.[97] For many women, the concert itself became a shared space that enabled women to gather and to express themselves freely in ways forbidden in everyday life. Thus, for instance, they cried openly and together at Louis Moreau Gottschalk's performances, or questioned patriarchal culture through subtle reinterpretations of the piano nocturne.[98]

This active public role of middle-class women in music after the Civil War prompted a crisis for some men, who sought to work against this "feminization of culture." While many middle-class men felt that cultural activities involving literature, art, and music were the foundation of any great civilization, the fact that culture had become the domain of women automatically meant that it was inadequate, a frail and pale imitation of civilization's promise. As one critic said, "Man's 'business interests' are running away with him, devouring him body and soul. And with him goes the rugged strength, the red blood corpuscles that we need to make our culture a living breathing reality. Without him we are weak, unstable, a soul without a body, a high, thin song without the sustaining notes of the organ accompaniment."[99] The growing visibility of the women's movement and new calls for women's suffrage exacerbated the situation.

Accepted ideas of culture and leisure became a subject for reform by public figures like William James, Theodore Roosevelt, and others toward the end of the century. In a time of increasing bureaucratic systems in corporations and industry, of "white collar" jobs which required one to sit all day copying and filing contracts, orders, and inventory lists, life seemed empty of purpose, edge, and power. Historian Jackson Lears explains, "The rationalization of urban culture and the decline of religion into sentimental religiosity further undermined a solid sense of self. For many, individual identities began to seem fragmented, diffuse, perhaps even unreal."[100] Sitting and listening to music, associated with elaborately ruled worlds of genteel refinement, church services, and lectures, seemed part of the problem rather than the solution. The deadening artifice of parlor etiquette, polite society, and "serious" culture had become no better than the stifling offices, shops, and warehouses of organized capitalism. In the new "cult of experience," where "intense experience became an end in itself," traditional culture was discarded for the more masculine pursuits of athletics, hunting, and hiking, as well as new kinds of thrills found outdoors in amusement parks and organized sports like baseball and football.

As with arguments about the elitism of music reformers, the "feminization of culture" and the influence of a "masculine" counter-movement can be overstated or generalized. Paul Knoper has warned that interpretations about the threat of consumption to the "producerly character of older Victorian manliness" need to be balanced by the "investment bourgeois males had in the domestic, or their recoil from pugnacious manliness."[101] Joseph Horowitz has argued that the general malaise—or following Jackson Lears's formulation, "weightlessness"—among the middle class in the Gilded Age was not gender specific and that women, as well as men, sought intense experience, exemplified by the cult-like intensity of Wagnerism.[102]

Still, there is evidence that women's extensive involvement in concert culture and reform at the end of the nineteenth century at least reinforced existing associations between femininity, passivity, and music. Women's search for intensity in Wagner was recognized and countered by some critics who attempted to claim Wagner for themselves, locating in his work a clear masculine discipline and virility.[103] Despite middle-class women's active role in the world of concert management, and shared sense with men of the malaise of modern urban life, anti-women attacks, especially associated with Wagnerism, only kept alive old stereotypes of women's passivity. A correspondent to *Dwight's Journal of Music* in 1874, for example, wrote a review of Wagner's *Die Walküre* that employed stereotypes of both passivity and over-emotionality that would have reflected badly on Wagner's growing legions of female enthusiasts: "The dramatic portion displays great monotony, is spun out to a weary length, affords no scope for anything but the extremes of passive listening and wringing the hands and tearing the hair."[104]

Emphasizing women's limited role in musical life—as ardent patrons and audience members but rarely composers, or conductors—was another means of indicating the passivity of women. The subject of "women in music" was a regular theme of editorials, letters to the editor, and other public forms of debate in the 1880s and 1890s. Some, like English philosopher John Stuart Mill, argued that the lack of woman composers was due simply to lack of access. "Women are taught music," he wrote, "but not for the purpose of composing, only of executing it: and accordingly it is only as composers, that men, in music, are superior to women."[105] On the contrary, there remained doubts that women could actually take on such an active, intellectual task of production. Edith Brower caused a great deal of controversy by asserting this position in the *Atlantic Monthly* in 1894. Despite open access to music, she argued, women have never produced much of value because of a lack of abstract imagination: "Woman ventures timidly, ofttimes boldly, into the shoreless deeps of the abstract. For a while she may disport herself prettily there—in the shallows, so to speak; but she is never quite happy nor at ease unless the terra firma of the concrete be at least within reach."[106] Brower's traditional message was clear: men create and produce great music, and women can only receive and consume it, because that's just how nature intends it.

Outside of the realm of music, this stereotype was also being promoted. Increased opportunities of consumption started to clash with the long-standing Victorian bourgeois worldview that espoused the value of personal achievement, industry, and work. Carl Roell, for example, traced the ways in which piano-makers in the 1890s, first supportive of the new technology of the player piano (which they thought would boost interest in piano playing generally) came to reject it as indicative of the passivity of "modern consumer culture."[107] In particular, consumption was often assumed to be the domain of women, who were taking advantage of newly available furniture, appliances, and home conveniences as part of their duties in shaping the "domestic sphere." Calls for more robust and masculine amusements that were active rather than passive, intense rather than polite, in the outdoors rather than the home, helped to promote the unification of femininity with passivity, consumption, and audiencing.[108]

Of course, anxiety about women's role in music culture was not new in the 1880s. Middle-class women had long been stereotyped as unable to engage in truly independent intellectual, critical, or creative activity. Especially in genteel society, it was generally thought that "a young woman . . . who consumed her vital force in intellectual activities was necessarily diverting these energies from the achievement of true womanhood."[109] While women were understood to be predisposed toward music and "sensibility," their frailty and passivity also raised the alleged problem of being unable to control themselves in the presence of music and thereby undermining the very project of refinement which society had made her charge.

The leading medical texts of the day alleged that the female nervous system was finer and more prone to over-stimulation than the male nervous system. Sentimentality, or emotion for emotion's sake, became a common complaint directed toward women's culture. Male critics, for instance, frequently and regularly denigrated reactions to sentimental art, like the tears and crying of women in the audiences for Louis Moreau Gottschalk's piano playing.[110] In general, women thus were vulnerable to accusations of over-emotionality, even as they were encouraged to develop their emotional sensibility—caught in a double standard, they could not help but reinforce their own inferiority in the eyes of middle-class critics.

Likewise, reconciling "manly" responsibility in the public sphere with a love for music had long been fraught with difficulty. Derek Scott recounts that when Charles Halle came to London in the late 1840s, if he "asked any gentleman belonging to society, 'Do you play any instrument?' it was considered an insult."[111] Such disdain for musical life was why a young Henry Higginson, the eventual founder of the Boston Symphony Orchestra, having to eschew his studies of music in Vienna in order to join his father's stockbrokerage business in Boston, noted to friends in the 1880s that he "never walked into 44 State Street without wanting to sit down on the doorstep and cry."[112]

At the turn of the century, new scholarly discussions of homosexuality created new stereotypes of the music-loving male as effeminate, and, at worst, a deviant.[113] This association was demonstrated, for example, in Willa Cather's 1905 short story, "Paul's Case: a Study in Temperament." It describes a wealthy young man, who, after school, works as an usher at Carnegie Hall. For him, nothing else matters: "The first sigh of the instruments seemed to free some hilarious and potent spirit within him. . . . He felt a sudden zest of life; the lights danced before his eyes and the concert hall blazed into unimaginable splendor." His enthusiasm is thwarted, how-ever, by the "practical" expectations of his parents and teachers. His teach-ers can't understand his slang, vague smile, or foppish dress. His family is conservative and distant; Paul sometimes stays out all night, seeking a glimpse of opera stars offstage, and dreads returning home to "his upstairs room and its horrible yellow wallpaper, the creaking bureau with the greasy plush collarbox, and over his painted wooden bed the pictures of George Washington and John Calvin." Eventually his father removes Paul from his usher job and puts him to work at the family business. Paul runs away and, after using up money he has stolen from his father, takes his own life by jumping in front of a train. Cather's framing of the story as a psychological "case," and her portrayal of Paul as a feminized outcast with a "secret love," directly suggested emerging stereotypes of homosexuality.[114]

Gendered rules for language and for participation in music (feminine and passive versus masculine and active) not only drew on similar arche-typal associations but also helped to form broad boundaries of conversa-tion and thinking in the latter half of the nineteenth century. However, that did not mean that they were always followed or used. Gender roles were cultural stereotypes, an official, public grammar that people, in the course of their everyday lives, could potentially suspend. Henry Higginson, for example, while despairing about his having to choose between the worlds of investment banking and music, did, in fact, choose music and went on to great success, founding the Boston Symphony Orchestra. Women were quite active in the music world, no matter what was thought about it in the press. In response to Edith Brower's assertion that women were not "ab-stract" enough for composition, Boston's *The Musical Record* reported "the curious announcement that, at the present moment, all of the students of the violencello at the Royal Academy of Music, London, are women" and that at a recent Academy concert the best piece was "a sonata in E for piano-forte and violin, composed by the Macfarren scholar, Miss Llewela Davies." The report went on to remark, "Although none of these facts are conclusive against the argument of the *Atlantic*'s essay, they at least go to prove that the final evidence as to the musical ability or disability of women is not yet in the hands of the theorists."[115]

What is most important is that the concert world in America in the latter half of the nineteenth century was clearly a place of heightened tension between women and men. What role would each play? How would the behaviors expected in the concert situation—managing, conducting, per-forming, listening, conversation, criticism—reflect expectations about mas-culinity and femininity? Mary Cassatt's painting, "In the Loge," from 1878, nicely demonstrates the array of associations attached to women attending a music performance during this transitional period.[116] While it is part of a series of works about women attending the opera in Paris in the 1870s, it nevertheless helps in sorting out similar aspects of the changing culture of opera attendance in the United States. The painting depicts a young woman at a Sunday matinee, dressed in black with minimal jewelry and with lace gloves, and holding a fan. She is seen in profile, with the viewer able to see both her and others seated in the balcony beyond. While she holds a lorgnette to her eyes and peers intently out at the stage, a gray-haired gentleman in a tuxedo, two or three boxes around the curve of the balcony, leans out and looks through his lorgnette at *her.*

At one level, the image depicts "self-confident New Women at the matinee," as Griselda Pollock has explained, facing down the legacy of forced erotic display created by open prostitution in the theater's notorious "third tier."[117] Like Lucy Lowell and other female music lovers, she is purposefully ignoring the social intrigue common to the theater among non-music lovers and giving full attention to the performance. She does this not only by rigidly looking elsewhere but also by *listening,* signified by the centrality of the woman's ear, its flesh-colored outline emphasized by the darkness of the woman's drawn-back hair and black bonnet and by a single diamond-stud earring.

At the same time, following the dictates of classical reform, she seems to be facing down her own passion, so to speak. Her matinee clothing is dour, literally straitlaced, something that rejects the expressive extravagance of "first night" fashion. And she is not standing and hurling bravos at the stage, she is not crying, and she does not appear dreamily intoxicated by the music or moved in any visible way. Yet she comes across as keenly interested in what is happening onstage. While the leering man is out of focus, fading lazily into a background of moving people and vague swirls of ostentation, the woman is close, crisp, unmoving, arched forward, and determined.

A Pre-History of Fandom

Irrational maniacs, uncontrolled mobs, over-emotional women—late nineteenth-century characterizations of music lovers would come to shape the discourse around musical audiences for the next century. How do we make sense of these changing and various characterizations and associations? It is important to note that music loving represented enough of a threat to accepted kinds of participation in social life that it necessitated attention in the first place. The excessive behaviors of new listeners—whether in the form of obsessive monomania, overly enthusiastic crowds, even women's agency—were all transgressive, violating and implicitly questioning the carefully inscribed borders of middle-class life.

Such violations had even more particular meanings in the context of rapid change during an era shaped by industrialization and urbanization. Irrationality, which had previously been interpreted in terms of European religious debates, acquired new meanings amidst the mechanization and rigidity of modern industrial life. The irrationality of mobs, previously associated with political expression, became indicative of uncontrolled overcrowding in cities, the alleged dangers of foreign immigrants, and worker revolts. Women's escalating participation in the concert world transformed former discussions of "sensibility" into debates about the meanings of production and consumption.

Music loving was an especially visible example, or symptom, of America's new marketplace of culture which, to some, was a place of unparalleled opportunity, and to others was a place of sensationalism and irrational impulses, shifting and sometimes confusing roles, and the manipulation of anonymous masses for profit. The entertainment and shopping districts of cities like Boston, New York, and Philadelphia were, for many Americans, strange, topsy-turvy places where government buildings, *and* churches, *and* concert halls, *and* department stores all made similar, grand, architectural statements, referencing classical Greek and Roman models. In fact, it is hard not to see the advent of permanent concert halls, publicly heralded as "temples" of transcendent art, as working simultaneously, in the realm of the everyday experience, within the frameworks of capitalism by providing independent and separate spaces for music consumption. If grand department stores of the turn of the century could evoke the gravity of meaningful social institutions like concert halls, the reverse could also be true: meaningful social institutions like concert halls could symbolize the commercial success of a community.[118] America's cities were also places where pianos and sewing machines were sold in the same salesrooms and even made by the same manufacturers. Sheet music, sewing machines, shoes, flour—music was just another commodity.[119]

The first music lovers in the antebellum era wholeheartedly embraced this mysterious commodification of musical experience. While one could certainly be a "music lover" in a rural community, participating avidly, for instance, in the local church choir or singing with family members and friends at home, the advent of commercial concerts in cities transformed the scope and profundity of the concept. Those interested in music were presented with choices for the first time, many of them thrillingly new and spectacular. This was the case with Nathan Beekley, for example, arriving in Philadelphia for the first time in 1849, or Francis Bennett, who seemed overwhelmed by the marching bands and sheer sounds of Boston in 1854. Even later, in 1874, seventeen-year-old Kenneth Allen could report about his friend who had moved to the Midwest: "Yesterday I received a letter from Charlie Pickard. He has been singing in the church choir, went with Mrs. Ferreira to see *Lucca* in Chicago, and, in fact, has gone crazy on music."[120]

For some, this embrace of urban musical life led to characterizations of music lovers as somehow diseased, addicted, overcome, "passive," easily manipulated. Well into the nineteenth century, many Americans perceived growing urban areas as unguarded and dangerous, divorced from the shared morality of family and community and instead reigned over by anonymity, laissez-faire attitudes, and unchecked freedoms. At worst, it was teeming with masses connected only by duplicitous contractual relationships and prone to violence. Clearly these ideas were at work in responses to the Jenny Lind mania of 1850, and to subsequent commercial musical ventures involving large advertising campaigns and unabashed doses of "humbug." In fact, such characterization of passive consumers, alienated from the production of music and confused about its meanings, would continue in twentieth-century Marxist critiques of mass culture.

To some extent, traditionalist worries were true: urban, public concerts, especially after 1850, had changed the fundamental social connections between musical performers and audiences. Musical experience was seemingly no longer something shared by a congregation or community in the local rituals of a church service, dance, or military muster; it had instead become a tangible product, made by those who were musically gifted, and easily exhibited and purchased by anyone with cash. Commercial concerts brought extraordinary access to music for many Americans in the new wage economy, and it made exhibitions and concerts into marked social events, but such concerts were based on an ephemeral flash that limited music's ability to signify deeply shared values and experiences.

In part, this was why classical reformers like Dwight wished to provide the American public with musical experiences of a different sort: not Christy's Minstrels but the Mendelssohn Quintette Club, not "Shoo Fly" but Beethoven's *Symphony No. 3*. For enthusiastic reformers like Dwight, commercial concert culture had to be balanced by other alternatives, mostly drawn from European "masters," that, once experienced by the public, would make clear the inadequacies of their previous delight with monster concerts and light music. As he enthused in the first issue of his journal, in 1852, "Think of fifteen hundred people, listening every week to orchestral rehearsals of the great symphonies and overtures!"[121]

Music lovers existing outside the community of critics and reformers, however, had already been heading in a different direction by the 1850s. While music lovers, too, could be critical of commercial concert culture, they nevertheless desired the opportunities it offered; they did not reject it but instead sought to redefine their own engagement with it. Many music lovers, for example, refused to accept the limited and temporary musical participation afforded by the purchase of a concert ticket; they sought instead to creatively imbue their listening experiences with lasting personal connection and depth of feeling. When the star system unmoored performers from localities and exaggerated stars' professional skills in the 1840s, music lovers sought to understand stars as authentic people with whom they had an intimate bond. While antebellum audiences tended to manipulate performance with frequent encores and outbursts of pleasure or displeasure, music lovers willingly allowed *performances* to control *them*, paying close attention to the physical sensations of listening. While most people returned to their daily lives after concerts ended, music lovers actively extended their audience role beyond the purchased frame of performance by seeking out music in churches, by attempting to see stars in the street, by making pilgrimages to significant sites, by performing their favorite pieces on home instruments, by collecting sheet music, and by meticulously recording descriptions of their listening experiences.

According to the frameworks of exchange in the new market economy, these behaviors were abnormal; music lovers did not abide by the equation of a ticket for a performance but sought rather to go beyond and around it, much like the alternative "shunpikes" that had turned up in the 1830s, snaking illegally around toll gates on many states' newly built roadways. While working outside some of the prescriptions of the marketplace, however, music lovers did not immediately or fully support reformers' "sacralization" of music, which focused on reverent rather than enthusiastic attention and on the significance of the "work" rather than the unique revelations of performance. Not surprisingly, such a stance invited critiques from reformers themselves: early music lovers' attention to sensation, personality, and the environment of the concert hall over the abstractions of the "sublime" meant that they were unaware of correct social behavior—that is, without "taste."

Public mockery and debate about music audiences between 1850 and 1885, as well as withering critiques of amateur music loving in 1870s by those like William Foster Apthorp, eventually hardened the lines between two different kinds of music engagement in the twentieth century: one based on the intellectual ecstasies of inner contemplation, fostered and supported by the performance of "good music," and one based on passionate participation in the world of stars, spectacle and collecting, relegated to the realm of "popular" culture. While *music lover* continued to be used to refer to enthusiastic patrons of classical music, practitioners of the older form of music loving were given a new name taken from sports: *fans*.

Not one of the music lovers I researched for this book called themselves "a fan." But in retrospect, mid-century music lovers and modern pop fans emerge as connected, across centuries, in their complex embrace of commodified participation. While the mechanisms and contexts may be different, the actions and broader meanings of music loving and music fandom, especially as examples of both excessive and resistant consumption, are the same.[122] The first music lovers, as witnesses to the beginnings of the commercialization of culture in the nineteenth century, were among the earliest to assume the role of the audience-consumer and to create the strategies many use today for understanding the world of stars, merchandizing, and spectacle.

Epilogue

+{·:·}+

In 1964, virtuoso pianist Glenn Gould, at the height of his career, ceased performing. Gould disliked the narrow expectations of audiences and promoters during concert tours, something that would likewise motivate the Beatles to eschew performance two years later. But Gould had another, deeper motivation: he was convinced that the future of musical creativity lay not in the role of the performer but in the role of the listener. As he provocatively explained in a 1966 essay in *High Fidelity Magazine*, "This listener is no longer passively analytical; he is an associate whose tastes, preferences, and inclinations even now alter peripherally the experiences to which he gives his attention, and upon whose fuller participation the future of the art of music waits." Citing the interpretive power of "dial twiddling," Gould argued that technology would shift "decision-making capacities" from musical establishment specialists to ordinary people, whose "properly self-indulgent participation" would transform the work from an "artistic to environmental experience." Musicality itself would be revolutionized: "In the best of all possible worlds, art would be unnecessary. Its offer of restorative, placative therapy would go begging a patient. The professional specialization involved in its making would be presumption. The generalities of its applicability would be an affront. The audience would be the artist and their life would be art."[1]

Such pronouncements were not uncommon in avant-garde circles in the mid-1960s (one might compare it to Roland Barthes's 1967 essay "Death of the Author"), but unlike most declarations about the future of art, Gould's predictions have largely come true. We live in a time when audiencing has become the dominant form of musicking for a majority of people in the Western world. Reggae and rap, with their recombination and layering of beats, refrains, and sounds from obscure tracks in the recorded history of music are essentially listeners' musics, dependent on a fan/listener's sensibility. The rise of easily exchangeable digital music files, made portable by ubiquitous iPods, mp3 players, and cell phones, has woven music even more deeply into previously "non-musical" experiences, including everything from jogging to doing the laundry. While listeners rarely twiddle dials anymore, Garage Band grooves, mash-ups, and other homemade remixes are evidence that ordinary people are, in fact, engaging in a great deal of decision making inside the music they *hear.*

Fandom, as both a personal and social expression of audience enthusiasm, was considered a suspicious activity as late as the 1980s, but today identifying passionately with a band is now an acceptable activity of self-definition, cultivated by Internet sites like MySpace and YouTube and even by a struggling record industry desperate to sell deluxe box sets and special concert promotions. Indeed, everyday life, which was formerly considered so separate from the institutionalized world of music as to necessitate a scholarly subfield, now seems to be the very ground on which music has significance. Recent work in sociology and ethnomusicology has shown clearly that listening, consuming, and audiencing have come to serve a number of meaningful functions for people in modern society, including developing self-identity, managing emotion, and establishing social relationships. As Tia DeNora says, we "aesthetize" ourselves through listening—we bring ourselves to life.[2]

Contemporary American culture does not get much respect in institutions of music education, where the idea of engaging in music *only through the act of listening* is at best a sign of dilettantism and at worst a symbol of our society's decreasing level of musical literacy. Despite their dedication to fostering an understanding about music through listening and analysis, departments of music at American colleges and universities are primarily vocational, focusing on the production of professional musicians and diminishing—through requirements and teaching techniques—knowledge of music created by listening. Most departments require at least two semesters of ensemble experience and/or keyboard proficiency for undergraduate majors, many have auditions for admission, and programs uniformly describe their mission in terms of musicianship, including photographs of their concert facilities and people playing instruments, either with master-teachers in a studio or on stage before an audience.[3]

Even the field of ethnomusicology, which was founded as an alternative to traditional musicology, and which one would think would be open to different sorts of musical experience, idealizes performance. In 1998, on the Internet discussion group run by the Society for Ethnomusicology, several scholars argued that the prevalence of music listening had made Americans less "musical" than people in other countries. As one said, "I think we tend to believe there are more people out there who can perform music or at least know something about it because we are constantly around people who can. Go meet people in the corporate world, down at the local Little League game, a restaurant, a small town church . . . you will find the majority of people there are lacking in musical knowledge."[4] I and a few others tried to argue in favor of the rich musical knowledge of popular music fans, but such efforts were met with disdain from another colleague:

It cannot be denied that actually performing music, playing an instrument or singing, opens up vast vistas of musical understanding. . . . Does a childhood spent surrounded by musical wallpaper in a shopping centre really inform a person IN THE SAME WAY as actually learning an instrument as a child? Should we really try to compare that kind of musical experience with that of an Aboriginal child who may spend a significant part of his or her life surrounded by parents, grandparents, uncles, brothers, and other assorted kin, all frequently involved in musical performance for weeks at a time?[5]

Music history doesn't fare much better, since listening is often understood with a definition of "music" that emphasizes performance, style, and technique and thereby misses entirely practices of listening that have been shaped around varieties of sensation, memory, and identity. As a well-known music education text from the 1990s explained, in a chapter section titled "passive listening":

The richness of American concert life led to passive participation. Music became a connoisseur art heard in concert halls, rather than an integral part of everyday life in which great numbers of people participated. School bands, orchestras, and choruses changed this somewhat throughout the twentieth century. Even so, despite their wealth of performing experiences as students, most of the children who participated did not continue to do so after completing their schooling. . . . For a time (until the 1930s) it was common for industry to sponsor choruses, bands, and orchestras comprised of its own employees; some industrial music ensembles still exist, but not to the extent of earlier years. This was a generous and humanistic aspect of some American industrial corporations, but most of these organizations have been replaced by piped-in "canned" music, selected for its ability to create an environment conducive to greater productivity. The loss of so many of these participative activities is a loss to American society.[6]

In his 2000 book on music in the daily lives of Americans between 1800 and 1861, musicologist Nicholas Tawa concluded that "similarities between then and now . . . exist. Music is still ubiquitous throughout the country. However, the tendency is toward more passive listening, not active participation."[7] In 2009, the Iowa Music Educator's Association, in response to the elimination of music programs in schools, argued for a "common sense" advocacy of the importance of musical performance as a bulwark against music consumption:

[One hundred] years ago, everyone sang with their families, at home, and in church. Since then, the advent of radio, television, and recorded music has transformed music from an active part of everyday life to a professional activity reserved for the "talented." In our elementary music classes, every child can and does make music, instrumental, vocal, solo, small group, and large group. They come to understand music making once again as an integral part of being human, as opposed to a form of passive entertainment.[8]

These are powerful assertions, but they make for neither good sociology nor history. To simply dismiss the audience activities of an increasing number of Americans as not really a form of participation, or to gloss over the complexities of listening as it has developed in history, reflects badly on music scholarship and is bound to weaken its ability to make a difference among both students and the general public. In particular, the binary of "active or passive" has lost whatever analytical meaning it once might have had, since its use (in the aforementioned excerpts, and others) rarely takes listening at face value, as it is practiced and experienced, but tends to reduce listening to an abstract, catch-all, anti-category of "not-playing" or "not-singing."[9]

In this book, I have tried to begin to recover the history of listening in America by exploring the potential origins of current practices that link audiencing, consumption, and musicality. Rather than framing that constellation of ideas as inherently negative or positive, however, I have attempted to focus on its meanings by examining the descriptive fragments left to us by early listeners themselves: young clerks struck by an "opera house" while making their way in the city, middle-class housewives exploring the limits of sensibility, brothers waiting impatiently to catch a glimpse of Jenny Lind outside her hotel. What kinds of conclusions might be drawn from seriously considering and valuing the musical environments in which these people lived and the decisions they made about their own participation in music?

Music lovers' diaries show that consumption was certainly an integral part of their experiences. Music listening emerged as a distinct and meaningful activity at a time when urban entrepreneurs were searching for ways to profit from music beyond the markets for instruments, music lessons, and sheet music; concerts were a means to demonstrate goods, create attention, and boost sales. Before concert programs came to feature serious aesthetic commentary about performances, they functioned as sensationalistic advertisements, guides to the availability of sheet music souvenirs, instruments similar to those played onstage, and seemingly random announcements for shoes, powders, and hats, as well as future acts—virtuoso singers, magicians, dancers, minstrel troupes—arriving in the city. Buying tickets reflected acquiescence to this marketplace of culture, and music lovers knew it, often tallying up their expenses and wondering about the worth of their purchases.

However, to see participation in a concert as an audience member as merely an example of people accepting the frameworks of the commercial market or as an example of encroaching passivity egregiously reduces the significance what was happening. Entrepreneurs' development of concert culture required a great deal of experimentation and public education, not to mention the coincidental rise of a middle class seeking to distinguish itself culturally, new transportation networks that facilitated building and movement of musical goods, and increased urban migration. These shifts cultivated a younger generation of new urban dwellers who were more willing than their parents or grandparents to try new behaviors.

For early music lovers, embracing cities' growing world of commercial entertainment was a thrilling act. Their fascination with "publicization" and exhibitions indicated a desire that was far more than a lust for goods. Audiences for singing families and other amateur performers in the 1840s, for example, extolled the private unseen practices of others as a means to confirm a shared, homegrown American culture, something that resonated in a changing society where standards for behavior seemed less rooted and such shared culture seemed absent. Reformers a decade later had similar concerns about American society—for them, listening was a means to a shared, uplifting, musical democracy. More selfishly, perhaps, concert-goers for much of the century simply expressed excitement about the possibility of using the marketplace of music to shape a sense of their own lives. This can be seen in the changing language of diarists, who, beginning at mid-century, talked about being able to *choose* to experience a particular performer or piece rather than simply "having music." It was also central to the earnestness with which music lovers were fascinated with performers who reflected their own changing thoughts, emotions, and ideals.

The social function of music listening has to be balanced, of course, with the fact that in the nineteenth century, it was never a single phenomenon of consumption but rather, like musical performance, an act that varied considerably and thus bore the weight of multiple, simultaneous—and sometimes contradictory—definitions and meanings. Behavior at any one concert varied, based on one's education, class, and the kinds of previous listening experiences and expectations one brought to balconies and the pit. Concert going had different meanings for single men, men and women of color, and married middle-class women. Even the criticisms of music loving were based on different fears and anxieties, about loss of individuality, crowd disorder, and transgressions of gender roles. Over time, the open and wide-ranging embrace of urban entertainment experienced by young men like Nathan Beekley in Philadelphia, or William Hoffman in New York City, or Francis Bennett in Boston was joined by the more educated, focused, and intense listening of George Templeton Strong or Lucy Lowell.

Beyond that: even while listening was one of the more extraordinary consequences of the commercialization of culture in the middle of the nineteenth century, it did not necessarily "force out" other musical behaviors. In fact, while listening was being institutionalized at concerts, piano manufacturing and amateur piano playing were also growing. Arthur Loesser estimated that in 1870 approximately one out of every 1,540 bought a new piano in the course of the year; that amounted to eighty persons a day investing in a large musical instrument for the home. Not surprisingly, piano playing and parlor performance were accompanied by a demand for sheet music, something that was satisfied by the publication of simplified "adaptations" of operas and concertos, as well as songs.[10] Music education grew, as well, with large numbers of piano teachers, singing instructors, and music tutors advertising their expertise for middle-class families.

Today, it might be natural to ask how, for instance, the rise of commercialized concert listening and the rise of amateur piano playing squared with one another. But this seems not to have been a problem for most nineteenth-century Americans, at least not until after the turn of the century. The best example of this might be the player piano, which first went on the market in 1895. It notably represented a combination of musical behaviors and values: it was a playback device, asking users to listen to it, but at the same time, it was a musical instrument, emphasizing the value of performance. Historian Carl Roell explains that the player pianos, before losing favor in the 1920s, were embraced by music educators as an important teaching tool and were sold alongside regular pianos in an effort to promote "musical democracy."[11] The phonograph was similar. While bandleader John Philip Sousa denounced it as a national threat, for much of the early 1900s the phonograph was generally understood as a powerful means to disseminate "good music" into the home or in schools. For some, record playing and instrument playing were explicitly linked, in that early Edison cylinder machines allowed amateur musicians to record and play back their own performances.[12]

Of course, I don't mean to suggest that every kind of musical engagement was valued equally; criticism of more exuberant types of music listening from Jenny Lind mania onward is enough to dispel such notions. And hardening distinctions of high/classical and low/popular culture from the

1880s would more concretely sort out and institutionalize the value of different kinds of performing and listening by the 1930s. But the introduction of regular opportunities to publicly hear music, alongside more traditional means of making music at home or in communal occasions, at least encouraged vigorous debate in the latter half of the nineteenth century about the nature of musical participation. "Music" was being defined in multiple ways simultaneously: singing in church choirs, attending lectures on Beethoven, going to an annual dance, taking piano lessons, getting a job as a musician, attending concerts, and so on. What did any musical interest or activity signify exactly about one's musical abilities or desires? What did it signify about one's culture? These questions were answered forcefully by reformers and critics in publications like *Dwight's Journal* or the *Atlantic Monthly* throughout the latter nineteenth century. Such questions, too, were pondered more privately by music lovers, and they did not always arrive at the same conclusions.

Glenn Gould suggested that the potential changes wrought by recording technology and the new power of listening would result, ultimately, in a "participational overlapping" where composers, performers, listeners, and even advertising men might take on the tasks and attitudes previously attributed to each other. Gould's notion of environmentalism was a bit too technologically determined; we don't necessarily need recording to arrive at such a situation. It was also too abstract—musical environments would likely only be sustained in specific contexts shaped by historical and cultural forces. But his point is well taken. Just as the introduction of listening suggested in the nineteenth century, our current moment—a digital world of fan mash-ups and virtuosic deejaying, where "participational overlapping" seems commonplace—suggests that there might be other ways to think about music.

We no longer need to be locked into the frameworks that abstractly privilege the performer and the work and instead have the opportunity to think more broadly about what "music" is, or how traditional roles might be transformed or reemphasized. Musicians and fans are certainly exploring the possibilities of participation, as are fellow scholars in law, sociology, and the sciences who are rethinking music copyright, cognition, and therapy. History is not immune; we can, if we wish, move away from what Gould would have called "artistic" accounts of the past to those that are more "environmental," those that more fully and seriously address the interrelationships of possible musical roles and activities in American society. My small attempt to recover and include the place of music listening in the everyday life of nineteenth-century Americans is, I hope, but one move toward that end.

Notes

Introduction

1. Edward Bellamy, *Looking Backward: 2000–1887* (New York: Penguin Books, 1982), 97–100.

2. Steven Levy, *The Perfect Thing: How the iPod Shuffles Commerce, Culture, and Coolness* (New York: Simon & Schuster, 2006). The National Association of Music Merchants (NAMM) reports that the percentage of households with at least one person who plays a musical instrument was 52 percent in 2006, with 42 percent participating in school music programs. See "2007 NAMM Global Report: A Statistical Review of the Music Products Industry," National Association of Music Merchants, www.nxtbook.com/nxtbooks/namm/2008musicusa. A Pew Research Center poll from the same year indicated that 34 percent of all Americans owned an mp3 player, with 61 percent among the age group 18 to 29. Data from 2009 indicates that ownership of mp3 players has risen significantly, with 43 percent of the adult population owning a digital playback device and 79 percent of those aged 12 to 17. See "Social Media Among Young Adults," February 2010, Pew Research Center, www.pewinternet.org/Reports/2010/Social-Media-and-Young-Adults.asp.

3. On the appeal of mechanical music in the nineteenth century, see Theresa Magdanz, "The Waltz: Technology's Muse," *Journal of Popular Music Studies* 18, no. 3 (2006): 251–81. For discussions of Edison's intentions for the phonograph, see Lisa Gitelman, *Scripts, Grooves, and Writing Machines: Representing Technology in the Edison Era* (Palo Alto, Calif.: Stanford University Press, 1999), 62–96; Emily Thompson, "Machines, Music, and the Quest for Fidelity," *Musical Quarterly* 79, no. 1 (1995): 131–71; and Andre Millard, *Edison and the Business of Innovation* (Baltimore: Johns Hopkins University Press, 1993), 162–66.

4. See, for example, Daniel Kingman, *American Music: A Panorama* (New York: Schirmer, 1979); Charles Hamm, *Music in the New World* (New York: W. W. Norton, 1983); H. Wiley Hitchcock, *Music in the United States: A Historical Introduction* (Englewood Cliffs, N.J.: Prentice Hall, 1988); and Gilbert Chase, *America's Music: From the Pilgrims to the Present* (Urbana: University of Illinois Press, 1992). Richard

Crawford's *America's Musical Life: A History* (New York: W. W. Norton, 2005) is a recent exception, offering a broader cultural account of music in the United States than is typical.

5. *Musicking* is a term, coined by musicologist Christopher Small, that accounts for "the act of taking part in a musical performance." It suggests a move toward an understanding of music not only as a thing to be performed but as one that encompasses a wider variety of actions and relationships involved in any performance, from rehearsing to performing to listening and dancing. See Christopher Small, *Music of the Common Tongue* (London: Calder Publications, 1987), 50, and *Musicking: The Meanings of Performing and Listening* (Middletown, Conn.: Wesleyan University Press, 1998). Following Small's lead, I employ the term *audiencing* in this book with similar intentions: to get away from a narrow modern idea of a listener, passively consuming a recording, and to move toward the wider array of behaviors that I describe in this book.

6. The subject of the phonograph is a good case in point. Many excellent histories of the phonograph interpret its invention as a determining moment that suddenly created new behaviors and perceptions, an analytical move that automatically makes consumption secondary to invention and production. See Jonathan Sterne, *The Audible Past: Cultural Origins of Sound Reproduction* (Durham, N.C.: Duke University Press, 2003), and Timothy D. Taylor, "The Commodification of Music at the Dawn of the Era of 'Mechanical Music,'" *Ethnomusicology* 51, no. 2 (2007): 281–305.

7. See Leon Botstein, "Toward a History of Listening," *Musical Quarterly* 82, nos. 3–4 (1998): 427–31. A notable exception is William Weber, *Music and the Middle Class: The Social Structure of Concert Life in London, Paris, and Vienna* (Aldershot: Ashgate, 2004).

8. Recent musicological works on European audiences include David P. Schroeder, *Haydn and the Enlightenment: The Late Symphonies and Their Audience* (New York: Oxford University Press, 1990); Thomas Forrest Kelly, *First Nights: Five Musical Premieres* (New Haven: Yale University Press, 2001); Dana Gooley, *The Virtuoso Liszt* (Cambridge: Cambridge University Press, 2004); and Antje Pieper, *Music and the Making of Middle-Class Culture: A Comparative History of Nineteenth-Century Leipzig and Birmingham* (Basingstoke: Palgrave Macmillan, 2008). Recent musicological works on historical American music audiences include Katherine K. Preston, *Opera on the Road: Traveling Opera Troupes in the United States, 1825–60* (Urbana: University of Illinois Press, 1993); Joseph Horowitz, *Wagner Nights: An American History* (Berkeley: University of California Press, 1994); Karen Alquist, *Democracy at the Opera* (Urbana: University of Illinois Press, 1997); and Nicholas Tawa, *High-Minded and Low-Down: Music in the Lives of Americans, 1800–1861* (Boston: Northeastern University Press, 2000).

9. An extraordinary and, to date, unique work in this vein is Vera Brodsky Lawrence's three-volume set on the musical life of New York attorney George Templeton Strong, based on his diary. See Vera Brodsky Lawrence, *Strong on Music*, vol. 1, *Resonances, 1836–1850* (Chicago: University of Chicago Press, 1988); *Strong on Music*, vol. 2, *Reverberations, 1850–1856* (Chicago: University of Chicago Press, 1995); *Strong on Music*, vol. 3, *Repercussions, 1857–1862* (Chicago: University of Chicago Press, 1998).

10. Keil introduced these terms in a keynote talk, "Moving and Grooving: Popular Music in the Lives of Children" (paper presented at the symposium "Around the Sound: Popular Music in Performance, Education, and Scholarship," University of Washington, 11 May 2000).

11. Leon Botstein, *Music and Its Public: Habits of Listening and the Crisis of Musical Modernism in Vienna, 1870–1914* (Ph.D. diss., Harvard University, 1985).

12. Carole Shammas, *The Pre-Industrial Consumer in England and America* (New York: Oxford University Press, 1990), 294.

13. James H. Johnson, *Listening in Paris: A Cultural History* (Berkeley: University of California Press, 1995), 281–84.

14. Work on the pacifying of American audiences includes Paul DiMaggio, "Cultural Entrepreneurship in Nineteenth-Century Boston: The Creation of an Organizational Base for High Culture in America," *Media, Culture and Society* 4 (1982); Lawrence Levine, *Highbrow/Lowbrow: The Emergence of Cultural Hierarchy in America* (Cambridge, Mass.: Harvard University Press, 1988); and John F. Kasson, *Rudeness and Civility: Manners in Nineteenth-Century America* (Hill & Wang, 1990).

15. Considering the "critical reception" of a specific work or composer, for example, has become a standard means for thinking about audience in musicology. Each book in Oxford University Press's "Studies in Musical Genesis, Structure, and Interpretation Series," for example, features an overview of a famed symphonic work, including its "critical reception."

16. My experiences with the distorted accounts of media fandom in contemporary journalism have made me suspicious of such sources in the past. See Daniel Cavicchi, *Tramps Like Us: Music and Meaning among Springsteen Fans* (New York: Oxford University Press, 1998), 3–21.

17. Weber, *Music and the Middle Class*, 120.

18. Richard Butsch, *The Making of American Audiences: From Stage to Television, 1750–1990* (New York: Cambridge University Press, 2000), vii.

19. Dena J. Epstein, *Sinful Tunes and Spirituals: Black Folk Music to the Civil War* (Urbana: University of Illinois Press, 1977).

20. Silent listening among European audiences has been taken up specifically in Botstein, *Music and Its Public*; Peter Gay, *The Bourgeois Experience: Victoria to Freud* (New York: W. W. Norton, 1995); and Johnson, *Listening in Paris*.

21. Susan J. Douglas, *Listening In: Radio and the American Imagination* (New York: Times Books, 1999); William H. Kenney, *Recorded Music in American Life: The Phonograph and Popular Memory 1890–1945* (New York: Oxford University Press, 1999); Andre Millard, *America on Record* (Cambridge: Cambridge University Press, 1995).

22. A good summary of the work in acoustic history can be found in Mark M. Smith, ed., *Hearing History: A Reader* (Athens: University of Georgia Press, 2004).

23. Cathy Davidson, *Revolution and the Word: The Rise of the Novel in America* (New York: Oxford University Press, 1986); Robert Darnton, *The Great Cat Massacre and Other Episodes in French Cultural History* (New York: Vintage Books, 1984); Jonathan Rose, *The Intellectual Life of the British Working Classes* (New Haven: Yale University Press, 2001).

24. Scott Casper, *Constructing American Lives: Biography and Culture in Nineteenth-Century America* (Chapel Hill: University of North Carolina Press, 1999).

25. See Steven Rendall, "On Diaries," *Diacritics* 16, no. 3 (1986): 57–65; Marilyn Ferris Motz, "Folk Expression of Time and Place: Nineteenth-Century Midwestern Rural Diaries," *Journal of American Folklore* 100, no. 396 (1987): 131–47; and Jane H. Hunter, "Inscribing the Self in the Heart of the Family: Diaries and Girlhood in America," *American Quarterly* 44, no. 1 (1992): 51–81.

26. Overviews include Robert Darnton, "History and Anthropology," in *The Kiss of the Lamourette: Reflections in Cultural History* (New York: W. W. Norton, 1990), 329–54; Clifford Geertz, "History and Anthropology," *New Literary History* 21, no. 2 (1990): 321–35; and Susan Kellogg, "Histories for Anthropology: Ten Years of Historical Research and Writing by Anthropologists, 1980–1990," *Social Science History* 15, no. 4 (1991): 417–55.

27. Rhys Isaac, *The Transformation of Virginia, 1740–1790* (Chapel Hill: University of North Carolina Press, 1982), 326.

28. Darnton, *The Great Cat Massacre*, 77–78.

29. For more recent thinking about the connections between the archive and the field, see Nicholas B. Dirks, "Annals of the Archive: Ethnographic Notes on the Sources of History," in *From the Margins: Historical Anthropology and Its Futures*, Brian Keith Axel, ed. (Durham, N.C.: Duke University Press, 2002), 47–65; William Kornblum, "Discovering Ink: A Mentor for Historical Ethnography," *Annals of the American Academy of Political and Social Science* 595 (Sept. 2004): 176–89; and Sue Waterman, "Collecting the Nineteenth Century," in *Representations* 90 (Spring 2005): 98–128. The process I describe may not be so strange to historians like John Lewis Gaddis, who reject the social scientific basis of history and emphasize its humanist aims. See John Lewis Gaddis, *The Landscape of History: How Historians Map the Past* (New York: Oxford University Press, 2004).

30. I have built on the ground-breaking diary research of Katherine Preston in both *Opera on the Road* and *Music for Hire: A Study of Professional Musicians in Washington, 1877–1900* (Hillsdale, N.J.: Pendragon Press, 1992), as well as Nicholas Tawa, *High-Minded and Low-Down*.

31. The increasing digitization of archival materials, coinciding with the full-fledged launch of Googlebooks in 2007 in the middle of my investigation, changed my initial practices immensely, offering the possibility of keyword searching of texts. While unpublished diaries and letters are not generally digitized, and while I believe that keyword searching cannot substitute for actual engagement with an entire text, digitization nevertheless enabled me to more easily investigate certain ideas and terms in the public record. The full ramifications of digitization have yet to be felt in scholarship; its merits and drawbacks will certainly be debated for years to come.

32. I have written previously about the methods of this project, including my site visits, in an online dialogue with literary scholar Barbara Therese Ryan, "History and Fan Studies: A Conversation between Barbara Ryan and Dan Cavicchi," posted March 2009, Confessions of an Aca-Fan: the Official Weblog of Henry Jenkins, http://henryjenkins.org/2009/03/a_conversation_between_barbara.html.

Chapter 1: "P. T. Barnum, Introducing Madelle. Jenny Lind to Ossian E. Dodge": Capitalizing on Music in the Antebellum Era

1. The opening narrative I offer, here, is based primarily on contemporary newspaper accounts, as well as descriptions in J. T. Trowbridge, *My Own Story, with Recollections of Noted Persons* (Boston: Houghton Mifflin, 1903); and Asmodeus, *The Jenny Lind Mania in Boston or, a Sequel to Barnum's Parnassus* (Boston: n.p., 1850). While I believe that the historical details are accurate, I nevertheless have taken descriptive liberties to evoke the moment, especially in the dialogue.

2. P. T. Barnum, *The Life of P. T. Barnum, Written by Himself* (Urbana: University of Illinois Press, 2000), 309.

3. The background details differ slightly between the lithograph and a later sheet music print. In the lithograph, there is clearly a mirror on the wall.

4. Neil Harris, Barnum's biographer, deftly articulated the idealized meanings of this particular scene for those who saw it in 1850s Boston by juxtaposing it with an editorial cartoon that depicted Jenny Lind's massive and unruly urban audiences. Neil Harris, *Humbug: The Art of P. T. Barnum* (Boston: Little, Brown, 1973), 127.

5. "Programme of Mademoiselle Jenny Lind's Concert: With the Words of the Airs in Italian, German, Swedish and English" (Boston: White & Potter, 1850), Theater Collection, Massachusetts Historical Society.

6. *Biographical, Historical, and Incidental Sketch of Ossian E. Dodge* (Boston: Wright & Potter, 1860).

7. Oliver Wendell Holmes, *The Professor at the Breakfast-Table* (Boston: Ticknor & Fields, 1860), 208.

8. The beginnings of concert life were first detailed in a book by Oscar Sonneck, *Early Concert Life in America, 1731–1800* (Leipzig: Breitkopf & Härtel, 1907). For more overviews of musical life in early America, see Kenneth Silverman, *A Cultural History of the American Revolution: Painting, Music, Literature, and the Theatre in the Colonies and the United States from the Treaty of Paris to the Inauguration of George Washington, 1763–1789* (New York: Thomas Crowell, 1976), and John Ogasapian, *Music of the Colonial and Revolutionary Era* (Westport, Conn.: Greenwood Press, 2004). Other useful summaries can be found in Chase, *America's Music*; Russell Sanjek, *American Popular Music and Its Business, The First Four Hundred Years*, vol. 2, *From 1790 to 1909* (New York: Oxford University Press, 1988); David Nicholls, ed., *The Cambridge History of American Music* (Cambridge: Cambridge University Press, 1998); and Crawford, *America's Musical Life*.

9. Attendance by free blacks was segregated and sometimes problematic. For an engaging exploration of African American participation in theater, see Marvin McAllister, *White People Do Not Know How to Behave at Entertainments Designed for Ladies and Gentlemen of Colour: William Brown's African and American Theater* (Chapel Hill: University of North Carolina Press, 2003).

10. For overviews of the development of the business and structure of American theater in the early 1800s, see David Grimstead, *American Theater and Culture, 1800–*

1850 (Berkeley: University of California Press, 1987); Don B. Wilmeth and Christopher Bigsby, *The Cambridge History of American Theatre*, vol. 1 (Cambridge: Cambridge University Press, 1998); and Rosemarie K. Bank, *Theatre Culture in America, 1825–1860* (Cambridge: Cambridge University Press, 2003). Musical theater in the antebellum era is specifically addressed by Julian Mates, *America's Musical Stage: Two Hundred Years of Musical Theater* (Westport, Conn.: Greenwood Press, 1987); Preston, *Opera on the Road*; Alquist, *Democracy at the Opera*; and Dale Cockrell, *Demons of Disorder: Early Blackface Minstrels and Their World* (Cambridge: Cambridge University Press, 1997).

11. See Nicholas Michael Butler, *Votaries of Apollo: The St. Cecilia Society and the Patronage of Concert Music in Charleston, South Carolina, 1766–1820* (Columbia: University of South Carolina Press, 2007), and Michael Broyles, *Music of the Highest Class: Elitism and Populism in Antebellum Boston* (New Haven: Yale University Press, 1992). Nathan Webb, a young man in Boston, wrote in his diary about establishing a music society in Boston in the 1790s; interestingly, the society decided to admit women. Nathan Webb, 10 March 1789 to 14 April 1789, diary, Nathan Webb Diary, Massachusetts Historical Society.

12. See, for example, the descriptions in Mary Caroline Crawford, *Social Life of Old New England* (Boston: Little, Brown, 1915).

13. Silverman, *A Cultural History of the American Revolution*, 37.

14. Eliza Susan Quincy, 17 January 1816, journal, *Quincy, Wendell, Holmes, and Upham Family Papers, 1633–1910*, microfilm edition, 67 reels (Boston: Massachusetts Historical Society, 1977), reel 5, Massachusetts Historical Society.

15. Lawrence, *Strong on Music*, vol. 1, 194.

16. The best overall explanation of the economic and social change of America after the War of 1812 remains Charles Sellers, *The Market Revolution: Jacksonian America, 1815–1846* (New York: Oxford University Press, 1991). The idea of a market revolution remains somewhat controversial, however. See, for example, Daniel Walker Howe's alternative conception in *What God Hath Wrought: The Transformation of America, 1815–1848* (New York: Oxford University Press, 2007). Daniel Feller also advocates caution in "The Market Revolution Ate My Homework," in *Reviews in American History* 25, no. 3 (1997): 408–15.

17. Alexis de Tocqueville, *Democracy in America*, vol. 2 (New York: Vintage Books, 1990), 51.

18. Scholars are only beginning to explore the cultural effects of the market revolution. See Scott C. Martin, *Cultural Change and the Market Revolution in America, 1789–1860* (Lanham, Md.: Rowan & Littlefield, 2004).

19. Sanjek, *American Popular Music and Its Business*, 16.

20. Quoted in Chase, *America's Music*, 102.

21. Thomas N. Baker, *Sentiment and Celebrity: Nathaniel Parker Willis and the Trials of Literary Fame* (New York: Oxford University Press, 1999), 107. See also Preston, *Opera on the Road*, 122–29.

22. Joseph Sill, 4 December 1840, Joseph Sill Diary, collection #600, vol. 2, The Historical Society of Pennsylvania.

23. Howard P. Chudacoff and Judith E. Smith, *The Evolution of American Urban Society*, 4th ed. (Englewood Cliffs, N.J.: Prentice Hall, 1994), 77–110.

24. De Tocqueville, *Democracy in America*, 157.

25. Alquist, *Democracy at the Opera*, 43–44.

26. R. Allen Lott, *From Paris to Peoria: How European Piano Virtuosos Brought Classical Music to America's Heartland* (New York: Oxford University Press, 2003), 5; Arthur Loesser, *Men, Women, and Pianos: A Social History* (New York: Dover Publications, 1990), 481.

27. Preston, *Opera on the Road*, 254.

28. Louis Moreau Gottschalk, *Notes of a Pianist* (Princeton: Princeton University Press, 2006).

29. Katherine Preston, "Art Music from 1800 to 1860," in Nicholls, ed., *The Cambridge History of American Music*, 192.

30. Stuart Blumin, "The Hypothesis of Middle-Class Formation in Nineteenth-Century America: A Critique and Some Proposals," *American Historical Review* 90, no. 2 (1985): 299–338. See also William Weber, "The Muddle of the Middle Classes," *19th-Century Music* 4, no. 2 (1979): 175–85.

31. Richard Bushman, *The Refinement of America: Persons, Houses, Cities.* (New York: Vintage Books, 1993); Seth Rockman, *Scraping by: Wage Labor, Slavery, and Survival in Early Baltimore* (Baltimore: Johns Hopkins University Press, 2008).

32. Brian P. Luskey, "Jumping Counters in White Collars: Manliness, Respectability, and Work in the Antebellum City," *Journal of the Early Republic* 26, no. 2 (2006): 174.

33. Thomas Augst, *The Clerk's Tale: Young Men and Moral Life in Nineteenth-Century America* (Chicago: University of Chicago Press, 2003), 175.

34. De Tocqueville, *Democracy in America*, 217.

35. Lucy Buckminster Emerson Lowell, 28 November 1845, diary, Lucy Lowell Diaries, Massachusetts Historical Society.

36. Karen Halttunen, *Confidence Men and Painted Women: A Study of Middle-Class Culture in America, 1830–1870* (New Haven: Yale University Press, 1988), xv.

37. John Evelev, *Tolerable Entertainment: Herman Melville and Professionalism in Antebellum New York* (Amherst: University of Massachusetts Press, 2006), 6.

38. The best scholarship on American genteel culture includes Mary P. Ryan, *Cradle of the Middle Class: The Family in Oneida County, New York, 1790–1865* (Cambridge: Cambridge University Press, 1981); Halttunen, *Confidence Men and Painted Women*; Stuart Blumin, *The Emergence of the Middle Class: Social Experience in the American City, 1760–1900* (Cambridge: Cambridge University Press, 1989); and Bushman, *The Refinement of America*.

39. Evelev, *Tolerable Entertainment*, 123. Bruce A. Kimball is emphatic that the term "professional" was limited to a small number of occupations in the antebellum era, but he concedes the presence of "interlopers into the professions," including those engaged in the "business of commerce." See Bruce A. Kimball, *The True Professional Ideal in America: A History* (New York: Rowman & Littlefield), 8.

40. Lawrence, *Strong on Music*, vol. 1, 169.

41. Julia Eklund Koza, "Music and the Feminine Sphere: Images of Women as

Musicians in 'Godey's Lady's Book,' 1830–1877," *Musical Quarterly* 75, no. 2 (1991): 103–29. See also Judith Tick, "Passed Away Is the Piano Girl: Changes in American Musical Life, 1870–1900," in *Women Making Music: The Western Art Tradition, 1150–1950*, Jane Bowers and Judith Tick, eds. (Urbana: University of Illinois Press, 1987), 325–48; and Ruth Solie, "'Girling' at the Parlor Piano," in *Music in Other Words: Victorian Conversations* (Berkeley: University of California Press, 2004), 85–117.

42. Phrases in programs for various concerts in Buffalo, N.Y., between 1850 and 1880 will suffice: "The Cornet used by Mr. Levy is the Celebrated 'Courtois Cornet.' Edward Hopkins, 861 Broadway, MY, Sole Agent in America" or "The magnificent Grand Piano used by Mr. Liebling has been obtained by Messrs. Wahle & Songs, from the celebrated Manufactory of Chickering & Songs, expressly for this occasion. Wahle & Songs, Sole Agts. for Buffalo, for Chickering & Sons' Grand Square and Upright Pianos, 355 Main Street." Collection of Concert Programs, Vertical File: Music Programs, Research Library and Archives, Buffalo and Erie County Historical Society.

43. Lawrence, *Strong on Music*, vol. 1, 347. Such native-born families were inspired by the 1839 tour of the Swiss Rainier Family, followed by a wave of subsequent European family singers, especially from Ireland and Germany. See Hans Nathan, "The Tyrolese Family Rainer, and the Vogue of Singing Mountain Troupes in Europe and America," *Musical Quarterly* 32, no. 1 (1946): 63–79.

44. Quoted in Robert D. Faner, *Walt Whitman and Opera* (Carbondale: Southern Illinois University Press, 1951), 36.

45. Van Wyck Brooks, *The Flowering of New England, 1815–1865* (New York: E. P. Dutton, 1937), 180.

46. Lawrence, *Strong on Music*, vol. 1, 129–30.

47. There is a clear need for a comparative survey of commercial music establishments in America's major cities in the antebellum era. City directories and local histories appear to be the best sources, but the work of sifting through the types of establishments (as well as the changes in ownership and name for the same building over time) is enormous and would require years of careful study. Useful works about Boston's changing performance venues include: William Clapp, *A Record of the Boston Stage*; John S. Dwight, "Music in Boston," in *The Memorial History of Boston, including Suffolk County, Massachusetts, 1630–1880*, 4 vols., Justin Winsow, ed. (Boston: James R. Osgood, 1881): 415–64; William Arms Fisher, *Notes on Music in Old Boston* (Boston: Oliver Ditson, 1918); H. Earle Johnson, *Musical Interludes in Boston, 1795–1830* (New York: Columbia University Press, 1943); Donald C. King, *The Theaters of Boston: A Stage and Screen History* (Jefferson, N.C.: McFarland Press, 2005); Moses King, *King's Handbook of Boston* (Cambridge: Moses King Publisher, 1878); R. L. Midgley, *Sights in Boston and Suburbs, or Guide to the Stranger* (Boston: John P. Jewett, 1856); Kate Ryan, *Old Boston Museum Days* (Boston: Little Brown, 1915); Douglass Shand-Tucci, *Built in Boston: City and Suburb, 1800–2000*, 3rd ed. (Amherst: University of Massachusetts Press, 1999); and Eugene Tompkins, *The History of the Boston Theatre* (Boston: Houghton Mifflin, 1908).

48. William E. Clapp, Jr., *A Record of the Boston Stage* (New York: Benjamin Blom, 1968), 439.

49. Lawrence, *Strong on Music*, vol. 1, 234.

50. See Lawrence, *Strong on Music*, vol. 1, 94–107 and 129–45. De Meyer's scheme is described in Lott, *From Paris to Peoria*, 11–28.

51. See Gooley, *The Virtuoso Liszt*; also Paul Metzner, *Crescendo of the Virtuoso* (Berkeley: University of California Press, 1998).

52. Description of Bottesini quoted in Clapp, *A Record of the Boston Stage*, 449. Quotations from Kowalski and Gungl quoted in Philip Hale, "Impressions of Visiting Musicians in New England, 1849–1875," *Proceedings of the Massachusetts Historical Society* 61 (1927–28): 105–16.

53. Loesser, *Men, Women, and Pianos*, 497.

54. H. Earle Johnson, *Musical Interludes in Boston, 1795–1830* (New York: Columbia University Press, 1943), 48–49.

55. Lott, *From Peoria to Paris*, 117.

56. Lott, *From Peoria to Paris*, 42. Arthur Loesser reports pianist Henri Herz hiring "carriages to stand or pass slowly before the doors of the hall just before concert time, so as to give an impression of bustle, on the principle that a crowd draws a crowd." See Loesser, *Men, Women, and Pianos*, 484.

57. Michael Broyles, "Music and Class Structure in Antebellum Boston," *Journal of the American Musicological Society* 44, no. 3 (1991): 451–93.

58. "Programme of Mademoiselle Jenny Lind's Concert."

59. Barnum, *The Life of P. T. Barnum*, 299–302.

60. Sherry Lee Linkon, "Reading Lind Mania: Print Culture and the Construction of Nineteenth-Century Audiences," *Book History* 1 (1998): 94–106.

61. Barnum, *The Life of Barnum*, 297.

62. Lind's appearance at a train station prompted an outcry from the guardians of high culture, who doubled their efforts to complete Boston's Music Hall. See Douglass Shand-Tucci, *Built in Boston*, 23.

63. Barnum's "artful deception" in the urban popular entertainment of the nineteenth century is summarized in James W. Cook, *The Arts of Deception: Playing with Fraud in the Age of Barnum* (Cambridge, Mass.: Harvard University Press, 2001). See also Leo Braudy's discussion in his book *The Frenzy of Renown: Fame and Its History* (New York: Oxford University Press, 1986), 498–506.

64. Bluford Adams, *E Pluribus Barnum: The Great Showman and the Making of U. S. Popular Culture* (Minneapolis: University of Minnesota Press, 1997), 37; P. T. Barnum, *Struggles and Triumphs, or, Sixty Years' Recollection of P. T. Barnum* (Buffalo: Courier, 1889), 495.

65. Trowbridge, *My Own Story*, 162.

66. See Cook, *The Arts of Deception*. In fact, there are interesting parallels between Dodge's career and that of another "comic vocalist" and eventual newspaper editor, George Washington Dixon, who was best known for popularizing the minstrelsy character of Zip Coon in the 1830s. See Cockrell, *Demons of Disorder*.

67. See *Biographical, Historical, and Incidental Sketch of Ossian E. Dodge* (n.p.). Dodge's egomania is rendered best in the actual text of the anecdote:

> On the company being seated at the table, Mr. Clay poured out two glasses of wine, and passing one of them to Mr. Dodge, remarked, in tones sufficiently loud for all to hear, "Mr. Dodge, let us pledge ourselves in a glass of old wine."
>
> Without touching the glass, Mr. Dodge replied, "Excuse me, Mr. Clay; I am a *strict teetotaler*, and with your permission I will pledge you in what is far more emblematical of the purity of true friendship—a glass of pure water."
>
> Mr. Clay slowly replaced the glass of wine upon the table, scanned with his eagle eyes the features of his guest, and discovering no expression but that of unbounded respect, reached across the corner of the table, grasped the hand of his honest friend, and exclaimed, "Mr Dodge, I honor your courage and respect your principles"; and then laughingly added, "but I can't say that I admire your taste."
>
> Mr. Dodge, with his usual promptness of retort, replied, "But is it not the doctrine that our orators are daily teaching us, Mr. Clay, to *throw aside taste for principle?*"
>
> Amid the shouts of laughter that followed, Mr. Clay exclaimed, "Handsomely turned—Charles, remove the wine from the table."

68. Quoted in Don C. Seitz, *Artemus Ward: A Biography and Bibliography* (New York: Harper & Brothers, 1919), 68–69.

69. J. T. Trowbridge [writing as Paul Creyton], *Martin Merrivale, His X Mark* (Boston: Phillips, Sampson, 1854), 179–84 and 232–34.

70. See Philip F. Gura, *C. F. Martin and His Guitars, 1796–1873* (Chapel Hill: University of North Carolina Press, 2003), 91–94.

71. *Literary World* 12: 191, cited in *A Collection of College Words and Customs*, Benjamin Homer Hall, ed. (Cambridge: John Bartlett, 1856).

72. Harris, *Humbug*, 123.

73. Charles G. Rosenberg, *Jenny Lind in America* (New York: Stringer and Townsend, 1851), 44.

74. Quoted in Rosenberg, *Jenny Lind in America*, 43.

75. *Biographical, Historical, and Incidental Sketch of Ossian E. Dodge*, III.

Chapter 2: "I Think I Will Do Nothing . . . But Listen": Forming a New Urban Ear

1. Philip Callow, *From Noon to Starry Night: A Life of Walt Whitman* (Chicago: Ivan R. Dee, 1992), 67.

2. Joel Myerson, ed. *Whitman in His Own Time: A Biographical Chronicle of His Life, Drawn from Recollections, Memoirs, and Interviews by Friends and Associates* (Detroit: Omnigraphics, 1991), 43.

3. Whitman's engagement with the commercial amusements of New York City is summarized in David S. Reynolds, *Walt Whitman's America* (New York: Vintage

Books, 1995), 154–93. See also Robert D. Faner, *Walt Whitman and Music* (Carbondale: Southern Illinois University Press, 1951) and John Dizikes, *Opera in America: A Cultural History* (New Haven: Yale University Press, 1993), 184–88.

4. This approach was established with Faner's *Walt Whitman and Music*. It was more recently articulated by Robert Hampson in a program for public television titled "I Hear America Singing," which focused on American concert song. "Thomas Hampson: I Hear America Singing," Public Broadcasting System, www.pbs.org/wnet/ihas.

5. Reynolds, *Walt Whitman's America*, 156.

6. Walt Whitman, *Poetry and Prose* (New York: Library of America, 1982), 55.

7. Quoted in Reynolds, *Walt Whitman's America*, 174–75.

8. Walt Whitman, *The Portable Walt Whitman*, Mark Van Doren ed. (New York: Penguin, 1973), 586.

9. Walt Whitman, *Poetry and Prose*, 53–54.

10. Walt Whitman, *Poetry and Prose*, 266.

11. While Whitman enjoys transcendent status as one of America's great poets, he was not unlike Ossian Dodge in his movement from one role to another in the new commercial world of publishing, including writing the first reviews of *Leaves of Grass* himself.

12. Reynolds, *Walt Whitman's America*, 49.

13. Gottschalk, *Notes of a Pianist*, 98.

14. See Mark M. Smith, "Producing Sense, Consuming Sense, Making Sense: Perils and Prospects for Sensory History," *Journal of Social History* 40, no. 4 (2007), 841–58. Key works include: Alain Corbin, *Village Bells: Sound and Meaning in the Nineteenth-Century French Countryside* (New York: Columbia University Press, 1994); Bruce R. Smith, *The Acoustic World of Early Modern England: Attending to the O-Factor* (Chicago: University of Chicago Press, 1999); Leigh Eric Schmidt, *Hearing Things: Religion, Illusion, and the American Enlightenment* (Cambridge, Mass.: Harvard University Press, 2000); Peter Charles Hoffer, *Sensory Worlds in Early America* (Baltimore: Johns Hopkins University Press, 2003); Richard Cullen Rath, *How Early America Sounded* (Ithaca: Cornell University Press, 2003); and Shane White and Graham White, *The Sounds of Slavery: Discovering African American History through Songs, Sermons, and Speech* (Boston: Beacon Press, 2005). Anthologies on the history of sound and listening include Michael Bull and Les Back, eds., *The Auditory Culture Reader* (Oxford: Berg Publishers, 2003); Veit Erlmann, ed., *Hearing Cultures: Essays on Sound, Listening and Modernity* (Oxford: Berg Publishers, 2004) and Mark M. Smith, ed. *Hearing History: A Reader* (Athens: University of Georgia Press, 2004).

15. Eighteenth- and nineteenth-century religious hearing is specifically addressed by Schmidt, *Hearing Things*, and Rath, *How Early America Sounded*. The class politics involved in the "objectification" of listening are analyzed by Mark Smith in *Listening to Nineteenth-Century America* and Sterne in *The Audible Past*.

16. John M. Picker, *Victorian Soundscapes* (New York: Oxford University Press, 2003), 14.

17. Francis Bennett, Jr., Diary, 29 August 1854, Octavo Vols. B, Manuscripts Collection, American Antiquarian Society.

18. Francis Bennett, Jr., Diary, 3 September 1849.

19. Francis Bennett, Jr., Diary, 5 October 1854.

20. Francis Bennett, Jr., Diary, 26 October 1854.

21. Francis Bennett, Jr., Diary, 14 November 1854.

22. R. Murray Schafer, *The Soundscape: Our Sonic Environment and the Tuning of the World* (Rochester, Vt.: Destiny Books, 1994), 43.

23. Samuel Wood, *The Cries of New York* (New York: S. Wood, 1808).

24. Dale Cockrell, *Excelsior: Journals of the Hutchinson Family Singers, 1842–1846* (Stuveysant, N.Y.: Pendragon Press, 1989), 129.

25. Quoted in *As I Pass O Manhattan!*, Esther Morgan McCullough, ed. (New York: Corey Taylor, 1956), 619. See also White and White, *The Sounds of Slavery*, 155–59. On vendors in Baltimore, see Barbara Jeanne Fields, *Slavery and Freedom on the Middle Ground* (New York: Oxford University Press, 1988), 45.

26. Joseph Sill Diary, vol. 1, 3 January 1832.

27. White and White, *The Sounds of Slavery*, 157.

28. Nathan Webb Diary, 11 March 1789.

29. Cockrell, *Excelsior*, 169.

30. Clapp, *A Record of the Boston Stage*, 28.

31. Anna Quincy Thaxter Cushing Papers, 4 August 1846, Octavo Vols. C, Manuscripts Collection, American Antiquarian Society.

32. William Hoffman, 26 October 1848, William Hoffman Diary, 1847–1850, BV Hoffman, William (MS 1543), New-York Historical Society.

33. Susan G. Davis, "Strike Parades and the Politics of Representing Class in Antebellum Philadelphia," *TDR/The Drama Review* 29, no. 3 (1985): 107. On Promenading, see David Scobey, "Anatomy of the Promenade: The Politics of Bourgeois Sociability in Nineteenth-Century New York," *Social History* 17, no. 2 (1992): 203–27.

34. Edmund Quincy, 6 October 1852, journal, *Quincy, Wendell, Holmes, and Upham Family Papers, 1633–1910*, microfilm edition, 67 reels (Boston: Massachusetts Historical Society, 1977), reel 11, Massachusetts Historical Society.

35. Glenn C. Altschuler and Stuart M. Blumin, "Limits of Political Engagement in Antebellum America: A New Look at the Golden Age of Participatory Democracy," *Journal of American History* 84, no. 3 (1997): 868. See also Glenn C. Altschuler and Stuart M. Blumin, *Rude Republic: Americans and Their Politics in the Nineteenth Century* (Princeton: Princeton University Press, 2000).

36. White and White, *The Sounds of Slavery*, 157–58.

37. William Smith, 6 September 1843, William Smith Diary, BV Smith, William (MS 2420), New-York Historical Society.

38. Thomas Whitaker, Unpublished Diary, October 1874, Folio Vols. W, Manuscripts Collection, American Antiquarian Society.

39. Lawrence, *Strong on Music*, vol. 1, 4–5.

40. *The Literary Museum* (31 July 1852): 119.

41. See Rath, *How Early America Sounded*.

42. See Dena J. Epstein, *Sinful Tunes and Spirituals: Black Folk Music to the Civil War* (Urbana: University of Illinois Press, 1977), 205.

43. *The Literary Museum* (10 July 1852): 89.

44. Quoted in Cockrell, *Demons of Disorder*, 142.

45. Mark Smith, *Listening to Nineteenth-Century America*, 119.

46. Quoted in Cockrell, *Demons of Disorder*, 143.

47. Mark Smith, *Listening to Nineteenth-Century America*, 95–118.

48. Henry Clay Southworth, 4 July 1850, Henry Clay Southworth Diary, 1850–1851, BV Southworth, Henry Clay (MS 2431), New-York Historical Society.

49. Susan G. Davis, *Parades and Power: Street Theater in Nineteenth-Century Philadelphia* (Philadelphia: Temple University Press, 1986), 30.

50. Alan Walker Read, "The First Stage in the History of O.K.," *American Speech* 38, no. 1 (1963): 11.

51. Susan G. Davis, "'Making Night Hideous': Christmas Revelry and Public Order in Nineteenth-Century Philadelphia," *American Quarterly* 34, no. 2 (1982): 188. The political uses of noise are also explained by Cockrell in *Demons of Disorder* and by Jacques Attali, *Noise: The Political Economy of Music* (Minneapolis: University of Minnesota Press, 1985).

52. From an 1840 playbill. See Cockrell, *Demons of Disorder*, 146.

53. Mark M. Smith, "Heard Worlds of Antebellum America," in *The Auditory Culture Reader*, Bull and Back, eds., 141.

54. David Shi, *The Simple Life: Plain Living and High Thinking in American Culture* (Athens: University of Georgia Press, 1985).

55. Lydia Child, *The Mother's Book* (Boston: Carter, Hendee, and Babcock, 1831), 18.

56. Shi, *The Simple Life*, 130.

57. Henry David Thoreau, *Walden: Or, Life in the Woods* (New York: Signet, 1960), 18.

58. Thoreau, *Walden*, 66.

59. Thoreau, *Walden*, 79–90.

60. Sterne, *The Audible Past*, 93–99.

61. These developments are astutely summarized by Sterne in *The Audible Past*. For other kinds of practical knowledge of listening in the nineteenth century, including that of the blind, and of thieves and pick-pockets, who could hear differences between coins, see William Gardiner, *The Music of Nature* (Boston: J. H. Wilkins & R. B. Carter, 1838).

62. J. T. Buckingham, "Music," *New England Magazine* 1, no. 6 (December 1831): 457.

63. William S. Porter, *The Musical Cyclopedia, or the Principles of Music Considered as a Science and an Art, Embracing a Complete Musical Dictionary* (Boston: James Loring, 1834), 136.

64. Francis James Fetis, *Music Explained to the World: Or, How to Understand Music and Enjoy Its Performance* (Boston: Benjamin Perkins, 1842); William Mullinger Higgins, *The Philosophy of Sound and History of Music* (London: William S. Orr, 1838); Joseph Bird, *Gleanings from the History of Music* (Boston: Benjamin B. Mussey, 1850).

65. *Arthur's Home Magazine* (September 1853): 167–70.

66. Sterne, *The Audible Past*, 98.

67. Walter Teller, ed., *Walt Whitman's Camden Conversations* (New Brunswick, N.J.: Rutgers University Press, 1973), 115.

68. Rath, *How Early America Sounded*, 104. See also Jeanne Halgren Kilde, *When Church Became Theatre* (New York: Oxford University Press, 2002), 11–21.

69. Biblical quotation is from Romans 10: 8–17. On preaching generally, see Susan Wabuda, "Preaching," in *Puritans and Puritanism in Europe and America: A Comprehensive Encyclopedia*, vol. 1, Francis J. Bremer and Tom Webster, eds. (Santa Barbara, Calif.: ABC-CLIO, 2006), 488–91.

70. Ola Elizabeth Winslow, *Meetinghouse Hill, 1630–1783* (New York: W. W. Norton, 1972), 91.

71. Quakers, who had a tenuous relationship with both Anglicans and Puritans, nevertheless built meetinghouses that likewise highlighted the primacy of acoustics and hearing. Quakers did not have a worship tradition of preaching but rather relied on the spontaneous contributions of participants, who remained silent until moved to speak. Such a practice required both clarity for all individual voices within, which was achieved through an open, rounded, room shape and concave ceilings, sometimes with sound-directing ceiling panels. See Rath, *How Early America Sounded*, 113–19.

72. Rath, *How Early America Sounded*, 119.

73. George Whitefield, *Directions How to Hear Sermons* (Boston: G. Rogers & D. Fowle, 1740).

74. Schmidt, *Hearing Things*, 40.

75. Alquist, *Democracy at the Opera*, 2–3.

76. For summary discussions of theater audiences in the antebellum era, see Butsch, *The Making of American Audiences*; Kasson, *Rudeness and Civility*; and Levine, *Highbrow/Lowbrow*.

77. Butsch, *The Making of American Audiences*, 59.

78. For a discussion of the antebellum star system in theater, see Bruce McConachie, *Melodramatic Formations: American Theatre and Society, 1820–1870* (Ames: University of Iowa Press, 1992), 69–90.

79. Butsch, *The Making of American Audiences*, 289–90.

80. Brooks, *The Flowering of New England*, 174.

81. Terry Baxter, *Frederick Douglass's Curious Audiences: Ethos in the Age of the Consumable Subject* (New York: Routledge, 2004), 68.

82. See Frederick J. Antczak, *Thought and Character: The Rhetoric of Democratic Education* (Ames: Iowa State University Press, 1985). Quoted in Baxter, 74.

83. Kilde, *When Church Became Theatre*, 27–37.

84. Kilde, *When Church Became Theatre*, 130 and note, 227.

85. Kilde, *When Church Became Theatre*, 116.

86. Kasson, *Rudeness and Civility*, 215–56.

87. Baxter, *Frederick Douglass's Curious Audiences*, 40–42.

88. Charles Grandison Finney, *Lectures on Revivals of Religion*, William G.

McLoughlin, ed. (Cambridge, Mass.: Harvard University Press, 1960), 218. On the theatricality of preachers, see R. Laurence Moore, *Selling God: American Religion in the Marketplace of Culture* (New York: Oxford University Press, 1992), 49–56.

89. Henry Clay Southworth, 16 June 1850, Henry Clay Southworth Diary, BV Southworth, Henry Clay, New-York Historical Society.

90. Caroline Wells Healey Dall, 27 September 1840, journal, *Caroline H. Dall Papers, 1811–1917*, microfilm edition, 45 reels (Boston: Massachusetts Historical Society, 1981), reel 32, Massachusetts Historical Society.

91. Moore, *Selling God*, 44–45.

92. Bruce C. Daniels offers a cogent summary of the role of music among Puritans in *Puritans at Play: Leisure and Recreation in Colonial New England* (New York: St. Martin's Press, 1995), 52–66. For discussion of regular singing and its ramifications, see Joyce Irwin, "The Theology of 'Regular Singing,'" *New England Quarterly* 51, no. 2 (1978): 176–92; Crawford, *America's Musical Past*, 125–38; and Anne Bagnall Yardley, "Choirs in the Methodist Episcopal Church, 1800–1860," *American Music* 17, no. 1 (1999): 39–64.

93. Samuel Gilman, *Memoirs of a New England Village Choir with Occasional Reflections, by a Member* (Boston: S. G. Goodrich, 1829), 35–37.

94. Nathaniel D. Gould, *Church Music in America, Comprising Its History and Its Peculiarities at Different Periods, with Cursory Remarks on Its Legitimate Use and Its Abuse; with Notices of the Schools, Composers, Teachers, and Societies* (Boston: A. N. Johnson, 1853), 198.

95. Gould, *Church Music in America*, 77.

96. *Father Kemp and His Old Folks, A History of the Old Folks' Concerts, comprising an Autobiography of the Author and Sketches of Many Humorous Scenes and Incidents, Which Have Transpired in a Concert-Giving Experience of Twelve Years in America and England* (Boston: published by the Author, 1868), 81.

97. Gilman, *Memoirs of a New England Village Choir*, 45–46.

98. Braham's concerts are noted in the collections of Yale University. See New Haven Concert Programs, Folder 2: 1840–1849, Special Collections, Irving S. Gilmore Music Library, Yale University.

99. Moore, *Selling God*, 59–60.

100. Gould, *Church Music in America*, 45.

101. Stuart Hall has usefully characterized production and consumption as a circuit defined by socio-cultural "meaning structures"; see "Encoding/Decoding," in *Media and Cultural Studies: Keyworks*, Meenakshi Gigi Durham and Douglas Kellner, eds. (Malden, Mass.: Blackwell Publishers, 2006), 163–73.

102. Dennis G. Waring, *Manufacturing the Muse: Estey Organs & Consumer Culture in Victorian America* (Middletown, Conn.: Wesleyan University Press, 2002), 48–76. On the piano as a domestic instrument, see also Richard Leppert, "Sexual Identity, Death, and the Family Piano," *19th-Century Music* 16, no. 2 (1992): 105–28.

103. Russell Sanjek characterizes the changing business of the era in terms of music publishing and copyright, citing the "printers, booksellers, engravers; instrument makers, repairers, and dealers; print-shop owners; umbrella manufactur-

ers; music teachers, professional musicians, bandleaders, composers, and songwriters." See Sanjek, *American Popular Music and Its Business*, 47. For a fascinatingly early description of the "music trades," see W. L. Hubbard, ed., *History of American Music* (Toledo: Irving Squire, 1908). Hubbard covers the "American inventiveness" of instrument making, music publishing, and, as a more recent development in 1908, "talking machine" companies.

104. See Roland Barthes, "The Death of the Author," in *Image, Music, Text* (New York: Hill & Wang, 1977), 142–48.

105. Loesser, *Men, Women, and Pianos*, 468.

106. *Oxford English Dictionary* (New York: Oxford University Press, 1989).

107. "Exhibitions of Musick" are especially prevalent in Oscar Sonneck's discussions of early American concerts among elites; see Sonneck, *Early Concert-Life in America*. On early museums, see John Elsner and Roger Cardinal, *The Cultures of Collecting* (Cambridge, Mass.: Harvard University Press, 1994).

108. *Psalms and Hymns for Christian Use and Worship, General Association of Connecticut* (Boston: Charles Tappan, 1845), 6.

109. George Hogarth, *Memoirs of the Musical Drama*, vol. 2 (London: R. Bentley, 1838), 231.

110. In fact, all exhibitions so depended on such authenticity that they, paradoxically, invited speculation and investigation. The open-ended attractiveness of "uncovering the truth," as James Cook has argued, was the basis for the widespread phenomenon of "artful deception" across all forms of antebellum entertainment culture, from the carnival to the trompe l'oeil paintings. See Cook, *The Arts of Deception*.

111. Metzner, *Crescendo of the Virtuoso*, 214.

112. Igor Kopytoff, "The Cultural Biography of Things: Commoditization as Process," in *The Social Life of Things: Commodities in Cultural Perspective*, Arjun Appadurai, ed. (Cambridge: Cambridge University Press, 1988), 64–91.

113. Iwan Rhys Morus, "Manufacturing Nature: Science, Technology, and Victorian Consumer Culture," *British Journal for the History of Science* 29, no. 4 (1996): 425. Much work in cultural or social economics has framed the development of consumerism away from traditional notions of increased production and "gratification" and toward a more nuanced understanding of the complex emotions and identity-work involved in the use of goods. For a recent summary of this work, see Joel Pfister, "Getting Personal and Getting Personnel: U.S. Capitalism as a System of Emotional Reproduction," *American Quarterly* 60, no. 4 (2008): 1135–41.

114. Evelev, *Tolerable Entertainment*, 123.

115. Daniel Roche has linked the rise of Western consumption specifically to the middle-class "autonomization of private life." See Daniel Roche, *A History of Everyday Things: The Birth of Consumption in France, 1600–1800* (Cambridge: Cambridge University Press, 2000), 19.

116. Barnum, *The Life of P. T. Barnum*, 99. Herman Melville notably satirized the confusing multiplicity of voices in the marketplace in *The Confidence Man: His Masquerade* (New York: Dix, Edwards, 1857). For a summary of duplicity in nineteenth-century consumption, see Cook, *The Arts of Deception*.

117. I don't believe it is a coincidence that exhibition practices were adopted by the mid-nineteenth century for the sales of goods in "show-rooms" and display counters. On middle-class anxiety about facades and acting, see Haltuunen, *Confidence Men and Painted Women*.

118. Lawrence, *Strong on Music*, vol. 1, 153.

119. Gottschalk, *Notes of a Pianist*, 155.

120. Kopytoff, "The Cultural Biography of Things," 73.

121. White and White, *The Sounds of Slavery*, 150–60.

122. Jon M. Kingsdale, "The 'Poor Man's Club': Social Functions of the Urban Working-Class Saloon," *American Quarterly* 25, no. 4 (1973): 480.

123. These new values of exchange are similar to those identified by Pierre Bourdieu among the twentieth-century French bourgeoisie in *Distinction: A Social Critique of the Judgment of Taste* (Cambridge, Mass.: Harvard University Press, 1987).

124. Peter G. Buckley, "Popular Entertainment before the Civil War," in *Encyclopedia of American Social History*, vol. 3, Mary K. Cayton, Elliot J. Gorn, and Peter W. Williams, eds. (New York: Charles Scribner's Sons, 1993), 1611.

Chapter 3: "Music Is What Awakens in You When You Are Reminded by the Instruments": Hearing a New Life at Mid-Century

1. N. Beekley Diary, 27 January 1849, Octavo Vols. B, Manuscripts Collection, American Antiquarian Society.

2. N. Beekley Diary, 9 October 1849.

3. N. Beekley Diary, 1 May 1849.

4. Henry Clay Southworth Diary, 1850–1851.

5. Charles Tracy, 1 September 1857, Charles Tracy Diary, 1856–1857, BV Tracy, Charles (MS 2901), New-York Historical Society.

6. The musical portions of Strong's diary were first published in Lawrence, *Strong on Music*, vol. 1.

7. Daniel Walker Howe, *Making the American Self: Jonathan Edwards to Abraham Lincoln* (Cambridge, Mass.: Harvard University Press, 1997), 8.

8. James A. Henretta, *The Evolution of American Society, 1700–1815: An Interdisciplinary Analysis* (Lexington, Mass.: D. C. Heath, 1973), 165.

9. Thomas Augst, "Composing the Moral Senses: Emerson and the Politics of Character in Nineteenth-Century America," *Political Theory* 27, no. 1 (1999): 91.

10. See Ralph Waldo Emerson, "Self Reliance," in *Selected Writings of Ralph Waldo Emerson* (New York: New American Library, 1965): 257–79. Emerson's changing understanding of the self between 1840 and 1860 is addressed by Augst in *The Clerk's Tale*, 120–28.

11. Jeffrey Sklansky, Charles Sellers, and Scott Casper see gradations in and negotiation around the idea of individual autonomy or sovereignty; Sellers, in particular, sees inequities in its application. Thomas Augst and Daniel Walker Howe tend to emphasize continuities and argue for democratization. See Jeffrey Sklansky,

The Soul's Economy: Market Society and Selfhood in American Thought, 1820–1920 (Chapel Hill: University of North Carolina Press, 2002); Sellers, *The Market Revolution*; Casper, *Constructing American Lives*; Howe, *Making the American Self*; Augst, "Composing the Moral Senses," 85–120. For a useful summary of some of the debates, see Charles L. Ponce de Leon, "Is There an American Self?," *Reviews in American History* 26, no. 3 (1998): 489–96.

12. E. Anthony Rotundo, *American Manhood: Transformations in Masculinity from the Revolution to the Modern Era* (New York: Basic Books, 1993), 20.

13. Howe, *Making the American Self*, 111; Lears, *Fables of Abundance*, 46.

14. A notable exception is Martin, ed., *Cultural Change and the Market Revolution in America*.

15. Augst, "Composing the Moral Senses," 113. Michel Foucault's ideas about self-formation are outlined in his essay, "Technologies of the Self," in *Technologies of the Self: A Seminar with Michel Foucault*, Luther H. Martin, Huck Gutman, and Patrick H. Hutton, eds. (Amherst, Mass.: University of Massachusetts Press, 1988), 16–49.

16. My focus on these groups is for analytical comparison only and not meant to suggest that ideologies of selfhood were not significant among the many other social groups (including working-class men and women, rural men and women, etc.) in antebellum America.

17. See Eugene Arden, "The Evil City in American Fiction," *New York History* 35 (July 1954): 259–79, and Halttunen, *Confidence Men and Painted Women*, 2–3.

18. Halttunen, *Confidence Men and Painted Women*, 12.

19. Trowbridge, *My Own Story*, n.p.

20. Cockrell, *Excelsior*, 112. Also quoted in Scott Gac, *Singing for Freedom: The Hutchinson Family Singers and the Nineteenth-Century Culture of Antebellum Reform* (New Haven: Yale University Press, 2007), 64.

21. See Evelev, *Tolerable Entertainment*. The classic outline of the weakening power of artisans in the antebellum era remains Sean Wilentz, *Chants Democratic: New York City and the Rise of the American Working Class, 1788–1850* (New York: Oxford University Press, 1984).

22. See Rotundo, *American Manhood*; and Michael Kimmel, "The Birth of the Self-Made Man," in *The Masculinity Studies Reader*, Rachel Adams and David Savran, eds. (Malden, Mass.: Blackwell Publishing, 2002), 135–52.

23. Daniel Webster to Habijah Fuller, 29 August 1802, in *The Writings and Speeches of Daniel Webster*, vol. 17. Edward Everett, ed. (Boston: Little Brown, 1903).

24. Quoted in Joseph Musselman, *Music in the Cultured Generation* (Evanston, Ill.: Northwestern University Press, 1971), 34.

25. Joseph Sill Diary, vol. 2, 11 November 1840.

26. Trowbridge, *My Own Story*, 114.

27. Trowbridge, *My Own Story*, 126

28. Trowbridge, *My Own Story*, 127–28.

29. William Hoffman Diary, 1 November 1850.

30. Otis Briggs Oakman, 19 July 1849 to 29 August 1862, diary, Otis Briggs Oakman Diary, Massachusetts Historical Society.

31. Loyed E. Chamberlain, 16 February 1877, diary, Loyed E. Chamberlain Papers, Massachusetts Historical Society.

32. Jean Matthews, "Race, Sex, and the Dimensions of Liberty in Antebellum America," *Journal of the Early Republic* 6, no. 3 (1986): 280. Daniel Walker Howe frames the desire for individual liberty a little differently, not in terms of inequality but in terms of definition: "Historians have reminded us that a majority of the population, including African-Americans, women, and others, were denied the full benefits of antebellum freedom. Yet if we widen the traditional universe of historical inquiry to include nonpolitical activities, we find that working-class people, women, minority groups, even slaves were able to participate to a degree in certain kinds of voluntary self-definition, through (for example) religion, manners, and self-discipline." See Daniel Walker Howe, *Making the American Self: Jonathan Edwards to Abraham Lincoln* (Cambridge, Mass.: Harvard University Press, 1997): 110.

33. Jean L. Matthews, "Race, Sex, and the Dimensions of Liberty in Antebellum America," *Journal of the Early Republic* 6, no. 3 (1986): 280–81.

34. Mary Kelley, "Reading Women/Women Reading: The Making of Learned Women in Antebellum America," *Journal of American History* 83, no. 2 (1996): 415.

35. See Petra Meyer-Frazeir, "Music, Novels, and Women: Nineteenth-Century Prescriptions for an Ideal Life," *Women & Music: A Journal of Gender and Culture* 10 (2006): 45–59, and Gillian Brown, *Domestic Individualism: Imaging Self in Nineteenth-Century America* (Berkeley: University of California Press, 1992).

36. For more discussion of the role of music collecting and the self, see Sheldon Cheney, "The Book-Plates of Musicians and Music-Lovers," *Musical Quarterly* 3, no. 3 (1917): 446–52.

37. The sheet music binders of both Nettie and Minna Brooker can be found in the Sheet Music Collection of The John Hay Library, Brown University, Providence, R.I.

38. See Halttunen, *Confidence Men and Painted Women*, 67.

39. Bushman, *The Refinement of America*, 366.

40. Anna Quincy Thaxter Cushing Papers, 29 September 1846.

41. Matinees were experimented with as early as the 1850s. As an announcement in Boston's *The Literary Museum* indicated on 19 June 1852: "The Germania Serenade Band have commenced a weekly series of afternoon concerts, at the Melodeon. These concerts are very popular, as an opportunity is given to ladies and their children to attend without requiring the presence of gentlemen."

42. Kathy Peiss, *Cheap Amusements: Working Women and Leisure in Turn-of-the-Century New York* (Philadelphia: Temple University Press, 1986), 4–5.

43. Adelaide Crossman Burr Diary, 1867. Octavo Vols. B, Manuscripts Collection, American Antiquarian Society.

44. Anna Quincy Thaxter Cushing Papers, 22 September 1850.

45. Caroline Barrett White Papers, 9 December 1851, 3 February 1852, 4 February 1852, vol. 3, Octavo Vols. W, Manuscripts Collection, American Antiquarian Society.

46. Quoted in Ora Frishberg Saloman, "Margaret Fuller on Beethoven in America, 1839–1846," *Journal of Musicology* 10, no. 1 (1992): 64. For Fuller's ideas on

selfhood, see Howe, *Making the American Self*, 212–34; and Sklansky, *The Soul's Economy*, 61–71.

47. James Oliver Horton and Lois E. Horton, *In Hope of Liberty: Culture, Community, and Protest Among Northern Free Blacks, 1700–1860* (New York: Oxford University Press, 1997), 160. On the African Grove Theater, see McAllister, *White People Do Not Know How to Behave at Entertainments Designed for Ladies and Gentlemen of Colour*. The life of James Forten is ably described in Julie Winch, *A Gentleman of Color: The Life of James Forten* (New York: Oxford University Press, 2002).

48. Horton and Horton, *In Hope of Liberty*, 115–16 and 154.

49. R. J. Young, *Antebellum Black Activists: Race, Gender, and Self* (New York: Garland Publishing, 1996), 57.

50. Young, *Antebellum Black Activists*, 67.

51. Michael O'Malley has written about the ways in which the classification of blacks as a lower "species" was predicated on the parallel rise in the social valuing of "specie," or money. See Michael O'Malley, "Specie and Species: Race and the Money Question in Nineteenth-Century America," *American Historical Review* 99, no. 2 (1994): 369–95.

52. Carla L. Peterson, "Capitalism, Black (Under)Development, and the Production of the African-American Novel in the 1850s," *American Literary History* 4, no. 4 (1992): 560.

53. Quoted in Linda M. Perkins, "The Impact of the 'Cult of True Womanhood' on the Education of Black Women," in *Black Women in United States History*, vol. 3, Darlene Clark Hine, ed. (Brooklyn, N.Y.: Carlson Publishing, 1990), 1066.

54. Young, *Antebellum Black Activists*, 149–52. Sojourner Truth's famous question at the 1851 Women's Rights Convention, "Ar'n't I a woman?," which reframed the more popular abolitionist phrasing of "Am I Not a Man?" is indicative of this gender difference. See Wilma King, *The Essence of Liberty: Free Black Women during the Slave Era* (Columbia: University of Missouri Press, 2006), 40.

55. King, *The Essence of Liberty*, 34–35.

56. See Elizabeth Clark, "The Sacred Rights of the Weak: Pain, Sympathy, and the Culture of Individual Rights in Antebellum America," *Journal of American History* 82, no. 2 (1995): 463–93.

57. Peterson, "Capitalism, Black (Under)Development, and the Production of the African-American Novel in the 1850s," 562.

58. Frederick Douglass, *Narrative of the Life of Frederick Douglass, an American Slave* (New York: Bedford Books, 1993), 55.

59. Fields, *Slavery and Freedom on the Middle Ground*, 34.

60. Eileen Southern. *The Music of Black Americans: A History*, 2nd ed. (New York: W. W. Norton, 1983), 103.

61. Southern, *The Music of Black Americans*, 111. Southern notes, "We cannot hope to know the full story about black bands and orchestras in the antebellum period, but judging from the numerous references in contemporary literature to such activities, the few names that have come down to us represent only the tip of the iceberg."

62. Juanita Karpf, "'As with Words of Fire': Art Music and Nineteenth-Century African-American Feminist Discourse." *Signs* 24, no. 3 (1999): 606. Black slaves, too, attended concerts, often with their owners, something that obviously had different ramifications. See Nancy R. Ping, "Black Musical Activities in Antebellum Wilmington, North Carolina," *Black Perspective in Music* 8, no. 2 (1980): 146.

63. Southern, *The Music of Black Americans*, 101–5.

64. Joseph Willson, *The Elite of Our People: Sketches of the Higher Classes of Colored Society in Philadelphia*, Julie Winch, ed. (University Park: Pennsylvania State University Press, 2000), 99.

65. Gloria C. Oden, "The Journal of Charlotte L. Forten: The Salem-Philadelphia Years (1854–1862) Reexamined," in *Black Women in United States History*, vol. 3, Clark Hine, ed., 1011. See also *A Free Black Girl before the Civil War: The Diary of Charlotte Forten, 1854*, Christy Steele and Kerry Graves, eds. (Mankato, Minn.: Capstone Press, 2000).

66. David McBride, "Afro-American Urban Culture and Intellectualism, 1840–1940," in Bette Ann Davis Lawrence et al., *Philadelphia African Americans: Color, Class, & Style, 1840–1940. An Exhibition Catalog* (Philadelphia: The Balch Institute for Ethnic Studies, 1988), 33.

67. James Oliver Horton and Lois E. Horton, *Black Bostonians: Family Life and Community Struggle in the Antebellum North* (New York: Holmes & Meier, 1999), 74.

68. Karpf, "'As with Words of Fire,'" 607.

69. Quoted in Frankie Hutton, *The Early Black Press in America* (Santa Barbara, Calif.: Greenwood Publishing, 1993), 83.

70. For a succinct account of the shifting ideologies of blackface, see Cockrell, *Demons of Disorder*.

71. Ronald Radano, *Lying up a Nation: Race and Black Music* (Chicago: University of Chicago Press, 2003), 150.

72. Sklansky, *The Soul's Economy*, 72.

73. David Haven Blake, *Walt Whitman and the Culture of American Celebrity* (New Haven: Yale University Press, 2006), 40–48.

74. Augst, "Composing the Moral Senses," 115.

75. Blake, *Walt Whitman and the Culture of American Celebrity*; Baker, *Sentiment and Celebrity*; Ezra Greenspan, *Walt Whitman and the American Reader* (New York: Cambridge University Press, 1990), 21.

76. Blake, *Walt Whitman and the Culture of American Celebrity*, 34.

77. Dwight, "Music in Boston," 443.

78. Joseph Sill Diary, vol. 2, 11 November 1840.

79. William Cullen Bryant, "To the Evening Post, Steamer Oregon, Lake Huron, off Thunder Bay, July 24, 1846," in *Letters of William Cullen Bryant*, vol. 2, William Cullen Bryant II and Thomas G. Voss, eds. (New York: Fordham University Press, 1975), 438.

80. Braudy, *The Frenzy of Renown*, 509.

81. *Oxford English Dictionary*, online edition (Oxford University Press, 2005). Found at www.oed.com. The word "star" was still used in quotation marks by the-

ater historian William E. Clapp, Jr., as late at 1853. See Clapp, *A Record of the Boston Stage*.

82. Quoted in Faner, *Walt Whitman and Opera*, 61.

83. Lucy Lowell, 8 May 1882, diary, Lucy Lowell Diaries, Massachusetts Historical Society.

84. Sarah Gooll Putnam, September 1882, diary, Sarah Gooll Putnam Diaries, Massachusetts Historical Society.

85. See Halttunen, *Confidence Men and Painted Women*.

86. Dizekes, *Opera in America*, 133.

87. Letters to Frieda Hempel about Jenny Lind, October and November 1924, Music of Jenny Lind and Her Contemporaries, Jenny Lind Collection, New-York Historical Society.

88. William Hoffman Diary, 21 September 1850.

89. Henry Clay Southworth Diary, 13 September 1850.

90. Caroline Barrett White Papers, 22 November 1851.

91. Lucia McMahon, "'While Our Souls Together Blend': Narrating a Romantic Readership in the Early Republic," in *An Emotional History of the United States*, Peter N. Stearns and Jan Lewis, eds. (New York: New York University Press, 1998), 66–90.

92. Quoted in Faner, *Walt Whitman and Opera*, 60.

93. Mortimer Brewster Smith, *The Life of Ole Bull* (Princeton: Princeton University Press, 1947), 67.

94. Gac, *Singing for Freedom*, 199.

95. Sara Chapman Thorp Bull, Ole Bull, and Alpheus Benning Crosby, *Ole Bull: A Memoir* (Boston: Houghton, Mifflin, 1882), 183.

Chapter 4: "How I Should Like to Hear It All Over Again & Again": Loving Music, 1850–1885

1. Lucy Lowell Diary, 14 April 1884.

2. Lucy Lowell Diary, 15 April 1884.

3. Lucy Lowell Diary, 16 April 1884.

4. Lucy Lowell Diary, 20 March 1882 and 13 May 1882.

5. Lucy Lowell Diary, 16 April 1884.

6. Lucy Lowell Diary, 17 April 1884. In Rose Fay Thomas's recounting of the festival program, Beethoven's 5th symphony is not listed; it may have been simply that Beethoven did not fit with the Wagnerian theme, so it was left out. She also, unfortunately, gives April 22 as the opening date of the festival, which was—by multiple accounts in Boston newspapers—a week later than it actually happened. See Rose Fay Thomas, *Memoirs of Theodore Thomas* (Whitefish, Mont.: Kessinger Publishing, 2004), 262.

7. Lucy Lowell Diary, 19 April 1884.

8. Performers who attempted commercial concerts during the War often faced unpredictable circumstances. Pianist Louis Moreau Gottschalk, for example, when scheduled to perform in Harrisburg, Pennsylvania, in 1862, found himself in a mad

race to reach the capital before the Confederate Army, during which he was swept up in the chaos of refugees, equipment convoys, and Union troops moving to defend the city. See Gottschalk, *Notes of a Pianist*, 129–43. A more general description of the War's effects can be found in Bruce C. Kelley, "'Old Times There Are Not Forgotten': An Overview of Music of the Civil War Era," in *Bugle Resounding: Music and Musicians in the Civil War Era*, Bruce C. Kelley and Mark A. Snell, eds. (Columbia: University of Missouri Press, 2004), 1–36.

9. On the rise of the private sphere and its relationship to music publishing, see Dale Cockrell, "Nineteenth-Century Popular Music," in *The Cambridge History of American Music*, David Nicholls, ed. (Cambridge: Cambridge University Press, 1998), 182–85.

10. Dwight, "Music in Boston," 445.

11. Theodore Thomas, *Theodore Thomas: A Musical Autobiography*, vol. 2, *Concert Programmes*, George Putnam Upton, ed. (Chicago: A. C. McClurg, 1905).

12. John Ogasapian and N. Lee Orr, *Music of the Gilded Age* (Westport, Conn.: Greenwood Press, 2007), 15 and 73.

13. Matthew Arnold, *Culture and Anarchy: An Essay in Political and Social Criticism* (New York: Macmillan, 1883), 38.

14. Lucy Buckminster Emerson Lowell Diary, 26 October 1845.

15. Lucy Lowell Diary, 1 January 1880. Lucy Lowell Diary quotations in following paragraphs cited by date only.

16. 4 February 1882.

17. 29 April 1882.

18. 28 January 1880.

19. 13 October 1887.

20. 4 January 1882.

21. 31 January 1884.

22. 13 April 1885.

23. 16 February 1887.

24. 15 February 1886.

25. 29 May 1886.

26. 4 January 1882.

27. 10 May 1882.

28. 12 February 1880 and 10 February 1882.

29. 7 November 1884.

30. 20 February 1886.

31. 23 March 1882.

32. 9 November 1885.

33. 23 February 1882.

34. 16 February 1887.

35. 10 May 1882.

36. 2 June 1882.

37. Peter J. Rabinowitz, "'With Our Own Dominant Passions': Gottschalk, Gender, and the Power of Listening," *19th-Century Music* 16, no. 3 (1993): 244 and 251.

38. Willa Cather, "A Wagner Matinee" in *Great Short Works of Willa Cather*, Robert K. Miller, ed. (New York: Perennial/Harper and Row, 1989), 51–62.

39. Joseph Horowitz, "Finding a 'Real Self': American Women and the Wagner Cult of the Late Nineteenth Century," *Musical Quarterly* 78, no. 2 (1994): 194.

40. Lucy Lowell Diary, July 1885.

41. Lucy Lowell Diary, 18 April 1885.

42. Elie Siegmeister, ed. *The Music Lover's Handbook* (New York: William Morrow, 1943), 736.

43. Helen Atkins, 17 June 1872, journal, Atkins Family Papers, Massachusetts Historical Society.

44. *Boston Herald Extra Edition*, third day of festival, from "Scrapbook containing newspaper articles and clippings relating to the National Peace Jubilee and Musical Festival, Boston, 1869," Massachusetts Historical Society.

45. *Frank Leslie's Illustrated History of the Great National Peace Jubilee and Musical Festival, held in Boston, Mass., June 15, 16, 17, 18, and 19 June 1869* (New York: Frank Leslie, 1869): n.p.

46. Mary E. F. Atkins, 25 June 1872, journal, Atkins Family Papers, Massachusetts Historical Society.

47. Quoted in Jennie Copeland, *Everyday but Sunday: The Romantic Age of New England Industry* (Brattleboro, Vt.: Stephen Daye Press, 1936), 244–45.

48. *Boston Advertiser*, fourth day of concert, from "Scrapbook containing newspaper articles and clippings relating to the National Peace Jubilee and Musical Festival, Boston, 1869," Massachusetts Historical Society.

49. "The World of New York," *Putnam's Monthly Magazine* 8, no. 48 (December 1856): 667.

50. Henry Clay Southworth Diary, 2 December 1851.

51. For a full account, see Nigel Cliff, *The Shakespeare Riots: Revenge, Drama, and Death in Nineteenth-Century America* (New York: Random House, 2007).

52. Walt Whitman, "Music for the Natural Ear," *The Brooklyn Daily Eagle*, April 1846: 2, http://eagle.brooklynpubliclibrary.org.

53. Caroline Wells Healey Dall Journal, 15 February 1840.

54. Joseph Sill Diary, vol. 2, 4 February 1841.

55. Lucy Lowell Diary, 16 May 1884.

56. Lucy Lowell Diary, 26 March 1886.

57. Michael Forsyth, *Buildings for Music: The Architect, the Musician, and the Listener from the Seventeenth Century to the Present Day* (Cambridge, Mass.: MIT Press, 1985), 205.

58. Gardiner, *The Music of Nature*, 289.

59. Alan Durant, *Conditions of Music* (Albany: SUNY Press, 1984), 34.

60. William Hoffman Diary, 19 November 1850.

61. Henry Clay Southworth Diary, 27 December 1850.

62. *Sketches and Business Directory of Boston 1860–1861* (Boston: Damrell & Moore and George Coolidge, 1861), 109.

63. Lucy Buckminster Emerson Lowell Diary, 29 October 1845.

64. Charles Pelham Curtis, 18 December 1874, diary, Charles Pelham Curtis Diary, Massachusetts Historical Society.

65. Anna Quincy Thaxter Cushing Papers, 21 November 1851.

66. Joseph Sill Diary, vol. 2, 2 December 1840.

67. Henry Van Dyke, *The Music Lover* (New York: Moffat, Yard, 1909), 5–6.

68. Gardiner, *The Music of Nature*, 125.

69. Whitman, *Complete Poetry and Collected Prose*, 875.

70. Sarah Gooll Putnam Diary, Summary of Winter 1884–85.

71. Gottschalk, *Notes of a Pianist*, 108.

72. See Rabinowitz, "With Our Own Dominant Passions," 242–52.

73. Whitman, *Complete Poetry and Collected Prose*, 54–55.

74. Jackson Lears, *No Place of Grace: Antimodernism and the Transformation of American Culture, 1880–1920* (New York: Pantheon Books, 1981), 172.

75. Lawrence, *Strong on Music*, vol. 1, 200.

76. Sarah Gooll Putnam Diary, 17 April 1884.

77. William Foster Apthorp, "Musicians and Music Lovers," *Atlantic Monthly* (February 1879): 151.

78. Schafer, *The Soundscape*, 103.

79. Lawrence, *Strong on Music*, vol. 1, 324.

80. Otis Briggs Oakham Journal, 4 November 1856. The lyrics are from the song "When Shall We Meet Again," in *Revival Melodies, or Songs of Zion. Dedicated to Elder Jacob Knapp* (Boston: John Putnam, 1842).

81. Charles D. Parker, 9 March 1870, Charles D. Parker Diary, 1870, Division of Rare and Manuscripts Collections, Carl A. Kroch Library, Cornell University.

82. Anna Quincy Thaxter Cushing Papers, 5 August 1846.

83. Kenneth Allen Diary, 9 March 1874, Octavo Vols. A, Manuscripts Collection, American Antiquarian Society.

84. Charles Tracy Diary, 27 August 1857.

85. Lucy Lowell Diary, 24 February 1880.

86. William Hoffman Diary, 8 July 1850.

87. Joseph Sill Diary, vol. 1, 23 November 1832.

88. Preston. *Opera on the Road*, 59–61.

89. Lawrence, *Strong on Music*, vol. 1, 318.

90. Lucy Lowell Diary, 16 April 1884.

91. Lawrence, *Strong on Music*, vol. 2, 38.

92. Letters to Frieda Hempel, 20 November 1924.

93. Chris Gibson and John Connell, *Music and Tourism: On the Road Again* (Clevedon, UK: Channel View Publications, 2005), 3–12.

94. Alice Drake, 26 October 1896 and November 1897, Travel Diary of Alice Drake, vols. 1 and 2, Special Collections, Irving S. Gilmore Music Library, Yale University.

95. Mark Twain, "Mark Twain at Bayreuth," *Chicago Daily Tribune* (6 December 1891).

96. Program for "Madame Henriette Sontag's Last Grand Performance," Boston Music Hall, 185[?], Massachusetts Historical Society.

97. Nancy Newman, *Good Music for a Free People: The Germania Musical Society and Transatlantic Musical Culture of the Mid-Nineteenth Century* (Ph.D. diss., Department of Music, Brown University, May 2002), 163.

98. Lawrence, *Strong on Music*, vol. 1, 194.

99. Lawrence, *Strong on Music*, vol. 1, 359.

100. Bonny H. Miller, "A Mirror of Ages Past: The Publication of Music in Domestic Periodicals," *Notes* 50, no. 3 (1994): 883–901.

101. See Leslie Gay, Jr., "Before the Deluge: The Technoculture of Song-Sheet Publishing Viewed from Late Nineteenth-Century Galveston," in *Music and Technoculture*, Rene T. A. Lysloff and Leslie C. Gay, Jr., eds. (Middletown, Conn.: Wesleyan University Press, 2003) 204–32; and Jon W. Finson, *The Voices That Are Gone: Themes in Nineteenth-Century American Popular Song.* (New York: Oxford University Press, 1997).

102. Loesser, *Men, Women and Pianos*, 531–36. Tin Pan Alley song promotion in the 1890s would reestablish the notion of linking particular songs with performers and performances, as would Edison's marketing of the phonograph in the early 1900s.

103. Lucy Lowell Diary, 29 May 1886.

104. Augst, *The Clerk's Tale*, 47–48.

105. In several diaries, in fact, "we had some music" or "went to concert" was simply listed next to "fixed fence" or "rained today."

106. N. Beekley Diary, 10–11 January 1849.

107. Lucy Lowell Diary, 1 March 1886.

108. Edith May Parks Scrapbook, accession no. SC1998.9, Ruth T. Watanabe Special Collections, Sibley Music Library, University of Rochester.

109. See Anna Quincy Thaxter Cushing Papers, American Antiquarian Society.

110. I previously discussed this quality of fandom in *Tramps Like Us*, 86–133.

111. Donald Grant Mitchell, *The Lorgnette: Or, Studies of the Town. By an Opera Goer* (New York: Stringer & Townsend, 1851), 149–50.

112. Gottschalk, *Notes of a Pianist*, 177.

113. Jean-Jacques Rousseau, *Dictionnaire de Musique* (Chez la Veuve Duchesne, 1768), 31.

114. *Oxford English Dictionary*, 2nd ed. (New York: Oxford University Press, 1989).

115. Charles Burney. *The Present State of Music in France and Italy: Or, the Journal of a Tour through Those Countries, Undertaken to Collect Materials for a General History of Music.* 2nd ed. (T. Becket, 1773), 76.

116. Edward Holmes, *A Ramble among the Musicians of Germany, Giving Some Account of the Operas of Munich, Dresden, Berlin, &c: with Remarks upon the Church Music, Singers, Performers, and Composers; and a Sample of the Pleasures and Inconveniences That Await the Lover of Art on a Similar Excursion* (Hunt & Clarke, 1828), 168 and 22.

117. Johnson, *Listening in Paris*.

118. Christopher H. Gibbs, "'Just Two Words. Enormous Success': Liszt's 1838

Vienna Concerts," in *Franz Liszt and His World*, Christopher H. Gibbs and Dana A. Gooley, eds. (Princeton: Princeton University Press, 2006); see also Gooley, *The Virtuoso Liszt*.

119. Weber, *Music and the Middle Class*, 68.

120. *The Musical Gazette*, 12 October 1846 (vol. 1, no. 19).

121. Charles Pelham Curtis Diary, 23 February 1877.

122. Sarah Spooner Bullard, 21 October 1892, diary, Rotch Family Papers, Massachusetts Historical Society.

123. Alice Drake Travel Diary, 20 December 1896.

124. Lawrence, *Strong on Music*, vol. 1, 504.

125. Francis Bennett Diary, 16 August 1854.

126. William Hoffman Diary, 1 September 1850.

127. Anna Quincy Thaxter Cushing Papers, 3 November 1846.

128. Lawrence, *Strong on Music*, vol. 1, 109.

129. Caroline Wells Healey Dall Journal, 18 June 1838.

130. John Van der Zee Sears, *My Friends at Brook Farm* (New York: D. Fitzgerald, 1912), 81.

131. George Willis Cooke, *John Sullivan Dwight, Brook-farmer, Editor, and Critic of Music: A Biography* (Boston: Small, Maynard, 1898), 64.

132. Lindsay Swift, *Brook Farm: Its Members, Scholars, and Visitors* (New York: Macmillan, 1900), 63. See also Cooke, *John Sullivan Dwight*, 66.

133. For more on the unifying effects of newspaper reading, see Benedict Anderson, *Imagined Communities: Reflections on the Origin and Spread of Nationalism* (London: Verso, 1999), 37–46.

134. *The Musical Gazette*, 2 February 1846 (vol. 1, no. 1): 4.

135. The *Literary Museum* (24 July 24 1852): n.p.

136. See Ralph P. Locke, "Music Lovers, Patrons, and the 'Sacrilization' of Culture in America," *19th-Century Music* 17, no. 2 (1993): 149–73.

137. Tuesday Musicale Scrapbook, 13 July 1892, Tuesday Musicale Collection, accession no. SC1998.7, Ruth T. Watanabe Special Collections, Sibley Music Library, University of Rochester.

138. Peter Gay, *The Bourgeois Experience: Victoria to Freud* (New York: W. W. Norton, 1995), 11–12.

Chapter 5: "Attempering This Whole People to the Sentiment of Art":
Institutionalizing Musical Ecstasy

1. William Allen Butler, *Barnum's Parnassus: Being Confidential Disclosures of the Prize Committee on the Jenny Lind Song* (New York: D. Appleton & Co., 1850), 10. The book is sometimes misattributed to Barnum himself. See, for instance, Henry Stevens, *Catalogue of the American Books in the Library of the British Museum at Christmas MDCCCLVI* (Chiswick: Chiswick Press, 1866), 46; or, more recently, Alan Walker, *Franz Liszt*, vol. 2 (Ithaca: Cornell University Press, 1997), 261, n. 102. At the same time, the extent to which Barnum may have known Butler and may

have helped in the book's publication is unclear. Barnum happily—a little too happily—noted Butler's wit and quoted extensively from the pamphlet in *The Life of P.T. Barnum*, 310–12.

2. W. H. C. West, *The Jenny Lind Mania—a Comic Song* (New York: Wm. Hall & Son, 1850).

3. Meaghan's interest in music blossomed after he was tried for obscenity in 1843 and convicted; he emerged from the episode as a composer and theater producer, publishing the 1849 comic song "California as It Is" (which mocked the hope of the gold-digging '49ers), and opening the new Olympic Theatre in New York in 1857. See Patricia Cline Cohen, Timothy J. Gilfoyle, Helen Lefkowitz Horowitz, and the American Antiquarian Society, *The Flash Press: Sporting Male Weeklies in 1840s New York* (Chicago: University of Chicago Press, 2008), 103–4.

4. Asmodeus, *The Jenny Lind Mania in Boston*, 12.

5. Mitchell, *The Lorgnette*, 231–34.

6. Franz Hinderoth, "The Second Deluge" (New York: W. Schaus, 1850). From the holdings of the Prints and Photographs Collection, Library of Congress, Reproduction number: LC-USZ62–1293.

7. Reproduced in Lawrence, *Strong on Music*, vol. 2, 43.

8. C. G. Bush, "Let Us Have Peace!," *Harper's Weekly* (3 July 1869): 392–93.

9. Augustus Hoppin, Thomas Bailey Aldrich and William Dean Howells, eds. *Jubilee Days: An Illustrated Daily Record of the Humorous Features of the World's Peace Jubilee* (Boston: J. R. Osgood, 1872). Illustrations from 27 June 1872, 44; 1 July 1872, 56; 2 July 1872, 60; and 3 July 1872, 64.

10. Lyra, "A Protest against Wagnerism," *The Critic*, no. 58 (7 February 1885): 66.

11. Mark Twain, "Mark Twain at Bayreuth," *Chicago Daily Tribune* (6 December 1891).

12. Henry Heathcote Statham, *My Thoughts on Music and Musicians* (London: Chapman & Hall, 1892), 324.

13. *Century Illustrated Monthly Magazine* 13, Josiah Gilbert Holland and Richard Watson Gilder, eds. (New York: Charles Scribner's Sons, 1877): 727. The origins of the term *longhair* are not clear. An item in a 1909 issue of *The Violinist*, however, states, "The reason why musicians wear long hair is revealed at last. According to a barber cited in the *Philadelphia Bulletin*, 'they wear long hair to protect their ears—their sensitive ears. All depends, with musicians on the ears, the same as all depends on the eyes with painters. And the ears of musicians are delicate, liable to take cold, liable to aches, inflammations, and what not. So they protect them with long hair, and you have no more right to laugh at the mane of a pianist or violinist than at the protective shields and pads of your favorite halfback.'" *The Violinist* 8, no. 5 (1909), 30.

14. Bushman, *The Refinement of America*, 411. See also Tom Lutz, *Doing Nothing: A History of Loafers, Loungers, Slackers, and Bums in America* (New York: Farrar, Straus & Giroux, 2006).

15. Nathaniel Hawthorne, "The Custom House: Introductory to the Scarlet Letter," in *The Scarlet Letter* (Boston: Bedford Books, 1990), 27.

16. William James, *Talks to Teachers on Psychology, and to Students on Some of Life's Ideals* (New York: Henry Holt, 1916), 70.

17. Phillip H. Ennis, "Ecstasy and Everyday Life," *Journal for the Scientific Study of Religion* 6, no. 1 (Spring 1967): 40–48. The "problem" of ecstasy and music is something that goes back to Plato, whose theories about the dangers of music are addressed in Susan McClary, "Same as It Ever Was: Youth Culture and Music," in *Microphone Fiends: Youth Music and Youth Culture*, Andrew Ross and Tricia Rose, eds. (New York: Routledge, 1994), 29–40. For a summary of the various meanings that might be associated with transcendent musical experience, see Harris Berger and Giovanna Del Negro, *Identity and Everyday Life: Essays in the Study of Folklore, Music, and Popular Culture* (Middletown, Conn.: Wesleyan University Press, 2004), 43–88.

18. Clapp, *A Record of the Boston Stage*, 368–69.

19. David Healy, *Mania: A Short History of Bipolar Disorder* (Baltimore: Johns Hopkins University Press, 2008), 1–23. The *Oxford English Dictionary* entry for *mania* cites the particular use of the term to form nouns referring not only to mental illness but also "passions marked by wild excess or delusion, enthusiastic (and often fashionable) participation in certain activities, or enthusiastic admiration for certain things or persons." It also notes that "about two-thirds of all words with this terminal element are first attested in the 19th century, nearly all of them formations in English. . . . Most compounds formed since 1900 are of infrequent occurrence." See "mania, comb. form," *Oxford English Dictionary*, online draft edition (New York: Oxford University Press, 2008).

20. Mitchell, *The Lorgnette*, 17.

21. Louisa May Alcott, *Psyche's Art* (Boston: Loring, 1868), 3.

22. See Penelope Gouk, "Raising Spirits and Restoring Souls: Early Modern Medical Explanations for Music's Effects," in *Hearing Cultures: Essays on Sound, Listening and Modernity*, Veit Erlmann, ed. (London: Berg Publishers, 2004), 87–105.

23. National Library of Medicine, *Medicine and Music* (Washington, D.C.: Department of Health, Education, and Welfare, 1977).

24. See Karen Ludtke, *Dances with Spiders: Crisis, Celebrity and Celebration in Southern Italy* (Oxford: Berghahn Books, 2009), 61–64.

25. Robley Dunglison, *A New Dictionary of Medical Science and Literature* (Boston: C. Bowen, 1833); John Forbes et al., eds., *The Cyclopaedia of Practical Medicine: Comprising Treatises on the Nature and Treatment of Diseases, Materia Medica, and Therapeutics, Medical Jurisprudence, etc, Vol. I* (Philadelphia: Lea & Blanchard, 1845), 434.

26. The debates over monomania in the nineteenth century are described by Jeffrey Geller, "Back to the Nineteenth Century Is Progress," *Journal of Philosophy, Psychiatry & Psychology* 15, no. 1 (2008): 19–21.

27. E. Esquirol, *Mental Maladies: A Treatise on Insanity*, trans. E. K. Hunt (Philadelphia: Lea & Blanchard, 1845), 200.

28. John Bouvier, in *A Law Dictionary Adapted to the Constitution and Laws of the United States of America, and of the Several States of the American Union; with Refer-*

ences to the Civil and Other Systems of Foreign Law, vol. 2 (Philadelphia: Childs & Peterson, 1856), 102–3, wrote, for instance: "Partial intellectual mania is generally known by the name of monomania. In its most usual and simplest form, the patient has conceived some single notion contrary to common sense and to common experience, generally dependent on errors of sensation. . . . In these cases the understanding is frequently found to be sound on all subjects, except those connected with the hallucination."

29. E. Esquirol, *Mental Maladies*, 342–51.

30. Forbes, *The Cyclopaedia of Practical Medicine*, 159.

31. Dunglison, *New Dictionary of Medical Science and Literature*, 64.

32. C. L. Gemmill, "Robley Dunglison's Dictionary of Medical Science, 1833," *Bulletin of the New York Academy of Medicine* 48, no. 5 (1972): 791–98.

33. Oliver Sacks uses the term *musicophilia* in his book of the same name. See Oliver Sacks, *Musicophilia: Tales of Music and the Brain* (New York: Random House, 2005).

34. See Leonard J. Davis, *Obsession: A History* (Chicago: University of Chicago Press, 2008); Marina Van Zuylen, *Monomania: The Flight from Everyday Life in Literature and Art* (Ithaca: Cornell University Press, 2005); Jan Goldstein, *Console and Classify: The French Psychiatric Profession in the Nineteenth Century* (Cambridge: Cambridge University Press, 1987), 152–55.

35. *The Musical World* 20, no. 35 (Thursday, 28 August 1845): 416.

36. Lawrence, *Strong on Music*, vol. 1, 182.

37. Francesca Brittan, "Berlioz and the Pathological Fantastic: Melancholy, Monomania, and Romantic Autobiography," *19th-Century Music* 29, no. 3 (2006): 227–28.

38. Louis C. Elson, "Richard Wagner: His Life and Influence," *Frank Leslie's Popular Monthly* 23, no. 5 (1887): 564.

39. Hector Berlioz, *Selections from His Letters, and Aesthetic, Humorous, and Satirical Writings*, trans. William F. Apthorp (New York: Henry Holt, 1879), 289.

40. Berlioz, *Selections*, 295–96.

41. Jon Mee, *Romanticism, Enthusiasm, and Regulation* (New York: Oxford University Press, 2005), 12. Critiques of enthusiasm are complex, involving minute distinctions of theology among Lutherans, Anglicans, Puritans, Deists, and various types of evangelicals, as well as Enlightenment philosophers. The standard overview remains Michael Heyd, *Be Sober and Reasonable: The Critique of Enthusiasm in the Seventeenth and Early Eighteenth Centuries* (Leiden: E. J. Brill, 1995). See also the special issue of the *Huntington Library Quarterly* titled *Enthusiasm and Enlightenment in Europe, 1650–1850*, 60, nos. 1 and 2 (1997), and David Herd, *Enthusiast! Essays on Modern Literature* (Manchester: Manchester University Press, 2007).

42. Lawrence E. Klein, "Sociability, Solitude, and Enthusiasm," *Huntington Library Quarterly* 60, nos. 1 and 2 (1997): 171.

43. Wordsworth, "Preface to the Lyrical Ballads," in *The Complete Poetical Works of William Wordsworth* (Boston: Houghton, Mifflin, 1919).

44. Herd, *Enthusiast!*, 20.

45. See Richard Leppert, "Cultural Contradiction, Idolatry, and the Piano Vir-

tuoso: Franz Liszt," in *Piano Roles: A New History of the Piano* (New Haven: Yale University Press, 2002), 206; Mirko Hall, "Friedrich Schlegel's Romanticization of Music," *Eighteenth-Century Studies* 42, no. 3 (2009): 413–29.

46. John Steinfort Kedney, *The Beautiful and the Sublime: An Analysis of These Emotions and a Determination of the Objectivity of Beauty* (New York: G. P. Putnam's Sons, 1880), 83.

47. See Martha Feldman, "Music and the Order of the Passions," in *Representing the Passions: Histories, Bodies, Visions*, Richard Meyer, ed. (Los Angeles: Getty Research Institute, 2003), 37–67.

48. Mee, *Romanticism*, 5.

49. Jon Mee has argued that this hesitance was also shared among some of the Romantic poets of England, including Samuel Taylor Coleridge. See Jon Mee, "Anxieties of Enthusiasm: Coleridge, Prophecy, and Popular Politics in the 1790s," *Huntington Library Quarterly* 60, nos. 1 and 2 (1997): 179–203.

50. Feldman, "Music and the Order of the Passions," 54. See also Otniel E. Dror, "Dangerous Liaisons: Science, Amusement, and the Civilizing Process," in *Representing Emotions: New Connections in the Histories of Art, Music, and Medicine*, Penelope Gouk and Helen Hills, eds. (Aldershot: Ashgate, 2005), 223–34. Middle-class understandings of the body and individuality can be usefully juxtaposed to understandings among those outside the middle-class world, namely white workers and African Americans. See, for example, Grant Olwage, "The Class and Colour of Tone: An Essay on the Social History of Vocal Timbre," *Ethnomusicology Forum* 13, no. 2 (2004): 203–26; or Charles Keil, "Motion and Feeling through Music," in *Music Grooves: Essays & Dialogues*, Charles Keil and Steven Feld (Chicago: University of Chicago Press, 1994): 53–76.

51. Anthony J. La Vopa, "The Philosopher and the Schwärmer: On the Career of a German Epithet from Luther to Kant," *Huntington Library Quarterly* 60, nos. 1 and 2 (1997): 92.

52. Mee, *Romanticism*, 16.

53. For a summary of these arguments, see Herd, *Enthusiast!*, 6–7.

54. Lawrence Klein and Anthony J. La Vopa, "Introduction," *The Huntington Library Quarterly* 60, nos. 1 and 2 (1997): 5.

55. See Mee, *Romanticisim*, 29; Clement Hawes, *Mania and Literary Style: The Rhetoric of Enthusiasm from the Ranters to Christopher Smart* (Cambridge: Cambridge University Press, 1996), 4–5.

56. Hawes, *Mania and Literary Style*, esp. 25–100.

57. David Lovejoy, *Religious Enthusiasm in the New World: Heresy to Revolution* (Cambridge, Mass.: Harvard University Press, 1985), 224–27. This reversal of an insult is interestingly similar to the Patriots' embrace of the satire in the British song "Yankee Doodle."

58. Gustave Le Bon, *The Crowd: A Study of the Popular Mind* (London: T. Fisher Unwin, 1903), 82. See also Richard Butsch's discussion of Le Bon and nineteenth-century crowds in *The Citizen Audience: Crowds, Publics, and Individuals* (New York: Routledge, 2008): 33–35.

59. Gustave Le Bon, *The Crowd: A Study of the Popular Mind* (London: T. Fisher Unwin, 1903), 57–59.

60. See Moore, *Selling God*, 76–78.

61. John F. Watson, *Methodist Error, or Friendly Christian Advice to Those Methodists Who Indulge in Extravagant Religious Emotions and Bodily Exercises* (Trenton, N.J.: D. and E. Fenton, 1819). For a classic caricature of a camp meeting, see "Religious Camp Meeting," Watercolor by J. Maze Burbank, *c.* 1839, Gift of William F. Havemeyer, Old Dartmouth Historical Society-New Bedford Whaling Museum, New Bedford, Massachusetts.

62. David W. Stowell, "Murder at a Methodist Camp Meeting: The Origins of Abraham Lincoln's Most Famous Trial," *Journal of the Illinois State Historical Society* 101, nos. 3–4 (2008): 221; see also Roger Robins, "Vernacular American Landscape: Methodists, Camp Meetings, and Social Respectability," *Religion and American Culture* 4, no. 2 (1994): 165–91.

63. William Cullen Bryant, *The Letters of William Cullen Bryant*, 438.

64. Caroline Wells Healey Dall Journal, 30 October 1850.

65. *Punch Magazine* (5 October 1850): n.p.

66. Asmodeous, *The Jenny Lind Mania in Boston*, 34.

67. "The Effects of Music," *New York Musical Review and Gazette* 8, no. 8 (18 April 1857): 117.

68. Rev. G. S. Weaver, *Hopes and Helps for the Young of Both Sexes* (New York: Fowlers & Wells, 1854), 37.

69. The tension between passion and refinement is discussed with a slightly different emphasis on sexuality in Maureen Needham Costonis, "The Personification of Desire: Fanny Elssler and American Audiences," *Dance Chronicle* 13, no. 1 (1990): 47–67.

70. Henry Lunettes, *The American Gentleman's Guide to Politeness and Fashion, or Familiar Letters to His Nephews* (New York: Derby & Jackson, 1858), 73.

71. Alfred Guillaume Gabriel d'Orsay, *Etiquette: Or, a Guide to the Usages of Society, with a Glance at Bad Habits* (New York: Wilson, 1843), 25.

72. Daniel Wise, *The Young Lady's Counsellor* (New York: Carlton and Porter, 1857), 22–23.

73. Bushman, *The Refinement of America*, 313.

74. Dr. J. Mainzer, *Music and Education* (London: Longman, Brown, Green & Longmans, 1853), 9.

75. Lucy Lowell Diary, 26 March 1887.

76. Lawrence, *Strong on Music*, vol. 1, 370.

77. Adolf Bernhard Marx, *The Music of the Nineteenth Century and Its Culture*, trans. C. Natalia MacFarren (London: Robert Cocks, 1854), 260.

78. Philip Ennis had identified later manifestations of this distinction in the social theories of both Karl Mannheim and Max Weber. See Ennis, "Ecstasy and Everyday Life," 40–41.

79. John S. Dwight, "Introductory," *Dwight's Journal of Music* 1, no. 1 (10 April 1852): 4.

80. See Levine, *Highbrow/Lowbrow*; Kasson, *Rudeness and Civility*; McConachie, *Melodramatic Formations*; Butsch, *The Making of American Audiences*.

81. William Foster Althorp, "Musicians and Music Lovers," *Atlantic Monthly* (February 1879): 150.

82. Criticism of Lawrence Levine's influential arguments about the elitism of reformers like Dwight and conductor Theodore Thomas can be found in Ralph P. Locke, "Music Lovers, Patrons, and the 'Sacralization' of Culture in America," *19th-Century Music* 17 (Fall 1993): 149–173; Joseph Horowitz, *Classical Music in America: A History of Its Rise and Fall* (New York: W. W. Norton, 2005), 242–62; and Newman, *Good Music for a Free People.* The ongoing debate about disciplining nineteenth-century music audiences is discussed in Steven Baur, "Music, Morals, and Social Management: Mendelssohn in Post–Civil War America," *American Music* 19, no. 1 (2001): 64–130. While Baur reemphasizes the institutionalization of social control by the 1870s and 1880s, I see far more variance and ambivalence in audience behavior and attitudes up until the early 1900s. That is, while the distinction between "commercial amusements" and "concerts" was certainly developing in this period, I would argue that the distinction was more readily employed by reformers and critics than by listeners.

83. Kasson, *Rudeness and Civility*, 251.

84. William Weber registers similar skepticism about silence among audiences, in response to Johnson's *Listening in Paris.* See "Did People Listen in the 18th Century?," *Early Music* 25, no. 4, 25th Anniversary Issue; Listening Practice (Nov. 1997): 678–91.

85. Buckley, *To the Opera House*, 145. William Weber, in *Music and the Middle Class*, has articulated this diversity in Europe by asserting different taste publics that did not correspond neatly to social class divisions.

86. Dwight, "Introductory," 4.

87. A piece in the *Atlantic Monthly* in 1874 stated that reform must proceed "by stealth, unsuspected by the audience" because "the music-likers have nevertheless their rights, and it behooves those who really love the art to see that they get them, and more; even that they be, if possible, changed to music-lovers and musicians. But such a change can by no means be brought about by violence nor by mere argument. Do not even debar them from hearing bad music, but, by giving them proper opportunities, lead them to find out for themselves that they like good music better than bad." See "Music," *Atlantic Monthly*, no. 197 (March 1874): 381–83.

88. Edward Dickinson, *The Education of a Music Lover* (New York: Charles Scribner's Sons, 1911), 282–83.

89. From an undated Gilmore Band program in Collection of Concert Programs, Research Library and Archives, Buffalo and Erie County Historical Society.

90. Nathan Webb Diary, 10 March 1789.

91. Max Maretzek, *Crochets and Quavers: Or, Revelations of an Opera Manager in America* (New York: S. French, 1855), 71.

92. Tuesday Musicale Scrapbook, 13 July 1892.

93. Quoted in Laura Whitesitt, "The Role of Women Impresarios in American

Concert Life, 1871–1933," *American Music* 7, no. 2 (1989): 177, n. 18. For a more recent account of women, reform, and music, see Derek Vaillant, *Sounds of Reform: Progressivism and Music in Chicago, 1873–1935* (Chapel Hill: University of North Carolina Press: 2006).

94. Ruth Solie, *Music in Other Words: Victorian Conversations* (Berkeley: University of California Press, 2004), 92.

95. Maretzek, *Crochets and Quavers*, 72.

96. Michael Broyles, "Art Music from 1860 to 1920," in *The Cambridge History of American Music*, David Nicholls, ed. (Cambridge: Cambridge University Press, 1998): 229. This development is also specifically emphasized in the work of Ralph P. Locke. See Ralph P. Locke, "Paradoxes of the Woman Music Patron in America," *Musical Quarterly* 78, no. 4 (1994): 798–825.

97. Adrienne Fried Block, "Matinee Mania," *19th-Century Music* 31, no. 3 (2008): 193–216.

98. See Steven Baur, "Waltz Me Round Again, Willie: Gender, Ideology, and the Waltz in the Gilded Age," in *Musicological Identities: Essays in Honor of Susan McClary*, Raymond Knapp, Steven Baur, and Jacqueline Warwick, eds. (Aldershot: Ashgate, 2008), 48–62; Rabinowitz, "With Our Own Dominant Passions," 242–52; and Kallberg, "The Harmony of the Tea Table: Gender and Ideology in the Piano Nocturne."

99. Quoted in Bailey Van Hook, *Angels of Art: Women and Art in American Society, 1876–1914* (Philadelphia: Penn State Press, 1996), 145.

100. Lears, *No Place of Grace*, 32.

101. Randall Knoper, *Acting Naturally: Mark Twain in the Culture of Performance* (Berkeley: University of California Press, 1995), 26.

102. Horowitz, *Wagner Nights*, 215.

103. Burton W. Peretti, "Democratic Leitmotivs in the American Reception of Wagner." *19th-Century Music* 13, no. 1 (1989): 20.

104. "Richard Wagner and His Theories, II," *Dwight's Journal of Music*, vol. 34, whole no. 867 (Saturday, 11 July 1874): 263; "Wagner's Last Opera," *Dwight's Journal of Music*, vol. 30, no. 14 (24 September 1870): 320.

105. John Stuart Mill, "The Subjection of Women," Political Science Study Series, vol. 1, no. 2 (September 1895): 340.

106. Edith Brower, "Is the Musical Idea Masculine?," *Atlantic Monthly* 73 (1894): 333.

107. Craig H. Roell, *The Piano in America: 1890–1940* (Chapel Hill: University of North Carolina Press, 1989), 45–58.

108. See Andreas Huyssen, "Mass Culture as Woman: Modernism's Other," in *After the Great Divide: Modernism, Mass Culture, Postmodernism* (Bloomington: Indiana University Press, 1986), 44–62.

109. Carroll Smith-Rosenberg and Charles Rosenberg, "The Female Animal: Medical and Biological Views of Woman and Her Role in Nineteenth-Century America," *Journal of American History* 60, no. 2 (1973): 337. This was the dilemma at the heart of Louisa May Alcott's 1868 novella *Psyche's Art*, in which a young and

talented woman artist, Psyche Dean, with "painfully prosaic" parents, must leave her art studio friends for a life of household drudgery when her sister takes ill. After her sister dies, Psyche allegedly matures, arguing that "doing one's duty *is* the way to feed heart, soul, and imagination; for if one is good, one is happy, and if happy, one can work well." It is an ambiguous ending, implying that Psyche is trying but not succeeding in convincing herself that her familial duty is paramount over her desire to assume a more independent and creative life.

110. Rabinowitz, "With Our Own Dominant Passions."

111. Derek B. Scott, "The Sexual Politics of Victorian Musical Aesthetics," *Journal of the Royal Musical Association* 119, no. 1 (1994): 93.

112. See Bliss Perry, *The Life and Letters of Henry Lee Higginson* (Boston: Atlantic Monthly Press, 1921), 267. See also Levine, *Highbrow/Lowbrow*, 123.

113. Susan Fast, "Gender Ideologies in Nineteenth- and Early Twentieth-Century Music Making," in *Music Cultures in the United States: An Introduction*, Ellen Koskoff, ed. (New York: Routledge, 2005), 82.

114. Willa Cather, "Paul's Case," in *Great Short Works of Willa Cather*, Robert K. Miller, ed. (New York: Perennial/Harper & Row, 1989), 75. Wayne Koestenbaum has interpreted the homosexual themes of the story in *The Queen's Throat: Opera, Homosexuality and the Mystery of Desire* (New York: Vintage Press, 1993), 28–29.

115. "Women and Music," *The Musical Record*, no. 392 (September 1894): 12.

116. Mary Cassatt, *In the Loge (at the Francais, a Sketch)*, 1878. Museum of Fine Arts, Boston. The image is available online at the Museum of Fine Arts website, www.mfa.org/collections/object/in-the-loge-31365.

117. Griselda Pollock, *Mary Cassatt: Painter of Modern Women* (London: Thames & Hudson, 1998), 145.

118. See Linda L. Tyler, "'Commerce and Poetry Hand in Hand': Music in American Department Stores, 1880–1930," *Journal of the American Musicological Society* 45, no. 1 (1992): 75–120. Though addressing the end of the century, see also the insights of Mark Claque, "The Industrial Evolution of the Arts: Chicago's Auditorium Building (1889–) as a Cultural Machine," *Opera Quarterly* 22, nos. 3–4 (2006): 477–511.

119. Loesser, *Men, Women and Pianos*, 560–64.

120. Kenneth Allen Diary, 23 January 1874.

121. Dwight, "Introductory," 4.

122. Cavicchi, *Tramps Like Us*, 60–85; Matt Hills, *Fan Cultures* (New York: Routledge, 2002), 27–45. Given the murky etymology and meaning of the term "fan" (see Cavicchi, *Tramps Like Us*, 38–39), it may be more useful, in thinking about the history of fandom, to start not with the emergence of the descriptive term "fan" but rather with the existing patterns of behavior that historically contingent term was meant to describe. As I have argued elsewhere (see Daniel Cavicchi, "Fans and Fan Clubs," *Encyclopedia of Recreation and Leisure in America*, vol. 1, Gary S. Cross et al., eds. (New York: Charles Scribner's Sons, 2004), 326–30), there is evidence of fan-like practices among people participating in the commodification of urban leisure in the industrial West before 1900, including the readers of mass-produced

books, opera lovers, urban theater-goers, and the members of fraternal baseball clubs. Music culture, in particular, is useful for opening up the history of fandom because it was at the forefront of both twentieth-century media technology (in the form of recording and broadcasting) as well as nineteenth-century urban entertainment (in the form of commodified performance and mass-published texts) and thus provides linkages between what typically has been perceived as different eras of audience behavior.

Epilogue

1. Glenn Gould, "The Prospects of Recording," *High Fidelity Magazine* 16, no. 4 (1966): 46–63.

2. Tia DeNora, *Music in Everyday Life* (Cambridge: Cambridge University Press, 2000).

3. E. Eugene Helm explained in a 1994 survey of musicology and ethnomusicology programs in America, "The main message of all undergraduate music curricula endorsed by the National Association of Schools of Music is that the student must be trained first as a practical musician. . . . If an undergraduate already happens to be an accomplished practical musician and wishes to set performance aside in order to take more courses in such subjects as foreign languages and history, NASM makes it very difficult for him or her to do so, as long as the university wants to keep its NASM accreditation." See E. Eugene Helm, *The Canon and the Curricula: A Study of Musicology and Ethnomusicology Programs in America* (Stuyvesant, N.Y.: Pendragon Press, 1994), 96.

4. Tommy Shapard, "Subject: Re: Outsider Take on Western Music," SEM-List, 22 July 1998.

5. Peter G. Toner, "Re: Americans' Alleged Ignorance of Music," SEM-List, 24 July 1998.

6. Michael L. Mark, *Contemporary Music Education* (New York: Schirmer Books, 1996), 10.

7. Tawa, *High-Minded and Low-Down*, 297.

8. The full text of the argument is available online at www.iamea.org. I would contend that the history offered in the excerpt, here, is wrong, ignoring the role of middle-class educators and reformers in professionalizing musical performance, long before recording technology even existed.

9. Sociologist Antoine Hennion has similarly critiqued the carelessness with which "passivity" and "activity" have been applied to various musical practices. See Antoine Hennion, "Music Lovers: Taste as Performance," *Theory Culture, Society* 18, no. 5 (2001): 1–22.

10. Loesser, *Men, Women and Pianos*, 520.

11. Roell, *The Piano in America*, 151–56. Roell expresses quite a bit of skepticism about this episode in the history of the piano business, suggesting that it eventually undermined the market for "regular" pianos. Yet at the same time, he admits (277–78), "The piano trade's experience demonstrates that the encroachment of consum-

erism is probably impossible to date accurately. It was certainly evident by the mid-to-late nineteenth century, definite by the first decade of the present century, and comfortably recognizable by the 1920s. This development was gradual, allowing time for adjustment to change as well as opportunity for even traditional businesses to profit, though not without risk."

12. For recent scholarship on the first musical applications of the phonograph, see Taylor, "The Commodification of Music"; Mark Katz, *Capturing Sound: How Technology Has Changed Music* (Berkeley: University of California Press, 2004), 48–71; and Kenney, *Recorded Music in American Life*, 3–22.

Bibliography

Unpublished/Archival Sources

Allen, Kenneth. Diary, 1874. Octavo Vols. A. Manuscripts Collection, American Antiquarian Society.

Atkins, Helen. Journal, 1872. Atkins Family Papers, Massachusetts Historical Society.

Atkins, Mary E. F. Diary, 1872–96. Atkins Family Papers, Massachusetts Historical Society.

Beekley, N. Diary, 1849. Octavo Vols. B. Manuscripts Collection, American Antiquarian Society.

Bennett, Francis, Jr. Diary, 1852–54. Octavo Vols. B. Manuscripts Collection, American Antiquarian Society.

Bullard, Sarah Spooner. Diary, 1892. Rotch Family Papers, Massachusetts Historical Society.

Burr, Adelaide Crossman. Diary, 1867. Octavo Vols. B. Manuscripts Collection, American Antiquarian Society.

Castle Garden. Daybook, 1843 May–1851 May. BV Castle Garden. New-York Historical Society.

Chamberlain, Loyed E. Diaries, 1876–77. Loyed E. Chamberlain Papers. Massachusetts Historical Society.

Collection of Concert Programs. Vertical File: Music Programs; Choral Music; Vocal and Instrumental Concerts (mixed); Band Concerts (includes Big Band). Research Library and Archives, Buffalo and Erie County Historical Society.

Curtis, Charles Pelham. Diary, 1873–85. Massachusetts Historical Society.

Cushing, Anna Quincy Thaxter. Papers, 1816–1918. Vols. 2–9. Octavo Vols. C. Manuscripts Collection. American Antiquarian Society.

Dall, Caroline Wells Healy. Journal. *Caroline H. Dall Papers, 1811–1917*. Microfilm edition, 45 reels. Boston: Massachusetts Historical Society, 1981. Reel 32. Massachusetts Historical Society.

Drake, Alice. Travel Diary, 1896. Special Collections. Irving S. Gilmore Music Library, Yale University.

Hoffman, William. Diary, 1847–50. BV Hoffman, William (MS 1543). Courtesy of New-York Historical Society.

Jenny Lind Collection, Manuscripts Collection. Irving S. Gilmore Music Library, Yale University.

Letters to Frieda Hempel about Jenny Lind, 1924. "Music of Jenny Lind and Her Contemporaries." Jenny Lind Collection. New-York Historical Society.

Local Music History Scrapbooks, Ruth T. Watanabe Special Collections. University of Rochester, Sibley Music Library.

Lowell, Lucy Buckminster Emerson. Diary 1845–48. Lucy Lowell Diaries. Massachusetts Historical Society.

Lowell, Lucy. Diary. Lucy Lowell Diaries. Massachusetts Historical Society.

New Haven Concert Programs, 1839–1912. Folders 1–6. Special Collections. Irving S. Gilmore Music Library, Yale University.

New Haven Musical Association Records, 1848. Special Collections. Irving S. Gilmore Music Library, Yale University.

Oakman, Otis Briggs. Diary, 1849–62. Massachusetts Historical Society.

Parker, Charles D. Diary, 1870. Division of Rare and Manuscripts Collections, Carl A. Kroch Library, Cornell University.

Parks, Edith May. Scrapbook. Accession no. SC1998.9. Ruth T. Watanabe Special Collections. Sibley Music Library, University of Rochester.

Program for Madame Henriette Sontag's Last Grand Performance. Boston Music Hall, 185[?]. Massachusetts Historical Society.

Programme of Mademoiselle Jenny Lind's Concert: With the Words of the Airs in Italian, German, Swedish and English. Theater Collection, Massachusetts Historical Society.

Putnam, Sarah Gooll. Diaries, Vol. 15, 1882–85. Sarah Gooll Putnam Diaries. Massachusetts Historical Society.

Quincy, Edmund. Journal, 1852. *Quincy, Wendell, Holmes, and Upham Family Papers, 1633–1910*. Microfilm edition, 67 reels. Boston: Massachusetts Historical Society, 1977. Reel 11. Massachusetts Historical Society.

Quincy, Eliza Susan. Journal [extracts], 1814–21. *Quincy, Wendell, Holmes, and Upham Family Papers, 1633–1910*. Microfilm edition, 67 reels. Boston: Massachusetts Historical Society, 1977. Reel 5. Massachusetts Historical Society.

Scrapbook containing newspaper articles and clippings relating to the National Peace Jubilee and Musical Festival, Boston, 1869. Massachusetts Historical Society.

Sill, Joseph. Diary, 1831–41. Vols. 1–10. Collection #600. The Historical Society of Pennsylvania.

Smith, William. Diary, February 1842–February 1851. BV Smith, William (MS 2420). Courtesy of New-York Historical Society.

Southworth, Henry Clay. Diary, 1850–51. BV Southworth, Henry Clay (MS 2431). Courtesy of New-York Historical Society.

Theater and Concert Programs, Miscellaneous Collection, Music Department, Boston Public Library.

Tracy, Charles. Diary, 1856–57. BV Tracy, Charles (MS 2901). Courtesy of New-York Historical Society.

Tuesday Musicale Scrapbook, 1891–94. Tuesday Musicale Collection. Accession no. SC1998.7. Ruth T. Watanabe Special Collections. Sibley Music Library, University of Rochester.

Webb, Nathan. Diary, 1788–91. Massachusetts Historical Society.

Whitaker, Thomas Arthur. Diary, 1874–78. Folio Vols. W. Manuscripts Collection, American Antiquarian Society.

White, Caroline Barrett. Papers, 1844–1915. Vol. 3. Octavo Vols. W. Manuscripts Collection, American Antiquarian Society.

Published Books and Articles

Adams, Bluford. *E Pluribus Barnum: The Great Showman & the Making of U.S. Popular Culture*. Minneapolis: University of Minnesota Press, 1997.

Alcott, Louisa May. *Psyche's Art*. Boston: Loring, 1868.

Alquist, Karen. *Democracy at the Opera: Music, Theater, and Culture in New York City, 1815–60*. Urbana: University of Illinois Press, 1997.

Altschuler, Glenn C., and Stuart M. Blumin. "Limits of Political Engagement in Antebellum America: A New Look at the Golden Age of Participatory Democracy." *Journal of American History* 84, no. 3 (1997): 855–85.

Altschuler, Glenn C., and Stuart M. Blumin. *Rude Republic: Americans and Their Politics in the Nineteenth Century*. Princeton: Princeton University Press, 2000.

Anderson, Benedict. *Imagined Communities: Reflections on the Origin and Spread of Nationalism*. London: Verso, 1999.

Antczak, Frederick J. *Thought and Character: The Rhetoric of Democratic Education*. Ames: Iowa State University Press, 1985.

Apthorp, William Foster. "Musicians and Music Lovers." *Atlantic Monthly* 43, no. 256 (1879): 145–53.

Arden, Eugene. "The Evil City in American Fiction." *New York History* 35 (July 1954): 259–79.

Arnold, Matthew. *Culture and Anarchy: An Essay in Political and Social Criticism*. New York: Macmillan, 1883.

Asmodeus. *The Jenny Lind Mania in Boston or, a Sequel to Barnum's Parnassus*. Boston: n.p., 1850.

Attali, Jacques. *Noise: The Political Economy of Music*. Minneapolis: University of Minnesota Press, 1985.

Augst, Thomas. *The Clerk's Tale: Young Men and Moral Life in Nineteenth-Century America*. Chicago: University of Chicago Press, 2003.

Augst, Thomas. "Composing the Moral Senses: Emerson and the Politics of Character in Nineteenth-Century America." *Political Theory* 27, no. 1 (1999): 85–120.

Axel, Brian Keith, ed. *From the Margins: Historical Anthropology and Its Futures*. Durham, N.C.: Duke University Press, 2002.

Baker, Thomas N. *Sentiment and Celebrity: Nathaniel Parker Willis and the Trials of Literary Fame*. New York: Oxford University Press, 1999.

Bank, Rosemarie K. *Theatre Culture in America, 1825–1860*. Cambridge: Cambridge University Press, 2003.

Barnum, P. T. *Struggles and Triumphs, or, Sixty Years' Recollection of P. T. Barnum*. Buffalo: Courier, 1889.

Barnum, P. T. *The Life of P. T. Barnum, Written by Himself*. Urbana: University of Illinois Press, 2000 [1855].

Barthes, Roland. "The Death of the Author." In *Image, Music, Text*. New York: Hill & Wang, 1977.

Baur, Steven. "Waltz Me Round Again, Willie: Gender, Ideology, and the Waltz in the Gilded Age." In *Musicological Identities: Essays in Honor of Susan McClary*, 48–62. Raymond Knapp, Steven Baur, and Jacqueline Warwick, eds. Aldershot: Ashgate, 2008.

Baur, Steven. "Music, Morals, and Social Management: Mendelssohn in Post-Civil War America." *American Music* 19, no. 1 (2001): 64–130.

Baxter, Terry. *Frederick Douglass's Curious Audiences: Ethos in the Age of the Consumable Subject*. New York: Routledge, 2004.

Bellamy, Edward. *Looking Backward: 2000–1887*. Boston: Ticknor, 1888; rpt., Harmondsworth, Middlesex, England: Penguin Books, 1982.

Berger, Harris, and Giovanna Del Negro. *Identity and Everyday Life: Essays in the Study of Folklore, Music, and Popular Culture*. Middletown, Conn: Wesleyan University Press, 2004.

Berlioz, Hector. *Selections from His Letters, and Aesthetic, Humorous, and Satirical Writings*. Trans. William F. Apthorp. New York: Henry Holt, 1879.

Biographical, Historical, and Incidental Sketch of Ossian E. Dodge, Including His Character, Phrenologically Considered, by His Old Friends, O. S. & L. N. Fowler. Boston: Wright & Potter, 1860.

Bird, Joseph. *Gleanings from the History of Music*. Boston: Benjamin B. Mussey, 1850.

Blake, David Haven. *Walt Whitman and the Culture of American Celebrity*. New Haven: Yale University Press, 2006.

Block, Adrienne Fried. "Matinee Mania." *19th-Century Music* 31, no. 3 (2008): 193–216.

Blumin, Stuart. "The Hypothesis of Middle-Class Formation in Nineteenth-Century America: A Critique and Some Proposals." *American Historical Review* 90, no. 2 (1985): 299–338.

Blumin, Stuart. *The Emergence of the Middle Class: Social Experience in the American City, 1760–1900*. Cambridge: Cambridge University Press, 1989.

Bourdieu, Pierre. *Distinction: A Social Critique of the Judgment of Taste*. Cambridge, Mass.: Harvard University Press, 1987.

Botstein, Leon. *Music and Its Public: Habits of Listening and the Crisis of Musical Modernism in Vienna, 1870–1914*. Ph.D. diss., Harvard University, 1985.

Botstein, Leon. "Toward a History of Listening." *Musical Quarterly* 82, nos. 3–4 (1998): 427–31.

Braudy, Leo. *The Frenzy of Renown: Fame and its History*. New York: Oxford University Press, 1988.

Brittan, Francesca. "Berlioz and the Pathological Fantastic: Melancholy, Monomania, and Romantic Autobiography." *19th-Century Music* 29, no. 3 (2006): 211–39.

Brooks, Van Wyck. *The Flowering of New England, 1815–1865.* New York: E. P. Dutton, 1937.

Brown, Gillian. *Domestic Individualism: Imaging Self in Nineteenth-Century America.* Berkeley: University of California Press, 1992.

Broyles, Michael. "Art Music from 1860 to 1920." In *The Cambridge History of American Music,* 214–54. David Nicholls, ed. Cambridge: Cambridge University Press, 1998.

Broyles, Michael. "Music and Class Structure in Antebellum Boston." *Journal of the American Musicological Society* 44, no. 3 (1991): 451–93.

Broyles, Michael. *Music of the Highest Class: Elitism and Populism in Antebellum Boston.* New Haven: Yale University Press, 1992.

Bryant, William Cullen, II, and Thomas G. Voss, eds. *Letters of William Cullen Bryant.* Vol. 2. New York: Fordham University Press, 1975.

Buckley, Peter G. "Popular Entertainment before the Civil War." In *Encyclopedia of American Social History.* Vol. 3, 1611–1625. Mary K. Cayton, Elliot J. Gorn, and Peter W. Williams, eds. New York: Charles Scribner's Sons, 1993.

Buckley, Peter G. *To the Opera House: Culture and Society in New York City, 1820–1860.* Ph.D. diss., State University of New York at Stony Brook, 1984.

Bull, Michael, and Les Back, eds. *The Auditory Culture Reader.* Oxford: Berg, 2003.

Bull, Sara Chapman Thorp, Ole Bull, and Alpheus Benning Crosby. *Ole Bull: A Memoir.* Boston: Houghton, Mifflin, 1882.

Burney, Charles. *The Present State of Music in France and Italy: Or, the Journal of a Tour through Those Countries, Undertaken to Collect Materials for a General History of Music.* 2nd ed. London: T. Becket, 1773.

Bushman, Richard. *The Refinement of America: Persons, Cities, Houses.* New York: Vintage Books, 1992.

Butler, Nicholas Michael. *Votaries of Apollo: The St. Cecilia Society and the Patronage of Concert Music in Charleston, South Carolina, 1766–1820.* Columbia: University of South Carolina Press, 2007.

Butler, William Allen. *Barnum's Parnassus: Being Confidential Disclosures of the Prize Committee on the Jenny Lind Song.* New York: D. Appleton, 1850.

Butsch, Richard. *The Citizen Audience: Crowds, Publics, and Individuals.* New York: Routledge, 2008.

Butsch, Richard. *The Making of American Audiences: From Stage to Television, 1750–1990.* New York: Cambridge University Press, 2000.

Callow, Philip. *From Noon to Starry Night: A Life of Walt Whitman.* Chicago: Ivan R. Dee, 1992.

Casper, Scott. *Constructing American Lives: Biography and Culture in Nineteenth-Century America.* Chapel Hill: University of North Carolina Press, 1999.

Cather, Willa. *Great Short Works of Willa Cather.* Robert K. Miller, ed. New York: Perennial/Harper and Row, 1989.

Cavicchi, Daniel. *Tramps Like Us: Music and Meaning among Springsteen Fans.* New York: Oxford University Press, 1998.

Cavicchi, Daniel. "Fans and Fan Clubs." In *Encyclopedia of Recreation and Leisure in*

America, 326–30. Vol. 1. Gary S. Cross et al., eds. New York: Charles Scribner's Sons, 2004.

Chase, Gilbert. *America's Music: From the Pilgrims to the Present*. Urbana: University of Illinois Press, 1992.

Cheney, Sheldon. "The Book-Plates of Musicians and Music-Lovers." *Musical Quarterly* 3, no. 3 (1917): 446–52.

Child, Lydia. *The Mother's Book*. Boston: Carter, Hendee, and Babcock, 1831.

Chudacoff, Howard P. and Judith E. Smith, *The Evolution of American Urban Society*, 4th ed. Englewood Cliffs, N.J.: Prentice Hall: 1994.

Clapp, William. *A Record of the Boston Stage*. New York: Benjamin Blom, 1968 [orig. 1853].

Claque, Mark. "The Industrial Evolution of the Arts: Chicago's Auditorium Building (1889–) as a Cultural Machine." *Opera Quarterly* 22, nos. 3–4 (2006): 477–511.

Clapp, William E. Jr. *A Record of the Boston Stage*. New York: Benjamin Blom, 1968 [1853].

Clark, Elizabeth. "The Sacred Rights of the Weak: Pain, Sympathy, and the Culture of Individual Rights in Antebellum America. *Journal of American History* 82, no. 2 (1995): 463–93.

Cliff, Nigel. *The Shakespeare Riots: Revenge, Drama, and Death in Nineteenth-Century America*. New York: Random House, 2007.

Cockrell, Dale. *Excelsior: Journals of the Hutchinson Family Singers, 1842–1846*. Stuveysant, N.Y.: Pendragon Press, 1989.

Cockrell, Dale. *Demons of Disorder*. Cambridge: Cambridge University Press, 1997.

Cockrell, Dale. "Nineteenth-Century Popular Music." In *The Cambridge History of American Music*, 182–85. David Nicholls, ed. Cambridge: Cambridge University Press, 1998.

Cohen, Patricia Cline, Timothy J. Gilfoyle, Helen Lefkowitz Horowitz, and the American Antiquarian Society. *The Flash Press: Sporting Male Weeklies in 1840s New York*. Chicago: University of Chicago Press, 2008.

Cook, James W. *The Arts of Deception: Playing with Fraud in the Age of Barnum*. Cambridge, Mass.: Harvard University Press, 2001.

Cooke, George Willis. *John Sullivan Dwight, Brook-farmer, Editor, and Critic of Music: A Biography*. N.p.: Small, Maynard, 1898.

Copeland, Jennie. *Everyday but Sunday: The Romantic Age of New England Industry*. Brattleboro, Vt.: Stephen Daye Press, 1936.

Corbin, Alain. *Village Bells: Sound and Meaning in the Nineteenth-Century French Countryside*. New York: Columbia University Press, 1994.

Costonis, Maureen Needham. "The Personification of Desire: Fanny Elssler and American Audiences." *Dance Chronicle* 13, no. 1 (1990): 47–67.

Crawford, Mary Caroline. *Social Life of Old New England*. Boston: Little, Brown, 1915.

Crawford, Richard. *America's Musical Life: A History*. New York: W. W. Norton, 2005.

Daniels, Bruce C. *Puritans at Play: Leisure and Recreation in Colonial New England*. New York: St. Martin's Press, 1995.

Darnton, Robert. *The Great Cat Massacre and Other Episodes in French Cultural History*. New York: Vintage Books, 1984.

Darnton, Robert. *The Kiss of the Lamourette: Reflections in Cultural History*. New York: W. W. Norton, 1990.

Davidson, Cathy. *Revolution and the Word: The Rise of the Novel in America*. New York: Oxford University Press, 1986.

Davis, Leonard J. *Obsession: A History*. Chicago: University of Chicago Press, 2008.

Davis, Susan G. "'Making Night Hideous': Christmas Revelry and Public Order in Nineteenth-Century Philadelphia." *American Quarterly* 34, no. 2 (1982): 185–99.

Davis, Susan G. "Strike Parades and the Politics of Representing Class in Antebellum Philadelphia." *TDR/The Drama Review* 29, no. 3 (1985): 106–16.

Davis, Susan G. *Parades and Power: Street Theater in Nineteenth-Century Philadelphia*. Philadelphia: Temple University Press, 1986.

DeNora, Tia. *Music in Everyday Life*. Cambridge: Cambridge University Press, 2000.

De Tocqueville, Alexis. *Democracy in America*. Vol. 2. New York: Vintage Books, 1990 [1844].

Dickinson, Edward. *The Education of a Music Lover*. New York: Charles Scribner's Sons, 1911.

DiMaggio, Paul. "Cultural Entrepreneurship in Nineteenth-Century Boston: The Creation of an Organizational Base for High Culture in America." *Media, Culture and Society* 4 (1982).

Dirks, Nicholas B. "Annals of the Archive: Ethnographic Notes on the Sources of History." In *From the Margins: Historical Anthropology and Its Futures*, 47–65. Brian Keith Axel, ed. Durham, N.C.: Duke University Press, 2002.

Dizekes, John. *Opera in America: A Cultural History*. New Haven: Yale University Press, 1993.

D'Orsay, Alfred Guillaume Gabriel. *Etiquette: or, a Guide to the Usages of Society, with a Glance at Bad Habits*. New York: Wilson, 1843.

Douglas, Susan J. *Listening In: Radio and the American Imagination*. New York: Times Books, 1999.

Douglass, Frederick. *Narrative of the Life of Frederick Douglass, An American Slave*. New York: Bedford Books, 1993 [1845].

Dror, Otniel E. "Dangerous Liaisons: Science, Amusement, and the Civilizing Process." In *Representing Emotions: New Connections in the Histories of Art, Music, and Medicine*, 223–34. Penelope Gouk and Helen Hills, eds. Aldershot: Ashgate, 2005.

Dunglison, Robley. *A New Dictionary of Medical Science and Literature*. Boston: C. Bowen, 1833.

Durant, Alan. *Conditions of Music*. Albany: SUNY Press, 1984.

Dwight, John S. "Music in Boston." In *The Memorial History of Boston, including Suffolk County, Massachusetts. 1630–1880*, 415–64. 4 vols. Justin Winsow, ed. Boston: James R. Osgood, 1881.

Everett, Edward, ed. *The Writings and Speeches of Daniel Webster*. Vol. 17. Boston: Little, Brown, 1903.

Elsner, John, and Roger Cardinal, *The Cultures of Collecting.* Cambridge, Mass.: Harvard University Press, 1994.

Emerson, Ralph Waldo. *Selected Writings of Ralph Waldo Emerson.* New York: New American Library, 1965.

Ennis, Phillip H. "Ecstasy and Everyday Life." *Journal for the Scientific Study of Religion* 6, no. 1 (1967): 40–48.

Epstein, Dena J. *Sinful Tunes and Spirituals: Black Folk Music to the Civil War.* Urbana: University of Illinois Press, 1977.

Esquirol, E. *Mental Maladies: A Treatise on Insanity.* Trans. E. K. Hunt. Philadelphia: Lea & Blanchard, 1845.

Evelev, John. *Tolerable Entertainment Herman Melville and Professionalism in Antebellum New York.* Amherst: University of Massachusetts Press.

Faner, Robert D. *Walt Whitman and Opera.* Carbondale: Southern Illinois University Press, 1951.

Fast, Susan. "Gender Ideologies in Nineteenth- and Early Twentieth-Century Music Making." In *Music Cultures in the United States: An Introduction.* Ellen Koskoff, ed. New York: Routledge, 2005.

Feldman, "Music and the Order of the Passions." In *Representing the Passions: Histories, Bodies, Visions*, 37–67. Richard Meyer, ed. Los Angeles: Getty Research Institute, 2003.

Feller, Daniel. "The Market Revolution Ate My Homework." *Reviews in American History* 25, no. 3 (1997): 408–15.

Fetis, Francis James. *Music Explained to the World: Or, How to Understand Music and Enjoy Its Performance.* Boston: Benjamin Perkins, 1842.

Fields, Barbara Jeanne. *Slavery and Freedom on the Middle Ground.* New York: Oxford University Press, 1988.

Finney, Charles Grandison. *Lectures on Revivals of Religion*, William G. McLoughlin, ed. Cambridge, Mass.: Harvard University Press, 1960.

Fisher, William Arms. *Notes on Music in Old Boston.* Boston: Oliver Ditson, 1918.

Forbes, John, et al., eds. *The Cyclopaedia of Practical Medicine: Comprising Treatises on the Nature and Treatment of Diseases, Materia Medica, and Therapeutics, Medical Jurisprudence, Etc.* Vol. 1. Philadelphia: Lea & Blanchard, 1845.

Forsyth, Michael. *Buildings for Music: The Architect, the Musician, and the Listener from the Seventeenth Century to the Present Day.* Cambridge, Mass.: MIT Press, 1985.

Foucault, Michel. "Technologies of the Self." In *Technologies of the Self: A Seminar with Michel Foucault*, 16–49. Luther H. Martin, Huck Gutman, and Patrick H. Hutton, eds. Amherst: University of Massachusetts Press, 1988.

Gac, Scott. *Singing for Freedom: The Hutchinson Family Singers and the Nineteenth-Century Culture of Antebellum Reform.* New Haven: Yale University Press, 2007.

Gaddis, John Lewis. *The Landscape of History: How Historians Map the Past.* New York: Oxford University Press, 2004.

Gardiner, William. *The Music of Nature, or, an Attempt to Prove That What Is Passionate and Pleasing in the Art of Singing, Speaking, and Performing upon Musical In-*

struments, Is Derived from the Sounds of the Animated World. Boston: J. H. Wilkins & R. B. Carter, 1838.

Garofalo, Reebee. *Rockin' Out: Popular Music in the USA.* Upper Saddle River, N.J.: Pearson, 2008.

Gay, Jr., Leslie, "Before the Deluge: The Technoculture of Song-Sheet Publishing Viewed from Late Nineteenth-Century Galveston." In *Music and Technoculture*, 204–32. Rene T. A. Lysloff and Leslie C. Gay, Jr., eds. Middletown, Conn.: Wesleyan University Press, 2003.

Gay, Peter. *The Bourgeois Experience: Victoria to Freud.* New York: W. W. Norton, 1995.

Geertz, Clifford. "History and Anthropology." *New Literary History* 21, no. 2 (1990): 321–35.

Geller, Jeffrey. "Back to the Nineteenth Century Is Progress." *Journal of Philosophy, Psychiatry & Psychology* 15, no. 1 (2008): 19–21.

Gemmill, C L. "Robley Dunglison's Dictionary of Medical Science, 1833." *Bulletin of the New York Academy of Medicine* 48, no. 5 (1972): 791–98.

Gibbs, Christopher H., and Dana A. Gooley, eds. *Franz Liszt and His World.* Princeton: Princeton University Press, 2006.

Gibson, Chris, and John Connell. *Music and Tourism: On the Road Again.* Clevedon, U.K.: Channel View Publications, 2005.

Gilman, Samuel. *Memoirs of a New England Village Choir with Occasional Reflections, by a Member.* Boston: S. G. Goodrich, 1829.

Gitelman, Lisa. *Scripts, Grooves, and Writing Machines: Representing Technology in the Edison Era.* Palo Alto, Calif.: Stanford University Press, 1999.

Goldstein, Jan. *Console and Classify: The French Psychiatric Profession in the Nineteenth Century.* Cambridge: Cambridge University Press, 1987.

Gooley, Dana. *The Virtuoso Liszt.* Cambridge: Cambridge University Press, 2004.

Gottschalk, Louis Moreau. *Notes of a Pianist.* Princeton: Princeton University Press, 2006 [1881].

Gouk, Penelope. "Raising Spirits and Restoring Souls: Early Modern Medical Explanations for Music's Effects." In *Hearing Cultures: Essays on Sound, Listening and Modernity*, 87–105. Veit Erlmann, ed. London: Berg Publishers, 2004.

Gould, Glenn. "The Prospects of Recording." *High Fidelity Magazine* 16, no. 4 (1966): 46–63.

Gould, Nathaniel D. *Church Music in America, Comprising Its History and Its Peculiarities at Different Periods, with Cursory Remarks on Its Legitimate Use and Its Abuse; with Notices of the Schools, Composers, Teachers, and Societies.* Boston: A. N. Johnson, 1853.

Greenspan, Ezra. *Walt Whitman and the American Reader.* New York: Cambridge University Press, 1990.

Grimstead, David. *American Theater and Culture, 1800–1850.* Berkeley: University of California Press, 1987.

Gura, Philip F. *C. F. Martin and His Guitars, 1796–1873.* Chapel Hill: University of North Carolina Press, 2003.

Hale, Philip. "Impressions of Visiting Musicians in New England (1849–1875)." *Proceedings of the Massachusetts Historical Society* 61 (1927–28): 105–16.

Hall, Benjamin Homer, ed. *A Collection of College Words and Customs*. Cambridge: John Bartlett, 1856.

Hall, Mirko. "Friedrich Schlegel's Romanticization of Music." *Eighteenth-Century Studies* 42, no. 3 (2009): 413–29.

Hall, Stuart. "Encoding/Decoding." In *Media and Cultural Studies: Keyworks*, 163–73. Meenakshi Gigi Durham and Douglas Kellner, eds. Malden: Blackwell Publishers, 2006.

Halttunen, Karen. *Confidence Men and Painted Women: A Study of Middle-Class Culture in America, 1830–1870*. New Haven: Yale University Press, 1988.

Hamm, Charles. *Music in the New World*. New York: W. W. Norton, 1983.

Harris, Neil. *Humbug: The Art of P. T. Barnum*. Boston: Little, Brown, 1973.

Hawes, Clement. *Mania and Literary Style: The Rhetoric of Enthusiasm from the Ranters to Christopher Smart*. Cambridge: Cambridge University Press, 1996.

Hawthorne, Nathaniel. *The Scarlet Letter*. Boston: Bedford Books, 1990.

Healy, David. *Mania: A Short History of Bipolar Disorder*. Baltimore: Johns Hopkins University Press, 2008.

Helm, E. Eugene. *The Canon and the Curricula: A Study of Musicology and Ethnomusicology Programs in America*. Stuyvesant, N.Y.: Pendragon Press, 1994.

Hennion, Antoine. "Music Lovers: Taste as Performance." *Theory Culture, Society* 18, no. 5 (2001): 1–22.

Henretta, James A. *The Evolution of American Society, 1700–1815: An Interdisciplinary Analysis*. Lexington, Mass.: D. C. Heath, 1973.

Herd, David. *Enthusiast! Essays on Modern Literature*. Manchester: Manchester University Press, 2007.

Heyd, Michael. *Be Sober and Reasonable: The Critique of Enthusiasm in the Seventeenth and Early Eighteenth Centuries*. Leiden: E. J. Brill, 1995.

Higgins, William Mullinger. *The Philosophy of Sound and History of Music*. London: William S. Orr, 1838.

Hills, Matt. *Fan Cultures*. New York: Routledge, 2002.

Hitchcock, H. Wiley. *Music in the United States: A Historical Introduction*. Englewood Cliffs, N.J.: Prentice Hall, 1988.

Hoffer, Peter Charles. *Sensory Worlds in Early America*. Baltimore: Johns Hopkins University Press, 2003.

Hogarth, George. *Memoirs of the Musical Drama*. Vol. 2. London: R. Bentley, 1838.

Holmes, Edward. *A Ramble among the Musicians of Germany, Giving Some Account of the Operas of Munich, Dresden, Berlin, &c: With Remarks upon the Church Music, Singers, Performers, and Composers; and a Sample of the Pleasures and Incoveniences That Await the Lover of Art on a Similar Excursion*. N.p.: Hunt & Clarke, 1828.

Holmes, Oliver Wendell. *The Professor at the Breakfast-Table*. Boston: Ticknor & Fields, 1860.

Hoppin, Augustus, Thomas Bailey Aldrich, and William Dean Howells, eds. *Jubilee Days: An Illustrated Daily Record of the Humorous Features of the World's Peace Jubilee*. J. R. Osgood, 1872.

Horowitz, Joseph. "Finding a 'Real Self': American Women and the Wagner Cult of the Late Nineteenth Century." *Musical Quarterly* 78, no. 2 (1994): 189–205.

Horowitz, Joseph. *Wagner Nights: An American History*. Berkeley: University of California Press, 1994.

Horowitz, Joseph. *Classical Music in America: A History of Its Rise and Fall*. New York: W. W. Norton, 2005.

Horton, James Oliver, and Lois E. Horton, *Black Bostonians: Family Life and Community Struggle in the Antebellum North*. New York: Holmes & Meier, 1979.

Horton, James Oliver, and Lois E. Horton, *In Hope of Liberty: Culture, Community, and Protest among Northern Free Blacks, 1700–1860*. New York: Oxford University Press, 1997.

Howe, Daniel Walker. *Making the American Self: Jonathan Edwards to Abraham Lincoln*. Cambridge, Mass.: Harvard University Press, 1997.

Howe, Daniel Walker. *What God Hath Wrought: The Transformation of America, 1815–1848*. New York: Oxford University Press, 2007.

Hubbard, W. L. ed. *History of American Music*. Toledo: Irving Squire, 1908.

Hunter, Jane H. "Inscribing the Self in the Heart of the Family: Diaries and Girlhood in America." *American Quarterly* 44, no. 1 (1992): 51–81.

Hutton, Frankie. *The Early Black Press in America*. Santa Barbara, Calif.: Greenwood Publishing, 1993.

Huyssen, Andreas. *After the Great Divide: Modernism, Mass Culture, Postmodernism*. Bloomington: Indiana University Press.

Irwin, Joyce. "The Theology of 'Regular Singing.'" *New England Quarterly* 51, no. 2 (1978): 176–92.

Isaac, Rhys. *The Transformation of Virginia, 1740–1790*. Chapel Hill: University of North Carolina Press, 1982.

James, William. *Talks to Teachers on Psychology, and to Students on Some of Life's Ideals*. New York: Henry Holt, 1916.

Johnson, H. Earle. *Musical Interludes in Boston, 1795–1830*. New York: Columbia University Press, 1943.

Johnson, James H. *Listening in Paris: A Cultural History*. Berkeley: University of California Press, 1995.

Kallberg, Jeffrey. "The Harmony of the Tea Table: Gender and Ideology in the Piano Nocturne." *Representations* 39 (1992): 102–33.

Karpf, Juanita. "'As with Words of Fire': Art Music and Nineteenth Century African-American Feminist Discourse." *Signs* 24, no. 3 (1999): 603–32.

Kasson, John F. *Rudeness and Civility: Manners in Nineteenth-Century America*. New York: Hill & Wang, 1990.

Katz, Mark. *Capturing Sound: How Technology Has Changed Music*. Berkeley: University of California Press, 2004.

Kedney, John Steinfort. *The Beautiful and the Sublime: An Analysis of These Emotions and a Determination of the Objectivity of Beauty*. New York: G. P. Putnam's Sons, 1880.

Keil, Charles. "Moving and Grooving: Popular Music in the Lives of Children." Paper presented at the symposium "Around the Sound: Popular Music in Performance, Education, and Scholarship." University of Washington, 11 May 2000.

Keil, Charles. "Motion and Feeling through Music." In *Music Grooves: Essays & Dialogues*, 53–76. Charles Keil and Steven Feld. Chicago: University of Chicago Press, 1994.

Kellogg, Susan. "Histories for Anthropology: Ten Years of Historical Research and Writing by Anthropologists, 1980–1990." *Social Science History* 15, no. 4 (1991): 417–55.

Kelley, Bruce C., and Mark A. Snell, eds. *Bugle Resounding: Music and Musicians in the Civil War Era*. Columbia: University of Missouri Press, 2004.

Kelley, Mary. "Reading Women/Women Reading: The Making of Learned Women in Antebellum America." *Journal of American History* 83, no. 2 (1996): 401–24.

Kelly, Thomas Forrest. *First Nights: Five Musical Premieres*. New Haven: Yale University Press, 2001.

Kemp, Father. *Father Kemp and His Old Folks, a History of the Old Folks' Concerts, Comprising an Autobiography of the Author and Sketches of Many Humorous Scenes and Incidents, Which Have Transpired in a Concert-Giving Experience of Twelve Years in America and England*. Boston: published by the Author, 1868.

Kenney, William. *Recorded Music in American Life: The Phonograph and Popular Memory, 1890–1945*. New York: Oxford University Press, 1999.

Kilde, Jeanne Halgren. *When Church Became Theatre*. New York: Oxford University Press, 2002.

Kimball, Bruce A. *The True Professional Ideal in America: A History*. New York: Rowan & Littlefield, 1996.

Kimmel, Michael. "The Birth of the Self-Made Man." In *The Masculinity Studies Reader*, 135–52. Rachel Adams and David Savran, eds. Malden, Mass.: Blackwell Publishing, 2002.

King, Donald C. *The Theaters of Boston: A Stage and Screen History*. Jefferson, N.C.: McFarland Press, 2005.

King, Moses. *King's Handbook of Boston*. Cambridge, Mass.: Moses King Publisher, 1878.

King, Wilma. *The Essence of Liberty: Free Black Women during the Slave Era*. Columbia: University of Missouri Press, 2006.

Kingman, Daniel. *American Music: A Panorama*. New York: Schirmer, 1979.

Kingsdale, Jon M. "The 'Poor Man's Club': Social Functions of the Urban Working-Class Saloon." *American Quarterly* 25, no. 4 (1973): 472–89.

Klein, Lawrence E., and Anthony J. La Vopa, eds. *Enthusiasm and Enlightenment in Europe, 1650–1850*. Special issue of the *Huntington Library Quarterly* 60, nos. 1 and 2 (1997).

Knoper, Randall. *Acting Naturally: Mark Twain in the Culture of Performance*. Berkeley: University of California Press, 1995.

Koestenbaum, Wayne. *The Queen's Throat: Opera, Homosexuality and the Mystery of Desire*. New York: Vintage Press, 1993.

Kopytoff, Igor. "The Cultural Biography of Things: Commoditization as Process." In *The Social Life of Things: Commodities in Cultural Perspective*, 64–91. Arjun Appadurai, ed., Cambridge: Cambridge University Press, 1988.

Kornblum, William. "Discovering Ink: A Mentor for Historical Ethnography." *Annals of the American Academy of Political and Social Science* 595 (Sept. 2004): 176–89.

Koza, Julia Eklund. "Music and the Feminine Sphere: Images of Women as Musicians in 'Godey's Lady's Book,' 1830–1877." *Musical Quarterly* 75, no. 2 (1991): 103–29.

La Vopa, Anthony J. "The Philosopher and the Schwärmer: On the Career of a German Epithet from Luther to Kant." *Huntington Library Quarterly* 60, nos. 1 and 2 (1997).

Lawrence, Vera Brodsky. *Strong on Music*. Vol. 1, *Resonances, 1836–1850*. Chicago: University of Chicago Press, 1988.

Lawrence, Vera Brodsky. *Strong on Music*. Vol. 2, *Reverberations, 1850–1856*. Chicago: University of Chicago Press, 1995.

Lawrence, Vera Brodsky. *Strong on Music*. Vol. 3, *Repercussions, 1857–1862*. Chicago: University of Chicago Press, 1998.

Le Bon, Gustave. *The Crowd: A Study of the Popular Mind*. London: T. Fisher Unwin, 1903 [1895].

Lears, Jackson. *No Place of Grace: Antimodernism and the Transformation of American Culture, 1880–1920*. New York: Pantheon Books, 1981.

Lears, Jackson. *Fables of Abundance: A Cultural History of Advertising in America*. New York: Basic Books, 1994.

Leppert, Richard. "Sexual Identity, Death, and the Family Piano." *19th-Century Music* 16, no. 2 (1992): 105–28.

Leppert, Richard. "Cultural Contradiction, Idolatry, and the Piano Virtuoso: Franz Liszt." In *Piano Roles: A New History of the Piano*. New Haven: Yale University Press, 2002.

Levine, Lawrence. *Highbrow/Lowbrow: The Emergence of Cultural Hierarchy in America*. Cambridge, Mass.: Harvard University Press, 1988.

Levy, Steven. *The Perfect Thing: How the iPod Shuffles Commerce, Culture, and Coolness*. New York: Simon & Schuster, 2006.

Linkon, Sherry Lee. "Reading Lind Mania: Print Culture and the Construction of Nineteenth-Century Audiences." *Book History* 1 (1998): 94–106.

Locke, Ralph P. "Music Lovers, Patrons, and the 'Sacrilization' of Culture in America." *19th-Century Music* 17, no. 2 (1993): 149–73.

Locke, Ralph P. "Paradoxes of the Woman Music Patron in America." *Musical Quarterly* 78, no. 4 (1994): 798–825.

Loesser, Arthur. *Men, Women, and Pianos: A Social History*. New York: Simon & Schuster, 1954; Dover ed., 1982.

Lott, R. Allen. *From Paris to Peoria: How European Piano Virtuosos Brought Classical Music to the American Heartland*. New York: Oxford University Press, 2003.

Lovejoy, David. *Religious Enthusiasm in the New World: Heresy to Revolution*. Cambridge, Mass.: Harvard University Press, 1985.

Ludtke, Karen. *Dances with Spiders: Crisis, Celebrity and Celebration in Southern Italy*. Oxford: Berghahn Books, 2009.

Lunettes, Henry. *The American Gentleman's Guide to Politeness and Fashion, or Familiar Letters to His Nephews.* New York: Derby & Jackson, 1858.

Luskey, Brian P. "Jumping Counters in White Collars: Manliness, Respectability, and Work in the Antebellum City." *Journal of the Early Republic* 26, no. 2 (2006): 173–219.

Lutz, Tom. *Doing Nothing: A History of Loafers, Loungers, Slackers, and Bums in America.* New York: Farrar, Straus & Giroux, 2006.

Magdanz, Theresa. "The Waltz: Technology's Muse." *Journal of Popular Music Studies* 18, no. 3 (2006): 251–81.

Mainzer, Dr. J. *Music and Education.* London: Longman, Brown, Green & Longmans, 1853.

Maretzek, Max. *Crochets and Quavers: Or, Revelations of an Opera Manager in America.* New York: S. French, 1855.

Mark, Michael L. *Contemporary Music Education.* New York: Schirmer Books, 1996.

Martin, Scott C., ed. *Cultural Change and the Market Revolution in America, 1789–1865.* Rowan & Littlefield, 2004.

Marx, Adolf Bernhard. *The Music of the Nineteenth Century and Its Culture.* Trans. C. Natalia MacFarren. London: Robert Cocks, 1854.

Mates, Julian. *America's Musical Stage: Two Hundred Years of Musical Theater.* Westport, Conn.: Greenwood Press, 1987.

Matthews, Jean. "Race, Sex, and the Dimensions of Liberty in Antebellum America." *Journal of the Early Republic* 6, no. 3 (1986): 275–91.

McAllister, Marvin. *White People Do Not Know How to Behave at Entertainments Designed for Ladies and Gentlemen of Color.* Chapel Hill: University of North Carolina Press, 2003.

McBride, David. "Afro-American Urban Culture and Intellectualism, 1840–1940." In *Philadelphia African Americans: Color, Class, & Style, 1840–1940. An Exhibition Catalog.* Bette Ann Davis Lawrence, et al. Philadelphia: The Balch Institute for Ethnic Studies, 1988.

McClary, Susan. "Same as It Ever Was: Youth Culture and Music." In *Microphone Fiends: Youth Music and Youth Culture*, 29–40. Andrew Ross and Tricia Rose, eds. New York: Routledge, 1994.

McConachie, Bruce. *Melodramatic Formations: American Theatre & Society, 1820–1870.* Ames: University of Iowa Press, 1992.

McCullough, Esther Morgan, ed. *As I Pass O Manhattan!* New York: Corey Taylor, 1956.

McMahon, Lucia. "'While Our Souls Together Blend': Narrating a Romantic Readership in the Early Republic." In *An Emotional History of the United States*, 66–90. Peter N. Stearns and Jan Lewis. New York: New York University Press, 1998.

Mee, Jon. "Anxieties of Enthusiasm: Coleridge, Prophecy, and Popular Politics in the 1790s." *Huntington Library Quarterly* 60, nos. 1 and 2 (1997): 179–203.

Mee, Jon. *Romanticism, Enthusiasm, and Regulation.* New York: Oxford University Press, 2005.

Melville, Herman. *The Confidence Man: His Masquerade.* New York: Dix, Edwards, 1857.

Metzner, Paul. *Crescendo of the Virtuoso*. Berkeley: University of California Press, 1988.

Meyer-Frazeir, Petra. "Music, Novels, and Women: Nineteenth-Century Prescriptions for an Ideal Life." *Women & Music: A Journal of Gender and Culture* 10 (2006): 45–59.

Midgley, R. L. *Sights in Boston and Suburbs, or Guide to the Stranger*. Boston: John P. Jewett, 1856.

Millard, Andre. *America on Record*. Cambridge: Cambridge University Press, 1995.

Millard, Andre. *Edison and the Business of Innovation*. Baltimore: Johns Hopkins University Press, 1993.

Miller, Bonny H. "A Mirror of Ages Past: The Publication of Music in Domestic Periodicals." *Notes* 50, no. 3 (1994): 883–901.

Mitchell, Donald Grant. *The Lorgnette, or, Studies of the Town. By an Opera Goer*. Vol. 1. New York: Stringer & Townsend, 1851.

Moore, R. Laurence. *Selling God: American Religion in the Marketplace of Culture*. New York: Oxford University Press, 1992.

Morus, Iwan Rhys. "Manufacturing Nature: Science, Technology, and Victorian Consumer Culture." *British Journal for the History of Science* 29, no. 4 (1996): 403–34.

Motz, Marilyn Ferris. "Folk Expression of Time and Place: Nineteenth-Century Midwestern Rural Diaries." *Journal of American Folklore* 100, no. 396 (1987): 131–47.

Musselman, Joseph. *Music in the Cultured Generation*. Evanston, Ill.: Northwestern University Press, 1971.

Myerson, Joel, ed. *Whitman in His Own Time: A Biographical Chronicle of His Life, Drawn from Recollections, Memoirs, and Interviews by Friends and Associates*. Detroit: Omnigraphics, 1991.

Nathan, Hans. "The Tyrolese Family Rainer, and the Vogue of Singing Mountain Troupes in Europe and America." *Musical Quarterly* 32, no. 1 (1946): 63–79.

National Library of Medicine. *Medicine and Music*. Washington, D.C.: Department of Health, Education, and Welfare, 1977.

Newman, Nancy. "Good Music for a Free People: The Germania Musical Society and Transatlantic Musical Culture of the Mid-Nineteenth Century." Ph.D. diss., Department of Music, Brown University, May 2002.

Oden, Gloria C. "The Journal of Charlotte L. Forten: The Salem-Philadelphia Years (1854–1862) Reexamined." In *Black Women in United States History*. Vol. 3. Darlene Clark Hine, ed. Brooklyn: Carlson Publishing, 1990.

Ogasapian, John. *Music of the Colonial and Revolutionary Era*. Westport, Conn.: Greenwood Press, 2004.

Ogasapian, John, and N. Lee Orr. *Music of the Gilded Age*. Westport, Conn.: Greenwood Press, 2007.

Olwage, Grant. "The Class and Colour of Tone: An Essay on the Social History of Vocal Timbre." *Ethnomusicology Forum* 13, no. 2 (2004): 203–26.

O'Malley, Michael. "Specie and Species: Race and the Money Question in Nineteenth-Century America." *American Historical Review* 99, no. 2 (1994): 369–95.

Peiss, Kathy. *Cheap Amusements: Working Women and Leisure in Turn-of-the-Century New York*. Philadelphia: Temple University Press, 1986.

Peretti, Burton W. "Democratic Leitmotivs in the American Reception of Wagner." *19th-Century Music* 13, no. 1 (1989): 28–38.

Perkins, Linda M. "The Impact of the 'Cult of True Womanhood' on the Education of Black Women." In *Black Women in United States History*. Vol. 3. Darlene Clark Hine, ed. Brooklyn, N.Y.: Carlson Publishing, 1990.

Perry, Bliss. *The Life and Letters of Henry Lee Higginson*. Boston: Atlantic Monthly Press, 1921.

Peterson, Carla L. "Capitalism, Black (Under)Development, and the Production of the African-American Novel in the 1850s." *American Literary History* 4, no. 4 (1992): 559–83.

Pfister, Joel. "Getting Personal and Getting Personnel: U.S. Capitalism as a System of Emotional Reproduction." *American Quarterly* 60, no. 4 (2008): 1135–41.

Picker, John M. *Victorian Soundscapes*. New York: Oxford University Press, 2003.

Ping, Nancy R. "Black Musical Activities in Antebellum Wilmington, North Carolina." *Black Perspective in Music* 8, no. 2 (1980): 139–60.

Pieper, Antje. *Music and the Making of Middle-Class Culture: A Comparative Study of Nineteenth-Century Leipzig and Birmingham*. Basingstoke: Palgrave Macmillan, 2008.

Pollock, Griselda. *Mary Cassatt: Painter of Modern Women*. London: Thames & Hudson, 1998.

Ponce de Leon, Charles L. "Is There an American Self?" *Reviews in American History* 26, no. 3 (1998): 489–96.

Porter, William S. *The Musical Cyclopedia, or the Principles of Music Considered as a Science and an Art, Embracing a Complete Musical Dictionary*. Boston: James Loring, 1834.

Preston, Katherine. "Art Music from 1800 to 1860." In *The Cambridge History of American Music*, 186–213. David Nicholls, ed. Cambridge: Cambridge University Press, 1998.

Preston, Katherine. *Opera on the Road: Traveling Opera Troupes in the United States, 1825–60*. Urbana: University of Illinois Press, 1993.

Psalms and Hymns for Christian Use and Worship, General Association of Connecticut. Boston: Charles Tappan, 1845.

Rabinowitz, Peter J. "'With Our Own Dominant Passions': Gottschalk, Gender, and the Power of Listening." *19th-Century Music* 16, no. 3 (1993): 242–52.

Radano, Ronald. *Lying up a Nation: Race and Black Music*. Chicago: University of Chicago Press, 2003.

Rath, Richard Cullen. *How Early America Sounded*. Cornell University Press, 2003.

Read, Alan Walker. "The First Stage in the History of O.K." *American Speech* 38, no. 1 (1963): 5–27.

Rendall, Steven. "On Diaries." *Diacritics* 16, no. 3 (1986): 57–65.

Reynolds, David S. *Walt Whitman's America*. New York: Vintage Books, 1995.

Robins, Roger. "Vernacular American Landscape: Methodists, Camp Meetings, and Social Respectability." *Religion and American Culture* 4, no. 2 (1994): 165–91.

Roche, Daniel. *A History of Everyday Things: The Birth of Consumption in France, 1600–1800*. Cambridge: Cambridge University Press, 2000.

Rockman, Seth. *Scraping By: Wage Labor, Slavery, and Survival in Early Baltimore*. Baltimore: Johns Hopkins University Press, 2008.

Roell, Craig H. *The Piano in America 1890–1940*. Chapel Hill: University of North Carolina Press, 1989.

Rose, Jonathan. *The Intellectual Life of the British Working Classes*. New Haven: Yale University Press, 2001.

Rosenberg, Charles G. *Jenny Lind in America*. New York: Stringer & Townsend, 1851.

Rotundo, E. Anthony. *American Manhood: Transformations in Masculinity from the Revolution to the Modern Era*. New York: Basic Books, 1993.

Rousseau, Jean-Jacques. *Dictionnaire de Musique*. Chez la Veuve Duchesne, 1768.

Ryan, Kate. *Old Boston Museum Days*. Boston: Little, Brown, 1915.

Ryan, Mary P. *Cradle of the Middle Class: The Family in Oneida County, New York, 1790–1865*. Cambridge: Cambridge University Press, 1981.

Sacks, Oliver. *Musicophilia: Tales of Music and the Brain*. New York: Random House, 2005.

Saloman, Ora Frishberg. "Margaret Fuller on Beethoven in America, 1839–1846." *Journal of Musicology* 10, no. 1 (1992): 89–105.

Sanjek, Russell. *American Popular Music and Its Business. The First Four Hundred Years*. Vol. 2, *From 1790 to 1909*. New York: Oxford University Press, 1988.

Schafer, R. Murray. *The Soundscape: Our Sonic Environment and the Tuning of the World*. Rochester, Vt.: Destiny Books, 1994 [1977].

Schmidt, Leigh Eric. *Hearing Things: Religion, Illusion, and the American Enlightenment*. Cambridge, Mass.: Harvard University Press, 2000.

Schroeder, David P. *Haydn and the Enlightenment: The Late Symphonies and Their Audience*. New York: Oxford University Press, 1990.

Scobey, David. "Anatomy of the Promenade: The Politics of Bourgeois Sociability in Nineteenth-Century New York." *Social History* 17, no. 2 (1992): 203–27.

Scott, Derek B. "The Sexual Politics of Victorian Musical Aesthetics." *Journal of the Royal Musical Association* 119, no. 1 (1994): 91–114.

Seitz, Don C. *Artemus Ward: A Biography and Bibliography*. New York: Harper & Brothers, 1919.

Sellers, Charles. *The Market Revolution: Jacksonian America, 1815–1846*. New York: Oxford University Press, 1991.

Shammas, Carole. *The Pre-Industrial Consumer in England and America*. New York: Oxford University Press, 1990.

Shand-Tucci, Douglass. *Built in Boston: City and Suburb, 1800–2000*. 3rd ed. Amherst: University of Massachusetts Press, 1999.

Shi, David. *The Simple Life: Plain Living and High Thinking in American Culture*. Athens: University of Georgia Press, 1985.

Siegmeister, Elie, ed. *The Music Lover's Handbook*. New York: William Morrow, 1943.

Silverman, Kenneth. *A Cultural History of the American Revolution: Painting, Music,*

Literature, and the Theatre in the Colonies and the United States from the Treaty of Paris to the Inauguration of George Washington, 1763–1789. New York: Thomas Crowell, 1976.

Sketches and Business Directory of Boston 1860–1861. Boston: Damrell & Moore and George Coolidge, 1861.

Sklansky, Jeffrey. *The Soul's Economy: Market Society and Selfhood in American Thought, 1820–1920*. Chapel Hill: University of North Carolina Press, 2002.

Small, Christopher. *Musicking: The Meanings of Performing and Listening*. Middletown, Conn.: Wesleyan University Press, 1998.

Small, Christopher. *Music of the Common Tongue*. London: John Calder, 1987.

Smith, Bruce R. *The Acoustic World of Early Modern England: Attending to the O-Factor*. Chicago: University of Chicago Press, 1999.

Smith, Mark M. *Listening to Nineteenth-Century America*. Chapel Hill: University of North Carolina Press, 2001.

Smith, Mark M. "Heard Worlds of Antebellum America." In *The Auditory Culture Reader*, 137–63. Michael Bull and Les Back, eds. Oxford: Berg Publishers, 2003.

Smith, Mark M., ed. *Hearing History: A Reader*. Athens: University of Georgia Press, 2004.

Smith, Mark M. "Producing Sense, Consuming Sense, Making Sense: Perils and Prospects for Sensory History." *Journal of Social History* 40, no. 4 (2007): 841–58.

Smith, Mortimer Brewster. *The Life of Ole Bull*. Princeton: Princeton University Press, 1947.

Smith-Rosenberg, Carroll, and Charles Rosenberg, "The Female Animal: Medical and Biological Views of Woman and Her Role in Nineteenth-Century America." *Journal of American History*, 60, no. 2 (1973): 332–56.

Solie, Ruth. *Music in Other Words: Victorian Conversations*. Berkeley: University of California Press, 2004.

Sonneck, Oscar. *Early Concert Life in America, 1731–1800*. Leipzig: Breitkopf & Härtel, 1907.

Southern, Eileen. *The Music of Black Americans: A History*. 2nd ed. New York: W. W. Norton, 1983.

Statham, Henry Heathcote. *My Thoughts on Music and Musicians*. London: Chapman & Hall, 1892.

Sterne, Jonathan. *The Audible Past: Cultural Origins of Sound Reproduction*. Durham, N.C.: Duke University Press, 2003.

Stevens, Henry. *Catalogue of the American Books in the Library of the British Museum at Christmas MDCCCLVI*. Chiswick: Chiswick Press, 1866.

Stowell, David W. "Murder at a Methodist Camp Meeting: The Origins of Abraham Lincoln's Most Famous Trial." *Journal of the Illinois State Historical Society* 101, nos. 3–4 (2008): 219–34.

Swift, Lindsay. *Brook Farm: Its Members, Scholars, and Visitors*. New York: Macmillan, 1900.

Taylor, Timothy D. "The Commodification of Music at the Dawn of the Era of 'Mechanical Music.'" *Ethnomusicology* 51, no. 2 (2007): 281–305.

Tawa, Nicholas. *High-Minded and Low-Down: Music in the Lives of Americans, 1800–1861*. Boston: Northeastern University Press, 2000.

Teller, Walter, ed. *Walt Whitman's Camden Conversations*. New Brunswick, N.J.: Rutgers University Press, 1973.

Thomas, Rose Fay. *Memoirs of Theodore Thomas*. Kessinger Publishing, 2004 [1911].

Thomas, Theodore. *Theodore Thomas: A Musical Autobiography*. Vol. 2, *Concert Programmes*. George Putnam Upton, ed. Chicago: A. C. McClurg, 1905.

Thompson, Emily. "Machines, Music, and the Quest for Fidelity." *Musical Quarterly* 79, no. 1 (1995): 131–71.

Thoreau, Henry David. *Walden: Or, Life in the Woods*. New York: Signet, 1960 [1847].

Tick, Judith. "Passed Away Is the Piano Girl: Changes in American Musical Life, 1870–1900." In *Women Making Music: The Western Art Tradition, 1150–1950*, 325–48. Jane Bowers and Judith Tick, eds. Urbana: University of Illinois Press, 1987.

Tompkins, Eugene. *The History of the Boston Theatre*. Boston: Houghton, Mifflin, 1908.

Trowbridge, J. T. *My Own Story, with Recollections of Noted Persons*. Boston: Houghton, Mifflin, 1903.

Trowbridge, J. T. [Writing as Paul Creyton], *Martin Merrivale, His X Mark*. Boston: Phillips, Sampson, 1854.

Tyler, Linda L. "'Commerce and Poetry Hand in Hand': Music in American Department Stores, 1880–1930." *Journal of the American Musicological Society* 45, no. 1 (1992): 75–120.

Vaillant, Derek. *Sounds of Reform: Progressivism and Music in Chicago, 1873–1935*. Chapel Hill: University of North Carolina Press: 2006.

Van der Zee Sears, John. *My Friends at Brook Farm*. New York: D. Fitzgerald, 1912.

Van Dyke, Henry. *The Music Lover*. New York: Moffat, Yard, 1909.

Van Hook, Bailey. *Angels of Art: Women and Art in American Society, 1876–1914*. Philadelphia: Penn State Press, 1996.

Van Zuylen, Marina. *Monomania: The Flight from Everyday Life in Literature and Art*. Ithaca: Cornell University Press, 2005.

Wabuda, Susan. "Preaching." In *Puritans and Puritanism in Europe and America: A Comprehensive Encyclopedia*. Vol. 1, 488–91. Francis J. Bremer and Tom Webster, eds. Santa Barbara: ABC-CLIO, 2006.

Walker, Alan. *Franz Liszt*. Vol. 2. Ithaca: Cornell University Press, 1997.

Waring, Dennis G. *Manufacturing the Muse: Estey Organs and Consumer Culture in Victorian America*. Middletown, Conn.: Wesleyan University Press, 2002.

Waterman, Sue. "Collecting the Nineteenth Century." *Representations* 90 (2005): 98–12.

Watson, John F. *Methodist Error, or Friendly Christian Advice to Those Methodists Who Indulge in Extravagant Religious Emotions and Bodily Exercises*, 1819.

Weaver, Rev. G. S. *Hopes and Helps for the Young of Both Sexes*. New York: Fowlers & Wells, 1854.

Weber, William. *Music and the Middle Class: The Social Structure of Concert Life in*

London, Paris, and Vienna between 1830 and 1848. Revised ed. Aldershot: Ashgate, 2004.

Weber, William. "Did People Listen in the 18th Century?" *Early Music* 25, no. 4, 25th Anniversary Issue: Listening Practice (1997): 678–91.

Weber, William. "The Muddle of the Middle Classes." *19th-Century Music* 4, no. 2 (1979): 175–85.

White, Shane, and Graham White, *The Sounds of Slavery*. Boston: Beacon Press, 2005.

Whitefield, George. *Directions How to Hear Sermons*. Boston: G. Rogers and D. Fowle, 1740.

Whitesitt, Laura. "The Role of Women Impresarios in American Concert Life, 1871–1933." *American Music* 7, no. 2 (1989): 159–80.

Whitman, Walt. *The Portable Walt Whitman*. Mark Van Doren, ed. New York: Penguin Books, 1973.

Whitman, Walt. *Walt Whitman: Complete Poetry and Collected Prose*. New York: Library of America, 1982.

Wilentz, Sean. *Chants Democratic: New York City and the Rise of the American Working Class, 1788–1850*. New York: Oxford University Press, 1984.

Willson, Joseph. *The Elite of Our People: Sketches of the Higher Classes of Colored Society in Philadelphia*. Julie Winch, ed. University Park: Pennsylvania State University Press, 2000 [1841].

Wilmeth, Don B. and Christopher Bigsby, eds. *The Cambridge History of American Theatre*. Vol. 1. Cambridge: Cambridge University Press, 1998.

Winch, Julie. *A Gentleman of Color: The Life of James Forten*. New York: Oxford University Press, 2002.

Winslow, Ola Elizabeth. *Meetinghouse Hill, 1630–1783*. New York: W. W. Norton, 1972 [1952].

Wise, Daniel. *The Young Lady's Counsellor*. New York: Carlton & Porter, 1857.

Wood, Samuel. *The Cries of New York*. 1931 [1808].

Wordsworth, William. "Preface to the Lyrical Ballads." In *The Complete Poetical Works of William Wordsworth*. Boston: Houghton, Mifflin, 1919.

Yardley, Anne Bagnall. "Choirs in the Methodist Episcopal Church, 1800–1860." *American Music* 17, no. 1 (1999): 39–64.

Young, R. J. *Antebellum Black Activists: Race, Gender, and Self*. New York: Garland Publishing, 1996.

Index

manhood, 80, 81, 95, 177, 179

mania, 157–58, 221n19; monomania, 159, 161; musicomania, 159–61, 171

Maretzek, Max, 175–176

Marshfield (Massachusetts), 85–86

Martin, C. F., 37

Marx, Adolf Bernhard, 171

Materna, Amalie, 109, 117, 125

McMahon, Lucia, 105

Meaghan, Thomas, 150, 220n3

Mechanics Hall (Boston), 107–109

medicine, 158–61. *See also* mania; tarantism

Mee, Jon, 164, 165

memory, 83, 131, 134

men: in antebellum city, 36, 40–41, 46–47, 54; concern about feminization of culture, 176–77; concert-going of, 75–77; as migrants, 46, 80–87, 145; music culture of, 73–74; in public sphere, 28. *See also* manhood

Mesmer, Franz Anton, 158

Metzner, Paul, 71

middle class: anxiety, 26–27, 37–38, 72–73, 156, 168; clerks, 26, 84, 109, 177; definition of, 26; domestic sphere, 28; myth of self-made man, 81; professionalism, 3, 27–28, 68; refinement, 7, 27, 32–34, 69, 72, 74, 90, 134, 155, 168–70, 172, 177; restraint, 128, 164, 168–69; suspicion of arts, 156, 170. *See also* cultural reform; listening; manhood; selfhood

military music, 51

minstrelsy, 21, 75, 76, 99, 110

Mitchell, Donald Grant, 140, 151, 158

mock performances, 130

monster concerts, 119, 152, 183

Moore, R. Laurence, 65, 68, 166

Mozart, Wolfgang Amadeus, 133

musical ear, 56–57, 58, 72

Musical Fund Society, 147, 160

musicality, 3, 74, 192

musical theater, 19–20, 21, 29–30

music dealer, 22–24. *See also* commercialization

music education, 146, 187, 191; instrument lessons, 2, 3, 23, 26, 28, 69, 89–90, 134, 191; singing lessons, 45, 87, 89, 112–13; teachers, 20, 28, 57, 65, 97, 102, 136. *See also* piano; singing schools

Music Hall (Boston), 126, 133

music history: audiences as part of, 5, 192; causation in, 6–7; generalization in, 7; methods for researching, 10–11, 196n31

music listening: centrality in modern life, 2, 187; in churches, 76, 132; definition of, 5–6; diversity of, 190; and ecstasy, 8128, 138; evidence for, 4, 8–9; individualized, 144, 164; as passive, 73, 187–89; and repetition, 131, 132; silent, 9, 124, 154, 173; and taste, 174–75; and technology, 1–2, 186, 192. *See also* audiences; concert-going; concert seating; consumption; listening

music lovers: connection to modern fans, 184–85, 227n122; developing opinions about music, 110, 115, 136, 140; diary-writing of, 135–36, 138; emergence of, in United States, 109–10; European, 142–43; extending performance, 132, 139; longing for music, 132, 138, *140*; mockery of, 149–57, 168–69, *169*, 183; vs. musicians, 172; noting audience, 123–25, 143; noting concert halls, 125–27; noting physical sensation, 127–29, 139; vs. ordinary audience members, 122–23, 139–40; social bonds between, 144–48; terms describing, 141–42, 154–55, 220n13. *See also* audiences; concert-going; Wagnerians

music magazines, 146–47

music-making: amateur, 20, 76, 114, 138; vs. concert-going, 1–4, 45, 73, 83, 134, 138, 191; domestic, 2, 28, 110, 134; local, 19–20. *See also* music education

music publishing, 133–34

music societies, 147–48, 175. *See also* Tuesday Musicale; women

National Peace Jubilee, 120–21, 152

Newton (MA), 111

New York City: Astor Place riot in, 123; Bowery b'hoy, 61; commercial amusements of, 40–41, 76; Lindmania in, 151–52; new migrants to, 80–85; parades in 51; streets sounds of, 48–49

New York Philharmonic, 21, 76, 147

Niblo's Garden (New York City), 76, 81, 82

noise: amateur performance as, 51–52, 57; and class prejudice, 52, 166; legislation against, 53–54; middle-class retreat from, 53; of monster concerts, 120, 152; as political resistance, 54; and racial and ethnic prejudice, 52–53. *See also* sounds

Oakman, Otis, 85–86, 130

opera, 75, 92, 115–18, 128, 130; in Europe, 142–

MUSIC/CULTURE
A series from Wesleyan University Press.
Edited by Harris M. Berger and Annie J. Randall

Originating editors: George Lipsitz, Susan McClary, and Robert Walser

ABOUT THE AUTHOR

Daniel Cavicchi is an associate professor of American studies and head of the Department of History, Philosophy, and the Social Sciences at Rhode Island School of Design. He is the author of *Tramps Like Us: Music and Meaning among Springsteen Fans* and coeditor of *My Music: Explorations of Music in Daily Life*. His public work has included "Songs of Conscience, Sounds of Freedom," an inaugural exhibit for the Grammy Museum in Los Angeles.